Inside Chinese Theater

MUSIC IN AMERICAN LIFE

The Music in American Life series documents and celebrates the dynamic and multifaceted relationship between music and American culture. From its first publication in 1972 through its half-century mark and beyond, the series has embraced a wide variety of methodologies, from biography and memoir to history and musical analysis, and spans the full range of musical forms, from classical through all types of vernacular music. The series showcases the wealth of musical practice and expression that characterizes American music, as well as the rich diversity of its stylistic, regional, racial, ethnic, and gendered contexts. Characterized by a firm grounding in material culture, whether archival or ethnographic, and by work that honors the musical activities of ordinary people and their communities, Music in American Life continually redefines and expands the very definition of what constitutes music in American culture, whose voices are heard, and how music and musical practices are understood and valued.

For a list of books in the series, please see our website at www.press.uillinois.edu.

Inside Chinese Theater

Community and Artistry in Nineteenth-Century California and Beyond

NANCY YUNHWA RAO

UNIVERSITY OF ILLINOIS PRESS
Urbana, Chicago, and Springfield

Publication of this book was supported by grants from
the H. Earle Johnson Subvention Fund of the Society
for American Music, the Judith McCulloh Endowment
for American Music, the General Fund of the American
Musicological Society, and the Rutgers University
Research Council.

Library of Congress Cataloging-in-Publication Data
Names: Rao, Nancy Yunhwa, author.
Title: Inside Chinese theater : community and artistry in
    nineteenth-century California and beyond / Nancy Yunhwa Rao.
Description: Urbana : University of Illinois Press, 2025. | Series:
    Music in American life | Includes bibliographical references
    and index.
Identifiers: LCCN 2024048522 (print) | LCCN 2024048523 (ebook)
    | ISBN 9780252046537 (hardcover) | ISBN 9780252088636
    (paperback) | ISBN 9780252047831 (ebook)
Subjects: LCSH: Operas, Chinese—California—19th century—History
    and criticism. | Operas, Chinese—California—San Francisco—
    19th century—History and criticism. | Theaters—California—
    San Francisco—History—19th century. | Chinese—California—
    History—19th century.
Classification: LCC ML1711.7.C15 R36 2025 (print) | LCC ML1711.7.C15
    (ebook) | DDC 782.10951/09794—dc23/eng/20241016
LC record available at https://lccn.loc.gov/2024048522
LC ebook record available at https://lccn.loc.gov/2024048523

Contents

Note on Chinese Names and Terms   vii

Prologue   ix

Introduction   1

1   First Encounters   19

2   Bringing Opera to the Mines and Railroad Chinese   41

3   Performing Chinese Opera in San Francisco   68

4   Cultural Capital: Theaters on Jackson Street   88

5   Prosperity: A New Theater on Washington Street   116

6   Education, Diplomacy Culture, and the Fourth Theater   136

7   Contesting Chinese Exclusion Laws: In re Ho King   153

8   Star Power and the Chinese American Theater   164

9   Picturesque Chinese Theater   187

10   Civil Rights, Owning Glamour, and Sonic Ethnology   218

Epilogue   239

Appendix A. Chronology of Chinese Theaters
in San Francisco   257

Appendix B. Stylistic Characteristics of Cantonese Opera
and a Transcription of *Golden-leaved Chrysanthemum*   259

Acknowledgments   267

Notes   271

Glossary   329

Bibliography   333

Index   357

Note on Chinese Names and Terms

Chinese immigrants came primarily from the Pearl River Delta in southern China, and their names, as well as terms and opera titles, were pronounced in Cantonese or Toisanese, rather than Mandarin Chinese. In written Chinese communication this does not pose problems because the written characters are the same, but when rendering in alphabetic spelling, confusions abound. When Chinese names of performers, theaters, and troupes were romanized in nineteenth-century English-language newspapers or travelogues, it was done casually and varied among individual writers. A hodgepodge of spellings resulted, often with multiple English versions of the same Chinese name. For example, the 1852 Cantonese opera troupe Tong Hook Tong could be found in at least a dozen varied spellings in different English-language newspapers. When tracing Chinese theater or troupe names in historical English documents or newspapers, therefore, one needs to allow for a range of spellings. In all quoted texts, the romanization in the original document will stay intact. Also, certain spellings of names occur in many English documents, such as theater names, so they will be kept as well.

In other situations, for the purpose of consistency, I use primarily standard Mandarin Pinyin romanization. Chinese person names and terms are romanized in the Pinyin system. The disadvantage of using Pinyin romanization, which renders unfamiliar many famous names traditionally romanized according to the Cantonese dialect, would be offset by the advantage of consistency and easy reference, both within this book and across other studies of this period. There are some exceptions, however. For prominent community figures and organizations in North America, the well-established Cantonese romanization of their names will be used, without reference to the Mandarin version in Pinyin, since the latter version would be of little use. A list of Chinese characters is provided for reference.

A chronological diagram of theater locations in San Francisco and both their Chinese and English names can be found in Appendix A. Cantonese opera titles are given in English translation; their romanization can be found in the glossary. Unless noted, all translations from Chinese to English are my own.

Prologue

Ah Quin, Theatergoer

In the last two weeks of December 1878, Ah Quin spent eighty hours visiting Chinese theaters.[1] After two years in Alaska, he had just returned to San Francisco, where he had arrived from China fifteen years previously. The thirty-year-old had become a Christian, devoting time every day to studying the Bible. He kept a diary in English, to which he occasionally added Chinese characters for the names of people and Chinese theaters, and once for a Chinese opera title.[2]

It was a lively time. According to the *Directory of Chinese Business Houses* that year, San Francisco's Chinese community was bustling, with 423 stores.[3] Ah Quin stayed from the end of 1878 to October 1880, the heyday of Chinese theaters in San Francisco. Three theaters were open concurrently in 1878; a major merger happened in mid-1879, and a fourth theater opened later the same year. Ah Quin divided his time among the three theaters, recording two of their names in Chinese as well as English—Quan Sun Yok, 崑山玉; Look Sun Fung, 祿新鳳; and Que Hing Log (no Chinese given). These Chinese characters in Ah Quin's diary are the earliest Chinese-language textual evidence of the prosperity and success of Chinese theaters in nineteenth-century America; their history will be the focus of this book.

Having left southern China when he was fifteen and having been away from San Francisco for six years (in Santa Barbara, San Diego, and Alaska), Ah Quin had seen little opera in the years past. When he left San Francisco, it had just one established Chinese theater, but interest in theater was high. On the day of his arrival in December 1878, he got off the steamer, paid a tax at the wharf, checked into a hotel and visited with relatives, then squeezed in an hour of Chinese theater before it closed at midnight. The next day he spent three hours in the afternoon at Look Sun Fung, and two more hours in the evening at Que Hing Log, until it closed. Que Hing Log was the city's oldest Chinese theater, built in 1868 on Jackson Street (as Hing Quen Yuan), whereas Look Sun Fung on Washington Street was the newest, built only a year previously. Ah Quin had a fondness for the latter, whose name appears frequently in his diary entries as L. S. F. Both theaters seated between 1,000 and 2,500. Ah Quin went to several theaters nearly every day. Not only were there matinee and evening performances daily, but the ticket prices were affordable: Ah Quin paid ten cents for one theater ticket, the same as he spent on a simple meal.[4] Since he was not a man of means, he evaded paying kinship association dues, but he did not skimp on theater visits.[5] These theaters produced Cantonese opera, the popular genre of the Pearl River Delta, a southern part of Guangdong province, where the majority of immigrants came from. Thousands of other men similarly enjoyed Chinese theater like Ah Quin.

Indeed, Ah Quin went to theaters at all different times of the day. The most time he spent in a single day was on December 24, 1878—a total of ten to eleven hours split between Que Hing Log and Look Sun Fung. So impressed was he by that day's performance that he added the Chinese characters 六國 in his diary for the opera title *Look Quok* (*Six Nations*). It is a grand opera, known as *The Joint Investiture of a Prime Minister of Six Warlords* (hereafter *Six Warlords*). Ah Quin's use of Chinese characters signaled a linguistic affinity that conveyed personal joy and pride.

> Get up at 10:30. The bre[akfast] at 11; go up to the house top[,] tell the glass man fix the sky light for Tom Out. Then I go see Que Thin Log till supper at 4; after go see Luk Sin Fung call Look Quok 六國 till another is dismissed at 12; read St. John the 7: the 7 [;] in bed at 1:25 A.M.[6]

Ah Quin's admiration is hardly surprising. *Six Warlords* is an opera of auspiciousness, with magnificent spectacle. It requires a full-fledged troupe with a large cast, acrobatic movements, and opulent costumes. Its production was a sign of prosperity, performed on celebratory occasions or when a troupe gave its first performance at a theater. The opera tells the story of Su Qin, a renowned politician of the Warring States Period (475–221 BC) who brought six antagonist states together against the powerful state of Qin. The positive outcome—Su Qin becomes prime minister of the six unified states—brings all the actors in the troupe onstage to celebrate the power of unity and the spirit of collaboration. The glamorous parade features the generals, imposing in their full regalia and each heralded by a banner that identifies his kingdom. With scenes such as "The Entrance of the Six Kings," "The Entrance of the Six Marshals," "Receiving the Imperial Decree," "The Departure of the Carriage," and "The Riding of the Carriage," the actors perform their individual feats, including the virtuosic "riding and pushing the carriage" routine by warriors and a prima donna. The ultimate triumph of the coalition sets the scene for a memorable exhibition of theatricality.

This theatricality enthralled audiences everywhere. In Guangxi, China, a Hunan-native official, Yang Enshou (1835–1891) was in awe when he saw *Six Warlords* on the opening night of a newly arrived troupe in 1865. "Over one hundred actors were on stage," he noted, "a dazzling sight with a conglomeration of splendid and beautiful things."[7] In San Francisco, *Six Warlords* was first performed by a 123-member opera troupe in 1852—the year that marked the beginning of significant Chinese migration to California, with 20,026 arrivals.[8] All through the second half of the nineteenth century, *Six Warlords* was performed often in California, generating considerable excitement. It was used frequently by the leading members and associations of the Chinese community to demonstrate China's advanced civilization, distinctive aesthetics, sophisticated drama, and physical and mental virility. Theaters and their troupes also aspired to produce *Six Warlords* as grandly as possible to display their strength, and, when necessary, to trump their rivals or combat racialized stereotypes. This opera drew such attention that the title *Six Warlords* (or *Six Kings* and *Feng Siang*) became a common term in the nineteenth century. It was the one Chinese opera title known to many American writers.

Chinese theaters were located in close proximity to each other. Two were across the street from each other on Jackson Street, and the other two were only several doors apart on Washington Street; theatergoers, most of whom lived nearby, enjoyed performances as part of their everyday activities. Ah Quin would stay as little as half an hour or as long as six hours on one occasion, slipping in and out of the theaters between other pursuits such as dining at restaurants, getting a haircut, gathering with friends or business associates, attending church activities, and visiting gambling houses and brothels.[9] His contemporary in southern China, Yang Enshou, similarly recorded a busy social life surrounding theatrical activities during his long-term sojourns in several provinces: performances for deities at temples, performances during festivals, and celebratory occasions at district associations (more on this below). Frequenting opera regularly, Yang would drop by midway through performances and stay for any length of time that fitted his day's official activities as a private magistrate adviser. "Watching opera," a scholar of Yang wrote, "has become an important part of their lives, a hobby, a way of life and living conditions."[10]

Theatergoers like Yang in Guangxi and Ah Quin in San Francisco had little difficulty following what was unfolding onstage, not only because Chinese theater "operates with a defined repertoire of gestures and situations" but also because happenings on the opera stage were closely tied to cultural memory.[11] The operas' plots and storylines were based on well-known fictional or historical accounts, and legendary figures on stage were household names. Entering or leaving performances midway did not diminish the viewing pleasure. One could expect to hear familiar aria types and percussion musical gestures. As anthropologist Barbara E. Ward concluded, Chinese theater could "mobilise not only sight and hearing, and not only minds and emotions, but also traditionally shared beliefs and attitudes at different levels."[12] Ah Quin's regular theatergoing, together with his daily Bible study—which he enhanced by attending group meetings and services at the Presbyterian Church on Stockton Street—reflected the emotional nexus on which he thrived in navigating the immigrant life in San Francisco.[13]

Ah Quin's theater attendance was interrupted two months into 1879, when he found full-time employment. He was hired as a live-in cook/servant by the US military, first at Angel Island and later at the Presidio, which was at the edge of the city and an hour away from Chinatown.[14] The distance required him to take boats, trains, or a long walk to return to Chinatown. The allure of Chinese theater remained: on his second daytrip back to Chinatown, Ah Quin spent two hours at Que Hing Log before returning to Angel Island by 4:30 for the dinner shift.[15] When finally making an overnight visit, he spent three hours or more at each of the two other theaters. His diary entry recorded the indulgence:

> I go see theatre 崑山玉 till 6; and back [to] Tom Out, and go to chi[nese] restaurant [to] have supper, and in 祿新鳳 again till 11:15 and in restaurant again [to] have 20 cent supper.[16]

It was in this entry that he wrote the names of two theaters in Chinese characters; previously, he had referred to them exclusively in English. Ah Quin's switch from the English alphabet to Chinese characters for the names of the two Chinese theaters—retrieving from memory and writing out the intersecting pen strokes in proper sequence and type (they were complex characters, too!)—was an affectionate gesture toward their cultural meaning, a gesture prompted by his elation at rejoining the scene. Through writing, he expressed a genuine connection to the joy of theater and subtly reclaimed the sounding identities and ideograms of his community.[17] It communicated the Chinese identity connected to "experiences that were expressive [and] intuitive," a contrast to English, which remained "a corrective device that straightened and twisted [him] to fit a new mold," to borrow an expression from the literary scholar Jing Tsu.[18] Theatrical performance emerged as a powerful medium through which Ah Quin experienced intimacy, and breathed and rejoiced in a worldview that was expressed and constructed in the Chinese language.[19]

Several months later, Ah Quin began serving as domestic help for army officers at the Presidio. Now that his commute involved only a train ride or a long walk, not a boat, his theater visits could be fitted neatly around his work

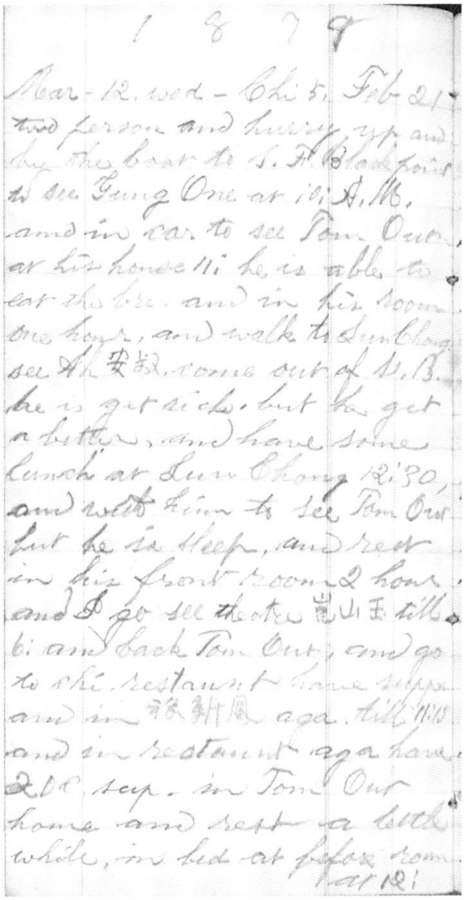

FIGURE P.1 Ah Quin, Diary, March 12, 1879. Courtesy San Diego History Center.

schedule: either three or four hours of a matinee between lunch and dinner, or two or three hours of an evening performance after dinner. Sometimes, when the army officers had outside social engagements, such as welcoming the former president Ulysses S. Grant on his return from Asia, he had an even more flexible schedule. By this time, a theater merger had been completed, and Wing Tie Ping was the only Chinese theater. In the first four weeks of autumn 1879, Ah Quin visited the Wing Tie Ping theater eleven times.[20] In October, when the city's fourth Chinese theater, Donn Quai Yuen, opened, Ah Quin was among the lucky ones who attended its bustling, grand opening. It was crowded beyond capacity. The exhilarated Ah Quin professed his elation with adjectives scarcely seen in his diary, "the Luk Quock [Six Warlords] is very nice and happy, and much [sic] people cannot get in."[21] The theater would still have a large crowd five weeks later, as an entry about the theater in November read "it is good many people and thick [sic]."[22]

Many nights, Ah Quin went home to the Presidio by rail or on foot after the theater closed at 12:00 a.m. One night, he began the walk home at 12:30 a.m., getting to bed at 2:00 a.m. and rising at 6:30 to work.[23] For Ah Quin, cleaning, ironing, and cooking were his livelihood, but theatergoing also was important as food for his soul. In May 1880, all but two of his thirteen visits to Chinese theaters followed activities at the church, such as singing hymns or listening to preaching. During his time in San Francisco, he occasionally befriended opera performers, noting the arrivals of new actors or jotting down their names in his diary.[24] In October 1880, Ah Quin landed a job as a labor contractor in San Diego for the California Southern Railroad and left San Francisco's vibrant Chinese theatrical life. Later, as a successful businessman and land developer, he visited Chinese theaters on trips to San Francisco and Los Angeles, the latter of which established its own Chinese theater in 1884.[25]

Throughout the second half of the nineteenth century, Chinese merchants recruited troupes and constructed theater buildings in California. Kinship and district associations and business organizations ensured the presence of theatrical troupes for a variety of reasons: to present offerings, to secure blessings, to celebrate the birthdays of patron deities, and so on. Their endeavors, investments, and resilience sustained the theaters over many decades. As a prominent cultural institution, Chinese theater would even play a significant role in the community's contestation of the 1882 Chinese Restriction Act, which is generally known as Chinese Exclusion Act (see chap. 6). As Virgil Ho notes, opera presentations brought "the kind of magico-religious blessing that performance is thought to confer on a community."[26] For both merchants and associations, presenting theatrical performances demonstrated their financial power, thus increasing their prestige. Chinese theater was where worship, communication, and entertainment, as well as commerce and power, converged.

If financial incentives were key to Chinese migration—whether gold mining, agricultural development, or railroad construction—maintaining the prospering community relied on cultural productions such as theater, temple (joss house) and kinship associations, all of which exemplified Chinese social belief systems and were models of moral etiquette and decency. Meanwhile, the everyday offerings of Chinese theater belonged intimately to thousands of theatergoers like Ah Quin. There they took what they could harness for their own flourishing. As the main daily attraction, operas were frequented by ordinary workers, the majority of whom were between twenty and thirty-nine years old. This dynamism was noted by the historian Yong Chen: "Chinese San Francisco's vitality came from its youthfulness."[27] The high demand for opera was reflected in the prosperity of theater businesses. During the heyday of production in San Francisco, when three fully operational Chinese theaters ran concurrently in the late 1870s, there were roughly forty-five hundred seats altogether. In this regard, Ah Quin's busy life as a frequent and enthusiastic theatergoer was not an exception but the norm.

Ah Quin's short, mundane diary entries give vibrant color to the faded image of nineteenth-century Chinese theater in San Francisco and pull us into its everydayness. His diary enables us to imagine the meaning of the theater's sounds resonating through the community, and to consider the theater institutionally as an expression of the transpacific community, opening up and mobilizing a way for immigrants to be in the world together. The operas encapsulated the "experience of [the performers] and of the listeners, all of the physiological, psychoacoustic, and sociopolitical dynamics that impact [their] perception of [themselves] and each other," to paraphrase the ethnomusicologist Katherine Meizel.[28] If Ah Quin's diary entries were short in expressing the theatrical effect of Cantonese opera, we can imagine his emotive response via the writer Yeng Pway Ngon's depiction of a Cantonese opera fan in the novel *Costume*: "He was completely enchanted. It wasn't just the performers in their magnificent costumes: their voices, their gestures, their expressions, even the music with its drums and cymbals had him spellbound."[29]

Linguistic Instability

The linguistic instability of "Chinese opera theater," the term used in this study, reflects its complex history in North America. It is an inexact translation of *xiqu*, a traditional Chinese theatrical genre that encompasses elements of drama, theater, stylized movement, acrobatics, classic lyrics, music, and song. It comprises more than three hundred regional varieties. As the Hong Kong scholar Siu Leung Li notes, "very literally, *xi* means 'play/drama' and *qu* 'song/music.'" The term *xiqu* can also refer to "[Chinese] drama" (literary drama), "[Chinese] theater" (stage, performance and the spectator-player interaction in the performing location) and "[Chinese] opera" (the whole tradition of the practice of musical theater in China and denoting various regional genres).[30] More specifically, Cantonese opera—the genre performed in North America—was from the Guangdong region. It is known colloquially in the Cantonese dialect as *daai hei* (great theater), *loh gu hei* (theater with percussion), or *Gwongfu daai hei* (great theater of Guangzhou), which signaled two performing contexts: ritual performances as important folk rites, and theatrical performances as entertainment.[31] Very few performances served only ritual purposes. For the most part, the opera repertoire is intended to entertain both humans and deities. Operas were performed during festivals celebrating birthdays of the deities as a form of worship, but at the same time, of course, entertaining the human audience. (It was assumed that the deities liked to be entertained as well.) As a popular genre that appealed to the masses, "Chinese opera theater" juxtaposes linguistic forms both high and low: poetic arias, literary lyrics, and dialogues that are approximations of more colloquial and plainspoken registers.

However, nineteenth-century American newspapers used terms in English such as "Chinese Theater," "Chinese Theatricals," "Celestial Drama," "Chinese Dramatic Company," and "Chinese Opera Troupe" to describe Chinese opera theater.[32] To be sure, the range of meanings associated with *xiqu* and *daai hei* cannot be captured in these English translations. The word *theater* was associated with nineteenth-century Western performance genres such as drama, opera, melodrama, pantomime, masquerade, minstrelsy, and other entertainments. Genres such as opera and drama had specific meanings and conventions as well. They carried certain values, attitudes, and expectations in American society, which often led to critiques or caricatures of Chinese theater's nonconformity to Western norms.[33] At the same time, the term "Chinese theater" carried a distinctive significance because it stood at the forefront of representing the community. This term's linguistic instability symbolizes the material existence and corporeality of Chinese opera theater in nineteenth-century America, a kind of schema that structured its everydayness and its hypervisibility. (The fact that Cantonese opera troupes at the time exclusively featured male performers, due to the prohibition of women on stage in China, contributed to their noteworthiness in American society as well.) Therefore, the history of Chinese opera theater in nineteenth-century America is not a history of the "origin" of *xiqu* and *daai hei*, or its copy in nineteenth-century America. Nor is it the performing history of a form of minoritarian identity politics. It is also not a history of the Euro-American craze for, or mockery of, an alien form of theatrical performance.[34] Rather, this is a history of the making and doing of Chinese opera theater in America.

Linguistic instability is manifested in archival activity. As the philosopher Michel de Certeau argues, "The transformation of 'archivistic' activity is the point of departure and the condition for a new history."[35] The historical record of Chinese theater is sparse. No business records have survived; early Chinese-language weekly newspapers had limited space, comprising mostly commodity prices, ship schedules, and brief government and local news items. The primary archive for this history is the English-language contemporaneous written accounts of Chinese theater. As a repository, these accounts reflect the perspectives of English-language writers tethered to and entrenched in their beliefs and listening practices. It is an archive full of mockery, ridicule, and charade. Excavating a reliable account of Chinese theater from these writings is nearly impossible. One must read against the grain in order to "centralize and animate information discredited," as Toni Morrison told us. It is necessary to mistrust "received reality," and to draw out the art form from "the silences and the distortions and the evasions in the history as received."[36] In this case, the archivistic activity would also mean listening for and imagining *daai hei* in the background, a process that Anne Laura Stoler calls the analytic tactics of "inversion and recuperation."[37] Meanwhile, whenever we encounter them, we also need to treat the rare Chinese-language sources in the archive—the ideograms—not merely as historical evidence for knowledge production, but also as a means to access the stored cultural memory, sonic genealogy, embodied experience, and unmediated meaning. Even in very brief linguistic slippages as in Ah Quin's diary, language constitutes the site of deepest resonance.

This book demonstrates how Chinese theater constituted the most prominent community space for Chinese immigrants of the nineteenth century, where Cantonese opera mesmerized audience of various kinds. Chinese theater experience intersected with nearly all facets of early Chinese immigrants' existence. The issue of language is an important consideration that runs through the book both as a bodily experience of belonging and as a sounded expression of the community. This history is the story of the transpacific network, encompassing the circulation of people, troupes, repertoire, stories, voice, instruments, costumes, stage performance, capital, and more.

The history of this sonic culture—its success, compromise, and prosperity, as well as its conflicts and obstacles—forms what Lily Wong calls a "transpacific genealogy."[38] This genealogy, rather than being imaginary and monolithic, has historical depth and aesthetic complexity. An important aim of this book is to demystify and to show the multifaceted engagement and multiphasic transformation of Chinese theaters throughout the second half of the nineteenth century. It also will explain transpacific sonic genealogy. The chapters recenter and explore transpacific and translinguistic perspectives to reconfigure historical knowledge about American music.

Some may ask why we, in twenty-first-century America, should care about the history of Chinese opera theater from so long ago, about a history that needs to be pieced together from fragments and impressions, a history that often needs to be excavated from crass jokes and ridicule. The reasons are many. The common narrative of nineteenth-century California depicts it as a frontier region where American pioneers followed the gold rush and the silver rush before pursuing such activities as logging, ranching, farming, and the construction of the transcontinental railroad. However, its history of Chinese theater offers an important perspective in the understanding of California as a heterogeneous and dynamic space importantly shaped by early Chinese immigrants and cultural forces via continuous transpacific crossings. The history of Chinese theater as a cultural production is marked by thriving theaters and traveling troupes; consequently it illuminates the significant presence and impact of Chinese communities in California. The sonic space of Chinese theater—often regarded as unrefined and of little import—holds a key to understanding the daily life of the Chinese immigrant community and its multifaceted interaction with cities and beyond.

Chinese opera theater in nineteenth-century America offers a distinctive lens through which to conceptualize the sonic world of Chinese immigrants. Given Chinese theater's complex role—as ritual offering, festive celebration, dramatic entertainment, and musical enjoyment—and the multitude of audiences it catered to—elite businessmen, women, their families, commoners, laborers, and non-Chinese artists and tourists—it provides a fascinating entry to a multifaceted (cultural) history of the early Chinese immigrant community. A crucial but too often neglected component of this history is sound. The development of Chinese theater not only encompassed the community's aspirations and flowering but was also deeply entwined with its challenges and obstacles. In the early days of the Chinese Exclusion Act, for example, Chinese actors vigorously contested this law in cases such as In re Ho King, earning significant victories. The history of Chinese theater is inseparable from the struggle and triumph of early Chinese in the United States.

Ultimately, however, this history is related to the ways we move through the world today. The treatment of certain images and sounds in our time has a complex history that sometimes can be traced back to the reception of Chinese opera theater in the nineteenth century. The early reception (historical listening) has a way of continuing the complex encryption of racial signs and signals into the twentieth- and twenty-first-century soundscape.[39] The book is a quest to render legible the vibrant history of Chinese opera theater in nineteenth-century America, to reclaim its complexity and sonic resonance from the grotesqueries created by mainstream English-language writers. This history also provokes us to acknowledge the rich stories and the people behind what has been taken as a stereotype or a simplistic notion of the joyless life of early Chinese immigrants. The wonder, glamour, and resonance within Chinese theater have a place not only in the historical narrative of Chinese America but also in the history of American music. Despite its significant influence and inherent ties to various facets of society, our understanding of its impact remains lacking. Although the scarcity of material documents is an unfortunate fact, the lack of means, conceptual frameworks, and inclination to think about a transpacific history of American music is a void that this study tries to address.

Inside Chinese Theater

.

Introduction

To comprehend the creation and development of Chinese theaters in nineteenth-century America, it is imperative to expand our perspective. Specifically, this involves situating the theaters within a broader context encompassing social, historical, cultural, theatrical, and visual dimensions. The trajectory of these theaters' history was intricately linked to a complex interplay of historical, cultural, and social forces on both sides of the Pacific. During this period, California matured from a young state and underwent significant shifts in social, economic, and political structures. San Francisco was transformed from a frontier town to a burgeoning metropolis. The story of Chinese theaters was deeply intertwined with these social and economic developments. Meanwhile, during the same period in China, Cantonese opera rose to become a distinctive regional culture. It experienced setbacks due to domestic and international factors, but ascended again by the mid-1860s and reached a pivotal point with growing mobility and expanded performing venues. As a result, opera troupes were accustomed to adapting to different environments and performing situations. With Chinese migration, they expanded their reach extensively into the Southeast Asian archipelago. Following the transpacific crossings, they came to play roles crucial to the success of early Chinese immigrants in California. The significant growth of the Chinese population in the United States, which tripled from about thirty-five thousand in 1860 to over one hundred thousand in 1890, greatly increased the demand for Chinese theaters.[1] The advancement of technology and efficient transportation allowed performers to continue traveling to and from San Francisco, further extending the influence of Cantonese opera across the Pacific.

On stage, the visual culture and theatricality intensified the sensorial qualities of Chinese theater. Chinese opera was well known for its symbolism and was typically performed with no curtain or scenery. Therefore, performers' skills in singing, recitation, acting, acrobatics, and stage combat, along with their painted faces and elaborate costumes rich in symbols, combined with instrumental accompaniment to create a system of signification to construct characters, convey stories, and express emotion. In particular, the opulence of Chinese opera costumes attested to the centrality of visuality—the distinct manifestations of visual experience—of Chinese theater. The materiality and physicality of Chinese theater activated many different modes of spectacle and many dramaturgical effects for the audience. Inevitably, they resonated with, or confronted, what the theater scholar Maaike Bleeker calls "the implications of already internalized modes of looking."[2] In other words, they worked to support or defy, and to reaffirm or challenge, expectations, desires and preconceptions. Regardless of the effect, Chinese opera costumes formed visual memories for nineteenth-century audiences and contributed to the ways in which individuals and society remembered and aspired to aesthetic ideals. This theatricality imbued cultural knowledge in individual and collective memory.

To explore the themes of network, institution, space, visuality, and theatricality, and to reinscribe the presence of Chinese theater into our understanding of the history of the American West, this introduction is organized in two parts. Part 1 will address issues concerning the institution. We will begin by reviewing the rise of the particular Chinese opera performing tradition and considering the primary performing venues and circulation networks. We then discuss the busy route of transpacific circulation, which established the central roles of San Francisco and Hong Kong. This will lead to a consideration of the four phases of Chinese opera theater's establishment and development in California and beyond. Part 2 will focus on the sensorial aspects. We will explore ways in which the visual practice of Chinese theater constituted an intense experience and left an indelible imprint on American society's visual culture. We will then consider how the theatricality of Chinese theater produced the illusion of the real, and how California might have influenced the theater's approach to its theatricality.

Part 1

Chinese opera: Temple Theater, Commercial Theater, and *Huiguan* Stage

Chinese opera troupes in California grew from the development of a regional opera genre in Guangdong, southern China. The late Qing period provided the background. From 1757 to 1842, Guangdong's primary port, Guangzhou, was the only designated one open to foreign trade, in response to perceived threats from abroad. During this period, Guangzhou became the largest commercial seaport, where products from all over the country were sent for export. As a result, in addition to foreign businessmen—including British, Dutch, French, Swedish, German, and other foreign nationals—Guangzhou also gathered a large number of prominent merchants of different trades from other parts of China, including Hunan, Jiangxi, Fujian, Jiangsu and Zhejiang. Vibrant opera cultures from these northern regions followed the merchants to Guangzhou as well.[3] This lively environment gave rise to the regional genre of Cantonese opera, which incorporated elements from the northern opera traditions with local characteristics. Gradually, Cantonese opera grew in prominence and became known for its strong sense of theatricality, visual opulence, large casts, and lively plots. An official, Yu Xunqing, made a special note of its distinctiveness and success: "There are a great many actors, and their stage properties and costumes are splendid and beautiful. The actors whose appearance, voice and skill are finest earn an income of up to 2,000 or 3,000 taels a year."[4] During the Taiping Rebellion (1851–64), the Cantonese opera profession suffered punitive sanctions for its entanglement with the political upheaval, but it rebounded and its troupes were again in high demand.[5] In 1867 the professional guild of Jiqing Gongsuo was founded in Guangzhou as the official organization that regulated the selection, contracts, and payment of troupes.

In a study of the social history of opera in the Ming and Qing periods, Li Hsiao-t'i observes, "The opera watching was a national pastime adopted by all different classes."[6] He particularly underscores the prominence of popular opera in the daily lives of China's common people, even though opera was also admired and patronized in private settings by the elite merchants, the gentry-literati, and even the ruling classes. Stages and venues for public performances were widely available, with differences depending on audiences and occasions. For Cantonese opera performance of the nineteenth century, there were three major categories of public performing venues:

1. Venues typically used for folk rites along the water routes of the Pearl River delta included stages in temple courtyards or temporary bamboo or mat-shed structures (see chap. 2) in rural village temples, to which the itinerant troupes traveled by boat. Religious observance played an important part in Chinese society, and opera performances routinely were offered as worship to deities on special holidays. Such folk rites constituted a major market for Cantonese opera troupes, which were particular in demand from after the fall harvest to the winter solstice, and then from the Lantern Festival (the fifteenth day of the first month in the lunar new year) to Duanwu (the fifth day of the fifth month). Troupes with busy itineraries could line up engagements one after another.[7]
2. Venues at *huiguan* (district, native-place, merchants,' or business associations), many of which had built-in stages or temporary structures and that held performances for festive occasions and auspicious

purposes. According to Li Hsiao-t'i, huiguan stages were immensely popular for many opera genres in the late Qing. He documented, for example, the existence of over four hundred huiguan in Beijing during the Ming-Qing period, noting that they often "provided fixed and sometimes even luxurious and splendid venues for opera performances."[8] Huiguan grew more significant as a venue for Cantonese opera with the increased migration of Cantonese people to other port cities both within and outside China.

3. Venues at purpose-built commercial theaters, a growing trend in urban spaces sustained by sizable regular audiences. The practice of building large commercial opera houses began around the 1860s and became more significant by the turn of the century. Hong Kong took the lead; thereafter, commercial theaters quickly began to appear as the main venues of public opera performances in cities like Guangzhou, Foshan, Hong Kong, and Macao (as it was then known). As entertainment in the urban environment, their business operations encompassed ticket sales, advertising, and vendors selling food and other services.

These different venues for Cantonese opera engendered varied modes of circulation. The network of the first type—the itinerant troupes—extended via waterways throughout Guangdong and Guangxi Provinces, offering opera performances at temple fairs or ancestral halls as a form of religious ceremony. It led to the legendary Red Boats (the wooden craft the performers used as conveyances and accommodations) in the last third of the nineteenth century.[9] For the second type of venue, theatrical troupes followed Cantonese merchants and migrants wherever they traveled and took up residence. This was significant because after 1841, many more ports were opened to foreign trade. Cantonese merchants led the way, migrating to cities such as Shanghai to meet the new demand for goods and services. Cantonese opera troupes followed suit and became closely tied to the huiguan in those cities. An old Chinese saying goes, "The commercial routes are also the theatrical routes," highlighting the close relationship between trade and entertainment in Chinese culture.[10] Furthermore, massive Chinese migration to the Southeast Asian archipelago also brought Cantonese opera to areas where Cantonese migrants settled. For the third type, the troupes circulated among the cities near the southern coastal region, where commercial theaters grew popular. Hong Kong, for example, built its first large theater in 1865 and had two more within five years. This expansion led to robust competition among theaters and transformed the operatic profession.

Through these three types of venues, Cantonese opera prospered in the second half of the nineteenth century, fostering a great deal of flexibility and fluidity in performance practices. Temporary bamboo stages for performances of folk rites could be seen in urban centers and huiguan; temples or ancestry halls could also have stages. These varied performance settings revealed the multiple roles they served in society: from worship to entertainment to camaraderie. As we will discuss below, the three types of venues also played important roles in the development and establishment of Chinese theaters in North America.

Transpacific Crossing

Attracted by the gold rushes, more than three hundred thousand Chinese emigrants went to the United States and British colonies in the mid-nineteenth century.[11] They were residents primarily of the coastal area near Guangdong, which, as a busy port of foreign trade, had a long history of openness to the outside world. As the Chinese missionary Rev. William Speer noted, when the news of gold reached them, "it was natural that they, above all Chinese, should rush to California."[12] Contrary to what has been often assumed, early Chinese emigrants to America did not all flee from hunger or come from impoverished families.[13] Some were seasoned merchants, and some were adventurous young men sent by their families for an opportunity to pursue their fortune and amass wealth. A few were also educated in missionary schools or engaged with missionaries in southern China. (There were about seventy mission schools around China by 1863.)[14] In a short time, routes and networks were established across the Pacific maritime world.[15] Hong Kong and San Francisco rose to become prominent nodes of the transpacific network. China, with significant mercantile expertise developed in Guangzhou and the South China Sea region, "provided large numbers of skilled merchants adept at complex cultural and political negotiation to go abroad, trade, settle and form communities."[16] Meanwhile, San Francisco also became a trade port where commercial ventures were fueled by the quickly increasing number of entrepreneurs, with gold as capital. The thriving network and flow of people and goods quickly transformed California. In addition to the so-called forty-niners from the eastern United States, the Pacific connection grew precipitously, satisfying California's immense market for products and urgent need for construction projects.[17] In 1868, to reinforce US trade interests in China, the Burlingame Treaty was signed to offer reciprocal protections and free travel for Chinese in the United States and Americans in China. More than thirty-five thousand Chinese arrived between 1868 and 1870.[18] More than twenty thousand Chinese arrived in 1873 alone.[19]

The transpacific circulation was a conduit not only for economics and commerce but for cultural production as well.[20] As California's Chinese population grew from 4,018 in 1850 to 75,412 in 1890, opera troupes and players from Guangdong arrived continuously and kept Cantonese opera culture thriving along the Pacific coast.[21] Chinese emigrants, as the historian Elizabeth Sinn notes, were "active agents, making decisions about their movements on many levels and strategizing their economic futures."[22]

Chinese theater in California was necessarily a transoceanic operation. The musicologist Yvonne Liao has underscored this point, noting that "[the culture of Chinatown opera] was practically dependent upon imperial networks."[23] Since the early nineteenth century, Great Britain and the United States had established a significant commercial presence in Guangzhou, importing opium from Turkey to China and transporting silk and tea from China to the United States, creating trade routes across the Indian and Atlantic oceans. British maritime and imperial trade expanded quickly through the nineteenth century, developing the "world's largest naval and mercantile fleets" and established shipping patterns and networks of trading routes.[24] Meanwhile, American merchants also developed an intra-Pacific trade of commodities with China, exchanging furs from the Pacific Northwest for silk, porcelain, and tea from China. According to the historian Eric Odell Oakley, by 1814, more than six hundred American vessels did business in Guangzhou, and Bostonian merchants extracted the wealth of the Northwest for their China trade.[25] The well-established route for China trade was one of the reasons that the gold rush had such a prompt and significant impact on southern China. Sinn notes, "Foreign shipping merchants in Hong Kong and Guangzhou actively seduced people in the region by circulating placards, maps, and pamphlets, presenting highly colored accounts of the 'Gold Mountain.'"[26] They came in large numbers: in August 1852, the *Daily Alta California* printed a list that recorded 68 vessels (37 British, 16 American, and 12 from other European and South American countries) arriving from China between January and August of that year, delivering 18,040 passengers from China.[27] That October, the British vessel *Berkshire*, which previously had served Boston, Bombay, Calcutta, Sydney, Geelong, and London, brought the first Chinese opera troupe, Tong Hook Tong, to San Francisco.[28] The ship *Berkshire* departed Hong Kong on July 29, and arrived at San Francisco on October 6.[29] The *Berkshire* endured a "succession of strong head gales" during the sixty-day journey, "lost topsail yard, topsail, &c." before arriving at San Francisco.[30] The opera troupe was committed to the transpacific crossing—both the potential benefits and the unknown dangers. In addition to its 166 passengers, the *Berkshire* also brought goods: 2,370 bags of rice, 50 casks of oil, 28,400 pounds of sugar, and 2,900 tiles.[31]

From then on, ships continued to carry opera troupes and performers, as well as trunks of costumes, to American shores. Like other emigrants, the actors crossed the ocean in search of prosperity, but they also came with the mission of entertaining, warding off evil spirits, eradicating misfortune, and enhancing the harmony and success of Chinese communities. Theatrical offerings were an important means by which merchants and huiguan (in North America they were not only district or kinship associations but also a type of mutual aid organization) could win over the communities and establish their legitimacy. Theatrical performances eased tensions in the fast-growing global world of exchanges, encounters, and disparate interests. Throughout the second half of the nineteenth century, the transpacific route grew steadily. Ships increased in carrying capacity and reliability; later, new technology made them speedier and cheaper. The route sustained the to and fro of ships, people, and goods between coastal southern China and the Pacific coasts of the Americas. In addition, the growing prominence and prosperity of Hong Kong and San Francisco as major ports in the transpacific network led to the flourishing of Cantonese opera performances in these two cities, reinforcing the mobility of the troupes.

On the US side of the Pacific, Chinese theater became part of a wide variety of theatrical entertainments that thrived throughout California during the mid-nineteenth century. "Amusements of all sorts were in demand," the theater historian Misha Berson notes. "Before [San Francisco] had decent streets or adequate food supplies, it had performances of circus troupes and Chinese operas; Shakespearean tragedies and knockabout minstrel shows; plays in French, Italian, and German."[32] In certain respects, Chinese theater had much in common with the other extensive parallel theater worlds of touring companies for various non-English-language immigrants in San Francisco and the mining towns.[33] As the musicologist John Koegel notes, "Almost all European immigrant groups and several Latin American and some Asian and Middle Eastern communities promoted their original homelands' non-English-language musical theatre traditions in their adopted country." On the one hand, these constituted important sources of entertainment, artistic edification, and national pride, and on the other, eased their transition into American society.[34] Chinese theater was among the earliest immigrant theaters in San Francisco. It participated in, negotiated, and helped shape theatrical entertainment in the city.[35] In 1853, under the headline "The Spanish Theatre," a reporter for the *Daily Alta California* wrote, "On Sunday last we took occasion to visit the Spanish play, another striking theatre in the theatricals of San Francisco, which had already presented very credible specimens of the English, German, French and Chinese drama."[36]

Yet Chinese theater was decidedly different from other immigrant theaters. The prevalence of anti-Chinese sentiment in the United States brought about numerous challenges for the theaters, making them constant targets of mockery, assaults, and the imposition of criminal charges. Although other immigrant theaters, such as Mexican theaters, faced their share of racist and discriminatory practices during the same period, these were likely not so severe as those endured by Chinese immigrants. In 1883, a news story titled "The Chinese Must Go" reported an attack on a Chinese theater in San Francisco, with stones thrown through the windows.[37] The Chinese theaters' ability to survive, endure, and ultimately prosper speaks volumes about their tenacity and the resilience of their communities. Chinese theater's institutions and modes of circulation led to distinctive phases of development, to which we will now turn.

Four Phases of Chinese Theater's Development in California and the United States

In California, Cantonese opera experienced four phases of development during the nineteenth century. The first phase of Chinese theater was closely connected to huiguan. These associations were established by merchants and community leaders for the purpose of uniting clans, protecting group economic interests, and performing charitable and social functions for compatriots away from home. Huiguan also provided assistance to newcomers, meeting them at the wharf and taking them to the association headquarters, where they would be registered.[38] As early as 1851, two huiguan were founded in North America: the Sam Yup Association and the Sze Yup Association.[39] The following year, the Young Wo Association was established; one of its founders, Norman Assing (Yuan Sheng), became a manager of Tong Hook Tong, the first Chinese opera troupe to perform in America. The *Boston Evening Transcript* noted the huiguans' power when it reported that "a number of wealthy Chinese residents have sent to China for a dramatic troupe. . . . The troupe numbers upwards of a hundred performers—tragic, comical and musical—who have made a reputation at home."[40] As in their work representing the Chinese community in negotiations with the governors and the state legislature of California, huiguan led the way in cultural production. One of the earliest references to Chinese theatrical performance in Sacramento described a space at the Sze Yup Association in 1851 that had one hundred seats.[41] As the number of Chinese immigrants continued to grow, quite a few huiguan were established to represent different constituencies within the community. This inevitably led to rivalries, split-offs, and reorganizations. Later, Chinese theaters would also become closely aligned with different huiguan.

The second phase of Chinese theater concerns the development of connections via waterways to San Francisco's hinterland. The transoceanic circulation brought the troupes not only to San Francisco; they continued upstream to the northern Californian mining towns and agricultural regions where the majority of Chinese lived.[42] Such an itinerant life was not new to Cantonese opera performers; in southern China, they traveled on boats to perform in towns and villages along the waterways throughout the Pearl River delta. Some smaller troupes also used other modes of transportation to visit places farther inland. There was even a name for such troupes, 過山班, meaning "cross-mountain troupe." Just as they skillfully shuttled among the temple fairs in various towns in China, the troupes adeptly toured the interior of

California on waterways and then on land via stagecoaches to mining and, later, railroad towns. Performances of Chinese theater were reported from the northern to the southern end of the delta region between the Sacramento and San Joaquin Rivers. The presence of the troupes signaled the prominence of Chinese in the locality. Unfortunately, very limited details about these performances survive today. Nevertheless, a rough sketch of the circulation of troupes through the hinterland can help us conceptualize afresh the reverberation of their voices.[43]

To be sure, the mining-town circuit was a common route for many types of groups, performing British melodramas, Italian operas, Irish plays, variety acts, and so on. It was very profitable and, as the historian Ronald Davis notes, "In their conscious effort to acquire the trappings of culture, the miners instinctively looked to Europe and to a heritage often incongruous with their own lives."[44] However, touring the mining towns held a particular significance for Chinese opera troupes. An important reason that Chinese communities engaged opera troupes, particularly in rural areas, was the belief that by drawing crowds and presenting lively, colorful spectacles, theatrical performances warded off evil spirit and brought good luck; in other words, one kind of bustling prosperity could induce another kind of prosperity. Ritual performances could eradicate misfortune. Barbara E. Ward explains that "the whole set of performance acts in general is a magical act, the very doing of which is supposed (*opus operatum*) to have a general, broad-spectrum, mystical effect for good."[45] The audiences' joviality at the theater also boded well for the community, bringing the aura of magical blessing (旺).[46] Although Ward was referring to performances at a fishing community in Hong Kong, the same effect applied to the mining, agricultural, fishing, logging, and railroad communities scattered in the foothills of northern California from the 1850s to the 1870s. And prosperous they became. The thrill of seeing these performances, which heightened opera troupes' popularity in villages along the Pearl River delta, also occured in the interior of California.

A notable example is Marysville, just north of Sacramento. By the end of 1869, Marysville had become an important center for supporting railroad construction, mining, and agriculture in the area.[47] In October of that year, a Cantonese opera troupe came to perform at the Marysville Theater, attracting a large number of attendees from the vicinity. With great success, its run was extended from one month to three. As it occupied the city's only performing venue, many other troupes were unable to rent the theater for their performances and were turned away, including the renowned Brignoli Italian Opera Troupe, which had had significant success in New York and San Francisco.

From one location to the next, the itinerant troupes would either hire existing public performing spaces, such as the Marysville Theater or construct their own theaters. For example, in 1856, the *Stockton Independent* reported on a Chinese theater made of a wood frame with a canvas covering; in 1857, another theater was reportedly constructed with frames and stakes for support.[48] As part of their itinerary, these troupes periodically held seasons of performances in San Francisco, using that city's theatrical spaces for a period of time before touring the interior of the state. Over time, their residencies in San Francisco theaters became longer and more continuous. Cantonese opera troupes, like other performing groups, benefited from the lucrative rotation between San Francisco and towns in the interior of the state. In addition to their regular performances, Chinese troupes occasionally were featured as special guests in prominent San Francisco venues, such as the Metropolitan Theater or Maguire's Opera House, which primarily produced European operas, operettas, concerts, comedies, and melodramas. Nevertheless, owing to their regular presence in northern California's mining towns and agricultural regions, Chinese troupes came to be touted as the "state's own," as seen in an advertisement for the Lyceum Theater (see fig. 3.6).

On the other hand, commercial theaters' purpose built by Chinese merchants firmly established Chinese theater's position in urban culture. Around the late 1860s in southern China, commercial theaters with seating capacities of fifteen hundred and two thousand were built for public performances of Cantonese opera. The first theater in Hong Kong, the Sheng Ping (昇平) Theater, was built in 1865. Similar developments began on the American side of the Pacific. The grand opening of the first purpose-built Chinese theater in San Francisco, in January 1868, marked the beginning of the third phase: large, commercial Chinese theaters. Before the end of the 1870s, four Chinese theaters were built in the city within blocks of one another, spurring the continued recruitment of troupes and performers from China. Theater advertisements, as well as actors' names and high salaries, began to appear in newspapers. This significant growth reflected the increase in the population of San Francisco, from 56,802 in 1860 to 149,473 in 1870 and 233,959 in 1880.[49] Meanwhile, as Misha Berson notes, the 1870s were a particularly remarkable era for the theatrical worlds of San Francisco, which saw the establishment of three grand venues: the California Theater, Baldwin's Theater, and Wade's Opera House.[50] The commercial Chinese theaters were ambitious and sizable as well, seating between fifteen hundred and twenty-five hundred. The third Chinese theater was built in a modern style; it shared the same architects as San Francisco's City Hall and the Nob Hill mansions of railroad tycoons such as Charles Crocker. Chinese theaters aimed to appeal to a more extensive audience beyond the Chinese community. As evidenced by newspaper advertisements, these theaters sought to compete with a diverse array of music theatrical entertainments, including European operas, concerts, melodramas, variety shows, and various other immigrant theaters. Over the years

Chinese theaters attracted visitors from a wide range of social and economic classes, including prominent figures such as the Austrian violinist and composer Miska Hauser (1853), President Ruthford B. Hayes (1880), the British princess Louise, Duchess of Argyll (1882), the Hungarian soprano Etelka Gerster (1884), the French actress Sarah Bernhardt (1887), and members of the Leland Stanford family (1887), to name only a few.[51]

The significance of Chinese theater also was enhanced by the advances in transportation and printing technology during the Industrial Era. With the completion of the transcontinental railroad in 1869, a year after the first theater was built, audiences from the East and the other side of the Atlantic could more easily reach San Francisco's Chinese theaters, making them a significant draw for westbound visitors seeking adventure. In addition, Chinese theater was an especially attractive visual subject for the surge in periodicals, particularly illustrated magazines, that resulted from advances in printing technology. Through images of various kinds, San Francisco's Chinese theaters gained widespread renown. One of the most notable illustrations was Joseph Becker's depiction of Chinese theater in the 1870s, commissioned by *Frank Leslie's Illustrated Magazine* as part of its series "The Coming Man" (see chap. 4).

During 1870s and eighties, the Chinese community also faced the rise of rampant anti-Chinese legislation, sentiment, and violence. In the 1871 Chinatown massacre, rioters in Los Angeles carried out one of the largest mass lynchings in US history. In 1877, the Workingmen's Party of California achieved political prominence with the rallying cry "Chinese Must Go." Yet Chinese opera theaters continued to thrive, becoming an integral part of the city's prominent artistic endeavors and theatrical entertainment. Artists, writers, actors, and groups such as the Bohemian Club visited the theaters and sought inspiration from them.[52] Attracting audiences from all over the world, Chinese theaters were a medium of representation for the Chinese community and San Francisco. Chinese opera troupes continued to arrive. Ah Quin's diary shows that he frequented all four Chinese theaters from 1878 to 1880, but the theaters and troupes had undergone significant turnover by the time he left San Francisco in October 1880. The world of Chinese theater also saw the influence of prominent actors: the first three theaters were founded by wealthy merchants, whereas an actor-manager led the establishment of the fourth.

The notability of Chinese theater led to the fourth phase of its development in the United States. This phase can be characterized as "sonic ethnology," a version of what Jann Pasler calls "sonic anthropology," which refers to the ethnographic and anthropological efforts to explore and transcribe non-European musical forms at the end of the nineteenth century.[53] The American public's general excitement and curiosity about the 1889 Paris Universal Exposition stimulated interest in viewing Chinese theater as a subject of study. It engendered new sensibilities in a society that craved knowledge about and analysis of ethnic others. Chinese opera performers and impresarios responded to this anthropological interest by expanding their networks across the continent and staging Chinese cultural conventions. Particularly important in this process was the connection to civil rights: Chinese theater gained the advocacy of Wong Chin Foo, a tireless Chinese civil rights activist in New York City. In 1889, with his endorsement, an eastbound Chinese troupe traveled across the continent and performed in the city's Windsor Theater; a portrait of a Chinese opera diva landed on the cover of *Harper's Bazaar*. The crowning event of this phase was a performance in Boston for the American Folklore Society. Although Bostonians' celebrated visit to the city's own Chinese theater might have been a nod to the Paris Universal Exposition, it underscored the burgeoning ethnographic interest. Chinese theater was placed in a more favorable light. Impresarios of Chinese opera continued to respond to the growing ethnographic interest in the United States by showcasing Chinese theater performances at world's fairs and exhibitions toward the end of nineteenth century, including the World's Columbian Exposition in Chicago in 1893.

San Francisco and northern California, where Chinese theater in the United States started and prospered, are the primary focus of this book. They were the locus of the most substantial and active theaters operated in the nineteenth century. Although this book does not include other cities along the Pacific coast, the establishment of Chinese theaters in Northern California was an impetus for continued arrivals of troupes and performers from China, which in turn facilitated further circulation along the Pacific coast: Victoria, British Columbia, had its first Chinese theater in the 1860s and its fifth by 1885; Portland's first was built in 1880; and in Los Angeles, a theater opened in 1884.[54] Gradually, a Pacific Northwest network was formed. Before San Francisco endured the catastrophic earthquake and fire in 1906, it still had two Chinese theaters, as the city's Chinese directory shows.[55]

During the 1920s, a second golden era of Chinese theater developed into an even more extensive yet intimately connected network encompassing San Francisco, Seattle, Vancouver, Chicago, New York, Havana, and Honolulu, the history of which is discussed in my book *Chinatown Opera Theater in North America*.[56]

Part 2

Visuality of Chinese Theater

Visual experience was one of the most significant sensory qualities of Chinese opera, a genre known for its symbolism. Accompanied by melodic and percussion instruments, performers animated the stage with their voices, choreographed dance, and other movements; their painted faces and their costumes embodied the roles, status, and predicaments of the characters. The whole created a complex system of signification. The opera costumes were particularly important, rich in symbolism from color and design, and played a crucial role in characterizing the various roles within the drama. They were an essential part of the apparatus of theatrical production, attesting to the centrality of visuality in Chinese theater. It is no surprise that nineteenth-century North American audiences found Chinese opera's costumes to be visually captivating. These costumes played a significant role in constructing the collective memories of individuals and society; their aesthetics and presence were something for viewers to aspire to. The opulence of the costumes constituted the visual spectacle of Chinese theater and further emphasized the role of theater in shaping cultural identity and experience.

Historically, opera costumes fulfilled an important function in reflecting and even propelling changes in Chinese society, particularly in connection with fashion trends, consumer culture, and social boundaries.[57] As a genre of the southern region, Cantonese opera was especially known for the extravagance of its costumes, whose fabric and embroidery reflected aesthetically both the lush vegetation and the climate in Guangzhou and the city's notable history as the only port accessible to foreign traders. Yang Maojian, a Cantonese writer known for his theatrical commentaries, wrote in 1842, "[Cantonese opera] costumes are extravagant and expensive. When appearing on stage, they shine mystically with gold and emerald, akin to the terraces of seven gems. With such dazzling brilliance one can hardly stare at them for long. Even opera theaters of the country's capital do not have such extravagance."[58] In 1866, another writer, Yang Enshou, gave a vivid description of the distinctive glamour associated with costumes for a Cantonese opera performance: "Seven ladies appeared in palace dresses, each presenting a dance. The palace dresses were double-sided with different colors. When they were quickly flipped during performance, it had the effect of colossal colorful clouds falling from the sky."[59]

Cantonese opera costume owed its glamour to exquisite Cantonese silk embroidery, whose salient features included "dense, decorative motifs; strongly contrasted, vivid colors; abundant use of gold thread; birds and animals depicted with the techniques [that simulated the texture of animal hair and outlined plumage and fur]; dragon scales and bird feathers rendered in [special stitching]; outlining in gold threads and horsehair threads; and the use of peacock feather threads."[60] Typically the embroidery's motifs and symbolic patterns signaled the status of the characters. For example, the armor of the generals could be densely embroidered in satin stitch, silk floss, and couched threads wrapped with gold-colored metal or heavily ornamented with silvered brass disks and hexagonal mirrors held by fitted metal frames.[61] These prized costumes were portable wealth for Cantonese opera troupes and accompanied the troupes' Pacific crossings. In California they attracted the attention of journalists and writers from the moment they arrived. As part of the Chinese theater presentation, the costumes affirmed the high value and desirability of the Cantonese silk embroidery that had traveled the trade routes to Europe and America, invariably collected as a sign of wealth and social status. "In the houses of the rich," an American magazine reflected, "Chinese embroidery was used for every purpose, even for furniture covering."[62] Imbued with dramatic power on stage, the costumes added to the allure of Chinese culture and objects, fueling the vogue and fantasy surrounding them. A news item in 1888 astutely encapsulated the public's fervent fascination: "One of the dresses of the outfit of a Chinese dramatic company, purchased for an opera in New York, contains over 4,000,000 stitches."[63] As the interest in Chinese opera costumes grew toward the end of the nineteenth century, various forms of "owning the glamour" arose on theater stages, at private parties, and in diverse social situations.

For the Chinese community, the glamorous opera costumes constituted an essential part of the performance identity of Chinese theater. It was an important factor in how the production of opera created spectacle. Richly elaborate, with complex symbolic designs, Cantonese opera costumes allowed actors to inhabit their characters' mental landscapes.[64] The costumes also enhanced their movements and gestures, imbuing the performers' bodies with meaning.[65] They performed the function of communication and were an extension of a performer's inner self to the textile. Rather than just a cover, they were the "second skin" of the performers, to borrow a an apt term from the literary scholar Anne Anlin Cheng.[66] The costume embodied the scenario associated with the role that the performer inhabited. Calling attention to what can be termed a "performative China," these representations concretized the public images of Chineseness.[67]

Opera costumes articulated the hypervisibility of Chinese theater and were the most prominent visual representations of the Chinese diaspora in the United States. Their beauty and glamour were a central attraction, and they played an important role in expanding the theater's influence beyond physical space to the commercial, cultural, and artistic realms of nineteenth- and twentieth-century America and beyond. It had a lasting impact. In the 1929 British silent film *Piccadilly*, Anna May Wong famously performed a long, sensational floor dance in a shiny, ornate costume that included a sequin-covered breastplate. In the background, the musicians played *sanxian* and *huqin*, traditional instruments of Cantonese opera accompaniment. Wong's stunning costume approximated Cantonese opera's armor of a warrior general, with novel twists.[68] Her headdress, with six fanning spears, simulated the headgear, with pheasant tail feathers and flags, typical of a general's attire. (See the discussion of the 1889 cover image of *Harper's Bazaar*, fig. 10.3.) These references to opera costume provided visual codes for her stage persona and identity. In the center of the spotlight, her costumed body projected brilliance and exercised a kind of performative agency akin to that of the glamorously clothed performers in Chinese theater.[69]

Theatricality

The stage of Chinese theater operates with a defined scenic repertoire of gestures, music, and scenarios. In the established tradition of Chinese theaters, where the stage was bare of scenery and stage props, the setting was indicated solely through the actors' movements, speech, and singing. In a study of Chinese theater of the Yuan dynasty, the scholar Patricia Sieber argues that the amalgamation of different rhetorical styles produces a wide range of emotional and moral stances. She listed the following rhetorical modalities used by a main female lead: "the language of filial tenderness, the language of filial counsel, the language of female decorum, the language of wifely care and worry, impassioned invective against the father, the language of wifely fidelity, the language of social satire, the poetic language of female longing, the invocation of Heaven, among others."[70] Indeed, it was such variety that created dynamic depth for the characters. Furthermore, comic roles on the Chinese stage interacted not only with each other but also with the audience, offering self-referential remarks, punch lines, assessments, and so on. They made "use of a plurality of voices within a play to make the audience laugh and reflect at the same time."[71]

The German dramatist Bertolt Brecht famously noted this essential theatricality after he encountered Chinese opera: "The feeling is produced in the audience by the manner in which the [actor] plays the scene."[72] In a similar vein, the theater scholar Samuel Weber noted that the primary interest of Chinese theater is not to advance the plot "but rather to use the action and plot to foreground the significance of the performance."[73] Whereas the repertoire of scenarios could be presented in infinite variations, at the center of the theatricality were the performers' renditions of music and speeches, as well as the mastery of gesticulation needed to portray the essence of characterization. Weber captured the fundamental core of theatricality in his description of the actors' body language during a Peking opera scene featuring boating, a popular scenario in Chinese theater, particularly Cantonese opera. His close observation is worth quoting at length.

> With one long oar as his sole prop, this rustic figure glides onto the stage in his (invisible) boat, suggested by the way he holds and moves the oar, as well as by the parallel, lateral movement of his feet, while his upper body remains rigid and unbending. With the suggested movement of the boat, there is inevitably that of the water itself, "visible" only in its effects: the rhythmic swaying of the man's body, rigid as it leans against the pole. The

boatman seems to sway in the water, going nowhere, yet constantly moving. Such going—nowhere—while-moving constitutes much of the magic of this scene. With the boatman's swaying, water invisibly enters the scene, taking (its) place less "on" than "as" the stage.[74]

Boating scenes were not only a popular element of scenic repertoire but often were incorporated into various dramatic plots in Cantonese opera. The emotion of taking the voyage was externalized through well-crafted gestures. As Brecht noted, the actor must "find a sensibly perceptible outward expression for his character's emotions, preferably some action that gives away what is going on inside him."[75] Such presentation of theatricality through gesture and symbolism is a major attraction for audiences and is considered a distinctive feature of Chinese theater. The reciprocal interplay among performers constitutes the exquisite theatricality of scenes on stage.

In a unique way, the Chinese theater in nineteenth-century America gave rise to a hybrid form of performance that combined the conventional performing gestures of Chinese opera with technological innovations in pursuit of realism on stage. An 1882 *San Francisco Examiner* report gave a vivid description of the doings of Chinese theater in a North American context.

> The curtains of the doorway on the right side of the stage parted and the junk walked in. In the bow of the vessel was Ah Sue, the celebrated actor, and in the stern another Chinaman, who also personated a woman. The junk was about eight feet long by four high, and was carried as the horsemen in burlesque scenes carry their steeds. . . . [H]e managed to have the junk outdo in agility anything ever seen on the waters of the Yang Tse Kiang. She bobbed up and down at the end of every verse of Ah Sue's song like a spavined streetcar horse, and twisted around as if the colic was working in her vitals. At every movement the theater roared with delight and amazement, and when Ah Sue and his partner picked up the waters of the Yang Tse Kiang, so as to leave their feet unobstructed, and with the naval constructor in close tow scooted back to the greenroom, the sensation reached its climax.[76]

In this visually striking scene of an entrance of a junk onto the stage, the elaborate mechanism of the junk, combined with the traditional theatrical movements of the actors, captivated the audience. The actors navigated the junk while moving the boat on the stage, eliciting delight and amazement from the audience. The traditional acting of a boating scene is known for its theatricality, which Brecht once described as "a true art of beholding."[77] Yet its convergence with machinery in the 1882 staging of Chinese opera in San Francisco reflected the dynamic interplay of cultural traditions and audience expectations. Chinese theater's bare stage and reliance on audience imagination had been frequently noted by the critics as reaffirming its primitive and inferior status. By presenting a life-size wooden boat on stage, this Chinese theater in California brought the representational object of realism to the stage while preserving the aesthetics of traditional symbolic performance of choreographed movements, a hallmark of Chinese opera. Furthermore, as an extension of the performers, the junk "boobed up and down . . . like a spavined streetcar horse." Theaters and actors embraced the challenges of navigating the terrain of novel entertainment and traditional stagecraft. Here, a key element of the entertainment was the unexpectedness of the new device as experiment. The spectators' delight came from both the surprise and the visualization of this innovative technology, combined with the familiar, traditional form of performance style.

This shift toward realism was shaped by the wider cultural and artistic movement in San Francisco, which was spearheaded by David Belasco. As the manager of the Baldwin Theater at the time, Belasco was renowned for his efforts to bring real-life fidelity to the stage, adding greater emotional depth to dramatic performances. During this time, Chinese theaters also created a unique style of theatricality that bridged different worlds, reaffirming the richness of Chinese theater in North America. Meanwhile, Chinese theater's presence in the cultural landscape also led to the absorption of various elements of Chinese opera's theatricality by other theaters and producers in San Francisco. This, in turn, led to the emergence of experimental theaters toward the end of the nineteenth century.

Chapter Overview

The chapters in this book proceed chronologically, largely following the four phases of the development of Chinese theater, primarily in California, and then across the continent as the fourth phase came into full scale. Chapter 1 considers the earliest history of Chinese music and opera in California. It traces the presentation of Chinese music to the early days of California's statehood (1850), demonstrating how the appearance of Chinese music and opera was closely connected to the agenda of the leaders of the first Chinese immigrant community. The establishment of Chinese opera theater was embedded in the rise of transpacific crossings and the operation of huiguan culture. Chapter 2 follows Chinese theater to the interior of northern California during the next fifteen years, the second phase of development. This chapter sketches out the circulation of troupes along California's waterways and the significance of Chinese theater for Chinese working in mining towns and on the railroad. It reinscribes the sonic presence of Chinese theater on the cultural landscape of the American West in the middle of the nineteenth century. Chapter 3 examines the parallel development of Chinese theater in San Francisco during the same period. It describes how, through the use of existing theatrical venues, Chinese opera remained an active presence in the city. Periodic performances in San Francisco grew more regular and constituted a prelude to the third phase of development.

Chapters 4 through 6 address the third phase. They detail the fascinating history of four commercial Chinese theaters in San Francisco that were built between 1868 and 1879. Chapter 4 begins with the grand opening of the first Chinese theater on Jackson Street: its audience, advertising, and reception. This theater, built a year before the completion of the transcontinental railroad, was made famous through an illustration by Joseph Becker (see fig. 4.1). The chapter also discusses city ordinances curtailing Chinese theaters' success. It then moves on to the second theater, built in 1874, and its key sponsor, doctor Li Po Tai. Chapter 5 begins with historical documents in Chinese: two rosters of eleven top Cantonese opera troupes printed in San Francisco's own Chinese newspaper. The chapter then considers the opening of the third theater amid intense anti-Chinese hostility after the Sandlot riot of July 1877. Chapter 6 considers music making in Chinese missionary schools and the impact of the first Chinese ambassador in 1878. A theater merger and the establishment of the fourth theater in 1879 brought the development of the third phase to an end.

Chapter 7 turns to the impact of the Chinese Exclusion Act (1882), detailing how Chinese theaters and actors presented some of the earliest challenges to the implementation of this law. Chapter 8 shows how star actors rose to become the public faces of Chinese theater and the community and discusses the appearance of the term "Chinese-American theater" in English-language newspapers. Chapter 9 considers the contemporaneous discourse about San Francisco's Chinese theater in print, both words and images. This chapter highlights the images created by Theodore Wores and Kenyon Cox, which have thus far received little attention. Chapter 10 considers the full-blown phase of sonic ethnology, which accompanied the movement of performers and troupes eastward, and its connection to the Chinese American civil rights advocate Wong Chin Foo. It examines the impact of the Paris Universal Exhibition of 1889 on Chinese theaters, culminating in the visit by the American Folklore Society to Boston's own Chinese theater. In an epilogue, we again consider the everydayness and social significance of Chinese theater through Ah Quin's eyes, exploring his entry about an opera in terms of both the text and the sonic possibilities. It is followed by discussion of archive and listening practice, examining three processes of erasure—conceptual identity, listening practice, and criminalization—and a reflection on transpacific history of American music.

CHAPTER 1

First Encounters

A Chinese music band appears in the lithographic print by Cooke & LeCount that commemorated California's July 4 celebration in 1852, along with other national groups (fig. 1.1). Published on July 5, this remarkable illustration showed the long, winding line of the parade snaking past the crowd of spectators in the foreground to disappear in the distance, linking "San Francisco, Cal" at the bottom of the page to the caption "Celebration of the 4th of July" at the top. A Chinese presence was prominently featured—more than eighty Chinese men, as well as six horses and two carriages. The meticulous rendering captured their different classes: mandarins and dignitaries in long coats with official headgear, commoners in gowns and trousers with conical hats or bowler hats, and hatless, burly men in martial gear. One wagon with a canopy is depicted at the left edge; the other, in the center, carries a band of four musicians, one holding a pair of cymbals. A billowing flag, the single largest object in the illustration, is flanked by people on both sides. This oversized triangular banner, depicting a dragon, suggests the bright yellow flag of imperial China. At the center of the drawing are three handsome horses carrying dignified Chinese men and the wagon carrying the Chinese band. With at least six other flags signaling the state's diverse constituents, the print presents an image of harmonious unity among diverse groups and a promising future. John McDougal, the governor of California in 1851, called the Chinese "one of the most worthy classes of our newly adopted citizens."[1]

This celebrated event was also reported in a lengthy article in the *Daily Alta California*, which included unequivocal praise of the Chinese contingent's impressive presence and patriotism:

[The] great and principal feature of the procession was the Celestials, who turned out in astonishing numbers. There were no less than three

FIGURE 1.1 Celebration of the Fourth of July, San Francisco, ca. 1852. Lithographic print by Cooke & Le. Courtesy Bancroft Library, University of California, Berkeley.

or four hundred of these singular beings, who took an active part in com-memorating this glorious day. Their procession was headed by four of their number bearing a large flag made of silk, on which was the figure of a dragon and having eyes made of looking-glass. It was one of the rich-est specimens of art we have seen, and the cost of it alone was $2000. Another banner in the procession, borne by some of their numbers, bore the emblematic words of "A rush for Republicanism" and "The 4th of July hereafter and forever a festival day for the Chinese." A carriage drawn by four grey horses contained a band of their native musicians, who with their unwieldy and strange looking musical instruments discoursed horrible harmony in an extravagant style. A large number of mandarins in carriages and on horseback were in attendance, whilst many followed on foot. The whole was under the command of Norman Assing, Esq., together with Sam Wo and several other of our prominent Chinese citizens. This was the great feature of the procession, and the manner in which it was gotten up by this portion of our Celestial population reflects great credit upon their generosity and patriotism. Mr. Tonga-Chick [*sic*], a young gentle-man well known to many of our merchants, took a prominent part in the proceedings.[2]

Excerpted and with the new title "Chinese Celebration of July 4th," this description was circulated in newspapers as far away as Louisville, Hartford, Portland (Maine), and Alexandria.[3] Norman Assing and Tong A-Chick were both leading members of the early Chinese community, and they would soon become the managers of a Chinese opera troupe.

Setting the Tone

Since their arrival, Chinese merchants and businessmen had participated in public ceremonies and parades like this to demonstrate their commitment to their new country. At a landmark celebration of California's formal admis-sion into the Union on September 9, 1850, Assing led the Chinese community in presenting a grand "triumphal car," drawn by six white horses and contain-ing thirty men, each holding a shield representing a state, and accompanied by a large, elaborate banner with the inscription "California—The Union, it must be preserved."[4]

The earliest currently known reference to Chinese performing musicians in the United States was their appearance at the celebration of George Wash-ington's birthday on February 22, 1852. California had become the thirty-first state only seventeen months prior, but the *Daily Alta California* reported the grandeur of the city's celebration as "unsurpassed by any city in the United States." This exhilarating event included firing a thirty-one-gun salute, the ringing of fire truck bells, and a long procession of horses, wagons, soldiers, engine (fire brigade) companies, and various other organizations. The *Daily Alta California* described the Chinese contingent.

> The citizens of the Celestial Empire turned out in large bodies under the command of Norman Assing, a well-known resident of our city. At the head of their body was a carriage containing several Chinese musicians, who dispensed harmony as they proceeded through the streets.[5]

Littell's Living Age reported that six Chinese musicians performed from an express wagon.[6]

Music was an important part of Chinese processions, which had different functions. Music enhanced auspiciousness, guided the processions, attracted attention, and intensified symbolic displays of prosperity.

Early Chinese leaders such as Norman Assing and Tong A-Chick received Western educations and traveled frequently in China, the United States, and the British colonies. Norman Assing (also known as Yuan Shen, 袁生) traveled from Macao to New York in the 1820s and lived in Charleston, South Carolina, where he became a naturalized citizen and a Christian. He returned to Hong Kong, then came to San Francisco after the gold rush began, becoming a successful restaurateur while also managing a trading company. Assing possessed an intimate knowledge of the US Constitution and continued to travel back and forth between China and the United States, becoming a bridge between the Chinese community and local California authorities.[7] The 1854 *San Francisco City Directory* lists Norman Assing as the representative of China among the twenty-seven foreign consuls.[8]

Tong A-Chick (also known as Tang Tinggui or Tong Mow Chee 唐廷桂, 1828–1897), was a native of Xiangshan in Guangdong, where he received an English-language education from 1839 to 1849 at the Morrison School, an American missionary school in Macao and Hong Kong, and then at St. Paul's College in Hong Kong. He was baptized and was sent by the Morrison School to work for a period as an interpreter for the British Consulate in Shanghai, after the Treaty of Nanking was signed and the British were granted the right to trade at the five treaty ports. Between 1847 and 1851 he was appointed police magistrate to the court in Hong Kong. He came to California in early 1852 and became the head of Tong Wo & Co., the largest Chinese business in San Francisco at the time.[9] Of his activity, Rev. William Speer, who arrived in October 1852, reported in his journal for the Presbyterian Church: "Achick [*sic*] is regarded by the American community here as a man of more than common ability. He received us in his office attached to the hall of the company whose chief he is. His dress is the native silk gown, close pants, and embroidered shoes. His address impresses strangers as both dignified and courteous."[10] Tong returned to China in 1873 to become the lead comprador (local representative) of the Shanghai branch of Jardine, Matheson & Co. Ltd.

Many other members of the large transpacific Chinese mercantile class also became prominent figures in trading ports. They formed the powerful organizations known as huiguan. One nineteenth-century writer described them as being "established at the metropolis by mandarins among compatriots or fellow-provincials for mutual aid and protection. . . . Later merchants formed guilds like those of the mandarinate, and now they exist in every province."[11] In California, huiguan were the principal vehicle for all public welfare. Assing founded one such organization, Yanghe huiguan (Young Wo) in 1852, one of the first three huiguan in California. It quickly became the largest one, with a membership of fourteen thousand in the 1850s.[12]

However, the triumphant and harmonious image in the Independence Day illustration above glossed over the rising anti-Chinese hostility that greeted these entrepreneurs. Unlike his predecessor, Governor John Bigler, who took office in January 1852, was virulently anti-Chinese. In April, he gave a formal address to the state assembly, requesting that the legislature stop "coolies" [sic, indentured laborers] from immigrating, at both the state and national levels, and imposed a tax on them. He alleged that Chinese were mostly "coolies," their families were held hostage, and they were a menace to public safety. Of course, none of these allegation were true. He also suggested that Chinese not be allowed to testify in court. Bigler's address was published in full in the Daily Alta California, and copies of it were printed and distributed in the goldfields.[13] A bill to reenact the 1850 Foreign Miners' Tax, targeted at Chinese miners, was introduced in the state legislature. The California State Assembly also issued a report declaring the Chinese a menace to the welfare and prosperity of the state.[14]

With his unsubstantiated charges, Bigler used a racial trope to compare "Chinese to black slaves, the antithesis of free labor, and thereby cast them as a threat."[15] These measures prompted immediate action from the Chinese. On April 29, Tong, together with Hab Wa, another merchant, wrote a scathing response to Bigler in the San Francisco Herald, refuting the notion that Chinese were "coolies," protesting the anti-Chinese measures, and reminding Governor Bigler of the benefits of the Chinese community in California.[16] On May 5, Assing published in the Daily Alta California an eloquent open letter stating, "We are not the degraded race you would make us."

> The effect of your late message has been thus far to prejudice the public mind against my people, to enable those who wait the opportunity to hunt them down, and rob them of the rewards of their toil. [. . .] You are deeply convinced you say "that to enhance the prosperity and preserve the tranquility of this State, Asiatic immigration must be checked." [. . .] But we would beg to remind you that when your nation was a wilderness, and the nation from whom you sprung barbarous, we exercised most of the arts and virtues of civilized life; that we are possessed of a language and

literature, and that men skilled in science and the arts are numerous among us; that the productions of our manufactories, our sail and workshops, fans no small share of the commerce of the world. [. . .] That our people cannot be reproved for their idleness, and that your historians have given them due credit for the variety and richness of their works of art, and for their simplicity of manners, and particularly their industry. [. . .] You say that "gold, with its talismanic power, has overcome those natural habits of nonintercourse we have exhibited." [But] thousands of your own citizens come here to dig gold, with the idea of returning as speedily as they can. We think you are in error, however, in this respect, as many of us, and many more, will acquire a domicile amongst you.

Assing goes on to reject the notion that California had the right under the Constitution to restrict immigration and closes with an unequivocal statement of the intent of the Chinese to settle in California like other people.[17]

These letters gained support from as far away as New York City. In a lengthy article entitled "John Chinaman vs. John Bigler," the *Daily Alta California* reported: "The N. Y. *Evening Mirror*, in a sensible, caustic and well written article on the famous Cooly [*sic*] Message of the present Executive of this State, cites the remonstrance of the citizens Tong Achick and Norman Assing, as an admirable example of the sound sense and logical reasoning which sometimes comes from despised and humble sources of intelligence to oppose and overthrow the pretentious wisdom and weak brained fulminations of would-be demagogues and rulers."[18]

Cultural articulation—the celebration of the history and value of any given culture—had an important role in Chinese leaders' attempts to push back against racist regulations and discrimination. Among the most popular public manifestations of Chinese immigrants in the nineteenth-century American West were its processions, often involving gongs, drums, and wind instruments, on occasions such as solemn religious rituals, public tribute, and celebration, as well as political and patriotic gestures. They were common wherever Chinese communities were established, whether rural or urban—even as far inland as Idaho—and were frequently commented on and depicted in American media.[19] In many historical photographs, we can see their long cavalcades amid various landscapes around the country. These processions both affirmed Chinese membership in American society and celebrated Chinese culture in the new nation.

Chinese community leaders were aware of their dual roles in facilitating both international and California business. As the historian Mae Ngai notes, "Their social influence was situated in two networks: their interaction and connection with American leaders of the city (and by extension, to the state), and more important, their position at the top of the organization of the huiguan."[20] Despite enacting restrictive laws to hinder the success of the

Chinese in the country, Americans also were interested in developing trade with China, which required the assistance of Chinese. Two early examples involve famous figures in American politics. In 1850, on the occasion of a commemoration of President Zachary Taylor, who had recently died, San Francisco's mayor invited Assing to send a contingent to participate in the ceremony and assigned it a prominent place in the procession.[21] Assing sent the mayor a letter after the event to express the Chinese community's "thanks for the kind mark of attention," adding that "they feel proud of the distinction shown them, and will always endeavor to merit the good opinion of the citizens of their adopted country.'"[22] The letter was reported in the newspapers. The depiction of a savvy Chinese merchant engaging in US politics was widely reprinted not only in America but also crossed the Pacific to appear in an English-language newspaper in China.[23] In August 1852, when city officials planned to hold a grand commemoration of Henry Clay—a renowned politician and the author of the Compromise of 1850, which had played a pivotal role in California's admission into the Union as a free state—Assing was again invited and led a Chinese procession with five hundred members.[24]

These active public engagements were facilitated through the huiguan, organizations without an American analog that fulfilled various significant social functions. For example, they made generous donations for good causes, such as a thousand dollars to the San Francisco Fire Department Fund, which was the third largest amount recorded at the time.[25] According to the sociologist Sue Fawn Chung, they also "served as brokers for goods, set prices for merchandise such as tea and dyed cloth, worked with government officials, hosted operas and other types of entertainment, and provided funerary arrangements and burial grounds."[26] Huiguan members staffed the processions, and these events became what can be called a "symbol of shared identity and mutual support" that bonded individuals in a wider sense of togetherness, to borrow an expression from the anthropologist Red Myers.[27]

The First Chinese Opera Troupe

By the summer of 1852, Chinese merchants and huiguan were working on bringing Chinese opera to California. This was partly due to its significance as entertainment and ritual for Chinese immigrants, the majority of whom came from southern China, where appreciation for Cantonese opera permeated all levels of society. It also was because the spectacle could appeal beyond the Chinese community, thus being profitable. The general American public had already gained glimpses of Chinese theater from reports of travelers, missionaries, and colonial officers. One such report appeared in a

September 1845 issue of the *American Penny Magazine, and Family Newspaper* (later *Dwight's American Magazine*), a magazine notably encyclopedic in its scope, with articles on world affairs, among other things. An illustration of Chinese opera warriors was on the cover (fig. 1.2). The lead article, "Chinese Play Actors," drew heavily on information from officials of Dutch and Portuguese colonies such as Macao, and in Indonesia, and the British colony of Hong Kong.[28] It discussed various aspects of Chinese opera, from storylines to wardrobe and music.

By the end of the summer of 1852, Assing confirmed for reporters that a Chinese opera troupe was coming.[29] Fully staged productions of opera were still uncommon in California; not until 1851 did San Francisco see its first fully staged opera, *La sonnambula*, by Vincenzo Bellini.[30] The performance,

FIGURE 1.2 "Chinese Play Actors," *Dwight's American Magazine* (1845).

by the Pellegrini Opera Company at the Adelphi Theatre, drew what Ronald Davis called a "motley collection" of frontiersmen. Although they "came to the opera merely to acquire the trappings of eastern society, many of them actually went away intrigued by what they saw and heard."[31] No European opera production was planned for the year 1852, but by midyear newspapers enthusiastically reported the imminent arrival of a Chinese opera troupe—Tong Hook Tong—and continued to update their readers on the event. In September, when the troupe was well on its way to San Francisco, a news report provided tantalizing details:

> A number of wealthy Chinese residents have sent to China for a dramatic troupe. They come provided with full theatrical costumes, decorations, scenes, and, in fact, all the singular contrivances with which they fit up their theatres in Canton. They are about to manage the affair in splendid style, and will spare no expense to put up a Celestial Theatre of the most approved order, and provide it with stars and starlets of the highest reputation. In course of time, as they find their enterprise successful, they will no doubt make regular engagements with the great Chinese tragedians and comedians who can run over here in forty or fifty days, and thus keep up, as our managers have it, a constant series of novelties. The company, we learn, have a capital of $40,000, with which they intend to erect a suitable and spacious theatre. The costumes they have ordered are said to be magnificent, and to have cost in China $27,000.[32]

The lavishness of Chinese silk and satin was well known as a result of the China trade, so people had reason to expect an extravagant show.[33] There would also be financial interest, because the impressive figure of the investment mentioned in the report implied the possibility of large profits.

Right before the opera opened, the city hosted another Chinese theatrical event: The Chinese Jugglers, a group of twenty Chinese magicians, tumblers, thrown-knife artists, and jugglers to perform at the American Theater for two days in early October. They reportedly arrived from Hong Kong. Managed by a prominent impresario John H. Gihon (known as the Western Barnum), this troupe created much excitement and drew significant audiences to the show.[34] On October 16, a preview of the Chinese opera troupe's opening night appeared in an advertisement in the *Daily Alta California* (fig. 1.3). To ensure that the audience could grasp the idea of the operas to be presented, the advertisement gave significant details, revealing a fully staged production with opera titles and a synopsis. This advertisement impressed the theatrical world, as it appeared three months later in a London weekly, the *Theatrical Journal*.[35] The arrival of Chinese opera on the American frontier was a notable affair to nineteenth-century societies from the United States to Great Britain.

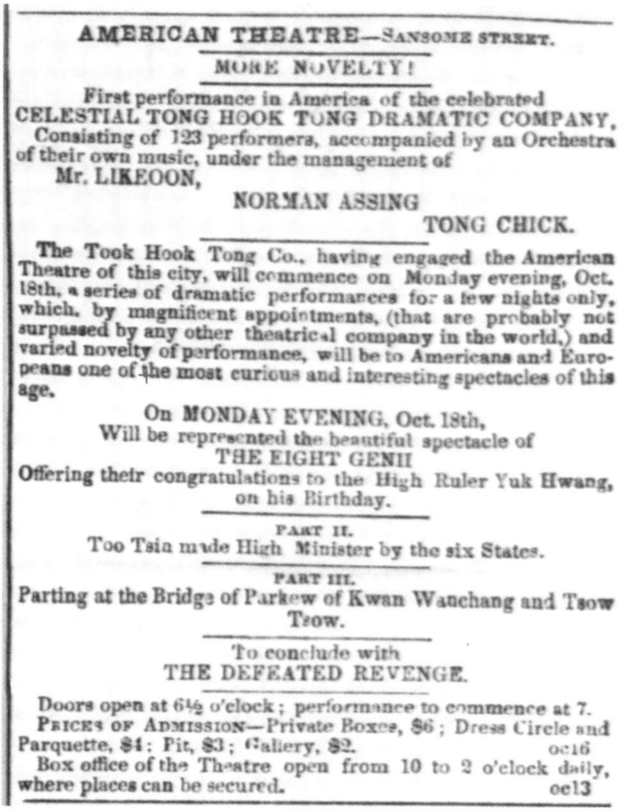

AMERICAN THEATRE—Sansome street.

MORE NOVELTY!

First performance in America of the celebrated
CELESTIAL TONG HOOK TONG DRAMATIC COMPANY,
Consisting of 123 performers, accompanied by an Orchestra
of their own music, under the management of
  Mr. LIKEOON,

NORMAN ASSING
TONG CHICK.

  The Took Hook Tong Co., having engaged the American
Theatre of this city, will commence on Monday evening, Oct.
18th, a series of dramatic performances for a few nights only,
which, by magnificent appointments, (that are probably not
surpassed by any other theatrical company in the world,) and
varied novelty of performance, will be to Americans and Europeans one of the most curious and interesting spectacles of this
age.

On MONDAY EVENING, Oct. 18th,
Will be represented the beautiful spectacle of
THE EIGHT GENII
Offering their congratulations to the High Ruler Yuk Hwang,
on his Birthday.

PART II.
Too Tsin made High Minister by the six States.

PART III.
Parting at the Bridge of Parkew of Kwan Wanchang and Tsow
Tsow.

To conclude with
THE DEFEATED REVENGE.

  Doors open at 6½ o'clock; performance to commence at 7.
Prices of Admission—Private Boxes, $6; Dress Circle and
Parquette, $4: Pit, $3; Gallery, $2.   oc16
  Box office of the Theatre open from 10 to 2 o'clock daily,
where places can be secured.   oc13

FIGURE 1.3 Advertisement for Tong Hook Tong Dramatic Company, *Daily Alta California*, October 16, 1852.

Tong Hook Tong premiered on the stage of the American Theatre on October 18. The opening performance's admission price was more than twice what the other theater, the Adelphi Theater (featuring a British melodrama) was charging. Tickets for Tong Hook Tong's opening night were two dollars for the gallery, three dollars for the pit, four dollars for the dress circle and parquet, and up to six dollars for the private boxes—about triple what the Chinese Jugglers had charged. The prices did not deter the audience; the *Sacramento Daily Union* opined, "the prices have been put up exorbitantly high, but they will probably draw full houses."[36] American audiences were not only curious but also felt the need to be more worldly; in the words of a writer newly moved to San Francisco, "I confessed I felt a very great curiosity to see how such [theatrical] exhibitions were conducted in China—a country of which we know so little, but are destined very soon to know a great deal more."[37] The troupe, reported the *Daily Alta California*, was "entertaining very good audiences, composed of their own countrymen as well as Americans."[38]

The performing venue, the American Theatre, was then the city's newest and best theater, built in October 1851. Its strongest competitor, the Jenny Lind Theatre, had just been sold to become the city hall. The American Theatre towered over its two lesser competitors, the Adelphi Theater and San Francisco Hall. Prominent and successful, it issued stock to its creditors, who got free admissions in return. The building had two balconies and a gallery, a dress circle, orchestra seats, and several stage boxes. Of its elegance, Albert Benard de Russailh, a French visitor, wrote:

> There is a great deal of typical English and American comfort. The carpets are thick and soft, and deaden your footsteps so that you can walk peacefully through the lobby and glance into the boxes without disturbing the audience.
>
> The house is nicely decorated with paintings and gilt-work. The boxes have red velvet curtains and the seats are upholstered in red plush. In many ways the luxury and good taste of this little theatre remind one of the Opéra Comique.[39]

Of the stage, the *Daily Alta California* reported, "The lights are arranged so as to extend from the two circles, there being no chandelier. On each side of the curtain and over the proscenium boxes two hanging lamps were suspended, each held up by an eagle's beak."[40]

To familiarize the enthusiastic audience with the program and to bridge the cultural gap, detailed playbills were prepared. A report in the *St. Louis Intelligencer* quoted in full the opening night's playbill, which included synopses of four operas. It was the earliest such document known in the United States, and is reproduced here:

> Monday evening. October 18. The entertainments of the evening will open with a favorite farce, in which the American company will appear. After which will be presented the four pieces of "The Eight Genii Offering their Congratulations," "The Six States making Soo Tsin their Great Minister," "The Parting at Park-Kew," and "The Defeated Revenge."
>
> Part 1. On the birthday of Yuh-twang, the High Ruler and Heavenly Majesty, the Eight Genii, whose names are Han chung-le, Nan-tsoi ho, Chang-ke-lo, Li-shua yang, Tswa kwok kan, Le techkwi, Hanslang tsy, and Hosie koo, come to congratulate him.
>
> Part 2. During the civil wars, B. C. 600, the Seven States were at war, of which the State of Tsin was the strongest. Soo tsin went around among the other six States of Tsi, Tsao, Hen, Ngai and Tsew to induce them to unite together and attack Tsin. This they did, and thus defeated Tsin. For it they made Soo Tsin their great Minister, and Generalissimo of their united forces.
>
> Part 3. During the Han dynasty, and the wars of the three States, A. D. 222 Kwan-wan-chang (a famous warrior) and Lau-pe were defeated by

Tsow-Tsow. The conqueror sent an officer to urge Kwan to submit; but the latter refused to come under his ruling, saying, "At present I can only dwell temporarily in your tent; when I have learned where Lau pe is, I must uphold the rightful majesty." Having learned that Lau-pe was with Yuan-shew, Kwan went to join him, and Tsow tsow made a parting feast at ParKew, and gave him a robe. On receiving it, Kwan put it on underneath one given him by Lau-pe. When Tsow-Tsow asked him the reason he replied, "A man of honor never forgets his old friends, but remembers the importance of the relations between Prince and Minister."

Part 4. The King and Queen of the Or pre-Hung country, while on a hunting expedition, shot a spirit which had assumed the form of a deer and wounded it in the leg. The spirit becoming angry, passed with the spirit of a fox into the forms of the father and daughter, making the father offer the daughter as a concubine to the King and intending, through her, to ruin the throne of the latter. A Buddhist Priest, named Tong-som chong, who was on his way to the Western Heavens, in order to get his prayer books, happened to pass by, and pacifying the anger of the spirit, secured peace to the King.[41]

For the Chinese audience, the first two operas were highly ceremonial offerings, routinely performed on a troupe's opening nights for good auspices. The first two, *The Eight Genii* (八仙賀壽) and *The Six States* (aka *Six Warlords*) are ritual operas. The latter, as noted earlier, calls for the troupe's full cast and the display of the best costumes. Typically, following the opening two ritual operas, is a selection from the traditional Kun-style opera, a classic version of Chinese opera. The troupe's choice, *Parting at Park-Kew* (aka *Farewell at Ba Bridge of Guan Gong and Cao Cao* (灞橋送別), was derived from the historical novel *Story of Three Kingdoms*. After this standard three-opera opening comes the main opera, typically a martial opera with fight scenes. The choice of the evening was *The Defeated Revenge*, from the classic novel *Journey to the West*. The opening night's program was quite orthodox.

The opening ritualistic presentations weren't mere entertainment. They offered both worship and entertainment to the deities as a plea for protection and harmony for the community. As Barbara E. Ward notes, such performances generally were believed to help make the community prosperous: "It is a rite in the magico-religious sense, and one in which the actors are the officiants."[42] Responses to the premiere at this respected theatrical venue were overall positive, though reporters wrote primarily of the visual spectacle. The *Daily Alta California* noted that "the American portion of the audience had to enjoy themselves in imagining what was going on, and in admiring the stage properties and the costumes of the numerous performers, some of which were really splendid. The performances were also diversified with some very agile and dexterous 'ground and lofty tumbling,' which seemed to be a portion of the plot. Upon the whole, the exhibition is a great novelty, and as such is, to 'outside barbarians' well worth seeing."[43] The *Nevada Journal* noted, "The dresses . . . are rich; the 'combinations' novel and extraordinary, and on the whole about as intelligible as the figures of a kaleidoscope."[44] The reviewer for *New York Herald* could hardly conceal his amazement:

> No company in the United States can at all vie with this in the splendor of its wardrobe. Indeed, I had formed no conception previously of the immense labor and expense expended in China upon such fabrics as these. The embroidery is wrought into the most beautiful figures, representing birds, flowers, leaves, etc., in endless variety and in the brightest and most tastefully blended colors. . . . Their shoes had wooden soles, about two inches thick, and turned up at the toe.[45]

Yet there were dismissive comments about the performance as well, which might have prompted the managers to tailor their presentation to local tastes. Over the course of its weeklong stand at the American Theatre (October 18–24), the troupe made many adjustments.[46] The American farce *My Neighbor's Wife* opened one evening; prices for admission returned to what the *Sacramento News* called the "old standard"; texts were added to the advertisement to highlight the acrobatic performances: "feats of skills, vaulting, tumbling and dramatic performance, which they hope will prove to their friends and the public generally, the most moral and interesting entertainment of the season."[47] The addition of the word "moral" to the description was meant to defuse recent accusations by Bigler and company of the Chinese as a menace to American culture.[48] By interspersing American acts with Cantonese opera, the theater offered an evening of varied theatrical experiences that allowed both genres to please its audiences.

A professional troupe, Tong Hook Tong arrived with a full range of standard repertoire. Judging from the titles that can be reliably translated from English back to their Chinese originals, they were the most popular standards in Cantonese opera at the time.[49] On the third evening they presented *Sung Kong: The Robber Chief of the Laong Hills*, the story of Song Jiang (宋江殺惜), from the classic novel *108 Outlaws at Mount Liang*. The fourth evening featured *Borrowing Soldiers*, likely *Shatuo Jiebing* (沙陀借兵), a story about the rise to fame of a young man born of the union of a human woman and a stone demon, one of the repertoire of "Eighteen Grand Operas" in the nineteenth century. The sixth evening included *Selling a Pig*, likely *Yalan Trades Pigs* (亞蘭賣豬), an old staple about a series of mix-ups by a buffoon sent by his wife to sell a pig.

The final evening featured a serious drama in four acts, *Rising of the Lions, or Looking at the Pictures* (舉獅觀圖), a popular opera about morality and chivalry. In Xue Jiao's youth, an enraged empress ordered his family to be executed. Xue Jiao escaped this fate only because a virtuous family friend, Xu Ce, swapped him with his own son in order to keep the family line going.[50] The friend raised Xue as his own son; the boy grew to be extraordinarily skilled in martial arts. One day, while playing, Xue moved the weighty stone lions in front of the house from one side to the other. On seeing his strength, Xu knew the appropriate time for revenge had come. He then took Xue to see the pictures of his real ancestors, told the secret of his family's tragedy, and helped him plot revenge. It was a popular play for the righteous middle-aged-male role type and reinforced core beliefs in Chinese culture, such as sacrifice, loyalty, patience, bravery, and justice.

Rising of the Lions brought the first full week of Chinese opera performances in San Francisco to an uplifting and triumphant close. The programming over the course of the week showcased standard repertoire of significant diversity and sophistication. The variety of characteristics and theatrical presentations included ritual performances, historical drama, chivalric drama, martial arts performances, melodrama, and tongue-in-cheek comedy. The repertoire demonstrates that the troupe likely performed to *kun* and *yiyang* tunes, the styles of the northern genres and dialect well-liked by merchant and elite classes in Guangzhou.[51]

Transpacific Opera as Commerce

The first performance of Chinese opera in America relied on the new transpacific reach of Chinese merchants. Tong Hook Tong's arrival in the United States reflected the complexity of historical forces at play surrounding the transpacific trade. A brief report by the *Sacramento Daily Union* on October 22 encapsulates the complexity of the moment well:

> The *Hong Kong Gazette* says that the principals in the project of sending the Chinese Dramatique corps, now performing at the American theater, to California, were certain native merchants of Canton who paid the charterer of the Berkshire £2000 for freight of theater, furniture, and passage money. The company are all shareholders in the concern. The *Gazette* thinks the "Bigler-rian government require something to charm them into rationality; and hopes that 'Chinese fiddling, piping and drumming' may have the desired effect."[52]

Chinese cultural production was entangled with the China trade, colonialism, and US racial politics. The writer cites a figure equivalent to more than $455,178 in today's currency.[53] But the anti-Chinese prejudice was also clear. The report drew from the quote of a tongue-in-cheek remark about the opera troupe by Hong Kong's leading English-language newspaper, the *Hong Kong*

Gazette, sneering at Chinese opera as an indigenous (i.e., "primitive") cultural form.

Tong Hook Tong intended to set up a business similar to others set up by Chinese immigrants. On October 17, shortly after the troupe's arrival, another news report noted: "Chinese Mandarins. Several carriage loads of the higher class of Chinese were passing through the streets yesterday, taking a survey of the improvements and wonders of the place. . . . [T]hey made themselves conspicuous the greater part of the day."[54] Around this time, there were about "twenty stores kept by Chinese merchants, who erected the buildings themselves," and sometimes ten thousand dollars worth of Chinese goods could be sold in a day, according to a Chinese clerk in an American store.[55] Tong Hook Tong was positioned at the nexus of British colonial influence, transpacific trade, Chinese immigration to America's newest state (and its anti-Chinese hostility), and the gold rush economy.

Elizabeth Sinn's study on Hong Kong's role in Pacific trade provides historical context crucial to the understanding of Tong Hook Tong's arrival. San Francisco became an official destination of Hong Kong exports in 1849, an indication of its sudden rise to significance. Export from and to San Francisco for the year reached 4,950 tons.[56] The goods included sugar, silk, tea, and rice, as well as building materials, such as bricks, lumber, window frames, grindstones, marble slabs, shovels and hoes, and tiles.[57] Since the Hong Kong-San Francisco trade offered a wide range of investment opportunities, British firms such as Jardine, Matheson & Co. were actively and intimately involved in transpacific commerce, giving them an even broader scope in Asia and South America. In addition to goods catering to the Chinese and American communities, Hong Kong businesses engaged in a wide range of activities. Opportunities arose for commission agents, charterers of ships, insurance agents, creditors, and so on.

The activity wasn't limited to trade in goods; Chinese laborers' skills in construction work were highly praised. One report noted, "A number of Chinese mechanics and laborers are now engaged on Parrot's splendid granite building on the corner of California and Montgomery streets. They appear to be a very steady, sober and industrious set-apparently very slow, but sure. The building on which they are engaged will, when completed, be the most magnificent structure in California."[58]

Information on Chinese activity around the Pacific was of great value to trading ports in the region. Hong Kong English-language newspapers such as the *Hong Kong Gazette* or the *Register* regularly arrived on ships from Hong Kong. Leading California newspapers such as the *Daily Alta California* typically kept them on file and frequently quoted them.[59] In Hong Kong, firms arose specializing in collecting and disseminating commercial intelligence to attract clients and to help merchants determine what to send to California.

In 1852, eighty-six ships sailed from Hong Kong to San Francisco, with a total of 17,246 passengers. Among them were the British vessel *Berkshire* with 166 passengers, including the members of the Tong Hook Tong troupe.[60] The *Berkshire* was owned by the prominent Toulmn Company. It sailed from Calcutta to Singapore in April 1852 and then to China in July.[61] The ship departed Hong Kong on July 29 and arrived at the port of San Francisco on October 6. The troupe brought along furniture and "the framework of a large theatre, with the intention of erecting it here," the *Daily Alta California* enthusiastically reported.[62]

The three managers listed in the *Daily Alta California* advertisement of Tong Hook Tong, Mr. Likeoon, Norman Assing, and Tong Chick [*sic*], were all Western-trained Chinese merchants. Tong Chick was likely Tong A-Chick. As discussed earlier, both Assing and Tong were prominent representatives of the community, fluent in English and well versed in Western manners. "Likeoon" was probably Lee Kan (or Li Gen; Li Akan), also a graduate of the Morrison School in Hong Kong, who would later become an associate editor of the bilingual newspaper the *Oriental* in San Francisco.[63] They and other merchants in San Francisco fulfilled important social functions of the huiguan, for example, establishing an essential venue for worship such as a temple as early as December 1851.[64] As the scholar Yucheng Qin notes, "Huiguan generally provided its members a place for worship," as many would be anxious for such space "in case misfortune stuck them."[65]

These prominent figures' advocacy for Chinese opera troupes signaled the importance of opera in establishing community. This was made clear when a procession of troupe members went to pay their respects at the Chinese cemetery at the end of October. Hundreds of participants jammed the streets of the Chinese quarter, balconies were crowded with spectators, and of course there was a band of musicians. Reporting on this event, American newspapers for the first time gave details about Chinese instruments: gongs, cymbals, drums, and stringed instruments.[66] Chinese instruments, together with "Roman, English, and German violin and guitar strings of the finest quality," began appearing in the advertisements of Atwill & Co. in the *Daily Alta California*.[67]

Constructing Spaces for Chinese Theater

As expected, after their performance at the American Theatre in October 1852, Tong Hook Tong used the construction materials they had brought to build a Chinese theater. In early December, Assing invited visitors to observe a ceremony performed by officials, priests, and a band of musicians, to bless the Chinese temple and the almost finished theater.[68] This ritual of dedication was held in the morning at the joss house (Chinese temple) across from the new theater, in honor of divinities that had come to be revered and worshiped by the community. The ceremonies included the performers welcoming deities and spirits to the temple and praying for their protection and blessing:

> The officials were dressed in the most gorgeous robes of embroidered satin and silk that can be imagined. . . . [T]he performers came forward, two at a time, to the front of the stage, and kneeling down, made adoration to a sacred tablet; then followed a recitation and chorus, and another performance by the band. . . . The sacred tablet was then introduced, and the high priest, after making to it an invocation, extended his arms and made to the audience a short address, to the effect, as we are informed, that all good friends of China wished success to the new house. After he had ceased speaking, the band struck up, an immense explosion of crackers succeeded, and the performance closed. . . . Opposite the house the new Chinese theatre is erected, which promises to be a very novel place of attraction.[69]

Temples are integral to Chinese communities. They are where rituals honoring a wide range of deities or ancestors are held, to ward off evil spirits, to seek religious guidance, to enlist protection and blessings, or to express gratitude. Since operas were often performed as offerings to express gratitude to the deities, many temples included theater stages or opera-related art as part of their decoration. The building of the Chinese theater across from the joss house, therefore, expressed a desire to engage in full-fledged social and cultural activities deeply rooted in Chinese culture.

As the theater scholar Tanaka Issei points out, performances of Chinese regional operas played a crucial role in a variety of seasonal ritual occasions, including celebrations of divine birthdays, propitiations for orphan souls, and prayers for a good harvest or for the protection of the community from flood and drought. The new theater created a space for this ritual connection and to some extent restored aspects of these cultural practices that otherwise would have been hard to sustain in California.[70]

A lithographic print of the drawing "Chinese Buddhistic Worship in San Francisco," by the famous German-born California artist Charles Christian Nahl (1818–1878), from 1855–56 gives a sense of the joss house in San Francisco (fig. 1.4). A room 22 by 40 feet and 14 feet in height, it had large, ornate incense and offering tables, brightly colored decorations, and furniture with embroidered upholstery that cost twelve thousand dollars in China.[71] The expense and ornate detail reflected the serious investment in their community by Chinese immigrants. Similarly, the erection of the Chinese theater was, as much a psychological and relational investment as it was a physical and material one.

During this time, Cantonese opera was performed by troupes either privately at the spacious villas of prominent families, or in public at temples for birthdays of deities and local festivities in villages along the Pearl River

CHINESE BUDDHISTIC WORSHIP IN SAN FRANCISCO.

Published by W. W. Kurtz & Co., Wide West Office, No. 162 Washington Street, San Francisco.

FIGURE 1.4 Chinese Buddhistic Worship in San Francisco (1850s). Lettersheet published by W. W. Kurtz & Co. Courtesy California Historical Society.

delta.[72] Performances for the public were typically held on open stages in temple courtyards or in temporary bamboo-shed theaters.[73] Or they were incorporated into huiguan, some of which included theater stages. Following the tradition of bringing good auspices to the community, this theater was constructed near the place of worship, the joss house.

From a detailed description in the *San Francisco Herald*, it is clear that the theater was well built and fully decorated.

THE CHINESE THEATRE IN SAN FRANCISCO

The building brought out by the company of Chinese, who performed sometime since at the American theatre, has been erected on Dupont street, near Green. Its interior is well worthy of being seen, not only for its decorations, but for the style of its architecture; displaying an unusual economy in the use of its material, though the structure presents every requisite of firmness and durability. The seats for the audience, arranged on an inclined plane in a manner that all will have a full view of the stage, will accommodate about a thousand persons. The front and larger portion is provided with backs and comfortably cushioned. This portion of the building will be lighted by twenty-two variegated Chinese lanterns or transparencies, and the walls are ornamented by numerous paintings. The orchestra will hold at least forty musicians, who constitute an important part of the performances. The stage, which is devoid of any wings or side scenes, presents a background of carved figures, Chinese characters, gilded and many colored, that forms the most striking part of the display.[74]

The unusual economy of materials noted likely referred to the practice in traditional Chinese architecture whereby timber frames are constructed with mortise-and-tenon joinery without nails, which creates semirigid structural joints that allow the wood structure to resist bending and torsion under high compression. The new theater was described by one visitor, John David Borthwick, as "a curious pagoda-looking edifice, built by them expressly for theatrical purposes and painted, outside and in, in an extraordinary manner."[75]

Eleven weeks after Tong Hook Tong arrived in California, it gave its first performance in a Chinese theater built at Dupont and Union Streets near what was then called "little China." The new theater opened on December 23, 1852, with a daily schedule of two performances at 11:00 a.m. and 7:00 p.m., at the prices of one dollar and two dollars. The opening night was reportedly cold and wet. "Heavy rains had transformed Dupont Street into a morass, but planks and stepping stones gave access to the new 'temple of the drama.'"[76] The theater was described by *The Golden Era*:

The interior is arranged in a manner quite different our own theatres and is, we imagine, a perfect model of the Chinese theatre. . . . The stage is ornamented in rather a fantastic manner with curious devices, the figures of men, hills, domestic animals, and all sorts of sea monsters. They use no scenery, other than a display of beautifully wrought shawls, raised silk work, etc.[77]

One newspaper report noted, "All Chinatown was out at the opening of the new Celestial Theatre. Such a rustling of loose breeches as took place, while the saffron colored audience selected their seats on the backless benches, never before has been witnessed within the limits of San Francisco."[78]

In February 1853, the Adelphi Theater was presenting Bellini's *La sonnambula*; San Francisco Hall featured several evenings of selections from Donizetti's *L'elisir d'amore* and *Linda di Chamounix*; the San Francisco Theater presented the American actress Caroline Chapman; and Armory Hall staged the New Orleans Serenaders performing burlesque opera. The new Chinese theater was offering performances of the Tong Hook Tong troupe. One paper noted that the receipt for a Sunday evening performance was reportedly fifteen hundred dollars.[79] The troupe was doing good business, which prompted multiple offers from "people speculating to bring them to New York and to realize a fortune from their exhibition."[80] A ten-month contract was signed on March 19 between Likeoon and a manager, George W. Beach, for a forty-member troupe, offering six thousand dollars per month in addition to travel expenses, with an advance payment of ten thousand dollars.

Eventually the theater building was put up for sale. Its auction notice gives some interesting details of what was for sale. Along with the 50 feet wide by 200 feet deep building itself, there was a large quantity of lumber, benches, cloth linings, fixtures, twenty-four Chinese lanterns, and forty lamps.[81] It was sold for $1,150 in March. After their last performance, on March 23, the troupe departed for New York by the steamship *Cortes* before April 1 via Panama, Jamaica, and New Orleans.[82] The *New-York Daily Times* reported the incoming attraction of the celebrated troupe, noting, "The historian in particular will gain a perfect insight into the habits, manners and customs of this wonderful race, so long shut out from the more enlightened nations of the earth."[83]

Prominent advertisements were placed in both the *New-York Daily Times* and the *New York Herald* two days before the performance, announcing "Li Keoon's Great Canton Tung [*sic*], Hook, Tong Chinese Historic and Dramatic Company" (fig. 1.5). They underscored the historical significance of the event. Another news article advised, "This company must not be confused with the recent Jugglery troupe at the Broadway."[84]

On May 20, Tong Hook Tong performed at Niblo's Garden in New York City, with translations by Rev. S. Wells Williams, a Chinese missionary. Its playbill was "conceived in the highest style of art," according to a writer for the *New York Tribune*.[85] The ritual operas, *Six Warlords* and *Eight Genii*, led the way. Two days after the premiere the *Tribune* wrote, "A complete Chinese Company, from the Celestial Empire, via California, performed, representing religious and other ceremonies, dramatic episodes, etc. The whole affair was

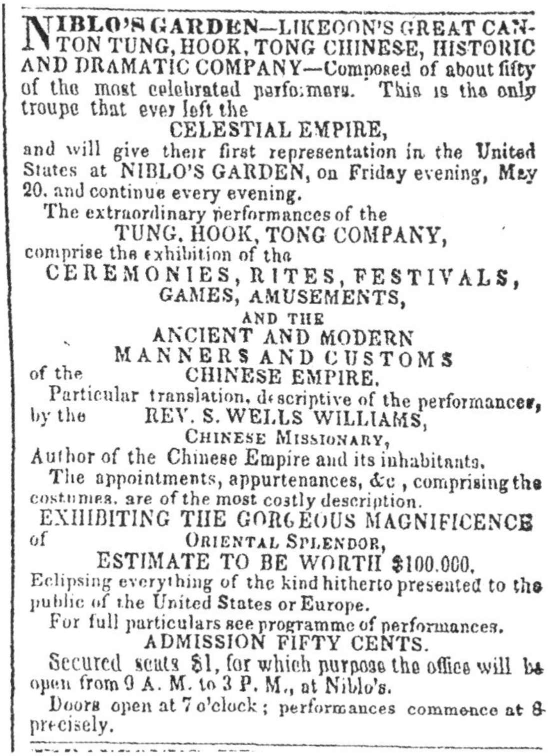

NIBLO'S GARDEN—LIKEOON'S GREAT CAN-
TON TUNG, HOOK, TONG CHINESE, HISTORIC
AND DRAMATIC COMPANY—Composed of about fifty
of the most celebrated performers. This is the only
troupe that ever left the
CELESTIAL EMPIRE,
and will give their first representation in the United
States at NIBLO'S GARDEN, on Friday evening, May
20, and continue every evening.
The extraordinary performances of the
TUNG, HOOK, TONG COMPANY,
comprise the exhibition of the
CEREMONIES, RITES, FESTIVALS,
GAMES, AMUSEMENTS,
AND THE
ANCIENT AND MODERN
MANNERS AND CUSTOMS
of the CHINESE EMPIRE.
Particular translation, descriptive of the performances,
by the REV. S. WELLS WILLIAMS,
CHINESE MISSIONARY,
Author of the Chinese Empire and its inhabitants.
The appointments, appurtenances, &c, comprising the
costumes, are of the most costly description.
EXHIBITING THE GORGEOUS MAGNIFICENCE
of ORIENTAL SPLENDOR,
ESTIMATE TO BE WORTH $100,000.
Eclipsing everything of the kind hitherto presented to the
public of the United States or Europe.
For full particulars see programme of performances.
ADMISSION FIFTY CENTS.
Secured seats $1, for which purpose the office will be
open from 9 A. M. to 3 P. M., at Niblo's.
Doors open at 7 o'clock; performances commence at 8
precisely.

FIGURE 1.5 Advertisement for Tung [sic] Hook Tong performance at Niblo's Garden, *New-York Daily Times*, May 18, 1853.

so utterly different from anything hitherto offered on our boards, [we] advise everyone who would not seek to be ignorant of some of the most salient points of the most ancient and peculiar people in the world, to go and see and hear it."[86] The writer concluded that the performers deserved a good reception, since they came afar, mirroring Chinese life and demonstrating "the magnetizing effects of California, of the opening glories of the Pacific." The performance was well attended in its weeklong engagement. One reviewer compared the audience's applause for the Tong Hook Tong troupe at Niblo's Garden to that for Max Maretzek's Italian Opera Company's performances at the Astor Place Opera House.[87] Reviews from many newspapers were written with a tone of regard for the ancient culture, although they expressed intense dislike of the music.[88] *The New York Herald* in particular heaped on ridicule and mockery of the music and performance. However, when the troupe's agent deserted the troupe and abandoned the signed ten-month contract, Tong Hook Tong was left stranded and broke.[89] Showing empathy with the troupe's misfortune, New York's benevolent forces came to the rescue, raising funds to send the troupe home.

The failure in New York notwithstanding, the success that Tong Hook Tong won in California aligned with the aspirations of the Chinese community leaders who had brought the troupe to the United States. Beyond being a business opportunity and a benefit for Chinese immigrants, the opera troupe also offered cultural representations that could strengthen their sense of belonging in the New World. From California's early days, Chinese theater—a form of transpacific cultural lineage—became part of the state's DNA. Californians considered Chinese theater their own, marking San Francisco as a distinctive cosmopolitan city imbued with Asiatic culture. As soon as the Chinese theater building was completed at the end of 1852, the *Daily Alta California* declared: "San Francisco boasts at the present time of three American Theatres, one French and one Chinese. We believe there is not another city in the world that can do the same. This is not the only unique trait we possess."[90] This sentiment might well have been the reason for the prominence of the Chinese contingent in the lithographic print of the July 4 parade that year.

CHAPTER 2

Bringing Opera to the Mines
and Railroad Chinese

The *Golden Hills' News*, a Chinese missionary bilingual newspaper, began publication in 1854. Its editorials repeatedly called for the fair treatment of Chinese immigrants, just like that accorded "the Anglo-Saxons . . . locating themselves on the shores and in the Cities of China."[1] While reporting on the continual arrival of Chinese for gold mining—for example, in July, a total of 1,813 Chinese arrived over seven days, all heading for the mountains—and significant yields from gold mines, the newspaper also frequently nudged its Chinese readers to consider the opportunities available in farming, stone quarrying, fisheries, lumber mills, and other industries.[2] In the years that followed, people arrived from southern China to pursue opportunities in gold mining, but also contributed in significant ways to the building of the infrastructure of the West Coast and the extension of the Central Pacific Railroad, which completed the first transcontinental railroad (1863–69). The shortage of labor resulting from the American Civil War (1861–65) further intensified the need for Chinese workers. As Chinese arrived en masse, opera troupes also began to circulate where they settled; opera performance was thus connected to the lives of thousands of Chinese engaged in this remarkable period of nation building.

This circulation constitutes the second phase of Chinese theater's development in California. During this period, iterant troupes traveled on waterways into the interior regions of northern California that had gained prosperity through mining, agriculture, railroad construction, and so on. Studies of Chinese theaters in America have paid little attention to their history away from larger cities like San Francisco, for two main reasons. First, San Francisco was the port where the troupes arrived and performed before venturing further inland. Due to the city's importance as the social and economic center of the

Chinese in America, its Chinese theaters are considered the most representative of that period. In contrast, mining or railroad towns seem inconsequential, as the transience of workers led to ephemeral Chinese communities in constant flux, both political and economic. Second, this period witnessed the growth of anti-Chinese hostility, harassment, racist attacks, and discriminatory legal measures. Mining towns were known to be the principal source of fierce anti-Chinese racial violence. They were seen by the public as places where Chinese miners and railroad workers toiled away and suffered a life of drudgery, leading to the assumption that cultural production in these communities would be rudimentary at best and therefore of little importance.

However, most early Chinese immigrants actually lived in the rural areas of California. The 1860 US census reports 34,933 Chinese in California, of whom only 2,719 were in San Francisco.[3] As the historian Sucheng Chan notes, "During the first two decades of Chinese immigration, an overwhelming proportion of the Chinese population located in the mining counties, first in the southern mines, and after the mid-1860s in the northern mines."[4] Newspaper accounts indicate that Chinese opera had a lively presence in the interior part of the state during these years. Not only did they answer the demand for entertainment that all frontier towns have, opera troupes brought solidarity and peace to Chinese all through the mining region. Scholars have noted that, wherever they settled to work, Chinese migrants in California brought vegetable seeds and herbs from home.[5] Theatrical performances were analogous food for the spirit.

The Gold Rush, Racial Politics, and Chinese Populations in Mining Towns

With the discovery of gold in 1848, California attracted people from all over the world. The number of Chinese increased sharply: 325 came in 1849, 450 in 1850, 2,176 in 1851, and 20,026 in 1852.[6] According to the historian Gordon H. Chang, between 1853 and the early 1860s, approximately six to seven thousand Chinese arrived every year.[7] Even after the initial gold rush ended, the number of miners continued to grow. Meanwhile, the warm weather and fertile soil of the Central Valley were particularly suited for agricultural development, employing a large number of Chinese workers. In particular, the agrarian-oriented Chungshan, Heunshan, and Toishan Cantonese headed there.[8] Two rivers connected the area: the Sacramento River, which is formed by rivers flowing out of the Sierra Nevada and flows into San Francisco Bay; and the San Joaquin River, which runs through the central and southern part of the region. As Chinese searched for mining opportunities and agricultural jobs, they were dispersed between the two river deltas and the surrounding region, taking on a wide range of occupations, becoming merchants, herbalists, barbers, launderers, restauranteurs, cooks, or farm laborers.

Anti-Chinese attitudes arose in mining counties in the region soon after 1852. Some mining districts had enacted local laws prohibiting Chinese from purchasing mining claims, such as the 1854 bylaws of Dutch Flat in Placer County, and the 1857 bylaws of Centreville and Helltown in Butte County. Others even forbade mining by Chinese, such as the 1856 bylaws of Columbia District in Tuolumne County.[9] Many more turned to violence to purge Chinese communities. In 1852, in Columbia, a mob of white miners, accompanied by a brass band, assaulted two hundred Chinese, forcing them to leave. In Sonora, "harassing the local Chinese had become a 'traditional sport.'"[10] The state legislature levied a tax on foreign miners, with heavier tax on those ineligible for citizenship (that is, the Chinese).[11] The resulting tax revenue was divided between the state and localities, with a fixed fee set aside for the tax collectors. This practice led to vengeful collectors, who freely used threat, harassment, and brutality in committing racial violence. The historian Jean Pfaelzer notes:

> The tax was a ticket to violent expulsion. One common sport was to tie Chinese miners together by their queues or use their long braids to tie them to trees, as the collectors wantonly looted their bedding, boots, and tools. The editor of the *Pacer Herald* reported that he witnessed a tax collector "corral" thirteen Chinese men at a stable in the town of Auburn, in order to "most energetically procure" the sum of four dollars.[12]

Because of the violence, some Chinese miners had to abandon their homes and were limited in the mining claims that they could purchase or stay to work. The instigators of violence generally were not held accountable for their crimes, due to legal decisions affirming individuals' power to remove Chinese laborers from their localities. This was what Pfaelzer calls the "first wave" of Chinese purges.[13]

The early technique of individual panning was gradually replaced by more industrial methods of hydraulic mining. Miners could no longer be entrepreneurial gold seekers but had to work as laborers for larger mining companies. As a result of work preferences, most of the miners who remained to pan in the mountains were Chinese. This brought a short window of reprieve: "The mass exodus of white miners from the gold fields during the late 1850s and early 1860s ended the first wave of Chinese purges. For several years Chinese miners were, more or less, left alone."[14]

Sucheng Chan's study of Chinese livelihood in three counties of California depicts a similar situation.[15] When white miners began their exodus from mining by the mid-1850s, Chinese miners mostly stayed, although some departed after 1863.[16] They typically formed their own companies, working rather successfully on what were called "preemption claims."[17] Chinese found their bonds of religion, tradition, and communal experience to be an effective basis for banding together in mining companies. As Chan notes in this study, "In California as a whole, 29.4 percent of all miners in 1860 were Chinese." By 1870, 37.2 percent of all miners were Chinese.[18]

To cater to the needs of these miners, there were a large number of Chinese entrepreneurs at transportation nodes that supplied the regions. Table 2.1 shows the distribution of Chinese in occupations in rural California, based on Chan's study of the 1870 US census. It forms a sharp contrast with the occupations of Chinese in San Francisco, as shown in Table 2.2.

The substantial demand for workers in mining and agriculture led to the continued presence of a large Chinese population in the Central Valley. As Jean Pfaelzer notes,

> Despite the ice and wind, the blackmail, the brutality, and the tax collectors, thousands of Chinese remained in the mother lode and thousands more continued to find their ways. In Placer County, at the end of November 1856, there were 12,540 white men, 1,860 white women, 400 male and female Negroes, and 125 Indians. But there were more than 3,500 Chinese men and women, almost one fifth of the population.[19]

Indeed, the 1860 US census shows that the Chinese were the single largest foreign-born ethnic group in California and comprised from 12 to 23 percent

TABLE 2.1 Occupations of Chinese in Rural California in 1870 after Chan, "Chinese Livelihood in Rural California"

Occupation	Miners	Truck gardeners and farmers	Nonagricultural laborers	Fishermen	Personal service	Independent business (artisans, professionals, and entrepreneurs)
Population	16,000	1,000	6,000	151	3,000	3,000

TABLE 2.2 Occupations of Chinese in San Francisco in 1870 after Chan, "Chinese Livelihood in Rural California"

Occupation	Extraction/ production (fishermen and miner)	Light manufacture	Nonagricultural laborers	Servants	Independent business (artisans, professionals, and entrepreneurs)
Percentage of employed Chinese	6%	27%	24.8%	14.8%	25.8%

of the population of various mining counties.[20] The number and percentage had grown significantly by 1870. The 1860 US census shows 10,648 Chinese miners in California, around a quarter of the total population of miners in the state (41,790); the 1870 US census shows 15,711 Chinese miners in California, 41 percent of the total population of miners in the state (37,451).[21]

Chinese Theaters in the Interior of the State

To meet the demand of the substantial Chinese population, the number of Chinese theaters grew significantly in the interior towns during the late 1850s and early 1860s. Newspaper reports showed that Chinese opera troupes traveled throughout the Central Valley and the Sierra Nevada gold mining towns.[22] This was despite the fact that traveling through the area presented significant challenges for Chinese troupes, who journeyed by steamboats, stagecoaches, and freight wagons and on foot. From the mid-1850s to the early 1860s, Chinese theaters appeared in towns of the interior, from Sacramento and north up to Chico, Oroville, Marysville, Grass Valley, Folsom, Placer, Auburn, and Drytown; to Stockton and south down to El Dorado, San Andreas, and Mariposa, as well as the Central Valley. Chinese theaters were established in no fewer than eighteen towns in the interior of the state. Between Placer in August 1855 and San Andreas in August 1857, the openings of seven full-fledged Chinese theaters were reported. To visualize the presence of Chinese theaters in the California gold rush landscape, figure 2.1 shows the locations of theaters in the interior of the northern part of the state over a fifteen-year period, based on reports from contemporary newspapers. As shown on the map, they appeared in both mining towns at the foothills, and cities that are important hubs of the waterway such as San Joaquin, Stockton, Sacramento, and Marysville.

Chinese troupes not only brought cultural production to widely dispersed communities; their performances were also celebratory occasions that drew Chinese immigrants from the vicinity. The attraction was so great that towns often did not wait for the completion of a troupe's performance run in another town before erecting theaters to host them. Like shops, restaurants, and gambling dens, which served a variety of daily functions, theaters were significant gathering places for the Chinese community. In 1855, Rev. Edward Syle wrote in his diary:

> October 31 (Wednesday) was spent at Auburn where the Chinese have established themselves in considerable number—seven or eight hundred, I should think, being about 25% of all the other population put together. Two gambling houses seem to be in operation night and day. Several brothels were open to the view of passers by and a Chinese theatre was filled with stolid listeners.[23]

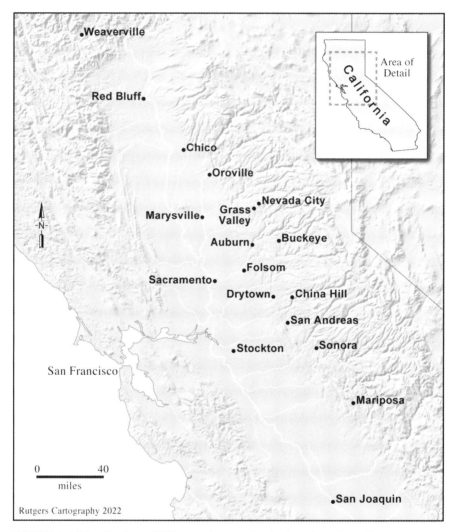

FIGURE 2.1 Distribution of Chinese theaters in the interior of northern California, 1850s–60s. Michael Siegel, Rutgers Cartography, 2022.

Auburn had a pivotal location connecting Sacramento with roads to the gold camps. With sizable population bases, towns such as Auburn hosted circuits of opera troupes. In some instances, the troupes brought performances to theaters in small towns for short runs; in other cases, the troupes erected theaters and stayed for a period of time, performing for captive theatergoers.

The theaters' appearances also signaled the relative cultural hierarchy of interior towns, places with a substantial audience base. Sacramento had the second-largest Chinese community in nineteenth-century America, as reflected in its Chinese name, Yee Fou ("Second City").[24] With its pivotal location at the confluence of two major rivers, Sacramento was a leading supplier for goldrush miners and other people passing through. Goods and supplies from the port of San Francisco were transported on steamboats to Sacramento, then were carried by riverboats or stagecoaches to supply the interior of the state. Becoming the city where the California state legislature resided in 1854, Sacramento grew in significance and became a major supplier of goods, reaching a population in 1860 of 13,785, from 6,820 a decade earlier.[25] The Chinese in Sacramento were mostly engaged in merchandizing and various trades; these occupations employed 49.4 percent of the 980 Chinese in the city in 1860.

Aside from San Francisco, Sacramento maintained the most substantial and constant presence of Chinese theater. As a gateway of the water route to Central Valley and the Sierra Nevada, it was also a significant hub for itinerant opera troupes traveling through the region. The Sze Yup Association, a huiguan established in 1851, had a hundred-seat room at the rear of its building set aside for entertainment such as puppet shows and, later, opera performances as well.[26] In February 1855, after a period of successful Cantonese opera performances, a theater opened on I street, announcing its presence with a fourteen-foot muslin sign saying "Canton Chinese Theater." Its popularity prompted the Sacramento Theater to recruit the troupe for a special performance in May, noting "Through the urgent solicitations of many persons, the [Chinese] Troupe have consented to appear for ONE NIGHT." An advertisement named Leong Ahghue as the manager, with ticket prices comparable to the most expensive theaters of San Francisco: dress circle and parquette [sic], two dollars; pit, one dollar; and private boxes, twelve dollars. They promised attendees "an entertainment at once rich, rare and racy" (see fig. 2.2).[27] It was the first such advertisement outside San Francisco. The English titles of the three operas do not readily indicate their Chinese originals; however, the "Birth Day Celebration of Three very Distinguished Men" seems to refer to a ritual opera with a similar title. In any case, the manager Leong officiated as interpreter.[28]

The performance at the Sacramento Theater was so popular that the theater brought the troupe back to its stage two weeks later, "in according with the request of many," as noted in the broadside of the theater of May 23 (fig. 2.3).[29] This is probably the earliest existing broadside for Chinese theater in the United States, printed in the typical style of theatrical entertainment of the period. Two operas were featured. The first, *The Mountain Wizard*, likely adapts the story of the Monkey King, a mythological character able to transform himself into any shape and who resides in a mountain. The Monkey King is a central figure in the classic novel *Journey to the West*, 西遊記, by Wu Cheng'en (Ming dynasty, sixteenth century). The second, *The Great Rebellion*, tells the story of Wang Yen-zhang (Wong Een Chuang, 王彥章), a historical figure. It is included in the *Eighteen Grand Cantonese Operas*, a

SACRAMENTO THEATER.

THE
CHINESE THEATRICAL TROUPE!
LEONG AHGHUE..........Manager and Interpreter.

Tuesday Evening, May 8th, 1855,
Through the urgent solicitations of many persons, the above Troupe have consented to appear for ONE NIGHT ONLY, at the SACRAMENTO THEATER, on which evening will be performed the very interesting Plays

THE BURGLAR!
THE BIRTH DAY CELEBRATION
of Three very Distinguished Men!
AND
THE WAR BETWEEN CHINA AND CHINESE TARTARY!

PRICES OF ADMISSION.
Dress Circle and Parquette, $2; Pit..............$1.
Private Boxes, $12.

Doors open at 7 o'clock. Curtain will rise at quarter before 8 o'clock.
Box Office open daily from 10 to 4 o'clock.   m5

FIGURE 2.2 Advertisement for a Chinese theatrical troupe, Sacramento Theater, *Sacramento Daily Union*, May 8, 1855.

repertoire of Chinese operas popular during the nineteenth century.[30] Both operas would offer a captivating spectacle, with the stage coming alive with high-energy sequences, showcasing a combination of acrobatics, choreography, and martial arts prowess. They would immerse the audience in a world of spirited performance and dramatic storytelling.

Two years later, the Sacramento Theater was converted into a Chinese theater, which highlighted the significance of the Chinese community in the city and the strong demand for opera performances. When it hosted a new troupe from China in April 1857, advertisements appeared for several days in local newspapers, though with no repertoire listed.[31] The confirmation of the theater's importance to the city's broader society and general population was reported in the *Daily Alta California*: "The only place of amusement opened in Sacramento on Thursday evening, says the *Journal*, was the Chinese Theatre; whereat were to be seen Hon. Senators and Assemblymen; nearly one-half the audience being Americans. Much of the acting is said to be of a superior character."[32] Many papers reported the troupe's successful run, one noting "upward of 100 Chinese women . . . at the performances."[33] The troupe performed for three successful weeks, according to a newspaper.[34] There were reports of occasional acts of hostility, as when one evening a group of newspaper men turned off the gas, resulting in a darkened theater and a suspended performance.[35] This was minor compared to the general enthusiasm accorded Chinese theater. The largest newspaper in town, the *Sacramento Daily Union*, entitled the report of the incident "Shameful."

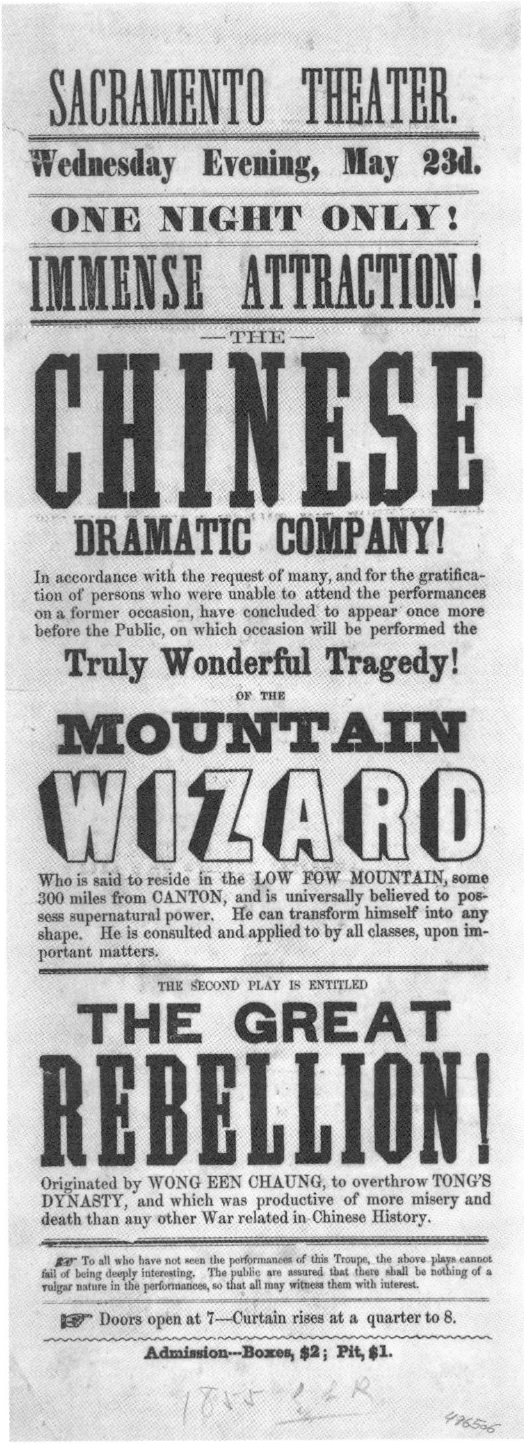

SACRAMENTO THEATER.

Wednesday Evening, May 23d.

ONE NIGHT ONLY!

IMMENSE ATTRACTION!

— THE —

CHINESE

DRAMATIC COMPANY!

In accordance with the request of many, and for the gratifica-
tion of persons who were unable to attend the performances
on a former occasion, have concluded to appear once more
before the Public, on which occasion will be performed the

Truly Wonderful Tragedy!

OF THE

MOUNTAIN

WIZARD

Who is said to reside in the LOW FOW MOUNTAIN, some
300 miles from CANTON, and is universally believed to possess supernatural power. He can transform himself into any
shape. He is consulted and applied to by all classes, upon important matters.

THE SECOND PLAY IS ENTITLED

THE GREAT

REBELLION!

Originated by WONG EEN CHAUNG, to overthrow TONG'S
DYNASTY, and which was productive of more misery and
death than any other War related in Chinese History.

☞ To all who have not seen the performances of this Troupe, the above plays cannot
fail of being deeply interesting. The public are assured that there shall be nothing of a
vulgar nature in the performances, so that all may witness them with interest.

☞ Doors open at 7—Curtain rises at a quarter to 8.

Admission—Boxes, $2; Pit, $1.

FIGURE 2.3 Broadside
of Sacramento Theater,
May 23, 1855, RB 496506,
Huntington Library, San
Marino, California.

"Celestial Theatricals in the Mines"

"Celestial Theatricals in the Mines"—this title led a May 1857 report in the *Daily Alta California* about a Chinese troupe in Auburn drawing crowded houses of four hundred to five hundred persons, in a large and airy theater building, "consisting of three or four ordinary sized houses converted into one."[36] The troupe of fifty performers was on tour, according to *Daily Evening Bulletin:* since they had left the Adelphi Theater in San Francisco, "they have visited a large portion of the state," including the three-week run in Sacramento.[37]

Many Chinese troupes had visited mining towns since the previous year, including San Andreas, Drytown, and Stockton, which they visited twice. The building methods and materials of Chinese theaters, in the traditional mat-shed structure, allowed for the swift construction of theaters for the troupes' visits. (In southern China, venues for itinerant troupes' performances during folk rites were typically mat-shed structures, made of bamboo, wood, hay, and mud.) In the fall of 1856, separated by only a few weeks, Stockton and San Andreas each erected a new theater. They were wooden frames of twenty-four by one hundred feet and forty-five by one hundred feet, respectively, with a canvas covering. They were equipped with carpeted stages and oil-burning lights suspended on iron poles, refilled every half hour.[38] Stockton's theater was about thirty feet in height and cost fifteen hundred dollars. Both theaters hosted the troupe of thirty actors, performing both afternoons and evenings.

After several visits to the theater, a writer for the *Stockton Independent* reported on its popularity and noted the troupe's plans to circulate among the mining towns: "From three to five hundred Chinese visit the house each performance, and they appear to be highly edified and pleased with the entertainment. Our interpreter told us that it would take the company three weeks longer to complete the play, and then the Theatrical Troupe would leave for other diggings."[39] The report provided a description of the play and depicted the scene: "The drop-curtain, side-wings and other scenery were stationary, and ornamented with tinsel, inscriptions and other insignia, illustrating the character of the play and announcing the *great success* of the Company." It was Stockton's second showing of Chinese theater that year, indicating both the city's significant Chinese population and the popularity of this entertainment. Several days later, another report noted, "A new feature in Thespian entertainments has been introduced in the interior of the State."[40]

In the early part of 1857, this successful entertainment started to attract wider attention in mining towns, as shown in reports of Chinese theaters in Chico, Placerville, and Auburn. In many towns, there were no more than a few Chinese-occupied buildings surrounded by primarily white-dominated downtowns.[41] And although towns such as Grass Valley had a large population of Chinese, they, not being allowed to own land, had to rent from non-Chinese. Often, they would build theaters to accommodate Chinese opera performances attracting audiences from both near and far.

In August, a Chinese theater building was constructed in San Andreas, a framed building of forty by 105 feet "covered with 'shakes'" [shingles].[42] Given that the construction cost of such theaters was considerable (the amount was reported as fifteen hundred dollars), we can assume that theatrical endeavors were highly profitable.[43] In April 1858, the *San Joaquin Republican* reported the performance of a twenty-five-member Chinese troupe in Mariposa and noted the Chinese in the county outnumber whites by two to one.[44] The troupe was scheduled to play for the season. When the growth of the Chinese population in Mariposa prompted expansion to a new site, a Chinese theater was part of the plan for the new village.[45] This new theatrical infrastructure in the interior of the state helped the formation of a touring network.

As Chinese troupes traveled through mining towns, mingling naturally occurred among different ethnic groups. It was often noted that many non-Chinese were among the audiences. Mixed-race social mingling of early Chinese is little documented, but we can gain a glimpse of it through an 1855 color lithograph by Frank Marryat, one of the first artists to depict in watercolor paintings and drawings the earliest gold rush days (fig. 2.4). He portrayed Chinese in a gambling saloon in Sonora, a scene he noted was

THE BAR OF A GAMBLING SALOON.

FIGURE 2.4 Frank Marryat, *The Bar of a Gambling Saloon* (1855). Lithograph by J. Brainard. Courtesy Bancroft Library, University of California, Berkeley.

quite common: "There is one or more at every Chinese digging."[46] (Sonora is sixty miles east of Stockton.) Of this drawing, one scholar noted, "Marryat's illustration exemplifies the 'men of all nations' trope."[47] Amid different ethnic groups, two Chinese men with conical hats, one with a queue, are making a transaction with the bartender. Although their boots might seem incongruous with the rest of their outfits, as early as April 1852, Tong A-Chick alluded to Chinese wearing boots. In his letter to John Bigler, to impress on the governor the variety of goods sold at the twenty stores run by Chinese in San Francisco, Tong wrote that "a great quantity of American goods [are sold in them], especially boots, of which every Chinaman buys one or more pairs immediately on landing."[48] They were common footwear of Chinese miners, as Marryat wrote: "Some of [the Chinese] adopt the European costume, and patronize patent leather boots and gold watchchains." They were shown in all Marryat's pictorial work where Chinese appeared, as in the watercolor "Sansome Street, San Francisco, 1850" and the lithograph "High and Dry," and are corroborated in accounts by the English traveler John Borthwick.[49]

The mixing of ethnic groups shown in the painting suggests the mixing of forms of popular entertainment. Saloons often provided various forms of entertainment to appeal to different senses, including the visual, sonic, and so on. Marryat noted, "On entering one of these saloons the eye is dazzled almost by the brilliancy of chandeliers and mirrors. The roof, rich with gilt-work, is supported by pillars of glass."[50]

At a local venue in Oroville, in August of 1857, musicians of a Chinese opera troupe appeared as entertainers of the evening:

> Chinese Entertainment—Deacon Sheldon is to give a grand Chinese concert at the old American Theatre building, this evening. . . . The music will be of the most refined and oriental nature.[51]

The event was so popular that two weeks later, the manager produced another saloon concert, with even more details.

> Another Celestial Concert—The Chinese Opera Troupe which sometime since was and still is, we believe under the management and control of that generous caterer to the public taste Deacon Shelden, played a "star engagement" last evening at the Arcade Saloon, for the especial benefit of "Bally." The house was of course crowded on the occasion, and Miss Ding Bats, the prima donna, and renowned Asiatic cantatrice belched forth most divinely and lugubriously, as did the other artists who accompanied her. The troupe will continue to play through the week.[52]

Although little is known about Chinese performances in such venues, they were likely in the nature of skits or short pieces, based on an advertisement put out by the same Deacon Sheldon earlier that month, "Grand Celestial

Concert at the American Theatre, Deacon Sheldon's Celebrated Chinese Band." Another advertisement mentioned "Chinese minstrels" whom he employed to "accommodate the musical taste of this community" and "to the edification and delight of hundreds of eager listeners."[53] Elsewhere, there were reports of Chinese actors performing knife-throwing or magic tricks, such as Ming Sing, first in Mariposa and later, 140 miles away, in Nevada City: "A company of Chinese actors gave an exhibition at the theater last evening, Ming Sing, the celebrated magician, (so the bills say) was the principal attraction."[54] Could it also be that individuals or smaller groups of actors, separated from the troupe of twenty-five actors who performed to a full house in Mariposa earlier that year?[55] The variety of performance venues and types shows the multitude of ways that Chinese troupes intermixed with the local community and catered to popular tastes in entertainment.

The Case of Grass Valley

Nestled in the heart of the Sierra Nevada foothills, Grass Valley was the richest mining district from the early 1850s.[56] A fire in 1855 burned down over three hundred buildings, and most Chinese in Grass Valley were urged to move away to the town of Auburn, but they returned as the city rebuilt. Other towns that on earlier goldmining methods dwindled, but Grass Valley continued to thrive with the newer method of quartz mining.[57] It became the "spiritual center for Chinese in the surrounding gold mining country" by the 1860s.[58] In December 1859, a Chinese theater opened: "[different plays] are announced, each successive day by placards posted in the theater in Chinese hieroglyphics," noted the local *Daily National Gazette*.[59] It gave a largely favorable account of the theatrical attraction with the help of an interpreter:

> The Chinese [theater] at the lower end of the town is pretty well thronged, both night and day, with great numbers of Chinese, besides a pretty good sprinkling of Americans. We spent an hour or so there on Thursday evening, when we were politely furnished with an interpreter, who took a seat beside us, and with whose assistance we were enabled to understand quite fully the general feature of the play as it proceeded. The performance on this occasion was of a historic melodramatic character, and of course in Chinese dialect. It appeared to have for its foundation a condition of things very much like the present state of affairs in China, when some powerful rebel chief was in arms against the regularly constituted Empire. During the performances, the Emperor was several times personified upon the stage surrounded by his counsellors, and high dignitaries. The great council of state was also presented in session. Prominent military characters were also introduced, as well as common soldiers of both contending parties. When fully understood there appears to be quite as much plot and machinery as

English pieces. . . . A large number of our citizens have attended the exhibitions from time to time, and several ladies have also been present. It is a novelty well worth seeing. We commend Mr. Ah Poo, the gentlemanly manager to the kind consideration of our citizens.

The reporter depicted the exciting theatrical presentation while using the performance to reinforce the perception of imperial China. Sometimes, reviews could imply racial prejudice even in the disguise of praise; several days earlier, another report viewed the production through the lens of racial stereotypes:

A Chinese Theatrical Corps, consisting of thirty-six performers, have been giving entertainments night and day, at this place, during the past week. These people are as anomalous in their theater doings as they are in everything else. They work on the stage as our miners do in the quartz mines—six hours on and six off. They are exceedingly "well up'" in their parts. . . . The operatic style prevails in all their plays, and their music is almost entirely on the minor scale, and not particularly attractive to English ears. This, however is merely a matter of taste. . . . All in all, the Chinese theater is an outre affair, which to be understood must be seen. The Stage manager is one indeed, for he is at work continually, arranging chairs and tables. . . . They are in this, as in everything else they do: barbarians in their very civilization. They attempt everything, and do everything almost, common to the highest civilized people—shipbuilding, printing, painting & [sic]—but it's all Chinese at last.[60]

Using indefatigability to describe the performers and the manager recirculated a stereotype associated with Chinese laborers at that time—that is, they were cheap and industrious, "anomalous" and almost mechanical, and took white laborers' jobs. Invoking stereotypes constituted a form of alienation, viewing the scene at the theater through the lenses of preconceived notions and prejudices about Chinese laborers.

Auburn received many visits from Chinese troupes. In 1855, locals erected a Chinese theater at nearby China Hill.[61] In 1857, it hosted a theatrical troupe from Sacramento.[62] In 1858, another Chinese troupe visited and was received extremely well. The *Mountain Democrat* reported on its popularity, as well as on the increasing Chinese population in the area.

A company of Celestials are giving Theatrical entertainments at Auburn to crowded houses—The [Auburn] *Herald* says there must be something intensely interesting to them in these exhibitions, as it can be observed that the Chinese are always attracted to the town in large numbers during the stay of one of their theatrical companies. Attend one of their exhibitions, Mr. *Herald*, and give us an account of it in Chinese [sic]. It also states that at the present time the Chinese population of Auburn and vicinity seems to be one hundred per cent greater than three months ago.[63]

As noted by this Placerville newspaper, the Chinese opera troupe attracted viewers from the expanding Chinese community of the entire area. In addition to entertainment, the performances brought together the congregation of Chinese immigrants from their disparate locations. Not unlike county fairs, it was a mix of wistful nostalgia and unabashedly commercial opportunity. But it also involved communal celebrations of religious practice, deity birthdays, and ritual observances.

Due to this era's lack of personal accounts from Chinese immigrants, the peripheral place of Chinese immigrants in American society, and the neglect of their perspectives in American historical narratives, few documents survive to provide information regarding the lives of Chinese miners. And as Gordon H. Chang reminds us, these communities were often the target of racist attacks, which destroyed their belongings and homes or forced them to flee, another reason for the lack of personal accounts. Yet they were not merely victims. These news reports of the lively scenes of Chinese theaters throughout the region from the early 1850s to the late 1860s are merely snapshots and occasional glimpses into the period, whose development extended well into the 1880s. Despite their fragmentary nature, these reports paint a picture of fully fledged communities that not only had access to daily essentials but also actively engaged in social activities and cultural production.

Chinese theatrical performances were more than entertainment. They served the communities of miners, agricultural workers, loggers, and so on as vital gathering places where members of the Chinese community could connect with each other, share news, and engage in other social activities. They provided a sense of continuity, deep-rooted connection, and confirmation of value system during a time of significant upheaval, hostility, and violence. Ritual opera offerings were considered propitious events and protection against malevolent forces. Thus, the circulation of the Cantonese opera troupes played a significant role in the lives of the Chinese population in the interior of the state. In turn, their continuing presence also suggests the vibrancy of the thriving communities.

Theater and the Political Climate in Mining Towns

This second phase of the development of Chinese theater was inevitably hindered by anti-Chinese hostility. One of the most obviously racist measures taken against Chinese immigrants during this time was the Foreign Miners' Tax, enacted in various forms with the heaviest burden on Chinese and other East Asians.[64] As the largest population of foreign miners in the state (10,648 in the 1860 US census), Chinese miners had a prominent presence and made a significant contribution to the state's fiscal health. Yet this did not stop anti-Chinese initiative. On February 23, 1859, the *Daily Alta California* reported that a Chinese theatrical troupe "in the town of El Dorado, [is performing] to crowded houses, for some time past, and is still in full blast." This was not surprising, giving the large Chinese populations in mining towns. Nevertheless, on the very same page was a discussion of a Chinese expulsion effort, originally published in the *Auburn Herald*.[65]

> Expel the Chinese and Bankrupt the State: We do not believe it practicable or desirable that the Chinamen shall be expelled immediately from the whole State or any particular portion of it, and we assert this upon the well-grounded conviction that the taxes at present derived from them are a necessity to the State; and therefore, any law that looks to their immediate expulsion from the mines, at the same time aims at the immediate cutting off of a large revenue from the several mining counties and the State government. The receipt into the State Treasury from Foreign Miners' License for the fiscal year ending June 30, 1858, was $129,958.91, over twelve per cent of the entire revenue of the State; and an equivalent amount has gone into the treasuries of the mining counties. From what source is this amount to be made up, if upon the instant Chinese are prohibited from mining and the collection on the licenses ceases? Have the public, the press, and legislators provided for the contingency? We think not! The financial view of this Chinese question should be of some moment to the Legislature when acting upon it.

Efforts to expel Chinese miners began early and continued. In 1853, Shasta County vehemently sought to expel Chinese miners; in 1855, Mariposa County passed a resolution forbidding Chinese to work in the mines. Amador County discussed measures of Chinese expulsion. In 1859, mobs at Shasta tried to expel two hundred fifty Chinese by force of arms before they were stopped by the sheriff.[66] As many contemporaries pointed out, these mobs were forcing out Chinese miners who had already paid the foreign miners' fee and were entitled to the state's protection.

But theaters continued to signal the perseverance of the Chinese community. For example, Lava Beds, near Oroville, had become the largest Chinese mining settlement in US history by 1874.[67] In the fall of 1873 the town of Chinese miners "contained 150 buildings, a dozen canvas tents, and a single brick store . . . [and] the construction of a brick Joss House." The following spring they added a theater, which cost three thousand dollars.[68] The *Weekly Butte Record* reported, "In the palmy days of Oroville when its mines were worked by white men, the legitimate drama was wont to flourish there. Of late years nothing but a circus dare open there. A Chinese theatre is largely patronized, however, and does a flourishing business."[69] The high cost of building the theater underscored its significance to the community. Performances lasted until the end of 1874, when the building was put up for sale. This example is later than the period under consideration in this chapter, but it affirms that

Chinese miners remained in the region despite the hostile environment and that Chinese theater continued to be of primary importance to them.

In February 1857, when a Chinese theater with forty-eight performers opened in Chico's Chinatown, the theater's proprietor and manager, Sing Yat, called on the *Weekly Butte Record* to offer free tickets to its staff.[70] This savvy diplomatic move was important to improving community relations and thwarting hostility. The ability of a Chinese troupe to perform hinged largely on the degree of local anti-Chinese hostility, and circumstances were subject to change. Whereas in 1859, Grass Valley had welcomed Chinese theater, as shown above, in October 1869 the situation was much dicier. In reporting the sensation a Chinese troupe caused in Marysville, the local newspaper noted, "if the 'political sky' at Grass Valley is favorable, we shall have the troupe at this place."[71] The writer was no doubt referring to the significant rise of the Anti-Coolie Association in Northern California, which had just held a large meeting at Grass Valley in September and was planning another.[72] These additional hostile situations placed constraints on Chinese theaters' existence, constraints that inevitably were beyond the Chinese community's control. Such circumstances made the wide circulation of Chinese opera troupes all the more remarkable. As the anti-Chinese movement gained momentum, fewer Chinese theaters were reported in mining towns, except in towns involved later in railroad construction.

We can learn three key points from this fragmented history. First, the dispersion of itinerant troupes in the Sacramento River delta resembled that in the Pearl River delta of southern China. Since Cantonese operas were often presented as worship and offerings to the deities, the circulation of the troupes in rural society was closely related to the cycle of deity birthdays and festivals. Accordingly, the itinerant troupes traveled from one performance location to another along the waterways. Whereas the tradition of the Red Boats (the wooden watercraft used as means of conveyance and accommodation by the actors) was developed to transport troupes in the Pearl River delta, regional circulation in California relied on a more arduous mode of transportation via steamboat or horsedrawn wagon or on foot. Nevertheless, in both cases, culture was brought from the coast inland, deepening the ties of scattered rural communities. Second, the troupes' and musicians' travels through the region facilitated the intermingling of Chinese with other ethnic groups. For example, a Chico newspaper report began, "A building is in process of erection in Chinatown, that is very shortly to be occupied by a company of Celestial devotees to Thespis. We are told that the company is to consist of forty-eight performers," and after a lengthy introduction to Chinese opera, made recommendations for its general readers regarding the logistics of their visits to the theater: "Tickets of admission can he procured at the various bookstores, and at the box-office of the theatre. The entire free list is suspended, excepting to the members of the press. Children in arms will not be admitted unless accompanied by a wet nurse."[73] These trivial reminders demonstrate that going to notable events such as Chinese theatrical performances was a matter of course and commonplace. Chinese theater catered to a mixed audience. Gordon H. Chang also found that the "local newspaper encouraged whites to enjoy the shows at the Chinese theater."[74] Racial barriers could be overlooked in the communal space of cultural entertainment when such opportunities were extremely limited. Third, since the dissemination of Chinese troupes was supported by the economy and by demand, the fast-growing market for Chinese theater attested to this region's significant and prominent Chinese communities. It pointed to the strength and autonomy of the region's thriving Chinese wealth and workforce; far from being passive, it actively organized its social system and customs. If the racial riots that would later drive the Chinese from these towns erased most traces of their success, the reports of these frequent Cantonese opera performances recall for us their economic and cultural prosperity.

It is worth noting the little-documented Chinese puppet theaters active during this time as well. Between 1854 and 1858, there were reports of Chinese puppet theaters in San Joaquin, Stockton, Chico, and Trinity. But given the scarcity of information, Chinese puppet theater of the goldmining era awaits further research.

Railroad Chinese

A pivotal part of California's state history was the 1860s' vast expansion in railroad construction, the transcontinental being the most important accomplishment. With the passage of the Pacific Railway Act in 1862, the Central Pacific Railroad Company (CPRR) began in 1863 to build the western portion of the first transcontinental railroad, starting from Sacramento and reaching east to meet the portion constructed by Union Pacific, starting from Iowa. A particularly difficult task for the CPRR was getting through the Sierra Nevada, which required blasting through rock, carving tunnels through long stretches of solid granite, and bridging canyons. These activities involved very high risks for workers. A shortage of white laborers compelled the company to hire Chinese workers, who became the most significant part of the workforce. "Railroad Chinese" were highly regarded for their stamina, discipline, and skill. The transcontinental railroad project in California began near the goldmining region, where the company drew first from Chinese miners in Auburn and other Sierra Nevada mining towns.[75] Many mining towns discussed earlier will also be considered here as railroad towns.

On October 26, 1863, in Sacramento, the CPRR laid the first track of what would be the transcontinental railroad. According to Chang, by spring 1865, two to three thousand Chinese worked on the line, mostly recruited from within the state.[76] They were not only laborers but also labor contractors, cooks, blacksmiths, teamsters, and waiters. Many helped to pave roads for access and supply transport. Chang's studies show that up to five hundred Chinese labor contractors and six thousand Chinese laborers worked for the CPRR in the first years of construction.

In the month before construction started, Hung Wah, a Chinese labor contractor living in Auburn, advertised from his office in Auburn in a local newspaper, the *Placer Herald*, "I will furnish any number of Chinese laborers to work on Rail Roads, Wagon Roads, or Mining Claim."[77] The following January, he and twenty-two other Chinese appear on the payroll of the CPRR.[78] In May 1865, he provided two hundred fifty Chinese workers; in July 1866 he provided nine hundred, almost a quarter of the construction workforce. The power of Hung Wah and other labor contractors grew quickly, as they not only supplied labor but also met those laborers' other needs such as wellness and social activities. When the CPRR began recruiting workers directly from southern China in 1865, the total number of its Chinese workers grew exponentially. It was estimated that at any one time as many as ten to fifteen thousand Chinese were working on the transcontinental railroad until it was completed at Promontory Summit on May 10, 1869.[79] Given the brutal working conditions faced by the railroad Chinese and their poor living conditions along the construction line, the endeavor to recover their experience is still an ongoing effort. Nevertheless, some news reports reflect the significance of Chinese theater during this era.

The Case of Marysville

In 1868 alone, Chinese theater activities were reported in Grass Valley, Marysville, Stockton, and Sacramento, all of which had expanded significantly in response to railroad construction. Among these, Marysville presents an interesting case study.

A significant town since the start of the gold rush, Marysville is situated where the Feather and Yuba rivers merge as the Feather, which in turn flows into the Sacramento River. Through river transportation it was well connected to Sacramento and San Francisco and was considered the merchant-oriented gateway to mining country, transporting gold, produce, and lumber, thereby becoming wealthy.[80] As noted above, the Chinese considered Marysville the "third city" in California. In 1870, the Chinese population of Marysville was 1,417, a bit less than 30 percent of its overall population of 4,738.[81] Many Chinese in Marysville were business owners, contractors, and traders who supplied other Chinese on their way to the Sierra. Flooding was a general problem, so levees were erected to secure more land from the swamp, and a bridge was built across the Feather River connecting Marysville to Yuba City. Over the years, railroad lines in the Sacramento and Vallejo valleys further raised its significance. The Oroville and Marysville Railroad began running in 1863, serving the mining communities of the northern Sierra as well as those in the lumber trades.[82]

After the celebration of the completion of the transcontinental railroad at Promontory Summit, the CPRR president, Leland Stanford, announced that the "Central Pacific will soon move men and teams to Marysville to commence the Oregon [Rail] Road."[83] This railroad line had been in discussion for nearly a decade. At the beginning of 1869, under an act of the state of Oregon, the California and Oregon Railroad Company was organized to connect Portland with Marysville. Construction began in mid-October 1869; by late November an Oregon newspaper reported the railroad was progressing rapidly from Marysville northward, with a workforce of six hundred Chinese men, and expected the railroad to reach Chico soon, continuing on to Shasta Valley and Yerba before reaching the Oregon border.[84]

Newspapers from around the country regularly noted the progress of the railroad's construction. A newspaper in West Virginia reported in January 1870 that the California and Oregon Rail Road had hired an additional two hundred fifty Chinese laborers and that one hundred more were expected to complete the forty-four miles between Marysville and Chico.[85] Marysville emerged for a while as a major nexus in discussions about the new possibility of traveling to the West, as the country eagerly explored the dramatic economic, technological, and cultural changes triggered by the new transcontinental railroad. The Central Pacific Railroad's advertisements in Idaho City included the following line: "The 6 a.m. passenger train connects at the Junction with the cars for Marysville and all points of Northern California and Oregon."[86] By October two trains ran daily between Sacramento and Marysville, and in November a daily train ran between San Francisco and Marysville. In early December, Yuba City was connected to Davis; it was reported that the Vallejo Rail Company was to bring two hundred Chinese men to work on another line from Woodland to Colusa. The trains also expedited the transportation of produce from the region to Sacramento and San Francisco.[87]

Work on bringing a large Chinese opera troupe to Marysville began at the same time as work on the California–Oregon railroad. On October 13, 1869, the *Marysville Daily Appeal* reported that a Chinese theatrical troupe of ninety-five members was to arrive on the river steamer *Flora* and had "leased the Marysville Theater, and the old Merchants' Hotel, between which they will play, sleep and eat."[88] The Marysville Theater was built in August 1865 at the heart of Marysville's business district, after an old theater was destroyed by fire the previous November. The theater seated nine hundred and had twelve basement dressing rooms lit by gas.[89] The paper gave frequent reports on the troupe, such as the performance of "Six Kings" (referring to *The Joint*

Investiture of a Prime Minister of Six Warlords). One noted that the theater had about two hundred audience members nightly, with Chinese, both male and female, sitting at the lower level, and private boxes filled with Americans. The reporter speculated on the positive impact of California–Oregon railroad construction:

> The Chinese grand opera troupe draw big houses. We suspect that we are indebted for this visit by Celestial theatricals to the fact that many hundreds of Chinese are now laboring on railroads in this vicinity. The house is well filled every night, and last evening was a complete jam. The same or a similar troupe visited this city last year, but did not make its fortune. The Oregon railroad Chinamen will save it this time? [*sic*][90]

The vibrancy of the city and its economic ties to the railroad were also reported in San Francisco, where the *Daily Evening Bulletin* wrote on November 8:

> From fifty to one hundred carpenters have arrived in this city during the last day or two, seeking work on the railroad bridges. They were recently employed upon the sheds of the Central railroad. Marysville is lively; sports and concomitants in town, and the hotels are crowded. The Chinese employed on the railroads give a support to the Chinese theatre.

While Marysville's reception of the Chinese troupe the year before might pale in comparison to the welcome of the 1869 troupe, it was due to the city's quick ascent to prominence in railroad construction rather than the size or significance of the troupes. The 1868 troupe, the San Nan Foo Company, was no less extravagant than the later one; it performed at the Marysville Theater for a month, and boasted a cast of eighty men and twelve women.[91]

The advertisement (fig. 2.5) underscored the splendor: "Each successive night new scenes in the eventful life of a Chinese emperor, more than 200 dresses."[92]

FIGURE 2.5 Advertisement for San Nang Foo company, *Marysville Daily Appeal*, September 24, 1868.

MARYSVILLE THEATER.

THE GREAT CHINESE

SAN NANG FOO COMPANY!

—CONSISTING OF—

80 MEN AND 12 WOMEN,

Have leased the Marysville Theater for one month, and will present on each successive night new scenes in the eventful life of a

CHINESE EMPEROR!

☞Their WARDROBE consists of more than TWO HUNDRED DRESSES, of the richest material and of great cost.

☞PRIVATE BOXES and DRESS CIRCLE will be RESERVED for the American portion of the audience. sep16-1w*

After attending the first performance, a *Marysville Daily Appeal* writer noted, "[W]e were favorably struck with the decency and good behaviour of these Mongolian actors, and we freely admit that they are quite equal to the reputation claimed for them by their own countrymen," then went on to describe two military plays.[93] The newspaper urged locals to take advantage of the show: "CHINESE THEATER.—Have you been to the Chinese Theater? If not, you are behind the age. The American audience increases every evening, which is quite conclusive of the merits of the exhibition. It is a rare curiosity, and well worthy of seeing once. The price of admission has been reduced from $1 to 75 cents."[94] A reporter observed on a second visit, "There was present a 'fashionable' audience of male and female citizens of the Celestial Kingdom."[95] Several similar observations suggest a significant class of wealthy merchants in the Chinese community. They formed an important part of the Chinese community of this busy interjunction, who likely sponsored and managed the monthlong performance. After its engagement in Marysville, the troupe moved on to Sacramento, where the Sacramento Theater recently had been refitted as a Chinese theater.

The troupe of 1869 appeared with more fanfare. The large troupe arriving in Marysville in October was praised all around: "The wardrobe of this troupe is magnificent, and when one becomes familiar with the Chinese language, their performances are interesting! At any rate, a man on the Pacific coast who has never seen a Chinese performance is behind the age."[96] In November, the *Marysville Daily Appeal* reported, with quite a bit of mockery, perhaps out of disbelief of its success or simply jealousy,

> The Chinese Theater—The play of the four emperors continues at the Marysville Theater—the institution running nightly till about 1 o'clock. The company is a good one—not forgetting the orchestra, which discourse heavenly (celestial) music. Among the leading actors there is a Forrest, Booth, McCullough, Barrett, et al. Old Forrest plays magnificently. He shakes his gray locks (beard) in the most approved nervous style, and dies half a dozen times a night as naturally as a man falls off a slippery log. The wardrobe (including the barrel of tea) is very good—some say their "morning gowns" are magnificent—and we understand that a few of first class ladies have occasioned private boxes several nights for the purpose of drawing patterns for their liege lords.[97]

The references here are to the actors John McCullough, Edwin Forrest, Edwin Booth, and Lawrence Barrett, then popular in San Francisco. But the hyperbolic presentation here was in the spirit of farce to elicit laughs and to achieve comic effects. It steered the audience away from an immersive experience of Chinese theater, given that farce is a dialogue "between aggression and flippancy."[98]

Unlike Sacramento (population 16,283 by 1870), which often offered several entertainment venues, Marysville, with less than a third of the population, had only one professional theater.[99] Since the Marysville Theater was the only venue for theatrical entertainment in town, performing groups could be turned away if it was occupied, as was the fate of the California Minstrels when they wished to have an engagement at the theater in October, when the Chinese troupe began its run in October.[100]

The continuing popularity of Chinese theater further precluded the appearance of many other entertainments and theater investors in subsequent months. Figure 2.6 shows two advertisements for the vibrantly successful troupe: one from its first week, the other from more than seven weeks into its run in Marysville. By the end of November, the troupe had decided to rent for another month, which prompted a paper to suggest "the building of a new theatre up town," noting "two or three first class companies" had been driven away.[101] The *Sonoma Democrat* reported in mid-December, "A Chinese theatrical troupe has been monopolizing the Theatre at Marysville for some time past."[102] Another reporter wrote in frustration, "The Wilton troupe, consisting of eight members, were in the city yesterday but compelled to go on to Davisville because unable to obtain a hall in the city. We are unable to say how many theatrical troupes have been prevented from playing in this city in consequence of the Marysville Theater being in possession of a heathen troupe of Chinese."[103]

FIGURE 2.6A Advertisement for San San Fong company, *Marysville Daily Appeal*, October 14, 1869.

FIGURE 2.6B Advertisement for the "Chinese Troupe," *Marysville Daily Appeal*, December 7, 1869.

The most famous among the acts turned away from the Marysville Theater due to the popularity of Chinese theater was the Pasquale Brignoli Italian Opera Troupe, regarded highly by critics on both coasts, performing Donizetti's *Don Pasquale* and Rossini's *Il barbiere di Siviglia* at the Metropolitan Theater in San Francisco.[104] Receiving rave reviews in San Francisco, the troupe announced a planned concert in Marysville on January 6, provided the theater became available; ten days later the manager canceled the planned concert.[105] The *San Francisco Chronicle* reported, "The Brignoli opera troupe were compelled to postpone giving a concert at Marysville, as the Chinese opera troupe have a lease of the theater."[106] Instead, the Brignoli company went to perform in Nevada City and Piper's Opera House in Virginia City.[107] When the Chinese opera troupe concluded its three-month performance run in mid-January, several papers reported that "the receipts of the Chinese theatrical company at Marysville aggregate $5,000 for the season, and was taxed $129."[108] The total revenue (the equivalent of $115,505 in 2024) was a significant record for this venture at the time, such that thirty years later the *Marysville Daily Appeal* reprinted the news to commemorate the city's history.[109] It was the city's longest theatrical engagement, proving the rich cultural life of a prominent Chinese community in a town made prosperous by railway construction. Marysville was not alone. Several years later, in 1874, Oroville would establish a Chinese theater as well.[110] They reveal the prevalence of Cantonese opera culture in California; just as important, they show that the social power of these Chinese communities cannot be underestimated.

Ritual, Rite, and Performance

One of the most important concerns of railroad Chinese was expressed in religious terms, in no small part owing to the high risk of accidents, illness, and death. The popular religious practice they were accustomed to was the worship of an amalgamation of folk deities and demigods from historical legends, such as Guan Gong (the god of war and brotherhood) and Tia Hou/Mazu (the empress of heaven), as well as aspects of Buddhism, Confucianism, and Taoism. Just as essential were rituals to honor ancestors and the recently deceased. Therefore, temples and altars were established where railroad Chinese lived. Many of these Chinese temples remain to this day. As the religious studies scholar Kathryn Gin noted, "The Chinese temples in the goldmining towns of Weaverville, Oroville, and Marysville, and in the fishing and farming village of Mendocino, persisted," and constitute today "windows into the nineteenth-century Chinese popular religion shared by gold rush era and railroad migrants."[111]

Cantonese opera performances played an important part in these religious practices. Traditionally, communities hired troupes to perform operas during religious or secular communal events such as the new year, the Mid-Autumn Harvest, and the "Rites of Purification for Thanksgiving and the Ghost Festival, the Initiation Ritual for Temples, and the Birthdays of Deities," as Sau-yan Chan notes.[112] "Traditional customs prescribe that the operas be performed to please the deities." Unlike in Christian churches, however, the presence of deities did not invoke a solemn atmosphere, and people were free to move around and engage in a variety of activities.[113] They included banqueting, gambling, commenting on the performances, offering incense or praying to the deities. Thus the festivals and rituals were carried out in a casual and secular atmosphere where "men and deities are being entertained simultaneously." Furthermore, Chan noted, "As the focal attraction within a series of rituals that are held to celebrate religious events, traditional Cantonese opera often features plots with happy endings." Indeed, the ritual plays typically included *Birthday Greetings from Eight Immortals*, *The Dance of Promotion*, *The Heavenly Maid Delivers Her Son*, all of which depict a search for good fortune in the forms of gaining longevity, prominence, and offspring, respectively. Depending on the occasion, the community would also choose opera repertoire whose subject matter involved "a happy reunion (whether on earth or in heaven), the birth or survival of a son, and the rise to an extremely prominent position." The audiences welcomed them. Such ritual occasions with opera performances benefited the community "by converging their emotions and thus strengthening their coalitions."

Gordon H. Chang's depiction of the celebration of *gui jie* (the Hunger Ghost Festival) at Grass Valley in August 1868 reflected the audience's active engagement in religious practice.

> A subscription of twenty-five cents would provide a Railroad Chinese special access to ceremonies. There would be plentiful food, cultural performances, and rituals performed by priests from San Francisco. . . . [L]ocal Chinese would have begun to practice their instruments for festival performances. . . . Special pavilions and stages were constructed to hold elaborate presentations.
>
> The local Chinese temple was festooned with rich tapestries, decorations, and calligraphy with propitiating inscriptions. Elaborately detailed, constructed deities large and small abounded: some ten feet tall, ferocious and threatening, others showing a benevolent demeanor. A huge god reigned over his court. Frightening images of displeased ghosts appeared everywhere, with long, thin necks because they were unable to eat on account of their misfortune. . . . Spiritual leaders were dressed in white robes with hoods made of light blue satin covering their heads. They engaged in long, mesmerizing incantations, while discordant music from Chinese reed and

string instruments, cymbals, and drums filled the air. Chinese men sang in a mournful nasal falsetto.[114]

In the following month, the *Weekly Butte Record* reported a three-day annual Chinese festival in Oroville with a significant religious component, which "consisted of a public theatrical exhibition, of vocal and instrumental music, worshipping in church [*sic*], and statuette scenes of life in the Celestial Kingdom."[115] The reporter depicted in great detail an exhibition of scenes of purgatory typical of Buddhist teaching, likely connected to the tradition of *Mulian Rescues His Mother* (目蓮救母), a tale of karmic punishment and redemption. Although sketchy and incomplete, such reports recorded ways that railroad Chinese continued and adapted popular Chinese religious practice to an environment of challenges, hardship and uncertainty. In this religious milieu, the presence of opera was both blissful and auspicious. The more spectacular the troupe's wardrobe and presentation, the more propitious the offering was.

Thus, in this second phase of its development in the interior of northern California, Cantonese opera constituted an important part of the soundscape of the American West. Through the end of the nineteenth century, towns such as Marysville, Oroville, Chico, and so on, as well as the important hub of Sacramento were frequented by Chinese opera troupes, and Chinese theaters were established intermittently for weeks or months at a time. Miraculously, despite the racial tension and violence, they were able to continue their performances successfully, bringing spiritual and emotional connections to the communities that nourished their wellbeing and flourishing. They sustained a regional operatic network along the waterways, which at its height was bustled with liveliness, color, and interactivity. In September 1868, a Sacramento reporter encountered them on the move: "One hundred and thirty-seven Chinamen came down on the steamer Flora from Marysville yesterday, bringing considerable baggage with them. On inquiry, we learned that they were members of the Chinese theatrical company which has leased the old Sacramento Theater."[116] Indeed, it was the San Nang Foo troupe discussed above. When three months later the troupe left for San Francisco, the Sacramento community was reluctant to part with them. At the pier, a reporter observed "their countrymen being assembled in considerable numbers at the steamer to see them off."[117] Yet Sacramento was not left without Chinese theater for long. Just eighteen days later, as noted by the *Sacramento Daily Union,* another Chinese troupe arrived. Such comings and goings must have become a norm for the Sacramento delta waterway.

> The steamer Capital brought up from San Francisco yesterday morning a Chinese theatrical company, numbering nearly one hundred performers. Their baggage, which formed quice [*sic*] an item in the steamer's freight, was gazed at with considerable curiosity by the white loungers about the

wharf. Last evening the troupe made their first appearance before a Sacramento audience in the "Old Drury" Theater, on Third street, near I, which
was packed full of Chinese, a few white people being also present. As actors,
the members of this company, as a general thing, are much superior to those
which were here a few weeks ago, and their wardrobes appear fully as rich
as those aired by the previous company.[118]

The steamer *Capital*, along with the *Flora* mentioned earlier, was part of
the California Steam Navigation Company, whose large steamships, with a
capacity of six hundred passengers and hundreds of tons of freight, served
the need of busy inland travels, transporting Chinese troupes regularly among
the interior towns.[119] According to news reports, many towns in the region
had Chinese theaters of significant sizes at various points. The performance
circuit in the interior of the state supported San Francisco as well, which will
be the topic of the next chapter.

CHAPTER 3

Performing Chinese Opera in San Francisco

As the seaport through which Chinese troupes entered California, San Francisco naturally became the first stop on their tours. But whereas in the interior of the state, Chinese theaters appeared one after another in different towns, the construction of a new Chinese theater building in San Francisco would have to wait until 1868 (fifteen years after that constructed by Tong Hook Tong was sold and repurposed in 1853). Meanwhile, Cantonese opera performances were held intermittently at existing San Francisco theaters, either the prominent Maguire Opera House and the Lyceum Theater or at less prestigious locations such as the older Adelphi Theater and the Union Theater (Bert's New Idea Melodeon). The latter hosted many different forms of popular entertainment such as concerts, opera, minstrelsy, and variety shows. In 1853, for example, the Austrian violinist Miska Hauser witnessed "eighty actors in glittering and expensive costumes" at the Chinese Theater.[1] By around 1860, the performances had become regular, and eventually required a permanent performing space by the end of the decade.

Between 1853 and 1867, there were numerous newspaper reports about appearances of Chinese theaters in the interior of the state, but most of them were brief. On the other hand, newspaper reports of Chinese theatrical activities in San Francisco appeared somewhat less frequently, but they tended to be longer. Many of these reports were advertisements associated with prominent theaters, showing that the demand from mainstream society might be partly responsible for the commercial success of Chinese theater in the city. Therefore, this chapter can be viewed as both a parallel development to the second phase of Chinese theater in California and a prelude to the third phase—the establishment of commercial Chinese theater.

Adelphi Theater: *We Have a Chinese Theater in Full Operation in Our City*

In June 1856, with no fanfare, a Chinese troupe of fifteen began performing at a venue on the east side of Dupont Street, near Clay. The *California Chronicle* brought attention to the opening: "It may not be generally known that we have a Chinese theater in full operation in our city."[2] The stage was a carpeted, raised platform, with the standard two doors to backstage. The orchestra sat onstage at the back, an adaptation to Cantonese opera. A long report described in detail the opera *The Siege of the House of Tso*.[3] It is a historical play with many twists: Chew Fung Yan is a highly respected warrior. After a failed attempt to assassinate the nefarious emperor, he escapes and endeavors to conceal himself in the house of a friend, Tso-ye. Soldiers come to arrest Chew but he gets away with the help of Tso-ye's sister-in-law, who claims Chew is her husband. It works because the two men greatly resemble one another. Later, however, she is ashamed of the act and dies of grief. Tso-ye is unaware of the situation, but when he discovers that the friend hidden in his house is the fugitive, he is torn between friendship and loyalty. Chew reminds him the importance of loyalty. They both agree that Chew Fung Yan is to be turned in to the emperor the next day. In the middle of the night, however, a patron deity comes to the rescue, removing a growth on Chew's neck, a feature that made him identifiable to the emperor. When Tso-ye turns in Chew the next day, the emperor releases him and grants him honor.

The story is filled with misunderstanding, bravery, loyalty, and moral justice. The audience was mesmerized. The writer noted, "[They] sit and listen for five long hours, with the gravest of countenances, and without opening their mouths or showing the slightest marks of disapprobation upon any occasion. There is never any applause, except sometimes a sort of involuntary grunt; but there is also never a hiss or a murmur." The report lamented that the opera did not have battle scenes but paid special attention to the female characters, performed by men. "The female characters are truly wonderful delineated to be played by males. The apparent meekness and modesty displayed, generally speaking, are remarkable." Overall, this review is a serious and meaningful engagement with the dramatic arts of Chinese opera.

In December 1856, the theater again appeared in the news; the number of performers had grown to thirty, with the added attraction of "a new, rich and extensive" wardrobe from China. The *Daily Evening Bulletin* wrote, "The dresses are made of a profusion of satin, silk and painted cotton stuffs, and are covered with tinsel, outlandish ornaments and barbaric display."[4] An advertisement in the *Daily Alta California* (fig. 3.1) declared, "Chinese Theatre: The Chinese Dramatic Company . . . will perform every night until further notice, at the Adelphi Theatre."[5] The company's indefinite residency was a

FIGURE 3.1 Advertisement for Chinese opera at Adelphi Theatre, *Daily Alta California*, December 4, 1856.

new arrangement for the city. This year, for the first time, Chinese Theatre was listed in the San Francisco City Directory.[6]

In the early 1850s, the Adelphi Theatre hosted the most prestigious performances in San Francisco, including the first opera season in 1851 with the first fully staged opera, Bellini's *La sonnambula*, by the Pellegrini Opera Company. This was the second Adelphi Theatre, built in fall 1852 after the San Francisco city fire of 1851 destroyed the first. It was located on Dupont Street between Washington Street and Clay Street, and seated about seven hundred. Prior to the residence of the Chinese opera troupe, it was overshadowed by larger theaters, such as Maguire's Opera House, but featured French drama, English theater, Dutch burlesque and farce.[7]

The performances were crowded and regularly drew American spectators.[8] They featured the celebrated ritual opera *Six Warlords*. An announcement brought attention to this grand opera (see Prologue). Again, the female roles drew special attention from the reporter: "Those intended to perform female characters cultivate soft soprano voices, tapering fingers and small feet. So completely feminine do they appear that the spectator feels a difficulty in believing them males."[9]

Various reports in the *Bulletin* expressed profound interest in the characters of the drama and the conventions of Chinese opera. In addition to *The Siege of the House of Tso* noted above, another reporter was engrossed in the intriguing stories of the classic opera *The Return of Sit Ping Quai* and gave it two long writeups.[10] It is interesting to note that although the opera included the character names and some key plots of this traditional play (also called *Pinggui Returning Home*), according to the reporter, the performed opera shortened the original story and incorporated plots from a different but also well-known legend.

The protagonist, Sit Ping Quai, bids farewell to his beloved wife, Wang, in answer to the emperor's call to fight the invading enemy. The original story has him conquer and come home triumphantly after years of difficult battles to his wife who, persevering through poverty, has patiently waited for him. But the story the reporter tells borrows parts of another legend (*Wenji Returning to Han*). According to the new plot, Sit Ping Quai is captured and wins the heart of Linfa, the enemy princess, whom he is forced to marry. After years of bliss, he hears from Wang, prompting him to recall his patriotism, feel remorse, and set off for home. Linfa captures him and lets him go twice, regretting her actions both times. The second time, she follows him on horseback. But her hope of persuading him to stay is completely crushed when he breaks a bridge to stop her. The reporter wrote of the bridge scene:

> He, however, before she could overtake him this time, had crossed the bridge of a mighty river, and seeing his wife galloping in a great cloud of dust behind him, he broke down the bridge as soon as he had passed it. Linfa approached on the wings of the wind, as it were, but finding the bridge broken and that her husband was now completely out of her power, she tore her hair, rent her garments, and at last fell down in a swoon, her attendants came up and carried her off to her own dominions.

The reporter also described the stage movement:

> The manner of crossing the bridge, we have already alluded to, Sit Ping Quai, having thrown down the bridge or board, stands upon one table and the princess upon the other, almost three feet apart; but the spectators understand, of course, that they are upon opposite sides of a mighty and impassible torrent. Linfa, after tearing her hair and rending her garments, moves backward towards the edge of the table and falls over upon the flat of her back upon the floor, a distance of four or five feet.

These detailed reports revealed that Chinese theater was taken as a serious, if less developed, dramatic form. The reporter concluded the review with a recommendation urging readers to visit this Chinese drama and perhaps take inspiration from it for the development of American drama.

> There can be doubt but that many of the Chinese plays are admirable in invention, and the conduct of the story [*sic*]. Even in the imperfect sketch, which we have given, some traces of deep insight into the human heart can be found without difficulty. It is a well-known fact that Shakespeare founded all, or nearly all his sublime production upon stories or plays, which existed before his time in an imperfect state. It is also known that almost all the plays which have lately appeared, and some of real merit, are adaptations from the dramatic literature of other countries, or of the author's own country. Considering these facts, it is in no way improbable that Anglo-Saxon authors will yet rummage over the old Chinese manuscripts and copies, and many future American dramas may be suggested and perhaps taken almost bodily from the hieroglyphic books of the Celestial Thespians.[11]

The review was written in an attentive manner similar to reviews for other contemporary theaters. During this period, San Francisco theaters featured Shakespeare frequently, thus the point of reference. There was no immediate response to the call to learn from Chinese drama, however.[12] Nevertheless, these reviews demonstrated a serious attempt in the late 1850s to engage with the dramatic art of Chinese opera—a quality that, unfortunately, would be sorely lacking in the subsequent decades.

The *Daily Alta California* also gave an extensive report on the theater scene. The writer, seated in a private box, gave an astute description of the Chinese audience separated by social class: "The audience was composed of Chinese of both sexes, the pit being filled with the plebians, while the aristocracy were in the boxes. Among those present we noticed some of our 'most prominent' Chinese citizens. . . . The female portion of the audience in the pit had their heads covered with beautiful bandana handkerchiefs, while those in the boxes had theirs covered with candle-grease."[13] Particularly interesting is the reporter's description of women. The candle grease and pomade were used to stiffen the elaborate hairstyles of Chinese women of the elite classes (see fig. 4.2). The reference to the women's colorful head covering likely related to prostitutes. According to the theater historian Carolyn Eichin, prostitutes were an important part of theater audiences in frontier towns.[14] The theater was established for, and supported by, the full spectrum of Chinese society, but the discrepancy in social and economic classes was readily comprehensible even to an outsider.

The Chinese opera performance run at the Adelphi Theatre was also part of a larger circuit. From June to December, the interval between these two news articles, Chinese theaters were reported in San Andreas, Stockton, and Drytown.[15] Troupes traveled from San Francisco to the interior towns, not unlike other traveling entertainment groups at the time. For example, the European Ravel and Martinetti variety troupes made an inland circuit in 1855–56 in conjunction with their San Francisco appearance; the Marsh Troupe of Juvenile Comedians went from San Francisco's Lyceum Theater to perform at Stockton, Placerville, Marysville and Sacramento in 1860.[16] As Eichin notes regarding their relationship, "The development of hinterland towns aided San Francisco, giving it a wider influence both economically and culturally."[17]

In San Francisco, Chinese opera performances were offered in celebration of the Chinese New Year in 1857.[18] A *Daily Evening Bulletin* report underscores the pride that the city took in its uniquely cosmopolitan entertainment scene and its connection to the hinterland:

> It is a strange country this California, where nearly at the same time people may see represented the national dramas of England and America, of France, Germany, Italy, Spain, and, though last not least, of China. For a considerable portion of the year Chinese theatrical performances are given

regularly in this city. When the "season" closes, the troupe take bag and baggage and visit the interior towns and mining camps. . . . Since the San Francisco troupe left the Adelphi Theater here, they have visited a large portion of the State. Of late they played for three successive weeks, to fair audiences, at the Sacramento Theatre, in Sacramento city.[19]

The numbers of Chinese immigrants increased annually; on average between three thousand and six thousand arrived from 1856 to 1868.[20] Entertainment was in increasingly high demand. Between 1857and 1867, several more major venues in San Francisco either became Chinese theaters or occasionally hosted Chinese troupes. They were the Maguire Opera House, the Lyceum Theatre, Bert's New Idea Melodeon, and the Union Theatre. Of these, the Union Theatre served as perhaps the longest and most frequent host and was eventually referred to as the Chinese Theater.

Meanwhile, theater impresarios began including Chinese opera troupes in their popular entertainment lineups. From 1859 to 1869, more than ten major theater venues operated in San Francisco.[21] In newspapers' classified ads, under the section "Amusements," notices for Chinese troupes, like other performing groups, followed the norm of listing programs, managers, and lead performers. Performances of Chinese troupes were interspersed with vaudevilles, Italian operas, and English plays and concerts. For example, a Chinese troupe at the Adelphi Theatre charged ticket prices of $1.50 and $1 in 1856, comparable to those of other theaters, such as the largest, the Metropolitan Theatre ($2, $1, $.50). Newspapers periodically reported on special features at Chinese theaters, such as fight scenes, acrobats, or exhibits of beautiful costumes.

Another opera troupe arrived in May 1858 and opened a theater across from the Adelphi Theater, which burned to the ground the following month, at the time a common fate of theaters.[22] A report in the *New York Clipper*, an entertainment newspaper, described the new opera troupe's appearance:

> Enter the place and you will find an audience of several rows of Chinamen ranged behind several rows of China women, all smoking, or eating peanuts, or laughing and talking perhaps, but still keeping their attention upon the drama. On one side of the stage are the orchestra, smoking and drumming away at their instruments; and at the other a lot of stage instruments in the shape of huge swords, battleaxes, flags, tables, chairs, and whatever else may be needed in the course of the play. There are no shifting scenes and no drop curtain, but the audience is called upon to imagine the "scene" by large signs in Chinese characters, which are changed with each change of scene. The actors make their entrances at a door at the back part on one side of the stage, and make their exits at a similar one on the other side. The language is said to be the Court language, and for that reason, as well as it is difficult to understand singing at its best, many of audience have trouble in keeping along with the thread of the story.[23]

Clearly the writer was provided with an interpreter who could share knowledge about performance practices, from the iconic two backstage doors for Chinese theaters (known in Chinese as *hudu men*) to more specialized knowledge, such as the use of court language, rather than Cantonese dialect, for Cantonese opera on stage. The latter observation also attested to the use of Central dialect by Cantonese opera troupes that came to America in the late 1850s.[24] Instead of the back of the stage, however, the orchestra was placed on one side of the stage. Quite a few reports similarly noted the use of placards with Chinese characters to announce the scenes or programs—a practice showing the high level of literacy of the audience, many of whom were merchants, business proprietors, or labor contractors.

San Francisco's Chinese theaters were helped by the active performing circuit in the interior of the state. Reciprocity likely developed between San Francisco and the interior towns' Chinese communities: on the one hand to offer city audiences a healthy rotation of troupes, and on the other to supply visiting troupes for the entertainment needs of scattered locations. One troupe performed in Sacramento in April 1857, at the Sacramento Theatre (discussed in the previous chapter), then made a visit to Auburn, performing for a month. It then returned to Sacramento in June before heading back to San Francisco.[25] Another troupe circulated through Oroville, San Andreas, and Chico later in the year.[26] A Chinese troupe of twenty-five performing in Mariposa in April 1858 was widely reported in connection with the construction of a Chinese village.[27] Later in the year, newspaper reports recorded Chinese troupes at Sacramento, Placerville, Nevada City, and Auburn. A Chinese troupe performed in El Dorado in 1859 and in Grass Valley, as previously noted.

This circuit ensured the prosperity of San Francisco's Chinese theater and ensured visits by Pacific-crossing troupes. Together the interior towns and San Francisco formed a larger route to attract better and larger opera troupes from southern China to California for longer and more profitable stays. It also made possible the employment of multiple troupes in the region that the city might not be able to sustain by itself. Each Chinese theater in a mining town became a node within the rapidly evolving and dynamic cultural network, which came to "resemble a spider web" with San Francisco at its hub.[28] Opera troupes were the carriers of cultural expression, connecting Chinese immigrants in dispersed locations of rural California to San Francisco through cultural expression.

At Maguire's Opera House

As a fast-growing cosmopolitan city, San Francisco in 1860 offered its residents a rich year of opera, such that it was termed a "year of wonders" in the annals of opera.[29] It also offered presentations of Chinese opera, which would find a skillful promoter in the city's most prominent theater proprietor, Thomas Maguire.

In March 1860, a Chinese troupe arrived to perform at the Union Theater on Commercial Street. Though the venue was no longer in its prime, the new arrival drew the attention of newspapers throughout the state. A paper praised that the troupe superseded any prior Chinese troupes in number, talent, costumes, and "silk stage decoration," with "single dresses being valued at $2,000 each."[30] According to the *Daily Evening Bulletin*, the troupe had a seven-member orchestra and gave nightly performances. Describing the performance of a historical play, the reporter wrote:

> The mandarins, governors and emperors were dressed in magnificent robes of silk embroidered with dragons, birds and snakes. . . . There is a tremendous flow of history during this scene. Sometimes a whirl means a generation, sometimes a somerset [*sic*] means a century. To represent the unmitigated martial glory of a dynasty, the warriors go tumbling and somerseting across the stage, performing gymnastics that the Turners themselves would be proud of. To intimate a dynasty famous for its orators, a warrior, dressed gorgeously, with feathers in his hair nearly of his own length, struts up and down for ten minutes, saying not a word but gesticulating powerfully, leaping aloft, smiting, striking and spreading the eagle—keeping time in all his gestures to deafening gong beats.[31]

A correspondent for the *New York Times* wrote a lengthy article after spending two evenings at the theater.[32] The writer, signing himself as "Glaucus," provided many details, particularly about the accompanying instruments, which included three stringed instruments, one wind instrument, several different gongs and a drum, as summarized in Table 3.1. In this table, I provide the instruments' names in modern Chinese, though not all are translatable. This 1860 report is the earliest depiction of instruments played in Cantonese opera in North American theaters.

In addition, the article describes a warrior "in gorgeous silk embroideries, with spread fans stuck in his hair, and feathers of his own length curving . . . from his head." The troupe had a well-stocked wardrobe chest.

A strict gender separation was also noted: "The first three seats of the dress-circle are sacredly surrendered to the women. The men behind, though crowded, leave one vacant seat between them and the females. Throughout the evening the sexes never interchange a word, scarcely a look. The women smoke long, elaborate pipes, or else cigarettes." A Chinese theater was listed in the San Francisco City Directory for the second time.[33]

The favorable reviews of Chinese theater were further enhanced by an extravagant community event. A wealthy merchant, Ah Ching, added Chinese opera to a lavish feast in May, with the help of the prominent Chinese interpreter, Charles Carvalho. The list of public figures and dignitaries included

TABLE 3.1 Instruments of the Orchestra

Instrument names in report	Number of musicians (7)	Summary of description	Instrument names (today)
ge-hee	2	two-stringed fiddle with a crescent bow	erxian 二弦
saw-heen	1	three-stringed banjo, played with the thumb and fingers of the right hand	sanxian 三弦
see-oo	1	hollow reed, with the mouthpiece to the left of the center—a rude, disreputable fife	dizi 笛子
law	1	gong suspended from the ceiling by a cord	gong 大鑼
koo-hoo	1	Stout oaken tub, top covered by a gong	
soo-law	1	small disc of bell metal, struck with a wooden hammer	small gong 小鑼
		two immense cymbals shaped like gongs	cymbal 鐃鈸
		globe of hardwood set on a frame, beaten with hammer	shagu 沙鼓

Source: According to a Report in *New York Times*, March 28, 1860.

two US circuit court judges, a *Herald* editor, and several leading businessmen and bankers, as well as leaders of the Society of California Pioneers, such as Selim Edwin Woodworth. An exquisite Chinese banquet was followed by a performance at the Chinese theater on Sacramento Street. Noted the *Herald*, "The last performance of the season being then given by the company, who are going on a tour through the interior. Private boxes were provided from whence the stage and audience could be distinctly seen. The dress circle was occupied entirely by women and the pit by the men. It would be impossible to convey anything like an accurate idea of the performances, but several of the actors exhibited wonderful agility in their combat scenes."[34] Little is known about this Chinese theater on Sacramento Street, however. Nevertheless, the report confirmed the seasonal nature of the Chinese opera troupe's performances in the city.

The buzz from this performance led to an opportunity with Thomas Maguire, one of the city's most eminent theater proprietors. On May 10, Maguire's Opera House announced a "Chinese Exhibition," presenting three evenings of "genuine" Chinese opera performances. With 1700 seats (700 on the main floor, 400 on the first balcony and 600 on the second balcony), the Opera House would be the largest venue where Chinese opera had been performed in California until that time.

Reflecting on Tong Hook Tong troupe's visit in 1852 and the recent Chinese troupe at the Union Theater, an announcement in the *Daily Alta California* by the theater reassured its readers of a different sort of presentation at Maguire's: "We are requested by the management of the Opera House, particularly to state that none of the objectionable features [introduced by the 1852 troupe] will characterize the approaching entertainments at Maguire's Opera House."[35] It was billed as a respectable cultural event, rather than a racial entertainment, and private boxes went for as much as ten dollars. The article went into more detail:

> The plays, of which three of the most interesting have been selected, are from the pens of eminent Chinese philosophers, inculcating high moral precepts, and are such as the most fastidious lady may witness with perfect safety. Ah Ching, the well-known and respectable Chinese merchant, has been engaged by Mr. Maguire to superintend the preparations of the three plays: but independent of that, Mr. Maguire would scarcely jeopardize the reputation of his Opera House by permitting any breach of propriety in this respect. These entertainments are prepared with special reference to the ladies and children. They will be innocent, amusing and instructive. All should have it to say, that they have seen the famous Chinese theatre.[36]

Maguire held sway in San Francisco as an arbiter of taste. His opera house, first opened in 1856, was the first San Francisco theater built for grand opera, with its big stage and large pit. It brought "many of the greatest actors" to San Francisco, according to a later article in the *San Francisco Call*.[37] Maguire's empire extended to the Central Valley and included the Marysville Theater, discussed in chapter 2.

Together with numerous previews, a weeklong advertisement preceded the show, giving details about the attractions and the twenty-nine Chinese performers. Figure 3.2 reproduces the advertisement of May 12 in the *Daily Alta California.*

Copies of the scripts in English translation at the performance were promised. The *Daily Alta California*, after introducing the plot of the evening's historical opera, *The Rebellion of Loo Fei, or the Chinese Joan of Arc*, wrote, "The dresses and general paraphernalia will be of the most gorgeous description. The entrance of the Opera House is to be hung with colored Chinese lanterns. We can promise our readers a rich evening's entertainment, the novelty of which must insure a large and fashionable house."[38] Major San Francisco newspapers reported on the opening night. The *Daily Evening Bulletin* excerpted the synopsis of the evening's performance, and verified its true historical origin. It noted the opera for the next day, *The Viceroy of Keang*, before another reassurance: "This is a rare chance presented to our citizens to see a Chinese play in all its glory, and where the management will take special care that everything objectionable to good manners is carefully removed."[39] The box office on the opening night was a complete success:

MAGUIRE'S OPERA HOUSE,

Washington street, above Montgomery.

PROPRIETOR......................................MR. T. MAGUIRE
Treasurer..Mr. C. V. HAND

UNEQUALLED AND NOVEL ATTRACTION

Arrival of the Chinese Dramatists

Gorgeous Mongolian Spectacle.

POSITIVELY FOR THREE NIGHTS ONLY

COMMENCING ON

THURSDAY EVENING,.........MAY 17th.

THE MANAGEMENT HAVE THE honor to announce that they have effected an engagement with the unrivalled Celestial Company lately arrived on the clipper ship Flying Mist, from Hongkong, en route for Paris, where they are engaged to appear before the Imperial Court of Louis Napoleon, and who have repeatedly performed before the Emperor of China and the grand dignitaries of Pekin

The magnificent stage of the Opera House will be brilliantly lighted, and hung with gorgeous tapestry of Chinese Silk, with

All the Varied Colors of the Rainbow.

A number of the dresses, brought from Pekin, are valued at UPWARD OF TWO THOUSAND DOLLARS A band of Chinese Musicians will be in attendance.

The performance will consist of Scenes, Combats, the most magnificent Processions, Battles, &c., and (in which the mystic creations of the Chinese Mythology and Superstitions will be illustrated,) Vaultings, Transformations, and all that is typical of the

Chinese Character and Magnificence of Costume.

The programme, which will be varied each night, will be particularly attractive to LADIES and CHILDREN and will be unequalled for splendor and rare beauty.

☞ There can positively be but three representations before the departure of the troupe for Paris via New York, on the 20th inst. And this will be the only opportunity ever offered outside of China for obtaining a perfect idea of Celestial theatricals.

PRICES OF ADMISSION.

Private Boxes...$10 00
Dress Circle and Orchestra........................ 1 00
Parquette... 50
Gallery.. 25

Box Office open from 10 A. M. to 4 P. M.
Doors open at 7 o'clock. Performance to commence at 8 o'clock.   my11-7

FIGURE 3.2 Advertisement for "Chinese Dramatists," Maguire's Opera House, *Daily Alta California*, May 12, 1860.

"The Chinese performance last night was witnessed by a crowded house," the *Daily Evening Bulletin* reported on May 16.[40]

The spectacle was highlighted in the advertisement of Maguire's Opera House: "The magnificent stage of the opera house will be brilliantly lighted, and hung with gorgeous tapestry of Chinese silk, with All the Varied Colors of the Rainbow. A number of the dresses, brought from Pekin, are valued at UPWARD OF TWO THOUSAND DOLLARS." All the announcements and reviews invariably called attention to the spectacle. The audiences might have been familiar with the opulence. Next to Maguire's Opera House was the famous store Chy Lung & Co., a top importer who was named as exemplar of success by Tong A-Chick in his famous 1852 letter. The bazaar's sizeable advertisement in the *Daily Alta California* listed an assortment of tapestries and apparel from China: "Canton Crape Embroidered; Silk Shawls; Satin Dress Pattern; Silk Bandas, Silk Sashes, etc."[41] Chy Lung was praised for "his commercial sagacity," and the business was considered "as great as that of any of our American or European merchants."[42]

"Next door to Maguire's Opera House" was noted on the bazaar's daily advertisements starting in June 1858.[43] Figure 3.3 reproduces an advertisement from May 1860. It was quite possible that Chy Lung helped produce the glamorous staging of Chinese opera at Maguire's. Figure 3.4 shows the storefront of Chy Lung & Co. in 1866.[44] The rich and continuous supply of goods from the transpacific China trade provided a support system for cultural

FIGURE 3.3 Advertisement for Chy Lung & Co., importers, *Daily Alta California*, May 11, 1860.

FIGURE 3.4 Chy Lung & Co. store, 1866. Stereograph by Thomas Houseworth & Co. Courtesy California History Room, California State Library, Sacramento.

productions. The storefront, with beautiful artifacts displayed, also reminded people of Chinese culture's splendor and glamour.

Being the first location outside Asia to feature its own Chinese theater, San Francisco took pride in this "authentic" identity, subsequently dispatching Chinese actors to other cities in the ensuing decades. Not only was Maguire's Opera House a mediating space between the Chinese quarter and the city's general audience but San Francisco became the conduit between China and the rest of California, and California the pathway from China to Europe. Maguire advertised the troupe's upcoming engagement in Paris, announcing that they were "to appear before the Imperial Court of Louie Napolean [*sic*], and who have repeatedly performed before The Emperor of China, and the Grand Dignitaries of Pekin!"[45] Chinese theater in San Francisco was pulled into cultural circulations (real or imagined) on a global scale.

Meanwhile, Chinese theater became a regular part of San Francisco's general entertainment scene; two days after the last presentation of Chinese opera, Maguire's Opera House featured its new Maguire-Lyster's Italian and English Opera Company, performing *Lucia di Lammermoor* by Gaetano Donizetti, sung in the original Italian.[46] They then presented the English opera *Maritana* by William Vincent Wallace. If, with Donizetti's opera produced by one of the most prominent impresarios of the time, the city could pride itself as being on a par with the East Coast, they certainly outshone the East Coast with the performance of genuine Chinese opera.

Figure 3.5 shows the opera house from later in the decade (1869), with its elegant exterior and oversized billboards promoting its program and groups.

FIGURE 3.5 Maguire's Opera House, 1869. Courtesy J. Paul Getty Museum, Los Angeles.

As the author of *Verdi at the Golden Gate* noted, "because in San Francisco no [immigrant] group by itself could support a resident company, the operas of all nationalities were forced to compete in the same few theaters for an audience."[47] The presentation of Chinese opera at Maguire's was all the more extraordinary, given the heated debate in the state legislature over a proposition for excluding Chinese from the mines, as well as issues of the "Chinese question" in general at the time.[48] San Francisco's taste for theatrical entertainment had increased. The Chinese opera troupe's style of theatrical glamour and spectacle was a point of attraction.

Furthermore, the vibrant transpacific circulation continued to facilitate the movement of people, economy, and culture from China. The discovery of gold in the Fraser River in British Columbia in 1856 encouraged many more Chinese to cross the Pacific. Chinese merchants and workers traveled from San Francisco north to British Columbia, expanding the network of Chinese culture and influence. In fact, some scholars posit that the hinterland of San Francisco expanded all through the Pacific Northwest corridor up to Victoria.[49] In June 1860, a newspaper in Marysville reported, "Since May eight vessels have arrived at San Francisco from China, with 3,143 Chinese immigrants on board."[50] Two months later, the paper again reported that the number of Chinese arrivals "for the past three months cannot fall short of seven or eight thousands. Nevertheless, the number who have left for Victoria and the British possessions in the north will probably equal those who have come."[51] The flow of Chinese migrants along the Pacific coast increased significantly. A paper reported that four thousand Chinese arrived in Victoria in 1860. Exports from San Francisco to Victoria were valued at $1,278,846 for the month of September 1860. Two Chinese theaters were built in Victoria during this time.[52]

Lyceum Theatre: The Chinese Theatrical Performers of the State of California

In 1860, Maguire's Opera House had one principal competitor in the city: the Lyceum Theatre, built in 1858 and seating nine hundred to one thousand. Their competition could be so severe that several times the latter offered the same plays as Maguire's on the same night.[53] The Lyceum did not let Maguire take the lead in its presentation of Chinese opera theater. Printed in a large boldface font, the words "The Chinese Theatrical Performers of the State of California" led the Lyceum Theater's advertisements in the *Daily Alta California* and the *Bulletin*.[54] It promised five days of performances (August 10–14), as opposed to Maguire's three days. The program was the famous Chinese story of Sam Kwok during the period of the tripartite division of China from 220 to 280 CE. This famous historic period inspired many operas featuring legendary figures, important battles, clever maneuvers, and so on.

The advertisement was larger and had more significant detail than that of Maguire's. Also notable was the Lyceum's language, underscoring its cosmopolitan self-image. At the end of the announcement, the *Bulletin* wrote, "Assuredly the stage is cosmopolitan in San Francisco. During the last few months, we have repeatedly had plays performed in English, French, Italian, German, Spanish and Chinese."[55] After all, in 1860, the foreign population constituted 39 percent of the state's total population.[56] The Lyceum's advertisement highlighted the repertoire, advertising the Chinese troupe in similar ways as advertisements for Italian operas or English plays. Building on the immense attention its rival received, the Lyceum's advertisement reassured readers, "They are far superior to the [Chinese] actors exhibited at Maguire's Opera House." It advertised a troupe of over fifty members, composed of five newly arrived actors along with the troupe then performing at the Union Theater (by which it meant the Chinese theater).[57]

The engagement at the Lyceum Theatre brought new attention to Chinese opera. The advertisement listed the names of the new actors: "King Ho, Wing Souey, Ah Lum Ah Foey and Ah Chow—Arrivals by the ship 'Moonlight,' considered the best actors in Canton, and who have come to these shores in pursuit of their profession."[58] It calls attention to the celebrated actor Ah Chow and introduces the female impersonator Wong Fong in much the same way that lead performers were typically highlighted in advertisements of European-language operas.[59]

The *Bulletin*'s reviews were lukewarm, whereas the critic of the *Herald* found value in the performance, comparing the troupe's performing style with that of a comic character from Shakespeare:

> All who have seen the Chinese dramatic troupe at the Lyceum unite in awarding them unconditional praise for their remarkable feats in vaulting, etc. Their dresses and stage furniture are really gorgeous and their acting is said by connoisseurs to be of a high order. Not being versed in the Chinese language we can give no very definite idea of the performance, which is carried on by a series of figurative representations very similar to those adopted by Bottom the Weaver, in "Midsummer Night's Dream." Viewed as a pantomime the entertainment will be found very amusing, and, in some respects, quite astonishing. No one will regret the time or money expended in seeing a performance or two of this company.[60]

The *Herald*'s general endorsement may have prompted more San Franciscans to check out the performance. The troupe began its run at the Lyceum on August 10 (a Friday) and was to run through August 14. On Sunday the theater cut ticket prices by half but extended the performances for two more days to August 16, which indicates its moderate success among general audiences.[61]

Overall, the well-curated presentation of Chinese opera troupes at Maguire's Opera House and the Lyceum Theatre within the short span of five

THE CHINESE

Theatrical Performers

OF THE STATE OF CALIFORNIA,

BEG RESPECTFULLY TO EXHIBIT before an American audience, the splendid and gorgeous history of

SAM KWOK.

They have added to their present Troupe,
KING HO,
WING SOUEY,
One of the Best Vaulters in the Province.

They are far superior to the actors exhibited at Maguire's Opera House some months ago.

They commence their engagement at the

LYCEUM THEATRE,

ON

FRIDAY EVENING,..........AUGUST 10th,

And will perform

FOR FIVE DAYS,

Ending August 14th, 1860.

The most Gorgeous Dresses, Richest and Choicest Garments, Fine Sceneries, excellent Chinese Music, Small Footed Women, and all the paraphernalia of

A REGULAR CHINESE TROUPE

As performed throughout the great cities of the Empire, will be exhibited before an American audience. The Vaulters display most extraordinary skill.

The history chosen by the performers, will be that of
SAM KWOK,
OR, THE HUNDRED YEARS WAR,
Wherein Heroes and Heroines, Warriors and Kings, Statesmen and Philosophers and all take part.
THE PLAY WILL LAST FIVE NIGHTS,
commencing on
FRIDAY EVENING.

But the chief attraction (exclusive of fine and gorgeous dresses,) will be

AH CHOW,
THE CELEBRATED VAULTER,
AND
WONG FONG,
AN ACTOR OF GREAT REPUTATION AND MERIT, who will appear in a female character representing the
HEROINE OF LOO NAN,
Victor in a hundred battles, and Pacificator of the Empire.

The patronage of the American and foreign residents is hereby respectfully solicited.

Dress circle..$1 00
Parquette.. 50
au9-6*

FIGURE 3.6 Advertisement for "Chinese Theatrical Performers," Lyceum Theatre, *Daily Alta California*, August 10, 1860.

months indicates that Chinese theater had become part of what the historian Katherine Preston calls "the constant changing potpourri of American popular musical theaters in the midcentury."[62] Chinese opera was incorporated into the large variety of theatricals that included drama, opera, burlesque, minstrelsy, melodrama, pantomime, and plays with songs, whose contents and formats were often flexible. Chinese opera began to infiltrate the city's theater scene. Not all left clear traces; the 1861 *City Directory of San Francisco* lists "Lee Tin Toy Co. (Chinese) theatre," west on Dupont Street between Sacramento and Clay Streets; little is known about this company, however.[63]

During the Civil War, an array of theatrical performances was held in San Francisco theaters.[64] Chinese theaters did not appear in the advertisement sections of San Francisco papers. However, their existence could be confirmed by references in the news, in both San Francisco and the interior of the state. For instance, a five-week performance run at the Folsom Theatre was given a close report.[65] In September 1864, the *Daily Alta California* reported that two actors, Liu Chiu and Chang Wang, Chinese theatrical performers on Commercial Street (the Union Theater), were heading to Paris.[66] In May 1865, the *Boston Investigator* reported that in San Francisco a sixty-member Chinese troupe was performing day and night "—the audience entering and departing at all hours, as best suits their convenient and taste for enjoyment," though in which theater is not clear.[67]

Theatrical activity grew livelier after the Civil War. In June 1865, the Globe Hotel on the corner of Dupont and Jackson was refitted for Chinese theater.[68] A report also noted that its manager had recently arrived from China, bringing a troupe of new performers, a new wardrobe, and new plays. No report of its opening or later activities can be found, but Chinese theater performances at the Globe Hotel were noted by General James F. Rusling. Touring the West in 1866–67, he wrote probably the last book about travel to the West by stagecoach, horseback, and steamer, *The Great West and Pacific Coast*. He was making this tour for the army, surveying various posts and depots in the West, with the aim of reevaluating federal expenditures. He devoted the last of his three chapters on San Francisco to the Chinese quarter, commenting quite favorably about the Chinese men whom he met at a grand banquet in honor of the sailing of *Colorado*, the first steamer of a new monthly line to Hong Kong. Attended by the city's dignitaries and Chinese leaders, the banquet room was decorated with flags of all nations, including the Stars and Stripes and the yellow dragon flag of China. Rusling's depiction of Chinese theater at the Globe Hotel is a rare account of this venue in the Chinese community at the time.

> We went first to the Chinese Theatre, an old hotel on the corner of Jackson and Dupont streets, that had recently been metamorphosed into an Oriental playhouse. We found two or three hundred Chinese there, of both sexes, but mainly males, listening to a play. . . . It was a history of the Flowery Kingdom,

by some Chinese Shakespeare—half-tragedy, half-comedy, like most human history—and altogether was a curious medley. The actors appeared to be both sexes, but we were told were only men and boys. Their dresses were usually very rich, the finest of embroidered silks, and their acting quite surprised us. Their pantomime was excellent, their humor irresistible, and their love-passages a good reproduction of the grand passion, that in all ages "make the world go around." . . . The general behavior of the audience was good; everybody, however, smoked—the majority cigars and cigarritos, a very few opium. Over the theater was a Chinese lottery-office, on entering which the proprietor tendered you wine and cigars, like a genuine Californian. He himself was whiffing away at a cigarrito, and was as polite and politic, as a noted New York ex-M.C., in the same lucrative business. Several Chinamen dropped in to buy tickets, while we were there; and the business seemed to be conducted on the same principle, or rather want of principle, as among Anglo-Saxons elsewhere.[69]

As Rusling depicts in his narrative, this venue was popular, offering a mix of Chinese theatrical performance, drinking, and gambling.[70] The Globe Hotel was a significant establishment, invested in the sale of liquor, cigarettes, and lotteries, as well as theatrical and musical entertainment.[71]

Union Chinese Theater: A "New Idea"

In 1867, a series of Chinese theater performances held from May to July at the International Exposition in Paris sparked more interest in the genre. In its special report in June on the Exhibition, *Frank Leslie's Illustrated Newspaper* provided an illustration and a description:

THE CHINESE THEATRE IN THE CHAMPS DE MARS

Among the attractions of the Paris Exhibition, one of the most curious is the Chinese theatre, of which was given an illustration, and where the natives of the "celestial kingdom" can be seen performing their wonderful acrobatic and juggling feats, with the surroundings that seem to transport the spectator to Pekin itself. Genuine Chinese plays are also here represented, but not as attractive as the gymnastic and other feats, the language being the great drawback.[72]

The *Boston Post* reported some details: "The greatest attraction of all—the one most exciting to the curiosity of the Parisians—was the Chinese Theatre, which was to give the exact imitation of the court representation of Pekin. Here were to have been the performances most in vogue in the great city, such as 'The Orphan of the House of Tihao,' 'The Vengeance of Pepaki.'"[73] Yet both the *New York Herald* and the *New York Times* raised doubts about the show's authenticity, noting that the Chinese theater at the exposition was "anything but Chinese," being staffed by French performers.[74] This was corroborated by many other contemporary papers. Although it provoked speculation about the possibility of opening a Chinese theater in London, that did not happen.[75]

Back in San Francisco, on September 21, 1867, the Union Theatre on Commercial Street announced the arrival of a Chinese theatrical troupe. Its advertisements were much simpler than those before the war, without details on either the troupe or the program, but the newspaper advertisement ran for a month (September 21 to October 20).[76] A variety theater, the Union was renamed "Bert's New Idea" in 1864 and periodically featuring minstrels, pantomime, and so on. It was then also known as the "New Idea" or "Old Union Theatre."

The Chinese Theatre at the New Idea benefited from the attention paid to Chinese theater at the Paris Exposition, as well as the large numbers of Chinese arriving in California to construct the transcontinental railroad. It was an immediate financial success. The theater quickly became the third-highest-earning venue of the city for September and October, trailing behind only the much larger two top theaters, Maguire's Opera House and the Metropolitan Theatre. For the next two months it was still ranked fourth, as shown in Table 2 and as published in the *Daily Dramatic Chronicle*.[77] With both the Globe Hotel and the New Idea Theatre as venues, Chinese theater was a significant form of entertainment in the city and highly profitable. However, despite the theater's success, the local papers were relatively quiet about it.

The *Chicago Tribune* gave a report of the vibrant scene: "I went around to the old Union Theatre, on Commercial street, which has recently been fitted up by the Chinese for a first-class temple of the Celestial drama. The house was crowded by Chinese, the men on one side, and the women on the other, and the company, which is a very large one and furnished with wardrobe the cost and magnificence of which would astonish an American manager, appeared to be doing well."[78] The writer also noted that the theater

FIGURE 3.7 Advertisement for "Chinese Theatrical Company," New Idea Theatre, *Daily Alta California*, September 23, 1867.

TABLE 3.2 Revenues (in Dollars) of Theaters of Popular Entertainment in San Francisco for the Last Quarter of 1867

Month	Maguire's Opera House	Metropolitan Theatre	Olympic	Bella Union	Chinese Theatre	Museum of Anatomy	American (occasional)	Temple of Music
Sept.	19,675	12,227	4,923	3,480	5,365	1,084	3,094	
Oct.	14,746	9,913		4,019	9,102	1,022	2,262	
Nov.	9,836	10,441		3,379	6,199	1,419	2,912	12,606
Dec.	8,275	21,643		3,079	4,026	893	2,635	6,470

Source: Compiled from "Theatrical Receipts in 1867," *San Francisco Chronicle*, January 25, 1868.

was superior to the Chinese theater ran concurrently at the Globe Hotel. This brief report was written as part of a larger article under the heading of "Celestial Entertainments," which also reported the crowded performance of the Japanese acrobatic troupe Hi-Yah-Tak-Kee. The thirty-one-member troupe included nine women and two boys and was the fourth Japanese troupe that recently performed in the city. The significant presence of transpacific theatrical troupes were gaining attention.

The *Daily Dramatic Chronicle* published a long article about the profusion of new places for entertainments in the city, showing that Chinese theater was incorporated into the city's entertainment scene through veteran theater managers' effort to expand their business. The New Idea Theater on Commercial Street was to be under the joint management of Sheridan Corbyn and Fred Bert.[79]

A further, notable indication of the success of Chinese theaters was the announcement in November of the construction of a two-story brick building for Chinese theater. The *Daily Evening Bulletin* reported that "The Chinese Theatrical Company of the city have just contracted with John Apel to build for them a new theatre on his lot on Jackson Street, between Kearny and Dupont. The building will be commenced immediately, and is to be a two-story brick one, costing about $40,000."[80] The *Examiner* also reported of the plan for the new theater and added, "There are now two Chinese theaters in the city, both of which, it is said, are doing a big business."[81] It was likely referring to the Globe Hotel and New Idea Theatre. The news theater was anticipated to be completed within ten weeks, and a new company of actors would be arriving imminently, with several celebrated stars.[82] The new theater would become the third venue in the city to host Chinese opera regularly. But it would also mark the beginning of new era in which Chinese opera troupes would have their own purpose-built theater. This was an important milestone, signaling the start of a new phase: commercial Chinese theater.

CHAPTER 4

Cultural Capital
Theaters on Jackson Street

The end of the gold rush era was followed by the quick growth of California through the construction of transportation systems and the quick development of agriculture and manufacturing. San Francisco would soon be immensely changed by the completion of the transcontinental railroad, as well as the signing of the Burlingame Treaty (see below) between China and the United States. In 1868, the Hing Chuen Yuen Theatre celebrated its opening as the first permanent home for Chinese opera, commencing a new era in the history of Chinese theater in North America. It was very different from the Chinese theaters built in mining towns, however. Rather than oil, it was equipped with gas lighting. Rather than a simple wood frame with a canvas top, it was made of brick, which accounted for only a quarter of newly erected buildings in San Francisco.[1] It was similar in size to the Lyceum Theatre, which previously had hosted Chinese opera.

The establishment of large commercial theaters began the third phase of the development of Chinese theater. Hing Chuen Yuen was the first of four Chinese theaters to be built in San Francisco before the end of the next decade—in all, six Chinese theaters were constructed in San Francisco between 1868 and 1925—even though a year after its opening, more than a dozen newspapers around the country erroneously reported that "San Francisco has ten Chinese theaters."[2] This exaggeration, however, reflected the noteworthiness of the theater's grand opening. In this chapter, we will consider the first two theaters, both built on Jackson Street. In addition, we will examine the two city ordinances that were introduced specifically to target Chinese theaters. These ordinances were part of the anti-Chinese measures that linked Chinese music with criminality and had a significant impact on the Chinese-American community.

A First-Class Theater: The Hing Chuen Yuen
on Jackson Street (North)

When Hing Chuen Yuen opened its doors, the transcontinental railroad was still a year and half from completion. The signing of the Burlingame Treaty, which promised the Chinese the right to immigrate to and travel within the United States, was still six months away.[3] But the significance of this newly built Chinese theater was already made clear by a reporter in the *Chicago Tribune*, whose words convey a sense of awe:

> The Chinese are now building a magnificent theatre on Jackson Street, between Kearney and Dupont, which is to eclipse anything ever attempted before by them on this Continent, and will compare not unfavorably with anything the Americans themselves have done in California. It is to be of brick, two stories in height, 70 feet front, and 160 in depth, and the bare building, exclusive of "scenery and stage effects," is to cost $40,000 in gold coin. A high-toned star company from the Central Flower Empire will arrive here by the next steamer from the Asiatic side, and will open the new histrionic temple on or about the Chinese New Year's, which falls this year early in February. The costumes and paraphernalia of one of these Oriental troupes are something marvelous in costliness and elaborate richness, and the new company expect to literally "astonish the natives."[4]

Three days prior to the opening, the *Daily Alta California* reported on a grand display of fireworks and ritual ceremonies of dedication, noting, "The new temple of the legitimate Celestial drama is to be known as the 'Hing Chuen Yuen,' and is intended to be a first class establishment throughout."[5]

On January 27, 1868, Hing Chuen Yuen (or Hing Ching Yuen; Hing Chung Yuen; Hing Chung Gue; 興全源 means "The Fountainhead of Prosperity") held its inaugural performance. According to news reports, the theater invited members of the press; the legal bench; and prominent members of the bar, the state legislature, and the city's board of supervisors to the opening banquet and performance, as well as various foreign consuls, merchants, and representatives of the army and navy. The grand banquet for a hundred guests, beginning at four o'clock, was said to match that of the famed farewell dinner in 1866 for Burlingame and Van Valkenburgh, the US ministers to China and Japan, respectively.[6] As at that dinner, the Chinese interpreter for the courts, Charles Carvalho, served as the master of ceremonies, offering the host's welcome and introducing the guests, many of whom gave speeches of appreciation on behalf of their groups. The inaugural performance began at seven; the theater, with a capacity of one thousand, was crowded to excess.[7]

Of the space, *Daily Alta California's* report drew attention to the architecture and opulence of the embroidery and silk used for the stage and the costumes:

> The theatre proper is in the rear, and quite disconnected from the front building. It is arranged in every particular like an American temple of the drama, having a pit or parquette, dress circle and galleries, and is lighted with gas throughout. The orchestra occupy an alcove in the rear of the stage . . . and the actors make their entrances and exits by side doors or openings, hung with the costliest bullion-embroidered silk curtains. . . . [T]he costumes are elaborate and costly almost beyond description. The play last night was a historic drama, and at times the whole stage was crowded with performers.[8]

It was clear to San Franciscans that Hing Chuen Yuen was planned as a theater on a par with other prominent venues. The vibrant performance of the full-fledged troupe, the magnificence of the costumes, and the other extravagances on the theater's stage indicated its prestige. This foretold a promising future for a premier theater.

Later, a correspondent for the *New York World* offered vivid depictions of both the orchestra and the stage movements, expressing a sense of bewilderment:

> The instruments, consisting of the instruments resembling the oboe in construction and the bagpipes in tone, several two-stringed violins, a kettle drum, an enormous pair of cymbals, a gong, a bell, a stone globe to pound with, sticks and a drum sounding much like our side drums. . . . Soldiers summoned and instructed to go in for a free fight. . . . Grand rumpus and powwow. Plenty of drums. Exit acrobatic diversion, sword combat. Combat with spears and swords; general free fight and whirligig arrangement, participated in by four Chinamen, who wear very long feathers in their caps. Finally loving couple are united, all the enemies of the Emperor are slain.[9]

An English visitor from Manchester gave additional context, greatly impressed by both the theater and the prosperous merchants of the thriving Chinese community: "The price for the whole theatre, exclusive of two boxes tenanted by Chinese aristocrats, was the same—half a dollar. The Chinese were making great progress here. They have built the Central Pacific Railway, but they do more than supply hands for hard work. There are wealthy mercantile houses owned and carried on by Chinese merchants."[10] The writer also noted the grand spectacle and the number of performances: "The properties and dresses were magnificent; the dresses, I am told, cost $45,000 in China. . . . There are now two Chinese theatres going in San Francisco, at which performances are given every afternoon and evening."[11]

The theater was crowded every night: in fact, the theater's success was so threatening to some community members that they wrote to the *Daily Alta California*, warning of the corrupting effect it would have on Chinese workers.[12] Still, English-language papers suspected the receipts might not be enough to cover the cost of the building, the fee for the costumes, "mostly of thick silk embroidered in gold and silver," the expenses of bringing in the troupe, and so on. A reporter observed that the wealthy owners maintained the new theater to entertain their large workforce.[13] Indeed, the proprietors' ambition was considerable; they continued to add more performers and recruited directly from China. In July 1869 the *San Francisco Morning Call* reported the theater manager's return from China with a new troupe of ninety and noted, "The fame of the company has gradually extended beyond Chinese circles, and every evening now sees quite a number of Americans in the audience."[14]

The inauguration of the transcontinental railroad in 1869 casted a fresh light on Hing Chuen Yuen. Following the summit, the famous New York publisher Frank Leslie dispatched his staff painter Joseph Becker to make drawings for a series entitled "Across the Continent."[15] While the first two of the series, "Passing Through the Valley of Great Salt Lake," and "The Snow Sheds on the Central Pacific Railroad in the Sierra Nevada," were about the railroad and natural scenery, the third, "The Coming Man," focused exclusively on the Chinese on the Pacific coast, including their manners, business and domestic lives, habits, religious rites, and amusements. In its overview, the paper's editorial noted, "Apparently affluent, they sustained three theatres, with large companies of actors; several temples," and powerful communal societies that led the companies who supplied Chinese workers for railroad construction. The paper assured its readers, "It will not be denied that [Becker] has succeeded, when the public become acquainted with the fine series of engravings."

Featured in a double-page supplement, the elaborate wood-engraving illustration entitled "The Great Chinese Theatre" was published in *Frank Leslie's Illustrated Newspaper* on May 7, 1870.[16] The picture is reproduced in figure 4.1 from one version that was colored (perhaps contemporary). The caption, "'The Coming Man' scene in the principal Chinese theatre, San Francisco, California, during the performance of a great historical play," accompanies the image. At 15½ by 20½ inches, the large, double-page spread gives us a detailed portrayal of the stage, performers, and diverse audience members. Thomas W. Knox, a travel writer who had previously toured China, supplied an accompanying article. In a single sentence, he captured the importance of the theater to the community: "Occidentals generally seek the theatre on their first night on shore, and the same is the case with Orientals."

FIGURE 4.1 Joseph Becker. "The Coming Man": scene in the Principal Chinese Theatre, San Francisco, California, during the performance of a great historical play." Engraved by Davis & Spee. *Frank Leslie's Illustrated Newspaper,* May 7, 1870. Private collection.

Echoing the illustration, Knox provided interesting details about the audience at the Hing Chung Yuen theater. The audience, which was widely varied, was mixed or segregated in different sections of the theater. The seating was clearly hierarchical:

> Up in the gallery the boys are turbulent, and require an occasional admonition from a policeman; in the boxes, on the right, and the second tier, on the left, there is better order, especially in the boxes, which are frequently occupied by Americans, drawn there by curiosity. The dress-circle contains a miscellaneous assemblage, with men and women mingled in most admirable confusion, and including here and there an American face. The women are painted quite gaudily, and their characters would not, in all cases, bear a strict examination. They talk and laugh very gayly, and pay little attention to the performance on the stage. Some wear their hair dressed with flowers, while others have it tied up with very little ornament; but in most instances it is plentifully oiled or made stiff with glue. Peddlers of fruit, bouquets, melon-seeds and sweetmeats, move among the spectators, and urge the purchase of their wares, which they carry in boxes, divided into compartments, as shown in the picture. Children in arms are by no means unknown, and sometimes add to the confusion by a little natural music of their own. Down before the stage the audience is more attentive than elsewhere, and when a farce is on the boards there is a great deal of laughter.[17]

With both their appearance and their demeaner, the colorful female audience drew Knox's attention. The women's stiff coiffures signaled their status and affluence, as we will discuss below.

In terms of the performance, Becker's drawing depicts ten supporting actors surrounding five main characters on stage. At the center is a seated general with pheasant feathers attached to his headdress; to his left a warrior raising a sword, to his right an older statesman gesturing. Two characters kneel in front, one of whom wears an official's hat. In the back is a group of musicians with various instruments. A large gong is hung on the wall, and a placard with Chinese characters is at the front of the stage. The events unfolding onstage resemble a Cantonese opera performance, albeit lacking liveliness in their portrayal. The actors' expressions are obscured in the panel-like presentation.

But the drawing brings the theater audience vividly to life, echoing Knox's depiction of the mixture of race, age, gender, and class. The box on the right is filled with Western spectators, and the dress circle is an assemblage of well-dressed men and women, as well as some youths. Several youngsters on the left are paying close attention to a tray of snacks held by a hatless vendor, and the stylish women with fans in the foreground are chatting and socializing. Whether these women were from wealthy merchant families or from brothels, their poise and colorful demeanor reflected the success and power of the community. They were significant patrons of Chinese theaters.

The hairstyles and attire of the women in the foreground provide clues and insights into the audience's fashion and cultural tastes, highlighting the connection between the prosperity of Chinese theater and its community. A few photo portraits of Chinese during the period could provide the context. A studio portrait taken around 1870 by the San Francisco photographer Carleton Watkins (1829–1916) shows a well-to-do Chinese woman, conveying a popular taste (see fig. 4.2). Her hairstyle is quite similar to that of one of the audience members with her back to the viewer in Becker's illustration. The elaborate embroidery on her clothing and her jewelry is similar to those of several women in the illustration. Although this portrait was no less carefully selected and composed than Becker's illustration, it also provides a reference point for the fashions of wealthy female theatergoers.[18] A portrait taken by the famous Bradley & Rulofson photo studio shows another Chinese woman in similar attire with elaborate embroidery and a stiff coiffure (see fig. 4.3). A portrait of a woman by Lai Yong, one of the earliest Chinese photographers in San Francisco, showcases the subject's perfect hair and attire, which speak volumes about her class and social privilege (see fig. 4.4).[19] Gordon H. Chang also underscores characteristics of this photo: the woman is "elegantly attired and coiffed and also comfortable. . . . She is composed and worldly."[20] Indeed, particularly interesting is the confident and relaxed smile captured in this photo, the kind of musing and contentment that resonated well with theatergoers. Another photo by Lai Yong captured a similarly confident pose, this one of a man with a dark silk tunic and the "dark trimmed black hat popular with city Chinese men at the time," according to Chang. One can easily imagine these Chinese women and men in the audience at Hing Chung

FIGURE 4.2 Carleton Watkins. "Chinese Lady." c. 1870. Print by I. W. Taber. Courtesy J. Paul Getty Museum, Los Angeles.

FIGURE 4.3 Bradley & Rulofson, San Francisco. "Chinese Woman." Carl Mautz Collection of Cartes-de-Visite Photographs Created by California Photographers. Yale Collection of Western Americana, Beinecke Rare Book and Manuscript Library, Yale University.

FIGURE 4.4 (left) "Chinese Woman" and FIGURE 4.5 (right) "Chinese Man." Lai Yong Photo Studio. Carl Mautz Collection of Cartes-de-Visite Photographs Created by California Photographers. Yale Collection of Western Americana, Beinecke Rare Book and Manuscript Library, Yale University.

Yuen.[21] A number of similar studio pictures of dignified and opulently dressed Chinese from around this time (by photographers such as William Shew, J. J. Reilly, and Carleton Watkins) depicted women and men of similar status in society.[22] The typically lavish surroundings—plush carpets, silk drapes, and expensive furniture—in these photos suggest an affluent American domestic interior, which enacted a sense of their prominent positions in the Chinese community.

Knox's article offers his readers a glimpse of the performance and stage, noting, among other things, the elaborate presentation of an emperor and his oratorical style. It also provides some details about the use of placards onstage.

> The historical pieces and tragedies are rather heavy, and contain a great many fine costumes. A stage emperor is an elaborate affair, and must be handled very carefully to guard against injury to his decorations. The declamation is quite oratorical in style, and some of the actors have excellent voices. They indulge only slightly in gestures, and their style would be accounted "slow" by the regular patrons of the Old Bowery. . . . The stage projects into the audience more than is the case in an American theatre. . . . The assistants stand around the ends and rear of the stage, and peep out from behind the screens and curtains. They are supposed to be invisible, and it would not be in accordance with etiquette to pretend to see them. Much of the scenery is imaginary, and I was amused, on my first visit, to see a man going through an imperceptible window. He stood near one side of the stage, and went through the motions of raising a sash, stepping inside, and closing the aperture after him. The audience considered it all right, and did not think to laugh at the occurrence. . . . The long rods depending from the wall, with horizontal arms, are for the support of screens, and also of bills that explain portions of the play.[23]

This article shaped the general public's understanding of Chinese theater by emphasizing the pantomime, the lack of scenery, and the property men walking around the stage. The notion of pantomime, which usually had comical overtones in Western culture, unfortunately compromised Westerners' understanding of the Chinese opera tradition. Its artistry and theatricality are vital to the essence of Chinese theater (see Introduction), yet they were frequently derided in news reports. These facets of the performance would be repeatedly mentioned in the American press in the coming decades.

Illustrated magazines such as *Frank Leslie's* and *Harper's* had a significant role in forming people's opinions about race through their pictorial portrayal. The "Coming Man" series ran from May 7 to July 30, 1870, and included more than a dozen illustrations based on Becker's drawings of various subjects and scenes. At this time, the circulation of *Frank Leslie's Illustrated Newspaper* was seventy thousand per issue, but a special edition could reach hundreds of thousands. Reproductions of the double-page illustrations as prints, many of which were hand colored, were popular.[24] As a reporter for the *Chronicle* put it sharply three days later, Hing Chuen Yuen was an "institution made famous by a wood cut in Frank Leslie's newspaper."[25] Conversely, this lavish illustration no doubt advanced the narrative in favor of the Chinese community and laborers, a solution sought by many to address the shortage of labor in the southern states during the Reconstruction Era.

Two weeks later, the famous impresario Phineas T. Barnum came to the Hing Chuen Yuen theater on his first visit to California, looking for acts to bring back east. The *Chronicle* reporter who accompanied him wrote, "The scene was an odd one for even the venerable showman. . . . [H]e exclaimed, 'Well, this beats all; I've never seen anything like *this* before.' . . . When tumbling commenced in the dreadful battle scene where scores of soldiers are slaughtered over and over again, and bravery consists in terrible falls and remarkable hand springs, he was quite carried away by the, to him, perfectly novel affair."[26] At the end, the impresario concluded that Chinese theater would not draw an audience in New York. Nevertheless, this renowned showman's visit was indicative of the high level of interest in Chinese theater at the time. The following month, the *Chronicle* covered the visit of the Boston Board of Trade to the theater, highlighting the widespread attention drawn by the theater.[27]

Chinese theaters were doing very good business. San Francisco's Chinese population in 1870 numbered 11,724, among them many merchants, store managers and importers. They collectively supported first-class Chinese theatrical performances. The 1870 US census recorded one Ah Sam as a theater proprietor whose personal assets were valued at fifty thousand dollars.[28] Joseph Becker left us several more drawings that attested to this vibrant community of affluent merchants, professionals, and artisans. One was of the theater. The Jackson Street front of the Hing Chuen Yuen theater was in fact occupied by shops; the audience entered the theater from an alley, accessible from Jackson Street. A sketch by Becker (fig. 4.6) depicts the entry to the theater, where a group of men and a boy are reading playbills and announcements posted in the alleyway. A woodcut engraving of it appeared in the May 7, 1870 issue of *Frank Leslie's Illustrated Newspaper*, with racialized facial features. In addition to verifying the alleyway entrance, the sketch reveals that the level of literacy in the Chinese community was at least at an average reading level. Several other Becker illustrations show Chinese people doing accounting and reading, as well as various, highly skilled kinds of work. All these illustrations contradicted the usual image of the Chinese as coolies and illiterate laborers.

Inevitably, a successful theater will face challenges from competition, and there were many competitors. In September 1868, five months after

FIGURE 4.6 Joseph Becker. "Entrance to Chinese Theatre, San Francisco."
Courtesy The Becker Collection, Boston College. The Chinese characters are
illegible.

Hing Chuen Yuen's opening, the New Idea Theatre hired the Yun Sing Ping
Company of eighty members from China.[29] The theater placed weeklong
advertisements in the paper. The same "Amusement" section also listed
La fille du regiment (Gaetano Donizetti) at Maguire's Opera House, *Robert
le diable* (Giacomo Meyerbeer) at the Metropolitan Theatre, and *La belle
Hélène* (Jacques Offenbach) at the Alhambra Theatre.[30] The New Idea Theatre clearly was poised to be part of the cosmopolitan entertainment scene.
Curiously, the Chinese-run Hing Chuen Yuen had not had advertisements
in the amusements section of newspapers, despite its newsworthy grand
opening in January and its immense success. However, this would change
very soon.

In 1869 the situation got quite complicated, with three Chinese theaters.
In January, a newspaper reported on a Chinese theater on Dupont Street,
likely the Globe Hotel (see chap. 3), which had been thriving for eight years.
Its recent engagement with the Sing Song Fung troupe, whose performances
ran till 3:00 a.m, was so successful that it caused a noise complaint to the city.[31]
In July 1869, however, Hing Chuen Yuen achieved even greater success with
the presentation of the Lung Quong Toy Dramatic Company, newly recruited
from China. The company's success prompted a three-day engagement at the

Metropolitan Theatre in September.[32] The event featured one hundred performers in total, which attracted distinguished guests such as Vice President Schuyler Colfax and General George H. Thomas.[33] The competition became intense when more troupes came, and friction between the two theaters was reported. In 1870 alone, the newspapers carried many advertisements of Chinese theaters on Dupont or Commercial Streets. In February 1870, the Quon Soon Tong company advertised its Chinese theater, claiming ownership of the entire Son Son Fong Troupe on Dupont Street.[34] Soon, the rivalry between the Globe Hotel's theater on Dupont and the more successful Hing Chuen Yuen grew so fierce that a large riot erupted between supporters of the rival theaters.[35] According to the newspapers, the rivalry was also deemed to be between different huiguan: Sze Yap (Siyi) was connected with the Globe Hotel on Dupont Street, whereas Sam Yap (Sanyi) was connected with Hing Chuen Yuen on Jackson Street. During this rivalry, the Dupont Street theater's operation was deeply hampered by the noise complaints (discussed below) as well. In May, the Ak Ling Tong Company advertised its Chinese theater, claiming it had purchased Quon Soon Tong.[36] In July, another advertisement announced the arrival of Ah Look at the Chinese theater on Commercial Street.[37] The details of these quick changes of ownership among theaters and troupes remain murky. That these advertisements of Chinese theaters all appeared in the Amusements section of the newspaper, next to Italian and French operas, English melodrama, circuses, and other attractions indicated the large demographic group these Chinese theaters aimed to attract.

Furthermore, in July 1871 an advertisement of a new Chinese theater on Washington Alley between Jackson and Washington Streets appeared in the *Daily Evening Bulletin*, announcing its opening on August 1. For four days the ad was printed next to the Metropolitan Theatre's ad for *Il trovatore*. Little is known about this Chinese theater, which was "remodeled in the first-class manner," except that the undersigned was Joseph Foy, Yee Yuen & Co. A map created in 1873 confirms the existence of this new theater, as well as showing the Globe Hotel and Hing Chuen Yuen.[38] Figure 4.7 is based on the 1873 map showing the locations of the these theaters. The New Idea Theatre is included, although by 1873 it had burned down. This map offers a sense of the spatial relationship among these theaters, positioned at the heart of the Chinese community. The flourishing of Chinese theaters underscored the allure of this theatrical entertainment, the substantial demand, and the affluence prevalent within the community.

Owing to the signing in 1868 of the Burlingame Treaty, which ensured reciprocal free travel of people in the United States and China, and the promising future brought by the completion of the transcontinental railroad in 1869, San Francisco's Chinese community grew exponentially in 1870.

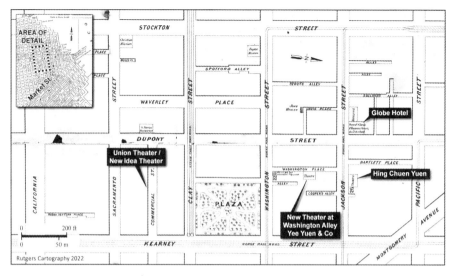

FIGURE 4.7 Locations of the Global Hotel, the New Idea Theatre, an unnamed new theater, and the Hing Chuen Yuen theater. Diagram based on an 1873 map of San Francisco's Chinatown. Michael Siegel, Rutgers Cartography, 2022.

Cantonese opera performance became ever more popular; at least five to six troupe names appeared in the newspapers in the span of three years (see table 4.1; the dates given refer to news reports). The mergers, splits, changes of ownership, renamings, and other transactions among troupes and theaters created a complicated and dynamic situation for Chinese theaters. It is undoubtedly true that the six troupes whose names are recorded in the newspapers (noted in table 4.1) were only a fraction of the Cantonese opera troupes that existed during this time. Many troupes came and went, creating a constantly evolving landscape on the theater scene.

San Francisco's Chinese theaters were the focus of attention not only for city residents but also for visitors and reporters arriving by train. News articles about the city's Chinese theaters turned up everywhere. In 1871, a correspondent for the London paper the *Era* gave an extensive report, noting the gambling saloons near the theaters and the performers' annual salaries of between four hundred and twelve hundred dollars.[39] Another London periodical cited a German-language newspaper in San Francisco, the *Abend Post*, which speculated that due to the low admission prices and the fact that recent Chinese immigrants were admitted free of charge, even a full house might not generate substantial profits.[40] On the other hand, a writer for the *Israelite*, a Jewish newspaper in Cincinnati, observed the theater's success, with "quite a number of Americans present, all of whom seemed greatly to enjoy the performance."[41]

TABLE 4.1 List of Chinese Opera Troupes and Theaters between 1868 and 1871 according to newspaper reports

City	Theater/street	Troupe/company	Troupe size	Date	Comments
Marysville	Marysville Theatre	San Nang Foo	80 men, 12 women	9/16/1868	
San Francisco	New Idea Theatre / Commercial Street Chinese Theatre	Yun Sing Ping	80	9/23/1868	
Sacramento	Sacramento Theatre	n/a	137	9/30/1868	From Marysville
San Francisco	Globe Hotel / Dupont	Sing Song Fung		1/12/1869	
Sacramento	Sacramento Theatre	n/a	100	1/13/1869	From SF
San Francisco	Hing Chuen Yuen / Jackson Street	Lung Quong Toy	90	7/23/1869	
San Francisco	Metropolitan Theatre	Lung Quong Toy	98	9/23/1869	For 2 days
Marysville	Marysville Theatre	San San Fong		10/15/1869	
San Francisco	Globe Hotel / Dupont	Son Son Fong		Pre-1870	
San Francisco	Globe Hotel / Dupont	Son Son Fong		2/8/1870	Run by Quon Soon Tong company
San Francisco	New Idea Theatre / Commercial Street Chinese Theatre	Ak Ling Tong		5/28/1870	Purchased Quon Soon Tong company
San Francisco	Theater on Washington Alley, between Jackson and Washington Streets	n/a		8/1/1871	Managed by Joseph Foy, Yee Yuen & Co.

The success and attention garnered by Hing Chuen Yuen caught the theater world's notice. In 1873, the *New York Clipper* declared that the Chinese theaters were outperforming their American counterparts in San Francisco. The latter often experienced cycles of closures and openings, with the exception of the California Theatre.[42] Clearly attracted by the potential of Hing Chuen Yuen's popularity, Maguire's Opera House presented another lavish performance of Chinese theater for its audiences in 1873, thirteen years after the first Chinese opera troupe had appeared on its stage (fig. 4.8). This time it showcased the "Royal Chinese Theatrical Company," a sixty-member troupe that claimed to hail from the imperial theater in Beijing. The advertisement highlighted its distinctive feature: "The performance differs entirely from any heretofore given in this country, introducing drama, battle scenes, court receptions and the most wonderful Acrobatic and Gymnastic feats."[43]

The *Daily Evening Bulletin* gave a substantial preview, noting an imperial wedding scene and the appearance of actresses: "There are three blooming Celestial ladies in the troupe, including two actresses of the modern school, who are under the direct control of the home Government, and a married lady with feet no larger than those of an infant."[44] The presence of actresses in Cantonese opera was unusual, considering the traditional casting of all roles to male actors, with women prohibited from performing on stage. Yet the cultural dynamics and audience preferences of California, coupled with

FIGURE 4.8 Advertisement for "Royal Chinese Theatrical Company," Maguire's Opera House, *Daily Alta California*, February 25, 1873.

the geographical distance from southern China, might have relaxed restrictions and given rise to diverse practices. In any case, after the successful engagement of the "Royal Chinese Theatrical Company" at Maguire's Opera House, troupes considered expanding business opportunities elsewhere in the United States. An advertisement seeking engagements for the troupe, managed by F. C. Pratt, appeared in the *New York Clipper* in April of that year, seeking engagements on the East Coast.[45] However, nothing came of this endeavor—not yet.

The 1870 US census provides a few clues about the Chinese theater business. In San Francisco, it recorded eighty-eight Chinese actors, six Chinese actresses, twenty-one Chinese musicians, and two theater manager/proprietors.[46] Members of the theatrical company typically lived together in accommodations arranged by the theater and formed a self-contained group. The census recorded two theater names (unrelated to those found in table 1), Sun Heen Lok Theater Company and Yang Fung Theater, their locations unknown due to the lack of street addresses recorded in the US census prior to 1880.[47] The manger of the Sun Heen Lok Theater was Sun Heen, with personal wealth valued at $10,000 (the equivalent of $239,828 in 2024). Forty-five people were listed for his theater, including the manager, twenty-four actors, ten musicians, five laborers, three carpenters, and two cooks. The chief actor was Ah Leung, forty years old, while the majority of the actors were under thirty. A self-contained, moderate-size operation, Sun Heen Lok could have been an older theater, either the New Idea on Commercial Street or the Chinese theater on Dupont Street. In contrast, Yang Fung Theater, whose proprietor, Ah Sam, had personal wealth value at $50,000 (the equivalent of $1,199,141 in 2024), listed sixty-one actors, six actresses, and four tailors. Nearly a full-size troupe by southern China standards, this could be the newer Hing Chuen Yuen theater. The census also recorded seven musicians residing at another location, and a "concert room" with four musicians and a keeper.[48] It is possible these musicians were associated with one of the two troupes. Despite the incomplete and fragmented nature of the information, the census records provide a glimpse into the vibrant musical life of the Chinese community in the city, revealing that at least 128 individuals were on record as working in the music and opera theater profession.

Noise Ordinances and Nuisance Complaints

During this period, the primary legal challenges faced by Chinese theaters in California revolved around recurrent noise complaints. As early as 1858, three Chinese musicians were arrested in San Francisco for making a disturbance while performing during New Year celebrations.[49] Such complaints multiplied as Chinese theaters gained more prominence. During the early years of Chinese theaters (1869–74), the city tackled noise complaints through two distinctive types of ordinance: a more general one that restricted the operating hours of theaters and another more explicit, direct one that prohibited music, particularly the use of gongs, which were employed only in Chinese music and theaters.

In January 1869, a representative of the Fourth Ward in the city filed a formal complaint about the noise created by the Dupont Street Chinese theater.[50] In response, the city Board of Supervisors required Chinese theaters to close by midnight; two weeks later the proprietors and owners of the Chinese theater on Dupont Street protested "against the late action of the Board requesting them to close up at 12 o'clock, unless the same rule should be applied to all other similar institutions in the city."[51] Although the curfew ordinance went into effect for all theaters, it was only enforced on Chinese theaters, with the Dupont Street theater specially targeted.

To protest this unfair treatment and to stop the proposed resolution from taking full effect, the Chinese managers of the theater and the white owners of the property filed formal petitions.[52]

> Your petitioners respectfully represent that they are the proprietors of the Chinese Theatre on Dupont Street; that they are licensed and have been for over eight years last passed; that during that time they have paid into the city and county treasury over the sum of $6,500 for said licenses; that they have recently erected their theatre at great cost, and pay a ground rent of $425 per month, gold coin, under a lease of ten years; that there are rival theatres in this city and that if resolution No. 9,407 is carried into effect it will altogether ruin this company; that other theatres will be kept open after twelve o'clock and will get all the custom.
>
> Your petitioners further respectfully represent that they do not object to any order that is general and applicable to all theatres, or if the honorable Board shall so determine, be applicable to all Chinese theatres, but they do strenuously object to any rule, order or regulation applying solely to them, and thus destroying their business for the benefit of rival establishments.
>
> [signed by Ah Sing & Co., Sam Yit & Co., Soong Sing, Ah Deen, Ah Loy, Yee Woo Jim, Ah Kee, Low Shi.]

> Your petitioners respectfully represent that they are owners or agents of property, or residents of the neighborhood of the Chinese theatre on Dupont street; that the said theatre does not injure the property in the neighborhood, but, on the contrary, benefits the same; that since the theatre has been built the rental of adjoining property has increased in value, in some instances to a great percentage, and that closing the said theatre, or interfering with its management so as to destroy its popularity among the Chinese, would depress the value of the greater portion of the property in the immediate neighborhood.
>
> Your petitioners further represent that if resolution No. 9,407 is carried into effect it will greatly injure the said theatre as a place of popular resort

among the Chinese of this city, and consequently will injure property in the vicinity.

Your petitioners further respectfully represent that the said theatre is not an annoyance to the majority of the people residing in the immediate neighborhood, and that the said majority do not object to it at all.

[signed by J. M. Baker, C. Wolf, J. Levy, C. Vaillant, D. McKay, I. Cohen, etc.]

The defense of Chinese theater underscored how the proposed policy would inflict financial damage on the business, emphasizing that the theater had already paid license fees for the right to stage performances. Cognizant of the noise-related concerns, it deliberately avoided delving into that particular topic. When the city sent a committee to investigate the theaters in February, its members engaged in a heated debate about the distinction between noise and music.[53] In April, a new noise complaint was registered, prompting the submission of a proposed ordinance to the city's Board of Supervisors. At the final argument in June, the *Chronicle* reported that the representative of the Fourth Ward, a Dr. Dole said that "he hoped it would pass if it would only stop with suppression of the abominable Chinese theater in the Fourth Ward: it was an intolerable nuisance," and "he said, 'It is not only that, but I abominate the whole race.'"[54] The disdain for Chinese music was often inseparable from extreme hostility toward Chinese people.

Dole was not alone. The Board of Supervisors passed an ordinance a month later, this time banning the use of gongs altogether. The following reproduces the ordinance in full.

RELATING TO THEATERS AND PLACES OF PUBLIC AMUSEMENT

The People of the City and County of San Francisco do ordain as follows:

[Beating upon a Gong or Gongs, etc., to Disturb the Peace, Prohibited.]

Section 1. No person participating in any exhibition or performance, in or about any theatre or place of entertainment or amusement in the City and County of San Francisco shall, at any time during such exhibition or performance, disturb the peace or quiet of any neighborhood, by beating or playing upon a gong or gongs, or by making an unusual noise of any kind, nor shall any person aid or abet in making such disturbance.

[Penalty]

Sec. 2. Every person convicted of a violation of any provision of section one of this Order shall be fined in a sum not exceeding two hundred dollars, or by imprisonment not exceeding two months.[55]

The absence of any reference to Chinese music could not hide the fact that this order was directed specifically at Chinese theaters. The *Chronicle* reported promptly on July 31, "The first arrests under the new ordinance respecting the beating of gongs in places of amusement were made by officers Taggart

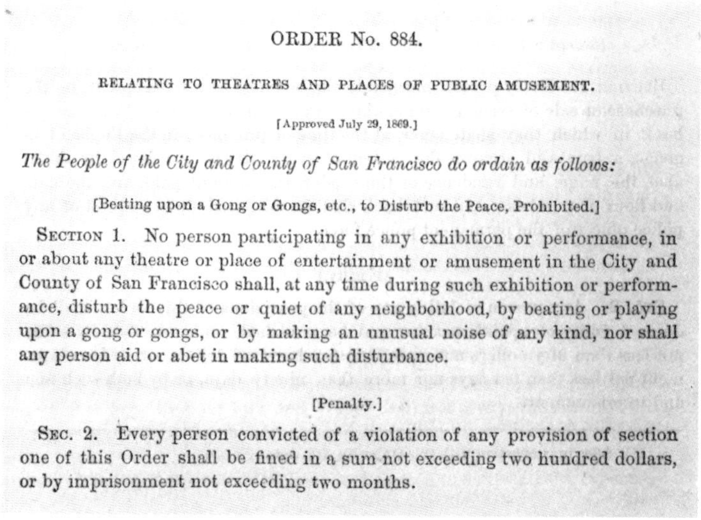

ORDER No. 884.

RELATING TO THEATRES AND PLACES OF PUBLIC AMUSEMENT.

[Approved July 29, 1869.]

The People of the City and County of San Francisco do ordain as follows:

[Beating upon a Gong or Gongs, etc., to Disturb the Peace, Prohibited.]

SECTION 1. No person participating in any exhibition or performance, in or about any theatre or place of entertainment or amusement in the City and County of San Francisco shall, at any time during such exhibition or performance, disturb the peace or quiet of any neighborhood, by beating or playing upon a gong or gongs, or by making an unusual noise of any kind, nor shall any person aid or abet in making such disturbance.

[Penalty.]

SEC. 2. Every person convicted of a violation of any provision of section one of this Order shall be fined in a sum not exceeding two hundred dollars, or by imprisonment not exceeding two months.

FIGURE 4.9 San Francisco City Ordinance Order No. 884, approved July 29, 1869. San Francisco Municipal Reports. San Francisco Board of Supervisors.

and Duffield, who arrested two Chinamen, Ah Look and Ah Keen, on this charge, for beating their gongs on Jackson street last evening."[56] The *Daily Evening Bulletin* also reported, "An ordinance has been passed in this city for the suppression of the 'music' of Chinese orchestra bands, and the first case under it was tried in the Police Court today," and "one of the musicians, a gong-beater, [was] arrested."[57] Although this news was widely circulated, the outcome of the trial of the "gong-beater" is unknown. But a judge did object to the ordinance, noting that "the Board had no right to pass such an order. The beating of gongs was just as necessary for them to conduct their business as was the playing of musical instruments in American theaters, and should the order be enforced it would virtually be a suppression of the theater. That they had no right to do."[58] Nevertheless, a modified version of the gong ordinance was introduced.[59] It was one of several ordinances designed to make life difficult for the Chinese in the city. In addition to the gong ordinance, a cubic air ordinance made it a crime to lease or live in rooms that contained fewer than five hundred cubic feet of air for each person dwelling in them, and a basket ordinance made it a misdemeanor for anyone on the city's sidewalks to carry baskets suspended from or attached to poles across the shoulders—the mode of transportation for Chinese laundry delivery.

Yet with the noise ordinance, the city categorized the timbre of gongs as noise and deemed playing them a criminal offense. Under the classification of unlawfulness, the Chinese sound had no legitimate standing, establishing a connection between the racialized timbre and criminality. The theater's music, categorized as noise, was targeted for silencing and punished by the city. Eight months later, on April 26, 1870, the theater musician Ah Ching was arrested by the police for playing music under the gong ordinance, and was fined twenty dollars. By May 1, Ah Ching was back in the theater, performing nightly—which, the *Morning Union* observed in amusement, would probably lead the theater to bankruptcy, as he was to be fined twenty dollars for each violation. The white owners of the Chinese theater, Glazier and Saligsberger, fought back in court to protect the value of their property. The *San Francisco Chronicle* reported their appeal shortly after:

> Chinese Theater Music. Mr. Story offered a communication from Glazier & Seligsberger, representing that they owned the property occupied by the Chinese Theater Company; that the use of the gong was absolutely necessary to the proper conducting of Celestial tragedies, and that the recent order prohibiting the pounding of gongs in the city had resulted in the entire demoralization of the Mongolian drama in this city, and the performances were necessarily suspended. To alter this building, so that it would be adapted to other purpose, would cost much and greatly reduce the rents, and seriously affect the valuation of contiguous property. Mr. Story introduced a resolution rescinding the original order.[60]

The *Daily Alta California* also reported the negative effects of the ordinance on the same day: "[The theater] had become less attractive, and the Chinese were gradually moving away from the locality, damaging the value of property."[61] However, the property owners' request "for permission to use Chinese gongs as music" was rejected by the Committee of Health and the police.[62] The *San Francisco Chronicle* made its agreement with the ruling clear, saying, "The Chinese Theater has made one more step toward civilization, by substituting a fife and drum for the usually execrable din of their gongs and squeak-tubes."[63] The writer of this sarcastic editorial gleefully replaced the racialized timbre with timbres of perceived whiteness.

The gong ordinance, like other anti-Chinese ordinances, was sporadically enforced. No arrests seem to have been made for the rest of 1870. But noise complaints were filed nearly every year. In 1871, the city formally passed an ordinance required all theatrical performance to close by midnight. All the managers of Chinese theaters came together to argue against the new restriction.[64] In early December 1872, a petition was filed again asking the Board of Supervisors to reduce the sound of the orchestra at the Chinese Theatre on Jackson Street; a few weeks later the police arrested Chinese orchestra musicians.[65] By 1873 the situation had become dire. Applying the cubic air ordinance, the police arrested 213 Chinese in April and 219 in May.[66] A newspaper in the Midwest reported bluntly, "The musicians of the Chinese Theater in San Francisco have been arrested and fined $20 each for making barbarous and unearthly noise." Another newspaper noted the drop in patronage at Chinese theater due to the cubic air ordinance.[67] The *San Francisco Chronicle* noted that the police took pride in their enforcement: "Officer Rogers is distinguishing himself and gaining public commendation by his

vigilance in putting down Chinese nuisances. The suppression of immorali-
ties in the heathen precincts has had such a depressing effect financially that
the Chinese theatre has been closed for a lack of patronage."[68] Fear of zeal-
ous police officers brought a halt to the new theater on Jackson Street; Hing
Chuen Yuen was closed and the property sold in July 1873, thus temporarily
ending the first permanent theater.[69]

Although the legal harassment continued, Chinese theaters would not be
stopped. Given that legal challenges grew during a time when anti-Chinese
politics gradually became a prominent national agenda—evident in various
anti-Chinese city ordinances and state laws and atrocities such as the Los
Angeles Chinese massacre in 1871—the resilience of Chinese theater was
extraordinary.[70]

The Second Theater: Sing Ping Yuen Theater on Jackson Street (South)

The lights of the Hing Chuen Yuen theater did not dim for long. The
theater was quickly rejuvenated by new management and opened for performance in mid-August. The successful operation by savvy veteran management was praised by the *Daily Evening Bulletin*, which reported a stunning
two thousand dollars in revenue for the opening three nights. It also offered
insights about the Chinese theater's goal in serving the community.

> The management of the theatre has always been characterized by discre-
> tion in the selection and production of plays and due regard for the tastes
> of the people, together with an unswerving adherence to popular prices for
> admission, thus encouraging the patrons of the drama to become regular in
> attendance and whetting the appetite of the young heathen. The properties
> of the theatre have attained a great value, the stock company has become
> one of the best of its kind in the world. . . . The business manager of the
> theatre, an urbane fellow of thirty summers, has just displayed rare tact and
> enterprise by bridging out from China a star of the first magnitude, who
> assumes female characters with startling fidelity, and has withal fine social
> qualities. The engagement is one of the greatest successes the theater has
> ever known. During the last three nights the performances have netted in
> the aggregate $2,000.[71]

The newspapers carried lengthy descriptions of the theater's activities well
into the next year, reflecting mainstream society's growing familiarity and
more probing inquiry about the performances. Invariably they noted the fully
packed theater. Despite its patronizing tone, one description provides a sense
of the aura of the place, in particular the crowded scene of enthusiastic fans.

> The pressure from the rear forced the portion of the audience in front to the
> very stage, and the young beaux who were tardy, when they were familiar

with the management or could claim relationship with the ushers, took advantage of the situation to advance upon the stage and secure positions where all that transpired could be seen and heard. The Caucasian spectator viewed the scene as resplendent with an ancient luster. The heathen devices upon the wall, the grotesque figures upon the stage attired in gilded costumes, the legion of warm, brown faces presented by the audience, all brought into strong relief by the soft light that poured in a steady flood through the dusty shades of venerable chandeliers, seemed to impregnate the atmosphere with an odor foreign to this age, and which refused to commingle with the regular and authorized smells of the place.[72]

Jackson Street's Chinese theater again dominated attention. A newspaper reported in January 1874 that of the two Chinese theaters in the city, the Jackson Street theater, identified as Hong Ting Yuen (probably Hing Chun Yuen), was the premier Chinese theater, whereas the smaller one on Washington Place was second class, not always in operation, and hosted traveling troupes.[73] The dynamics of Chinese theaters would change in a few months.

In late June 1874 a new theater, seating twelve hundred to sixteen hundred—Sing Ping Yuen 昇平院—was completed on the south side of Jackson Street, across from the older one on the north side. Newspapers reported that fifty thousand dollars was spent on its construction. The inaugural performance on June 21 lasted from 7:00 p.m. to 3:00 a.m., drawing an audience reported to be eighteen hundred.[74] The opening of the new theater was again a celebrated event in San Francisco. This time, the Chinese-run theater placed a two-week-long advertisement in the *Daily Alta California*. It highlighted the

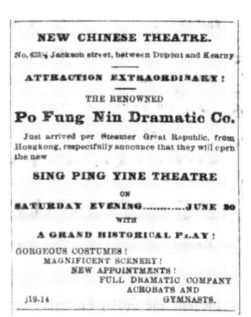

FIGURE 4.10 Advertisement for the Po Fung Nin Dramatic Company, Sing Ping [Yuen] Theatre, *Daily Alta California*, June 21–28, 1874.

Po Fung Nin Dramatic Company 普豐年, newly arriving from China (fig. 4.10). The troupe shared the name of a famous Cantonese opera troupe in China.[75] For the next three years, it would be the primary rival to the old Jackson theater, which was to be renamed the Royal Chinese Theatre three months later.

The theater owners were not ordinary merchants but rather what the *Evening Bulletin* called "elegant and superior members" of the community: Dr. Li Po Tai; Ah You, ex-inspector of the Sam Yup [Yap] Company; Ho Man, of the firm of Kum Wo; Ah Jarek, of the firm of Yee Tuck, and Ah Yung, agent for Dr. Li Po Tai.[76] An agent of the theater noted that the goal was for it to "be finished in elegant style, according to Oriental taste, and specially adapted to the demands of his countrymen resident here."[77]

Widely recognized as the most successful herbalist and apothecary in San Francisco, Dr. Li had a practice in a prominent building in Chinatown, and he counted Californians such as the railroad tycoons Leland Stanford and Mark Hopkins among his patients.[78] A contemporary writer noted, "His rooms are thronged with visitors of all conditions and nationalities, who come to consult him touching their various ailments."[79] The *Chronicle* claimed that he "has a larger and more lucrative practice than any other doctor in the city."[80] Only two years previously, he had built a new temple on Dupont Street that was considered the most extravagant of the existing six temples.[81] The theater on Washington Place that opened in the early 1870s was only several doors from Dr. Li's practice on Washington Street (see fig. 4.7). The 1870 census records him as forty-two years old, owning $40,000 of real estate and having $12,000 in personal worth. The city tax records of 1875 showed that his personal assets ranked thirteenth in the Chinese community, with an annual income of $75,000.[82] This prominent, erudite doctor, possessing wealth and esteemed social status within both the Chinese community and the larger city, was a dedicated enthusiast and major supporter of Cantonese opera.

A grand banquet offered prior to the theater opening had an exclusive guest list that included a Municipal Court judge, the chief of police, the fire marshal, various members of the bar, and the press. Each seat was decorated with a small vase of flowers, and the guests ate exquisite delicacies of Chinese cuisine, accompanied by Dr. Li's commentary. The dishes ranged from fancy fruit, bird's nest soup, shark-fin stew, and fresh oysters, to roast pig. Li's special and elevated status could be confirmed in a portrait when he was in his fifties (fig. 4.11). He donned Qing dynasty court attire, a typical civil official's surcoat with a court insignia badge in front. The necklace and the embroidered pheasant signaled a second-rank civil servant of the Qing empire, a prestigious position for scholar-officials in the imperial bureaucracy. Advertisement of his practice appeared in the *San Francisco China News*, the only local Chinese newspaper at the time. Li Po Tai's practice was

FIGURE 4.11 Li Po Tai at fifty years old. Foo and Wing Herb Company, *The Science of Oriental Medicine* (Los Angeles: G. Rice and Sons, 1897), 3.

one of the fourteen business advertisements in the paper. Below is the translation of the Chinese advertisement. The address of the medical practice is marked on the 1873 map.

Li Po Tai, Extending His Gracious Medical Services

Doctor Li took residence earlier at Changrong Yachu and has since returned to no. 747 Washington Street. He shall be at your service for patient consultations from noon until two daily. Pray, bestow on the clinic your esteemed presence.[83]

The new theater's troupe, Po Fung Nin Dramatic Company, claimed to have 122 performers. Opening night began with the traditional inauguration play, *Six Warlords*. It was followed, however, by a unusual performance, featuring two cows played by performers enveloped in cow skins and decorated in horns. The drama included sixteen acts. The *San Francisco Chronicle* gave a report of the convoluted plot.

A husband and wife appeared upon the scene, the former accompanied by two cows—represented by small Chinamen with beast's heads. The wife has lofty aspirations, and does not like her liege lord because of his devotion to agricultural pursuits. Enter the heavy villain in the guise of an invalid, as a destroyer, of the felicity of the hearthstone. He gets access to the discontented wife, and elopes with her. Enter husband with the two cows—which he instructs to live in harmony, and feed on the green grass, otherwise matting. He falls asleep and they fight it out on that line. Enter a vile robber in miserable dress. He gathers the two cows by the horns and, is making off with them, when their owner awakes and rescues his property. Exit husband. Enter gay seducer with recreant wife. Emaciated thief beats the gay seducer, and secures the unfaithful baggage to himself. Reenter deserted husband, recovers his wife, and finally put her to death with unheard-of tortures. After having expired in agony, the faithless wife deliberately gets up and coolly walks off the stage. Another general war, and so on ad libitum.[84]

Many newspapers reported the inauguration: an audience of eighteen hundred was noted, including many American ladies.[85] All commented on the special attraction of the two cows. No doubt it was an attention-grabbing and immensely popular event.

The incorporation of two "cow" characters onto the stage was unconventional for Cantonese opera, quite unlike other plays seen thus far that drew from the traditional repertoire. Prior to the premiere, this deviation from tradition was forecast in the *Daily Evening Bulletin*, which reported: "In order to run a lively opposition to the theater on the opposite side of the street, which is now doing a fine business, [the theater managers] have secured the services of an eminent Chinese to write an original play of the historical school, founded on incidents of life in China and California."[86] The inventive use of headgear and costumes to depict cows, along with the dramatic twist, contributed to the novel spectacle. These innovations demonstrated how Cantonese opera adapted to local demand, catering to the audience's desire for novelty, incorporating influences from the entertainment culture of California, and gaining a competitive advantage. This is the first record of its kind: the creation of a Chinese opera reflecting life in California.

A depiction of a Chinese theater by the Englishman Reverend Samuel Manning, made a year later, might well portray the opening night of Sing Ping Yuen (fig. 4.12).[87] This illustration was printed in 1875 in *Scribner's Monthly*, in the long article "The City of the Golden Gate," by Samuel Williams, a popular writer and editor of the *Daily Evening Bulletin*, who was regarded by contemporaries as "prominently identified with journalism on this coast."[88] The drawing depicts the interior of a theater featuring a stage design and pit/gallery structure that is notably distinct from that portrayed in "The Coming Man." It has a smaller stage and two plainer doors leading to the backstage, where the characters for "entry" and "exit" can be read above the two doors. The gallery and private box are smaller as well. The stage matches various descriptions of Sing Ping Yuen. For example, the orchestra, which is typically located at the back of the stage, is roughly visible behind a screen; the stage

FIGURE 4.12 Samuel Manning. "A Chinese Theater." Reprinted in "The City of the Golden Gate," *Scribners Monthly* 10, no. 3, July 1, 1875.

props and property man are in a corner of the stage visible to the audience; and there is a perpendicular display of Chinese characters.

Still more suggestive are the details of the stage scene. Several performers stand onstage, among them the leading man, an official with a gauze hat, and the leading woman in a robe at the center. On their sides are squatting figures. Judging from their headpieces and unusual poses, they could be the two actors playing cows in the plot described by the *Chronicle*.[89] Such headpieces and attire might have been inspired by the outfits of the tiger-soldiers of the Qing dynasty: according to the China historian Steven Platt, were a "unit of highly trained foot soldiers in the imperial Qing army [who] wore hats, tunics and trousers with tiger-stripe marking."[90] Regardless, this stage was depicted as abundantly rich in theatrical interactions between the cow characters and the husband-wife pair.

In August, a *San Francisco Chronicle* article gave readers a tour of the theater space and the daily routine at Sing Ping Yuen:

A large lamp marks the entrance of the theater, a brick building on Jackson Street. To enter the theater, one takes the steps up to a staircase landing, buys a ticket ($.50) through a window, then hands it to a Welsh doorman who puts it into the slit on a box he sits on. Behind the theater stage in the basement is a large kitchen providing food for the entire staff, and sleeping quarters for the actors. There is an altar where a flame is kept constantly burning within a glass globe before the images of deities of several religious rites. On the level of the stage, behind the orchestra, is the green room, about the same size as the stage, where a large number of silk, heavily embroidered costumes, as well as other garments and headpieces, or pieces such as large feathers, flags, and spears are kept. There the performers get robed and changed with the help of two staff persons, and wait for their scenes. A separate room with face paint is where actors put on the elaborate makeup. There is no prompter or director backstage, and the actors constantly pass out and in through the two entrances to the stage without special direction from anyone.[91]

To be sure, the costumes and adornments of Chinese opera performers involved complicated layers of clothing. The conventional process of dressing performers, depending on role types and plots, required detailed knowledge of different steps and methods of layering, tying, and so on. Putting on the formal costumes usually required the assistance of experienced staff. This report of the green room confirms the highly professional level of the troupe. The writer provided the names of a partial list of the cast and the musicians of the accompanying orchestra. Table 4.2 summarizes the list, with Chinese translation of the instruments. This newspaper article constituted the earliest record of a Cantonese opera cast in America. Although the restoration of these actors' names to their original Chinese forms is unattainable, the list offers insight into the organizational structure of the early Cantonese opera troupe in California.

The audience expressed their adulation of performers readily, as observed by another reporter, who wrote, "Each actor was greeted on his appearance by many marks of approbation from his immediate circle of friends."[92] There was good reason for their enthusiasm. Po Fung Nin (or Bo Fung Lin, Pu Fengnian, 普豐年) was famous in China; a Chinese official in Guangdong recorded in 1873 that it was one of the top three Cantonese opera troupes in southern China (to be discussed in chap. 5). The Chronicle reporter drew attention to what he called "females of suspicious maidenhood, with bright red cheeks and lips, loosely dressed in glossy black cotton skirts, each carrying in her pudgy right hand a bandanna as large as a ship's mainsail, and having her shiny hair done up in bowie knife fashion on the cone of the occiput, are forever streaming in and out."[93] The depiction implied activities of prostitution in the neighborhood of the theater.

The rival theater on the north side of Jackson Street did not sit idle in the face of this competition. It was renamed the Royal Chinese Theatre

TABLE 4.2 Partial List of Cast and Musicians in the Po Fung Nin Troupe

Name	Role	Name	Instrument	Chinese terms
Ah You	First General	Liu Yi	lo	鑼 (large gong)
Ah Hop	Second General	Ah Say	sam yin	三弦 (sanxian)
Ah Ti	Mandarin	Ah Sop	yot kom	月琴 (yueqin)
Ah Quong	Mandarin	Ah Jon	yee hin	二弦 (erxian)
Ah Sin	Mandarin	Ah Hong	shay koo	沙鼓 (shagu)
Ti Sor	Mandarin	Ah Look	ti loy	提鑼 (handheld gong)
Ah Quong	Emperor	Chin Lung	tien sok	弦索 (bowed or plucked stringed instrument)
Li Hong	Comedian (including demons and dragons)			
Ah Poom	Leading woman			
Ah Bart	Second woman			
Ah Chow	Coquette			
Ah Bo	Third woman (middle aged)			
Ah Dot	Old woman (comic)			

Source: *San Francisco Chronicle*, August 30, 1874.

and featured the newly arrived Yu Henn Choy (堯天彩) troupe, beginning September 8. It even placed a weeklong advertisement in the *Daily Evening Bulletin*, listing seventy-five cents as the admission fee.[94] Both theaters were reportedly always crowded, so together they drew an audience of at least two to three thousand to the surrounding area every evening. The vibrancy of theatrical activities prompted complaints about noise and hours of operation all through the autumn, and another petition for ordinance was brought before the Board of Supervisors.[95] This time, evidently, the prestige of the owners of Sing Ping Yuen swayed the board's opinion. After pushing back on the complaints and promising to abate the sound, the theaters did not have to yield very much.[96] The police officer in charge of the street was replaced; passage of the ordinance was postponed indefinitely. As for the reason, the *Daily Evening Bulletin* wrote in December, "The enterprising proprietors of the theatre belong to the progressive class of heathen."[97] The high social standing of Chinese elites became the most effective shield or deterrent against efforts to criminalize the lively scene of their opera theaters.

CHAPTER 5

Prosperity

A New Theater on Washington Street

The 1870s were a remarkable time in Chinese American history. A large number of Chinese had been recruited for the construction of the transcontinental railroad in the 1860s. Afterward, a significant number of them went to San Francisco for manufacturing and service jobs. The signing of the Burlingame Treaty in 1868 established free travel between the United States and China, which led to a new surge of Chinese immigration. According to a report by the *San Francisco Chronicle*, between 1868 and 1875, Chinese entered the country at an average of around 12,000 annually, with 18,448 arriving in 1875 alone.[1] Transpacific commerce between America and China grew significantly as well: "In 1878 total imports from China jumped to $18,128,042, while exports to China reached $23,079,586."[2] In the 1870s Chinese mining companies, such as Hong Fook Kong & Co. and the Man See Company, made significant profits; the Chinese bourgeoisie entered the field of manufacturing with cigar and boot factories.[3] This was a time of vibrant growth for the business ventures of the Chinese community of San Francisco.

Meanwhile, the anti-Chinese activities that had been most prevalent in mining towns and the interior of the state gradually spread to the cities as well. Politicians, urban white workers, and union leaders began to organize anti-Chinese initiatives with remarkable zeal, aided by several newspapers that fueled the flames with editorials and condemnations. California felt the prolonged national depression of 1873–76; according to the historian Mae Ngai, by 1876 there were fifteen thousand unemployed white workers in San Francisco. All these conditions added fuel to the anti-Chinese movement.[4] In a quantitative study of the anti-Chinese politics of the 1870s, the sociologists Eric Fong and William Markham identify three primary approaches in anti-Chinese legislative activities: first, obstructing Chinese business activities through taxes and regulation; second, denying the Chinese civil rights, including voting, naturalization, testifying, and education; and third, taking legal action against Chinatowns, including targeting living spaces, gambling dens, and theaters. Fong and Markham note that the city or urban environment supported these activities. Urban areas—where working-class whites were concentrated—"[made] it easier for antiminority forces to organize" and achieve a high level of organization "to use the political system to discriminate."[5]

Opposition and resistance to these anti-Chinese activities were common, if not altogether effective in slowing their rise. Members of society at large, missionaries, white employers, landlords, and merchants profiting on Chinese trade brought petitions against anti-Chinese measures. State and county officials were also protective of the revenues from discriminatory taxes, on which they had grown dependent.[6] In the Chinese community, leaders or district organizations brought lawsuits or petitions on constitutional grounds. They worked to uphold the 1875 Civil Rights Act's prohibition of discrimination on the basis of race or color, or treaty agreements guaranteeing immigration rights. The Chinese government also sent its first ambassador to the United States to address issues related to these measures.

Miraculously, despite this tumultuous political and social environment, two more Chinese theaters were built in San Francisco before the end of the decade. Both were on Washington Street and even more elegant and ambitious than the previous two theaters. It would not be an exaggeration to say that these theaters were ushered in by racial hostility. But in this act to counter anti-Chinese laws, the new theatrical endeavor, presenting as the public face of Chinese community, raised its respectability. It was all the more important at a time when significant initiatives were advanced to vilify and cast aspersions on the Chinese. New theaters opened largely in response to high audience demand, offering the community a fantastic and electrifying cultural life, as well as a potentially lucrative business opportunity.

This chapter examines the establishment of the third phase of Chinese theater in the late 1870s, which demonstrated more glamour and professionalism. It also discusses the impact of police raids and violence on everyday life as well as the portrayal of Chinese theater in print media. To explore these topics in depth, it is crucial to examine a fascinating Chinese-language resource: two lists of top Cantonese opera troupes that were published in a local Chinese newspaper. As the earliest such record, these lists provide valuable insights into the flourishing Cantonese opera culture in San Francisco, unmediated by English-language writers.

Eleven Top Troupes! Cast Lists in *Tangfan Gongbao* (*The Oriental*) 唐番公報

Chinese (or Chinese-English) newspapers began publication in San Francisco in the mid-1850s.[7] The number of Chinese newspapers grew after more

Chinese moved to the city following the completion of the transcontinental railroad. In July 1874, the *San Francisco China News* (舊金山唐人新聞紙) began publication. A year later, *The Oriental,* with the Chinese name *Tangfan Gongbao* (唐番公報), commenced the publication of a four-page weekly newspaper (in Chinese only) on September 11, 1875. It would become the longest-lived Chinese newspaper in nineteenth-century America. It was written by hand with Chinese brush and, and the printing was done through lithography. The content encompassed commodity prices, steamship schedules, interior train and freight schedules, local and China news, advertisements, and miscellaneous public notices and stories. Its coverage addressed the needs and concerns of the transpacific, mobile, and prosperous community of Chinese merchants, traders, and workers.

In the third issue of *The Oriental,* on September 25, 1875, a remarkable list of Cantonese opera troupes and actors took up the top half of the third page (fig. 5.1a). Across the top of the page, the source of the list was given: "Cast List of Eleven Newly Formed Top Troupes copied from Jiqing Gongsuo, the first year of Emperor Guangxu." Jiqing Gongsuo (吉慶公所) was a professional organization in Guangzhou serving as a clearing house. The next row lists thirteen categories of opera role types, from warriors to scholars, maidens, and comic roles. Underneath them are eleven rows listing the troupes, each of which begins with the troupe name, followed by its actors neatly listed under the thirteen role types. It is the earliest and most significant existent nineteenth-century Chinese-language document related to Cantonese opera in North America. Table 5.1 is a summary of the role types and the corresponding number of actors in each type.

In the list, each troupe features around 28–32 members under the thirteen role types.

These are the essential performers in the troupe's cast. Among them are no fewer than ten famous actors of the time.[8] Most famous are Bengya Qi

TABLE 5.1 Summary of Role Types in the Cast List in Fig. 5.1a

Role types	Number of actors	Role types	Number of actors
Wusheng (bearded warrior)	2	*Zongsheng* (middle-aged scholar)	3–4
Xiaowu (young warrior)	5	*Xiaowu* (young warrior)	2–3
Huadan (young belle)	5–6	*Gongjiao* (bearded old man)	1–2
Wuadan (young belle warrior)	2	*Da Huamian* (villainous man)	1–2
Zhengdan (decorous middle-aged woman)	2	*Er Huamian* (tempestuous man)	2
Zhengsheng (dignified middle-aged man)	1	*Nanchou* (male comic role)	1
		Nüchou (female comic role)	1

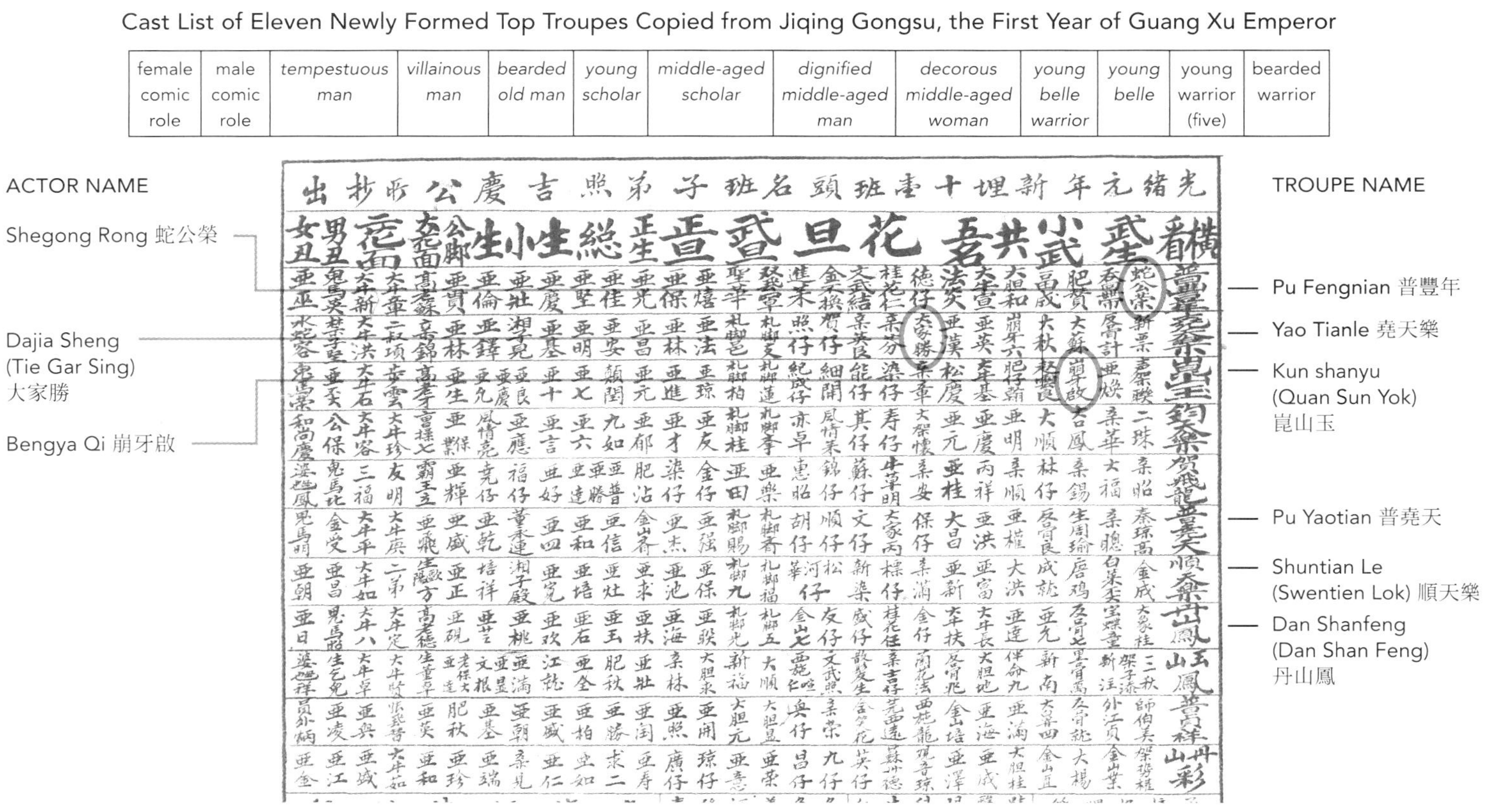

Cast List of Eleven Newly Formed Top Troupes Copied from Jiqing Gongsu, the First Year of Guang Xu Emperor

female comic role	male comic role	tempestuous man	villainous man	bearded old man	young scholar	middle-aged scholar	dignified middle-aged man	decorous middle-aged woman	young belle warrior	young belle	young warrior	young warrior (five)	bearded warrior

ACTOR NAME

Shegong Rong 蛇公榮

Dajia Sheng
(Tie Gar Sing)
大家勝

Bengya Qi 崩牙啟

TROUPE NAME

— Pu Fengnian 普豐年

— Yao Tianle 堯天樂

— Kun shanyu
(Quan Sun Yok)
崑山玉

— Pu Yaotian 普堯天

— Shuntian Le
(Swentien Lok) 順天樂

— Dan Shanfeng
(Dan Shan Feng)
丹山鳳

FIGURE 5.1A Cast list of eleven newly formed top troupes copied from the Jiqing Gongsu, in the first year of the Guang Xu emperor. *The Oriental*, September 11, 1875.

(崩牙啟), the young warrior; and Shegong Rong (蛇公榮), the bearded warrior; the latter had an illustrious career in southern China extending to the early twentieth century.

Located in Guangzhou, China, the Jiqing Gongsuo functioned as the primary clearinghouse for opera troupes. Established in 1868, it was the first official guild organization for Cantonese opera troupes. During this period, Cantonese opera flourished in rural communities and started to attract growing audiences in cities, both in southern China and elsewhere. As the historian Wing Chung Ng notes of its founding, "[T]he Jiqing Gongsuo was as much a corporate business agency for the itinerant troupes as their marketing hub. Through advanced booking, the brokerage function helped minimize competition among the participants and allowed them to maximize their exposure and profitability."[9] At the guild's headquarter, troupes put up wooden plaques or badges displaying information on their rosters and repertoires.[10] The organization's staff, senior members of the profession, handled inquiries and brokered deals between prospective buyers and the troupes, ensuring ethical practices and preventing unseemly competition, providing business protection for both parties. It anchored both the operation of itinerant engagements and structures of cooperation and solidified the system of role types, each of which developed its particular vocal style, makeup design, costume, gestures, and formulaic acts.

Because the Jiqing Gongsuo was the governing body that regulated Cantonese opera in China, such a list of the top eleven troupes in the profession, copied from the organization's own documents, would have carried the institutional seal of approval, signaling its credibility and authenticity. Eighteen seventy-five was also the year that the Guangxu Emperor established his reign title.[11] A year later, on September 9, 1876, another new Jiqing Gongsuo list appeared (fig. 5.1b). These two lists share five troupe names (marked on the right of fig. 5.1b); a handful of prominent actors reappear on the second list. As documents of the Jiqing Gongsuo, these two lists affirm the system of Cantonese opera in southern China during this time. Their importance resonated across the Pacific.

What might be the reason that the new, weekly Chinese-language newspaper used an eighth of its total print space to publish these cast lists? Did these eleven Cantonese opera troupes, with their total of around 350 actors, intend to perform in California for the season? Did they actually do so? Despite the vibrancy of Chinese theaters in San Francisco and the interior of the state, as discussed earlier, it is unlikely that they needed to or could accommodate eleven troupes. Moreover, it is improbable that the eleven top troupes from southern China would all be performing in California simultaneously.

Cast List of Eleven Newly Formed Top Troupes Copied from Jiqing Gongsu, the Second Year of Guang Xu Emperor

female comic role	male comic role	*tempestuous man*	*villainous man*	*bearded old man*	*young scholar*	*middle-aged scholar*	*dignified middle-aged man*	*decorous middle-aged woman*	*young belle warrior*	*young belle*	young warrior	bearded warrior

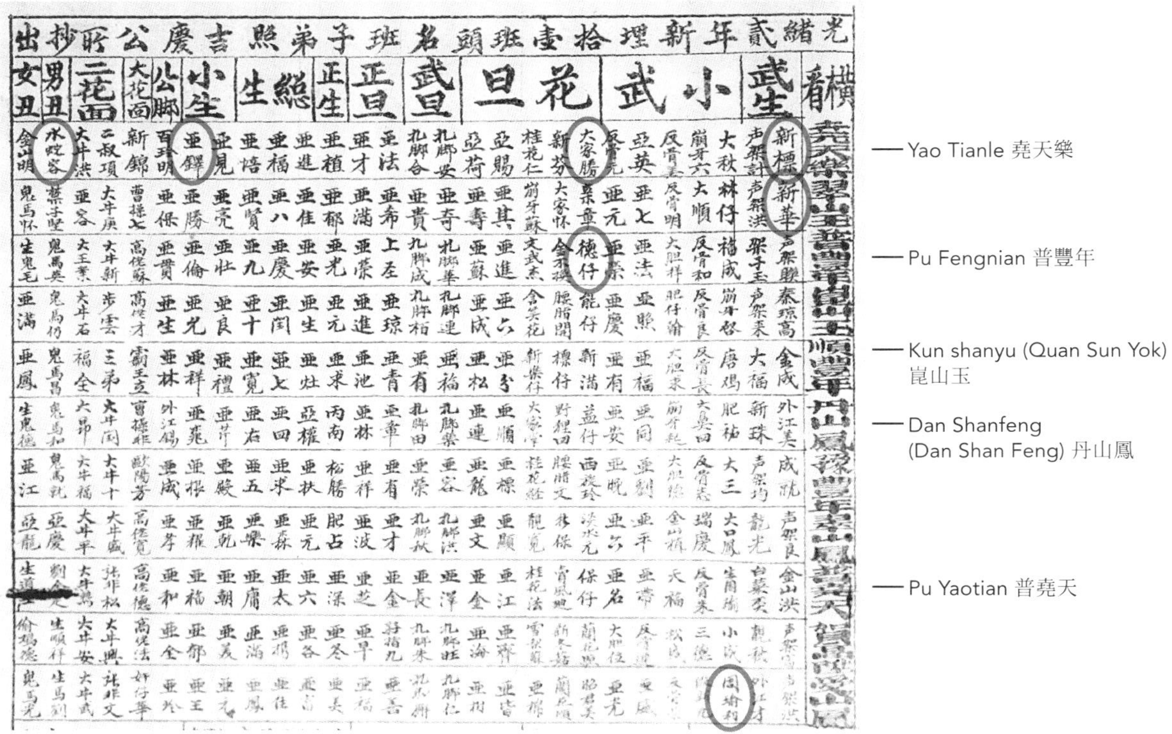

光緒貳年新理拾壹班頭名班子弟照吉慶公所抄出
橫看
武生
小武
花旦
武旦
正旦
正生
總生
小生
公腳
大花面
二花面
男丑
女丑
Yao Tianle 堯天樂
Pu Fengnian 普豐年
Kun shanyu (Quan Sun Yok) 崑山玉
Dan Shanfeng (Dan Shan Feng) 丹山鳳
Pu Yaotian 普堯天

FIGURE 5.1B Cast list of eleven newly formed top troupes copied from the Jiqing Gongsu, in the second year of the Guang Xu Emperor. *The Oriental*, September 9, 1876.

There are three potential explanations for the publication of these two lists in San Francisco's *The Oriental*. First, the lists could have been advertisements of troupes for hire from China, functioning similarly to other commercial lists in newspapers that detailed unit prices of commodities such as rice, spices, fur, copper, and fuel. After all, opera troupes were a part of transpacific commerce. Therefore, the lists could be seen as an extension of the Jiqing Gongsu's influence and operation across the Pacific, but replacing wooden plaques with newsprint. The printing of the lists reflects the value and seriousness with which Chinese theater in North America was viewed in the mid-1870s. Indeed, at least one actor on both lists, the female impersonator for the young belle role, Dajia Sheng (大家勝, or Tie Gar Sing), did make the voyage to San Francisco (see figs. 5.1a and 5.1b). We will meet him again in chapter 6, where we will learn about his success and enormous influence as an actor-manager in the San Francisco opera scene.

Second, the lists could have been printed to affirm the prestige and fame of the troupes then performing in San Francisco. The first entry that topped the 1875 list—Pu Fengnian, 普豐年—was identical to the name of the troupe performing at the Sing Ping Yuen Theater, which had opened just a year before.[12] (The English-language newspapers used the romanization Po Fung Nin.) It was a famous name: in Guangzhuo, Du Fengzhe, a government official, considered the troupe a premier choice to honor his mother's birthday celebration.[13] The Pu Fengnian troupe's activities in China also extended beyond Guangdong, Hong Kong, and Macao to Shanghai, where it performed in 1874.[14] Granted, however, such affirmation would most likely be merely symbolic. In reality, the cast members of the Pu Fengnian troupe on the 1875 and 1876 Jiqing Gongsuo lists may bear little resemblance to those of the Pu Fengnian troupe performing at the Sing Ping Yuen theater in San Francisco. It is impossible to establish a connection between the cast list for the theater, presented in the *San Francisco Chronicle* (see table 4.2) and the Chinese names of the Po Fengnian troupe in the Jiqing Gongsuo lists. Nevertheless, the Sing Ping Yuen theater could take pride in showcasing a troupe with a famous name that topped the Jiqing Gongsuo lists—an honor that its rival, the New Chinese Royal Theatre, could not claim.[15]

Finally, the Jiqing Gongsuo lists may be a form of commendation, by elite enthusiasts of the community, for the top Cantonese opera troupes and actors. It underscored excellence in theatrical arts. The sense of commendation may be comparable to the celebration of other accolades from the home country that also concerned the community. Also published in *The Oriental* are a list of thirty-two students selected for the Chinese Educational Mission to study in the United States and a list of sixty-four names of youngsters awarded the top places in the Imperial Examination of Military Service for the Guangdong region.[16] The inclusion of long honor rolls of youngsters in the four-page newspaper indicates the earnestness of the paper to enshrine success on the home front. Regardless, these two troupe lists, printed a year after the grand opening of the second Chinese theater, signaled the vital importance of Chinese theater within the community.

The New Chinese Royal Theatre was featuring the Yu Henn Choy troupe (or Yao Tian Cai in Pinyin). The Chinese name of the Yu Henn Choy troupe emerged in a later news report in *The Oriental*. In a record of the everyday life of harassment, and comprising only two lines in the four-page weekly, a news report confirmed the Chinese characters of the troupe's name: 堯天彩 (Yao Tian Cai).[17] Another troupe name, related to a police raid, appeared in January 1876: 高天彩 (Gao Tian Cai).[18] Neither appears on the Jiqing Gongsuo lists, but they undoubtedly belonged to the extensive roster of opera troupes that came to California and presented performances in Chinese theaters.

We can safely say that the official lists of 1875 and 1876 copied from the Jiqing Gongsuo are not meant to indicate Cantonese opera troupes performing in California, as some have previously assumed.[19] The lists nonetheless points to the lively Cantonese opera culture in San Francisco and the full range of role types employed in opera performances. More important, they constitute the critical historical Chinese-language record of the high level of professionalism and prosperity of Cantonese opera troupes in the San Francisco of the 1870s. Through the printed text, these lists linked Chinese theaters in San Francisco more closely to the scene of Cantonese opera in southern China.

Although photographs of Cantonese opera performers in San Francisco from the 1870s are unavailable, the portraits of Cantonese opera actors captured by the Hong Kong photographer Lai Fong 黎芳 provide valuable visual insight.[20] As the owner of the Ah Fong Studio 華芳照相館 in Hong Kong, Lai Fong was active in the 1870s. He took many portraits of notable figures, such as the governor of Hong Kong, Sir Arthur Kennedy, or comprador-merchants of bank corporations. (Comprador-merchants were Chinese managers of foreign firms in China treaty ports, who constituted a new business class.) He also captured the glamour of Cantonese opera performers in several works; we can assume they were from the premier troupes. Figure 5.2 reproduces two of such portraits.[21] Figure 5.2a features a female warrior (on the left) and a young male warrior. Figure 5.2b features a middle-aged bearded warrior (on the right) and a young warrior. Their poses convey artistry and strength. The elaborately embroidered costumes and finely made headdresses demonstrate the opulence of Cantonese opera performance. The embroidered tiger-head panel worn over the abdomen of the warriors' armor, typical of Cantonese opera costumes, "a powerful and fearsome spirit known for guarding the gates to the underworld, is an apotropaic image that protects the performers and the audience from evil spirits," according to the art historian April

Liu.[22] Such tiger-head armor was often decorated with shiny gold couching swirling around brass and mirrored discs. The woman warrior's headdress is adorned with long pheasant feathers, which could swing in the air as the warrior spun across the stage, and "may be manipulated in a wide range of movements to express anger, intense thought, or anticipation."[23] Figure. 5.2b also shows the "one table two chairs," the most essential props of Chinese opera performances. They have a wide range of uses, serving as tables and chairs on different occasions, as well as substitutes for mountains, buildings, beds, and doors. The chair and table covers have glamorous textile designs, with beautifully embroidered flowers and animals. Such opulent textiles and costumes were often singled out for praise in reports in English-language newspapers.

These portraits are the earliest visual documentation of Cantonese opera performers.[24] In subsequent chapters covering the 1880s, we will encounter similarly dignified poses in exceptional illustrations of Cantonese opera

FIGURE 5.2A
Lai Fong.
Cantonese opera
performers in
Hong Kong.
c. 1870s. Courtesy
of Moonchu
Foundation.

FIGURE 5.2B Lai Fong. Cantonese opera performers in Hong Kong. c. 1870s. Courtesy of Moonchu Foundation.

performers in San Francisco. For the 1870s, both the Jiqing Gongsuo lists and the artistic portraits of actors by Lai Fong in Hong Kong attest to Cantonese opera during this era in southern China, which, as noted by Wing Chung Ng, went through periodic highs and lows yet demonstrated "considerable resilience and creativity."[25] The troupes' glamour, adaptability, and ingenuity played a crucial role in successfully facilitating the opera's expansion across the Pacific. Today, these lists and images also allow us to conceptualize the stages of Chinese theater in San Francisco and envision the spectacle of their performances and full casts. They counteract the prevalent negative portrayal and denigration of Chinese theater and opera performance in the contemporary English-language press. As we will see below, these excellent theaters would face increased adversity with the rise of the anti-Chinese movement.

Raids, Disasters, and Other Trouble

Earlier, we discussed San Francisco's use of city regulations (cubic feet of air and sidewalk ordinances) to harass the Chinese and to reduce their presence. The cubic-air ordinance made it a misdemeanor for living spaces to be less than five hundred cubic feet for each adult person sleeping or dwelling there. It targeted San Francisco's Chinese inhabitants, who tended to live communally and/or in smaller spaces than their white counterparts. The sidewalk ordinance made it a misdemeanor to carry baskets suspended from or attached to poles carried across one's shoulders, which targeted Chinese fish and vegetable street hawkers. Noise and curfew ordinances targeting Chinese theaters accomplished similar goals. But starting in 1875, the police's enforcement of these ordinances became a prominent excuse for assault, sometimes even leading to lethal outcomes.

Between 1875 and the end of 1877, when the third Chinese theater in San Francisco was built, the city police carried out five largescale raids on Chinese theaters. A squad of policemen would surround the theater and bar the doors, in the name of enforcing an ordinance. They would then arrest a large number of Chinese and place them in custody. At the court the Chinese would be fined from $10 to $150 or serve jail time. During the raids the police were often accompanied by reporters who wrote sensational accounts of the action.

By the end of October 1875, the city's Board of Supervisors had approved an ordinance requiring theaters to close by 1 a.m.[26] The ordinance, as the *Chronicle* acknowledged, was explicitly directed at Chinese theaters.[27] To enforce the ordinance, the police captain gathered a dozen officers one evening to raid the theaters and invited reporters to come along. Just after 1:00 a.m., they sounded a shrill whistle, which prompted the audience to scramble out of the theater through doors, windows, and even via adjacent roofs. The officers remained hidden during the stampede, and then moved on to the second theater. There they shut the doors and barred the audience from getting out. The performance came to a halt, and the police captain and officers went to the stage and the dressing rooms to make arrests. Altogether fifteen actors and a dozen audience members were arrested and put in jail.[28] Whereas theaters' violations of the ordinance had previously resulted in fines or the arrest of performers or the proprietor, regular raiding of crowded theaters for ordinance violation was something new.

There was no shortage of ordinances the police could use as excuses to harass Chinese theaters, but the curfew ordinance remained the most convenient and common. In the next raid, in December, searching for concealed weapons was the main purpose, but the pretext remained curfew ordinance violations.[29] The following May, the cubic air ordinance was used to justify large police raids; sixty-two actors were arrested at the theater for this violation.

When passing the ordinances, the Board of Supervisors might not have anticipated the degree to which they could be exploited by the police and harm people. These highly public raids both humiliated and endangered the

Chinese community and kept theater audiences on edge even while enjoying performances. Ultimately, in October 1876, tragedy struck, perhaps connected with the high levels of anxiety.[30] At the Royal Chinese Theater (on the north side of Jackson Street), a false alarm of "fire" was called during a well-attended benefit performance, with an estimated crowd of two to three thousand in attendance. The audience panicked and all rushed for the single exit, causing the floor to collapse. Nineteen people were injured, and twenty died. This horrible incident attracted wide attention and reinforced the negative image of a "restless torrent of yellow humanity" about Chinese, as the *New York Tribune* laid out in an "objective" analysis of the incident.[31] Afterward, the city added building regulations to ensure the sound structure of theaters.

At times, anxiety was expressed in fights within the community. Internal discord frequently arose in the community. The competition between the two theaters over division of patronage or performer contracts could cause friction. As public spaces, Chinese theaters could also hardly avoid the fate of being the places where members of rival groups sought to solve their disagreements or grudges or inflict harm on opponents. Fights broke out in the theaters, and arrests were made from time to time.[32]

The Third Chinese Theater: Poo Hing Hee Yung (Luk Suhn Fung) on Washington Street

In 1877, due to the increase of Chinese migration, the number of Chinese theaters in the Americas increased. New theaters were reported in places such as Panama, Lima, and Havana.[33] In San Francisco, community discord, city ordinances, police raids, and anti-Chinese agitation didn't stop Chinese theater. Not only did the community erect a new building for its third Chinese theater but it was extravagant, in response to intense interest. The *Chronicle* first reported the plan on July 22, 1877: "[A] new Chinese Theater is about to be erected on Washington Street, between Dupont and Stockton, at a cost of $30,000. It . . . will rank a grade higher in respectability and be devoted to the production of the standard heathen operas at the outset."[34]

In a twist of fate, this unremarkable but buoyant report of the prospective Chinese theater appeared just one day before the infamous San Francisco Riot of 1877, a socialist rally of eight thousand people at the sandlots near city hall that degenerated into a three-day riot against the city's Chinese community. After several weeks of rumors of impending violence, a mob of six to seven hundred rioters set Chinese laundries on fire, stoned the Chinese mission, and threatened to burn the dock of the Pacific Mail Steamship Company, a major transpacific firm.[35] It caused $100,000 in damage to the Chinese community, and many Chinese were injured or killed. The riot is now considered a historic turning point, as it established the importance of the fledgling Workingmen's Party and its leader Denis Kearney, an Irish immigrant. The associated slogan "The Chinese Must Go" was used to mobilize hatred and violence, and the party continued to hold large rallies. On October 16, Kearney published a Workingmen's Party manifesto in the *Chronicle*, proclaiming, "To an American, death is preferable to life on par with the Chinaman."[36] A week later, the State Senate called on the US Congress to recommend a ban on Chinese immigration and to abrogate the treaty with China.[37] On November 3, the leaders of the Chinese Six Companies wrote to the mayor of San Francisco, calling attention to "large gatherings of the idle and irresponsible elements. . . . [T]he population of this city are nightly addressed in the open streets by speakers who use the most violent, inflammatory, and incendiary language, threatening in plainest term to burn and pillage the Chinese quarter and kill our people unless . . . we leave this 'free republic.'"[38] The committee leaders warned that, if attacked, they would not be able to restrain Chinese residents from defending themselves.

Despite the continuance of the intense threat and anxiety, however, the new Chinese theater was built. In August, the *Baltimore Sun* reported, "A new Chinese theater is to be erected in Washington street, San Francisco. The present theatre is always crowded and their increasing numbers require the new structure."[39] In mid-October, the *Chronicle* reported with enthusiasm that the new theater "will greatly surpass the dimensions of either of the two on Jackson street, and will be finished in superior style, approaching the fashion of some of the pretentious theatres patronized by the civilized community . . . The theater manager, Ah Wang, is now on the way hither from Hong Kong, and will arrive by the next steamer with a full company of carefully selected artists numbering ninety-two actors and six cooks."[40]

On December 4, four months after the July 1877 riot, the theater on Washington Street held its inaugural performance. The *Daily Alta California* gave a lengthy report:

> A new Chinese theatre, "Yung Kee Luck Shun Fun," opened last night at the corner of Church Alley and Washington Street, between Dupont and Stockton. It is understood that Tom Poy, Pin Choo and others are the head of the company which is name Poo Hing Hee Yung. The land is owned by Dr. Stout, who leased it to Ah Fook Wing for five years. The theater company sublease from Wing. Their building is substantial brick, 42 × 108, with thirty-two feet clear in the ceiling. The theater was planned by Laver & Curlett, architects and built by John E. McFadden, contractor. The interior is arranged in modern style, gallery and hanging gallery. . . . Another feature of the interior, are the four octagon ventilators, twelve feet in diameter, and as many high, from the ceiling to the roof. . . . The stage is thirty feet deep; above it is a Joss Temple, and underneath, in the basement, are the

property rooms. Looking from the Joss House to the stage, is a window, through which the tumblers perform the skillful feat of turning to the stage below, a distance of about twenty-three feet. It is the intention to fresco the interior. The entire building is supplied with water and gas. It will seat 1500 persons, and accommodate 500 more by standing room. The entire cost has been about $16,000. The company engaged numbers nearly a hundred members, and formerly played at the theater on the south side of Jackson street. Burke is the special officer employed at this new theater. The schedule of prices at the Theatre is both sagacious and equitable. The price of admission is reduced with each hour of the progress of the performance, until, as it approaches the termination, a visitor can enter for ten cents. In this way the box office catches a great deal of patronage, which it would not if the full price was demanded throughout the evening. It is understood that the Theatre is largely patronized by Chinese business men, as well as their countrymen of the common sort. The Chinese Theatre is always a source of curiosity to visitors from abroad.[41]

All the major newspapers in San Francisco reported in detail on the modern features of the new, grand theater. Some also recognized its implication—the Chinese "mean to stay there some time longer" as the *Jewish Messenger* concluded.[42] The land was leased to the theater proprietors at $350 a month for five years, and they could buy it for $60,000 when the lease was up.[43] Safety was a grave concern for both the city and the community; the tragedy at the Royal Chinese Theatre of the previous October was still fresh in people's minds because of recent events commemorating its anniversary. The new design had various safety features. A special design feature was two private boxes with cushioned seats, a curtain, and an entrance, for white visitors. The theater had high-profile architects: Laver & Curlett. Augustus Laver, a Canadian, was then one of the most celebrated architects on the Pacific coast and the designer of city hall in San Francisco, then under construction; William Curlett, from Ireland, joined Laver as a partner in 1877 and designed many extravagant mansions.[44] The following year he would design a mansion on Nob Hill for Charles Crocker, a railroad tycoon, and later many public and bank buildings in the city. This project raised Chinese theaters' respectability. In January, the city granted the theater special permission to erect two lamps and lampposts on the outer edge of the sidewalk in front of the theater.[45] The new theater sought to raise its visibility, literally and symbolically.

Noticeably missing from the news reports, however, were the festivities and extravagant banquet usually associated with the inauguration of a new Chinese theater. Built in the shadow of the anti-Chinese riots, the new theater was not ostentatious about its grandiosity or the richness of its offerings. The *Chronicle* noted only that opening night was crowded with the Chinatown elite and performed the auspicious *Six Warlords*; the *San Francisco Examiner* even reported that the audience was quite small.[46] The lack of fanfare and the chilly reception of the third theater's inauguration beyond the Chinese community were in sharp contrast to those of Hing Chuen Yuen in 1868 and Sing Ping Yuen in 1874, when the houses' openings were crowded with the city's dignitaries as honored guests. Nevertheless, the fact remained that amid the anti-Chinese hostility, the community inaugurated a third grand Chinese theater with a more modern and stylish design. The new theater's name was given different spellings: Poo Hing Hee Yung, Yung Kee Luck Shun Fun, Look Sun Foong, Luk Suhn Fung, and in Chinese 禄新鳳.

The newspapers reported on a ritual ceremony held privately, in the early morning of the opening day. The *Examiner* wrote:

> [The Chinese] believe that the moment a building is turned into a show-house it becomes filled with evil spirits, white, red, black and yellow, and that if any person not a member of the theatrical Company should visit the place before the Company gave an expurgatorious performance, the spirits would throw an evil spell before him, and that within a year he would die a violent death. The members of the Company, in order to [exorcise] the evil one, at four o'clock yesterday morning gave an initial performance, which lasted one hour. The actors were all stripped to the waist, and had their faces and bodies painted in livid colors, to frighten away the evil spirits, who, it is said, flee from the building at such a sight, and watch the players from the windows and the doors. When the performance drew to a close, the head player made the announcement that the house was cleared of spirits and that it was ready for opening. This fact was made known by posters on the dead walls, and at seven o'clock the theater was opened without further ceremony.[47]

This ceremony was typically performed prior to the premiere of a troupe at a new location. A ritual to expunge evil spirits, the ceremony is called "Sacrifice to the White Tiger," a "break stage" ceremony to fend off disaster. It was based on the belief that if the disaster spirit is allowed to manifest itself, misfortune or accidents will follow. Given the violence and threat that the community had faced in recent months, the ceremony had a broader goal: to receive the benediction of the deities for a prosperous and peaceful life. An important function of Cantonese opera was to seek protection and blessings from the deities for the community.

Luk Suhn Fung placed an advertisement in the classified ads in the "Amusements" section of the *Chronicle* on December 13, highlighting its cast of great acrobats, and listing prices for general admission (50 cents) and boxes (two dollars and 50 cents). It was not the only Chinese theater to advertise that day. Above it was the Royal Chinese Theater's advertisement, promising the well-known and glamorous opera *Six Warlords*.

Although the printing of advertisements for Chinese theaters was not new to the *Chronicle*—in 1870 it ran an advertisement of Chinese theater for the old Union Theatre—the appearance of a pair of Chinese-run commercial Chinese theaters together was unprecedented.[48] They joined the advertisements in the "Amusements" section for the usual five to six San Francisco theatrical venues, such as the California Theatre, Maguire's Opera House, and so on. But just as remarkable, this pair of ads disappeared after only one day, a sharp contrast with the common practice of multiday advertising. The short-lived Chinese theater ads after the 1877 riot remind us that the "Amusements" section in the newspapers was, after all, a space of privilege that signaled legitimacy. Only three years previously, the newspaper *Morning Call*, after reviewing San Francisco's Chinese theaters, scornfully warned that the "Amusements" section would not allow such illegitimate theaters to advertise anytime soon: "The day may come when Hong Ting Yuen may form a 'side head' under the title of 'amusements' in the daily press. . . . [B]ut that day is at present a few centuries down the dim vista of futurity."[49] The appearance of a pair of Chinese theater ads in December 1877 ran counter to the intense hostility toward the Chinese and the political climate, as reflected plentifully in other sections of the *Chronicle*. Nevertheless Luk Suhn Fung tried again. On January 26, 1878, the advertisement for the new theater reappeared but again disappeared after just one day. The Workingmen's Party was acquiring political clout, its members were elected city mayors of both Oakland and Sacramento, and the party held its first state convention on January.[50]

In its first months all reports on the new Chinese theater were infused with more mockery and ridicule than usual. San Francisco's newspapers embraced anti-Chinese rhetoric, even if they disliked Kearney. The *Chronicle* reprinted a piece from the *Stockton Independent* with the title "Encouraging Lawlessness."

[A] portion of the press of San Francisco seem disposed to encouraging [Kearney] in his wild schemes, and apparently for the purpose of getting the approval and support of him and his followers, they are willing to pander to the vanity and ambition for notoriety of a man whose every utterance shows him to be either an idiot or maniac. Every sensible person will admit that the field for labor in this State is limited, and that the Chinese are filling many positions that would gladly be taken by white men, but Kearney and his crowd have not suggested any way to remove the Chinese except by mob force.[51]

With more newspapers and politicians in California and elsewhere adopting this stance, the anti-Chinese agenda quickly grew from a local initiative to a national platform. This outside hostility made Chinese theaters even more crucial for the inhabitants of the Chinese community. There, they could find not only pleasure but also belonging. The collective experience engendered strength that the individuals could harness for themselves.

In subsequent months few details about the new theater and its performance were reported in English-language newspapers. On the other hand, the Royal Chinese Theatre on Jackson Street, still the largest venue, received renewed attention as a result of an article about San Francisco's Chinese quarter by Miriam Leslie (the wife of the publisher Frank Leslie, discussed previously), published in March 1878. It appeared in the family's new, cheaper magazine, *Frank Leslie's Popular Monthly*. Along with a reprint of the "Coming Man" woodblock engraving of 1870 (see fig. 4.1) and amid mostly unfavorable observations about the theater, the article mentions the ticket pricing and class: "The drama is one of the greatest luxuries of the Chinaman, who frequents it constantly when in funds; nor does this imply great wealth, since the admission fee is two bits—twenty-five cents at the beginning, fifteen cents toward the middle, and only ten cents near the end of the performance."[52] The fantastic world of the opera stage was accessible to ordinary audiences of modest means, as we have seen with Ah Quin. The historian Yong Chen writes, "The theater, which was open during the daytime and until late at night, was a convenient place for Chinese immigrants to recuperate from their daily toil. In the cozy environment of the theater hall that often recalled a familiar past, they could also forget hostile realities."[53]

Miriam Leslie's article came from her book *California: A Pleasure Trip from Gotham to the Golden Gate*, a travelogue of the famous "Across the Continent" excursion of Leslie and company from 1876 to 1878.[54] Her use of Becker's old engraving of the Chinese theater reflected its significance in the popular imagination. Several months later, in the August 24, 1878 issue, the weekly *Frank Leslie's Illustrated Newspaper* published another account of the Chinese theater, this time with two arresting illustrations of the theater stage: "Interior of the Royal China [*sic*] Theatre during a Performance," and "The All-Night Supper Spread in the Dressing Room of the Royal Theatre."[55] Drawn by the staff artists Henry Alexander Ogden and Walter Yeager, these two images are necessarily fantasized versions of Chinese theater. In viewing them, we must understand that the illustrators depicted Chinese theatrical scenes according to preconceived, racialized notions. This is why it is good to keep the photographs in figure 5.2 in mind.

The first features at its center are the whirling movement of a majestic bearded warrior, in armor with headdress, flags, and long pheasant feathers and holding a lance (fig. 5.3a). The stage is crowded with four energetic soldiers waving their red-tasselled spears, and a dignified mandarin. At the back of the stage are five musicians. Next to the seated musician closest to the center is a percussion instrument unique to Cantonese opera during this era—*shagu*, a drum—placed on a wooden stand (see table 4.2).[56] That musician

FIGURE 5.3A Henry Alexander Ogden and Walter Yeager. "Interior of the Royal China [*sic*] Theatre During a Performance." *Frank Leslie's Illustrated Newspaper*, August 24, 1878, 421–22.

plays a *yueqin*; beside him, another musician with crossed legs played the *sanxian* (three-stringed lute). The pair of large cymbals held by the musician off to the side was also characteristic of Cantonese opera accompaniment. The house is shown as full, with the higher of the two balconies occupied by women. This illustration depicts a vivid opera scene. The accompanying commentary provided a narrative about the "God of War" and the warriors, which further enlivened the illustration: "the God of War himself . . . comes prancing and stamping out, screaming at the highest grating pitch of his voice, and performs a pirouette on one leg exactly in the centre of the stage. . . . [T]he half-naked warriors chase each other round and round the stage, throwing double and triple somersaults high in the air, forward and backward, alighting on their feet, on their hands, and flat on their backs with their feet stretched out straight and their arms close on their sides."[57]

The second picture depicts nine performers standing around a green room over a late meal, with a roast pig on the center table and fancy lanterns hanging from the ceiling (fig. 5.3b). It is likely a composite of different spaces and people, both real and imagined. Nevertheless, a few items in the picture are quite real: the actor with the painted face at the center, the long beard accessory hanging on the wall, and the Manchu horse-hoof shoes of an actor (second from left) in a female role. Most peculiar is the actor on the right, with an animal mask and long white beard.[58] The mask recalls the cow headpiece

FIGURE 5.3B Henry Alexander Ogden and Walter Yeager. "The All-Night Supper Spread in the Dressing-Room of the Royal China [*sic*] Theatre." *Frank Leslie's Illustrated Newspaper*, August 24, 1878, 421–22.

at the opening of Sing Ping Yuen theater, discussed in chapter 4. These two illustrations reappeared in many later publications and played an important role in shaping visual representation of Chinese theater during this decade.

With the photographs of contemporary Cantonese opera actors shown in figure 5.2 in mind, we can see that these illustrations are distorted, racialized, and sensationalized depictions of Chinese performers and the opera stage. They were fantasies of grotesque scenes. In great contrast to this depiction, Chinese theaters in San Francisco were staffed with professional opera troupes rather than being performance venues for circuslike, rowdy shows as these illustrations would have the readers believe. Yet for American general readers, these illustrations of racialized performances and actors made the Chinese theaters in California "real" and tantalizing.

In wide circulation, reports about the eye-catching scenes and the novelty of Chinese theater contributed to San Francisco's reputation as a picturesque megacity of the West, a worldly urban center. Rising to the attention of the metropolis, Chinese theater seemed to be a cosmopolitan feature. Under the heading "The Demand for a Chinese Theatre in Boson," a critic for the *Boston*

Daily Globe opined in 1877 that establishing a Chinese theater would be "a step forward in the march of progress." The writer advocates for establishing a Chinese theater in Boston as a matter of civil rights, providing equal opportunities for diverse populations. It also emphasizes that the new sensations and scenes in Chinese theater could help American drama overcome the limitations imposed by traditional stage conventions. Situating a Chinese theater in American soil, the writer notes,

> It would be simply carrying out the principles of the civil rights law, giving equal privileges to men of all colors and races. We have German theatrical often; French theatricals occasionally; Italian opera comes semi-occasionally; we have been dosed with the Ethiopian drama and the Irish drama, ad nauseam; even the Swedes have had their innings and I see no reason why the oldest nation on earth should not have a chance to display its dramatic talents. In San Francisco there is at least one regular Chinese theatre, and as [Chinese] is rapidly becoming an established institution with us, why shouldn't he have his theatre.

> [There] would be something novel and original about the style of play presented, which Mr. Boucicault might find worth adapting for his next comedy, and embellishing as he does everything he adapts. Perhaps, also, a new style of dramatic construction might be introduced. Hitherto they have been hampered, cabined, cribbed, confined, by the exigencies of the established tradition of the stage, and have been unable to present to the five or six acts deemed admissible anything more than an outline of history and a series of isolated tableaux of salient points in the episodes chosen.[59]

In a lighthearted, pleading tone, the author advocates for the opening of a Chinese theater in Boston, foreseeing that its presence could catalyze a new and original approach to drama, injecting vitality into Western theatrical arts. Another publication echoed a similar happening in Berlin. In June 1878, the *Los Angeles Herald* reported that Berlin would have its Chinese play with "scenery, dresses, and all" and even a translation of the play.[60]

Together, these articles illustrate the widespread acknowledgment of the cosmopolitan model set by San Francisco. The establishment of commercial Chinese theaters, one after another over ten years, totaling three by 1878—each distinguished by opulent designs and enlivened by the continuous arrival of opera troupes—solidified their distinct role as a premier attraction in the city's theatrical culture. The distinctive characteristics of Chinese theater became inseparable from the city's entertainment landscape. Meanwhile they were also seamlessly integrated into the urban scene, as we will see in the next chapter.

CHAPTER 6

Education, Diplomacy Culture, and the Fourth Theater

As the 1870s drew to a close, San Francisco saw the opening of a fourth Chinese theater. Whereas the earlier Chinese theaters were built in response to the growth of the city and the prosperity of the Chinese community, a recent significant diplomatic event led to a cultural milieu that paved the way. This was the arrival of the first consul of the Qing government in 1878. The enthusiasm and grand ceremonial reception accorded the Chinese minister and his delegation captivated the public's imagination and kindled appreciation for Chinese civilization and culture. It effectively invigorated Chinese performing culture in San Francisco and contributed positively to the establishment of the fourth theater. To begin, we will consider an interaction between Chinese theater and the city's Chinese mission, which reflected Chinese integration in the urban scene, as well as the musical talent and environment of second-generation Chinese (born in the United States).

Performances at the Methodist Chinese Mission School and the Second Generation

The Reverend Otis Gibson, a missionary to China in 1855–65, led the Missionary Society of the Methodist Episcopal Church beginning in 1870 and was an outspoken critic of the anti-Chinese movement. In less than a year after the Sandlot riot, he moved the annual celebration of the mission school to the public space most representative of the Chinese community. In June 1878, the newest Chinese theater (on Washington Street) hosted an anniversary celebration of the Methodist Chinese Mission School. At the ceremony, seventy-five students, both male and female, were seated on the stage, where the sign "China for Christ" was hung prominently. The *Chronicle* reported, "Half of the large auditorium was reserved for Caucasians and every seat was filled with ladies and gentlemen."[1] The rest of the auditorium and the galleries were filled with Chinese, reported the paper, suggesting the success of the missionary work. The performance, primarily in English, included essays, orations, recitation, dialogues, hymns and songs, and instrumental music. The reporter proudly noted,

> Standing near the door when the Sabbath-school songs were being sung, it was noticeable that nearly every Chinaman would hum the air in a very correct manner. The recitations, dialogues, etc., were nearly perfect, not the slightest hesitation being shown in their delivery, and several of the pupils spoke English with a purity that was remarkable.... Some of the solo singing was so good that it would have been difficult to have distinguished that an American was not singing.[2]

The occasion prompted a *Daily Alta California* reporter to marvel at the power of education, particularly in music: "[T]he musical part of the programme, especially to those who were only accustomed to the nasal twangs and bagpipe noise of the ordinary Chinamen, demonstrated clearly the fact that with proper training, this race possessed voices of melody and power."[3] After praising the performance of several individuals, the reporter concluded,

> It would also be difficult to find among our American schools much better signing than was given by these Chinese scholars in the hymns, "Pull for the Shore," "Dark is the Night," The Gospel Ship," "The Clear," "Precious Jewels," The Bell Doth Toll" . . . and "The Sweet By and By." Nor must there be forgotten "The Whistling Farmer Boy," in which the Chinamen puckered up their lips and whistled in harmony, nor the solo, "Outside the Gates," of a Chinese maiden which developed the most extraordinary notes of sweetness and volume.[4]

The report concluded with a student's direct rebuttal of the anti-Chinese movement: "George Howe, an American citizen, but with Chinese blood in his veins, made a brief address, in which he argued that anti-American[s] were worse than Chinese. . . . [H]e thought Kearney, that barking dog, had done more to injure labor and reduce wages than all the Chinamen." Indeed, during the infamous 1877 Sandlot riot, the Chinese Missionary School was stoned.

The celebration was a notable social event for San Francisco, especially for those who disagreed with the anti-Chinese movement. Although the Missionary School's annual events were usually held at the schoolhouse, a special point was being made by moving it to Chinese theater at this difficulty time for the community.[5] Even if indirectly, it also legitimized the new Chinese theater in the eyes of society. In his annual report to the Missionary Society of Methodist Episcopal Church, Rev. Gibson made a special note of this: "The anniversary of these schools was held in the month of June in the Chinese theater. The scholars acquitted themselves so well and manfully as to win favorable criticisms, even from a hostile press."[6] This episode reveals the influence of missionary work, as well as the growing significance of youth education in the Chinese community. One report points out that Chinese youth did not attend public school; they were excluded from any but the colored school: "Here is an instance of taxation without representation. It is estimated that the Chinese in San Francisco pay one-twentieth of the total taxation, amounting this year [1867] to $120,000, and of this amount $14,000 goes to the school fund."[7]

According to available data, as early as 1867 San Francisco had 179 Chinese between the ages of five and fifteen. The Chinese community also offered Chinese youth the opportunity to learn Chinese music. In early 1877, the *Chronicle* reported the opening of a music conservatory by Lee Tom to teach Chinese instruments to youngsters, possibly to prepare them for Chinese opera.[8] On the second floor of a building on Washington Street, students learned Chinese instruments. Reporters were invited to attend their rehearsals. This reporter remarked insightfully about the flow of the music: "The principle of Chinese music is not generally understood, and an explanation will prove interesting. It is governed by no rules of time whatever, but is simply adapted to the narrative or drama which it accompanies, or the varying depths of emotion which it is intended to express." References to the teaching of Chinese music instruments in the community, as in this report, are quite rare. However, they are an important reminder that, even if little documented, vibrant music making in the community, as in Chinese theaters, led to the development of homegrown talent and amateur music making. The music making of the second generation, whether Christian church hymns or Chinese tunes, also contributed to the soundscape of Chinese communities in everyday life.

The First Chinese Minister

In the summer of 1878, the first minister to the United States from China, Chen Lanbin (Chun Lan Pin), arrived in San Francisco with more than two dozen officials in his entourage, on his way to Washington, DC to establish the first Chinese embassy in the United States. The arrival of the first diplomatic corps from the Qing empire attracted national attention. A seasoned and distinguished diplomat and statesman, Chen was widely expected to hold a stern position concerning treaty agreements and to discuss the restrictions on Chinese immigration with the US government. The *Chronicle* noted the excitement at his arrival: "[T]he temples, restaurants, Company headquarters and mercantile houses [were all flying] red, blue and piebald dragons in the air suggesting a carnival of delirium tremens on a colossal scale."[9] Americans were awed but bewildered by the first official sent from the Chinese empire.[10]

The grand welcome in San Francisco reflected the utmost respect for a dignified mandarin representing the Qing empire. In the official chronicle, *Brief Record of a Mission to America*, Minister Chen wrote of the historical moment. It provides a rare Chinese perspective of this important event.

> The steamship passed Oakland and finally arrived San Francisco. By then it was already 9. The secretary of Sam Yip Huiguan, Liang Nan, came on board, informing us that the directors of the Six Companies had prepared the horse carriages to receive us, and asked us to remain on the ship. At 11, the directors and business managers, over a hundred of them, came on board. More than ten of them were dressed in the imperial Qing court robes with surcoats of mandarin badges, while others dressed in the formal long robes with jackets. They stood in line at the wharf to receive us. The wharf was crowded with an audience of men and women, both Chinese and Westerners, some of whom had traveled by train for hundreds of miles to get a good view of the dignified and impressive manner of the empire of Han. After landing, we saw that the yellow flags of the Qing court with the emblem of the azure dragon were already flying on top of the Chinese huiguan and hotels. We stayed at the Plaza Hotel on Montgomery Street (where the Qing dragon flag was also erected).[11]

The Review of the Times, a Chinese-language newspaper published by a missionary in Shanghai, reported,

> Chinese merchants and huiguan hired forty carriages to receive the minister; the Palace Hotel prepared another eighteen carriages. The minister and company proceeded toward the hotel. The procession had the minister in the largest carriage at the center, on his sides were carriages with consular and secretaries. All dressed in official attire, the ceremonial was grand and impressive, while Chinese merchants waited for the procession respectfully and police guarded the way. San Franciscans gathered to watch the procession. While intermittently there are outlaws looking with hostility, they don't dare to make a move, because of the close control. There are also Westerners who lift their hats and salute.[12]

The activities of the Chinese delegation in San Francisco were reported in great detail in all major newspapers. Minister Chen received a large number of visitors, toured around the Chinese quarter and institutions, and visited a photo studio, where photos of the entire party were taken. The *Chronicle* opined that "the sending of this imposing Embassy" was to counteract the growing aversion to Chinese laborers.[13]

Chen traveled to the East Coast via railroad, where the train's passing through cities was "heralded by the telegraphs for several days."[14] People gathered to catch a glimpse of the Chinese minister often pushing to the edge of station platforms. Because he was a high-class mandarin, his etiquette,

FIGURE 6.1 "His Excellency Chun Lan Pin." 1878. Chen Lanbin is depicted in the photograph at the top center. California Historical Society.

wardrobe, and official garments—as well as the symbolism of color and decoration on his robes and jackets—were scrutinized closely. Even though the minister did not stop in Chicago, a report took up more than half of page 5 in the *Chicago Daily Tribune*, with descriptions and analyses as well as interviews with his entourage, providing vivid depictions of the crowded train stations.[15] The *New York Herald* also ran a long report with the headline "The Youngest Nation to the Oldest."[16] The delegation met with President Rutherford B. Hayes in Washington in September and was feted with a ceremony akin to those for "other foreign Ministers."[17] Minister Chen's arrival drew significant attention to all things Chinese: culture, history, trade, and the transpacific connection. The weight of civilization was clearly the undertone. This prompted many Americans to have a closer look at, and even develop more respect for, their own Chinese theaters. For their part, Chinese theaters tried to recalibrate their image in order to capitalize on the attention. Two months after Minister Chen left San Francisco, Chinese opera would appear on the stage of the city's largest opera house.

Quon San Yok at the Grand Opera House

The biggest news for San Francisco's theatrical world in the autumn of 1878 was a new troupe from China, Quon San Yok 崑山玉, one of the opera troupes on the 1875 list from Giqing Gongsuo printed in the *Oriental*. Its leading actor, although unnamed, attracted much attention, as his celebrity status was reflected in the theater's special arrangement for him: a salary of $7,000 (the equivalent of $219,923 in 2024) for each of the two years in his contract; a servant; and a room decorated with carpets and American furniture that cost $180. On October 18, the New Chinese Theater (Sing Ping Yuen) on Jackson Street (the south side) reopened with this new troupe. The opening, however, was marred by commotions caused by the rival theater across the street (now named the Royal Chinese Theatre), causing one offender to be jailed for 120 days.[18] The rivalry was due to both business competition and family associations between Sam Yup (New Chinese Theater) and See Yup (Royal Chinese Theater).

Four weeks later, Quon San Yok also appeared on the stage of the Grand Opera House, then the largest theater in San Francisco, for three nights and one matinee. Built in 1876, the opera house seated three thousand, with twelve proscenium boxes and twenty-two mezzanine boxes. Advertisements for Quon San Yok's performance at the Grand Opera House appeared in major newspapers for five consecutive days, updated with new content daily. The notability garnered by the visit of the first Chinese minister could be seen in the advertisements. In particular, the advertisements used titles such as "Imperial Troupe" or "Imperial Theater, Canton, China" to underscore the authenticity of the presentation. Although many newspapers printed the opera house's advertisements, the *Daily Alta California*'s design was most eye catching. In large font, the troupe name stands out amid the sea of classified ads (fig. 6.2). Under the "Amusements" section, this lengthy ad took up a full third of the newspaper column. The smaller print reads:

> The managers of the above Company have the honor to announce to the citizens of the States of America that after a great deal of trouble and through the intercession of high officials in the Empire of China, they have succeed, at a great outlay, in obtaining the "Quon San Yok" Company of Dramatic, Acrobatic and Gymnastic Performers, from Government Theatre, Canton, where they have lately exhibited their marvelous feats before the Emperor and full Court, as well as the Council of Foreign Ambassadors there assembled. . . . As they are under contract to appear in Paris before the close of the present year, their stay in San Francisco is limited to a few days only.[19]

Drawing from the public's fascination with the recent arrival of the minister, the ad takes a ceremonious tone with a diplomatic-sounding form of address. The company sought to distinguish itself by suggesting the troupe's official affiliations, adding value to its artistry while suggesting exclusivity and status. The same entertainment enjoyed by elites and aristocrats from China to Paris could now be had at the opera house, the ad promised.

The depiction of the interior of the Grand Opera House (fig. 6.3) provides a sense of the space where Quon San Yok performed in November

ANNOUNCEMENT
Extraordinary.

THE GREAT

QUON SAN YOK

Dramatic, Acrobatic and Gymnastic Company,

FROM THE

IMPERIAL THEATRE,
CANTON, (CHINA,)

Comprising the largest and most wonderful Company of First-class Male and Female Artists that have ever left

THE FLOWERY KINGDOM.

The managers of the above Company have the honor to announce to the citizens of the United States of America that after a great deal of trouble and through the intercession of high officials in the Empire of China, they have succeeded, at a great outlay, in obtaining the "QUON SAN YOK" Company of Dramatic, Acrobatic and Gymnastic Performers, from the Government Theatre, Canton, where they have lately exhibited their marvelous feats before the Emperor and full Court, as well as the Council of Foreign Ambassadors there assembled. This Troupe is the largest (forty in number) that has ever left China. They are all artists of the highest rank and bear no resemblance to the mountebanks and common street performers that have preceded them to this country. Their costumes are the richest ever seen out of China, and are all new, having been made expressly for this tour. As they are under contract to appear in Paris before the close of the present year, their stay in San Francisco must be limited to a few days only. They have the honor to announce that they have secured the

GRAND OPERA HOUSE,

As the only fitting place for the proper display of their

GRAND ACTS
AND
GORGEOUS COSTUMES,

And that they will appear for

Three Nights Only
AND
ONE MATINEE,

COMMENCING ON

WEDNESDAY EVENING...........NOV. 13

In consequence of the immense outlay necessary to introduce this great novelty to the American public, the prices will be :

Dress Circle, Orchestra and Parquette.........$1 00
  Reserved Seats, 50 cents extra.
Mazonein Boxes.............................$6 00
Private Boxes....................$8, 10 and 12 00
Balcony...............................50 Cents
Gallery..................................25 Cents

Box Office open daily at the Grand Opera House, where seats and boxes may be secured.

Admission to Matinee, 50 Cents,

To all parts of the House.

Reserved Seats, 35 cents extra.

LAI KING,
LEE SING,
WONG TAI,
no12-1   Directors.

FIGURE 6.2 Advertisement for the Quon San Yok company at the Grand Opera House, *Daily Alta California*, November 12, 1878.

1878. Leveraging the respect that Americans felt for the ancient Chinese civilization was an effective strategy for the troupe. The reception at the Grand Opera House was enthusiastic; as the *Daily Alta California* reported after the first evening, "[The company] gave a very novel entertainment at this theatre last evening, which afforded a great deal of amusement to a very respectably-sized audience, which will no doubt be greatly increased this evening."[20] The highest price for the private boxes was twelve dollars. And the wide range of ticket prices catered to theatergoers of all classes: the general seats were one dollar, and the lowest price was twenty-five cents for the gallery, ensuring a large audience. The day after the last performance, the *Daily Alta California* reported that Quon San Yok had departed for the east. The *Chronicle*, too, noted, "Their acrobatic feats are very neatly and skillfully done. They proceeded hence to Europe."[21] In fact the troupe did not go to Paris but returned to the New Chinese theater on Jackson Street.[22] Yet the illusion of the Chinese troupe's appeal in Europe was part of its allure.

Ah Quin, who returned to San Francisco in December 1878, visited Quon San Yok regularly. His personal accounts might seem so trivial as to be on the verge of insignificance. Yet the frequency and regularity of his visits, as he recorded in the diary, connect the mapping of the performing activities of the theaters to an individual whom these performances served. Indeed, he attended them all. The theater establishment and its offerings were an

FIGURE 6.3 The interior of the Grand Opera House, San Francisco. Date unknown. British Library Common.

essential part of the daily life of the community, whose residents such as Ah
Quin hustled and bustled, gaining various kinds of necessities and entertainment. The performances and socialization that theaters provided gave
residents like him immense enjoyment, comfort, and inspiration, a crucial
reason for the theaters' popularity. In fact, it is through Ah Quin's words that
we witness, in the prologue, the grandiose opening of the next theater. The
activities and events—and the competition—of Chinese theaters discussed in
the following sections constitutes the backdrop to Ah Quin's lived experience
of 1878–80 in San Francisco.

A Merger: Wing Tie Ping Theater

A new type of plaintiff appeared in the Fifteenth District Court in 1879.
They were Chinese actors and theater proprietors trying to settle disputes
regarding contracts and theater properties. In February, the proprietors (Ug
Fook et al.) of Poo Hing Hee Yung (Luk Suhn Fung) on Washington Street
sought to stop the star actor Leong Yow from performing at the Royal Chinese
Theatre or any other theater, citing an unfinished contract. Leong Yow, however, claimed he had not been paid. The judge first ruled for the proprietors
but later dismissed the case. The legal proceeding made Leong Yow famous:
the amount of his salary, $6,700 per year (the equivalent of $210,497 in 2024),
was made public.[23] The news spread nationwide, prompting mockery of its
incongruence with stereotypically cheap Chinese labor.

Given the intense rivalry among the theaters, this discord was the tip
of the iceberg. In June the previous year, the Royal Chinese Theatre was
accused of imprisoning those of its performers who had signed a contract
to perform with a rival theater. The court ruled the Royal Chinese Theatre
in the wrong, and that it owed significant damages to both the performers
and the rival theater. A similar incident happened in March 1879: a theater
locked performers in the green room to keep them from appearing in a rival
theater, though they were released quickly.[24]

To address the vicious competition, a merger was proposed by spring 1879.
The *Chronicle* reported the merger, noting that, although the community had
supported "three theaters—the Yew Hin Look, or Royal Chinese Theatre, on
the north side of Jackson Street, between Kearny and Dupont streets, the Quan
Sun Yoke or Gem of Mount Quan, on the south side of Jackson street, and
the Look Sun Fung or Peacock, on Washington street, between Dupont and
Stockton," the expenses of all three had exceeded their profits. Therefore "the
three theaters will be under the control of the Wing Ti Ping, or 'The Company
of Eternal Peace.'"[25] As a result of the merger, many actors were let go.

A public notice appeared in the *Daily Alta California* on June 28, and for
the subsequent month (fig. 6.4). To cut costs, the new company dismissed

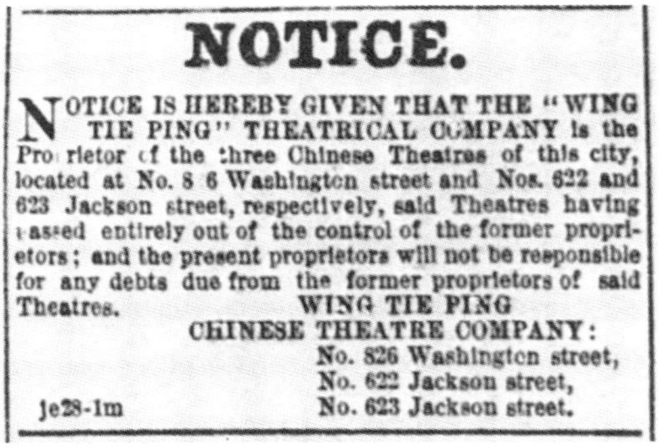

FIGURE 6.4 Notice of the merger of San Francisco's Chinese theaters to one theater, Wing Tie Ping, *Daily Alta California*, July–August 1879.

NOTICE.

NOTICE IS HEREBY GIVEN THAT THE "WING TIE PING" THEATRICAL COMPANY is the Proprietor of the three Chinese Theatres of this city, located at No. 8 6 Washington street and Nos. 622 and 623 Jackson street, respectively, said Theatres having passed entirely out of the control of the former proprietors; and the present proprietors will not be responsible for any debts due from the former proprietors of said Theatres.
WING TIE PING
CHINESE THEATRE COMPANY:
No. 826 Washington street,
No. 622 Jackson street,
je28-1m   No. 623 Jackson street.

eighty actors, including some expensive star actors. It planned to continue performances at all three theaters but found that it didn't have enough remaining actors for concurrent performances. The theaters consolidated further, retaining only enough actors to perform in each of the three theaters consecutively. On June 19, the first performance based on the new arrangement was expected to take place at one of the theaters on Jackson Street. That afternoon, the discharged actors, numbering one to two hundred, together with their supporters, formed a mob of three hundred that converged on the street to disrupt the performance and stop Wing Tie Ping's monopoly. The riot was called off after leaders in the Chinese community stepped in as mediators, and the police came to maintain order.[26]

The trouble in San Francisco was the gain of theater-loving audiences elsewhere: Sacramento's Chinese theater began to feature celebrated actors; a group of eighty actors arrived in Honolulu with the same name as one of the theaters in San Francisco, Look Sun Fung Company.[27] An advertisement published in the *Pacific Commercial Advertiser* on September 20, 1879 is reproduced in figure 6.5. Given the similarity in the names, it was likely the troupe had been excluded from the merger on their way to China. Since Honolulu had just opened a Chinese theater at the beginning of the year, the arrival of this troupe was understandably welcome. Because Honolulu was on the transpacific route, the lively cultural energy brought by the troupes also helped that city become pivotal as a midway stop for Cantonese opera troupes on transpacific crossings and sustained frequent presentations of Chinese theater. By 1898 Honolulu would have two Chinese theaters.[28]

In San Francisco, however, the monopoly continued to be contested. Dissatisfied by their dismissal from the merger, the star actor Ti Gar Sing and a group of performers sought investment from wealthy merchants.[29] They were soon joined by other top actors disadvantaged by the monopoly. The group quickly acquired the necessary funding and formed a stock company, building a new theater on Washington Street facing Waverly Place.[30] Enterprising star

FIGURE 6.5 Advertisement for the Look Sun Fung company at the Chinese Theatre, Esplanade, *Pacific Commercial Advertiser*, September 20, 1879.

performers were beginning to use their high status as leverage. They were starting to gain notability and could capitalize on their star power.

The consolidation effort of Wing Tie Ping was short lived, but it, too, gained impressive community support. On September 30, 1879, as the construction of the new theater was under way, the Royal Chinese Theatre transformed its space for a festive event with a grand banquet in honor of the birthday of the first Chinese consul general in San Francisco, Chen Shutang 陳樹棠, a former comprador for the China Merchants Steamship Navigation Company in Shanghai. Only five days earlier, Chen Shutang and prominent Chinese merchants had been granted the honor of meeting the former president Ulysses S. Grant on his arrival in San Francisco, returning from a visit to Asia.[31] The meeting was an important victory for the Chinese community, since Grant had publicly declined to meet with Denis Kearney. It was a risky decision for the former president, as his biographer noted:

> General [Irvine] McDowell, commanding the Military Department of the Pacific, gave General Grant a reception. . . . It was while at the house of General McDowell that the delicate question, whether or not General Grant should receive a delegation from the Chinese of San Francisco, was decided. The Chinese are not loved in California, and so, when it was proposed

to present him with an address from the Chinese merchants, there were strong objections from some quarters, for fear that it would give offense to the people of California. When the matter was submitted to General Grant he said that the kindness he had received from the statesmen and rulers of China was so remarkable that he would be only too happy to return it by any courtesy he could show to Chinamen in America. . . . [After their meeting and mutual addresses], there were visits to the theater, and a very pleasant day at Oakland.[32]

No doubt it was the Wing Tie Ping Theater that President Grant visited. He had attended opera performances many times while in China and expressed appreciation for the culture and country. The *New York Times* wrote acerbically about Grant's public humiliation of Kearney, whom most thought Grant would have been wise to court. The *Times* warned, "The news that Gen. Grant has insulted Mr. Denis Kearney, by refusing to receive him, will create such a whirlwind of indignation and will be accepted as so true a revelation of his despotic instincts, that his factitious popularity will vanish at once and forever."[33]

After the victory of the highly publicized meeting with Grant, the consul general's birthday festivities were a full-blown affair. The presentation of Cantonese opera performances was a fitting gesture for Consul General Chen, who was a Cantonese native. The celebration at the theater was attended by three hundred Chinese merchants and their families, as well as a handful of American guests, though no government officials. The theater was decorated with fourteen eight-foot-long scrolls of laudatory verses, silk banners of paintings and large lanterns on the balcony. It also offered opera performances, as well as a twenty-course banquet.[34] Such grand gestures, combining a banquet with opera performances, were a common cultural practice in southern China as expressions of gratitude or marks of respect on celebratory occasions. The spotlight thus also shone on Wing Tie Ping, which hosted the grand event.

The Fourth Chinese Theater: Donn Quai Yuen on Washington Street

Undeterred by the prominence of Wing Tie Ping, the new theater opened its doors on October 12, 1879, and San Francisco had its fourth Chinese opera theater less than three months before the end of the year. The new theater, managed by the actor-manager Ti Gar Sing, broke the monopoly. We have already encountered his name as Dajia Sheng on the Jiqing Gongsuo lists published in *The Oriental* (see figs. 5.1a and 5.1b). ("Ti Gar Sing" reflects the Cantonese dialect, whereas "Dajia Sheng" is Mandarin Pinyin.) An ambitious undertaking, the theater was regarded by the *Daily Evening Bulletin* as "the largest and most aristocratic" of the theaters.[35] The theater was a three-story brick building, 92 feet by 52 feet, with an impressive iron front 35 feet high. It had three balconies, one on each side, with a seating capacity of twenty-five hundred.[36] The construction cost was $40,000.[37] Given the hostile political climate, similar to that surrounding the opening of the third theater two years prior, little fanfare in the English-language press greeted the new theater's arrival. But the opening performance was well attended, with three thousand attendees reported.[38] As usual, the opera *Six Warlords* was performed. Ah Quin recorded in his diary a joyful eyewitness account of the inauguration of the new theater. His term "Luk Quock" refers to *Six Warlords*.

> I go enter the new theatre house Donn Quai Yuen, which is called Goe Quon You, the head Actor is named Sie Kar Sing, then I past in the door, is very hardly most torn me down, the Luk Quock is very nice and happy, and much people cannot get in, It is dismissed at 12:30.

> [I go enter the new theatre house Donn Quai Yuen, which is called Goe Quon You, the head actor is named Tie Kar Sing. Then I passed the door and got in; it was very hard and I was almost torn down by the crowd. The opera Six Warlords was very nice, and made us all happy. Many people could not get in. The theater was dismissed at 12:30.][39]

The press referred to the new theater by several different names during its first few months: Gee Quuen Yung 義群英 (referring to the troupe name in the *Daily Evening Bulletin*), Donn Quai Yuen (the Chinese name of the theater 丹桂院 in Cantonese pronunciation) and Grand Theatre (the English name of the theater).[40] We will use "Donn Quai Yuen" hereafter. It was the first Chinese theater in San Francisco that we know was managed by the actors themselves; it attracted the patronage of their fans and was probably deeply engaged in cultivating community support. Ti Gar Sing reportedly received a salary of $10,000 (the equivalent of $314,175 in 2024) a year. Several months later, the theater recruited new performers from China to perform on its stage, attracting another full house of three thousand.[41] Figure 6.6 shows the interior of the theater. The romanized Chinese name can be seen at the center of the stage, "Donn Quai Yuen."

Ah Quin, the diary-keeping theater lover, was a regular patron of Wing Tie Ping, attending the theater twelve times between September 6 and October 10. But for the remainder of October, he went to the new theater eight times before revisiting Wing Tie Ping at the end of the month.[42] The novelty of a new theater and its modern, iron structural design must have been important attractions then, as was the atmosphere, which was full of vim and vigor. The two doors on the wall leading backstage were decorated with sculpted designs above the door frame, in the style of European architectural

FIGURE 6.6 Chinese Grand Theatre, Washington Street. Courtesy
California History Room, California State Library, Sacramento.

ornament. At the rear of the stage, an alcove for the orchestra was adorned
with elaborate wood carvings in the exquisite Chinese style. As shown in
figure 6.6, the interior design integrated styles of multiple traditions rather
than the plainer design typical of earlier theaters. In late December it was
reported that the new theater was doing good business and offered three
performances daily, at 1 p.m., 4 p.m. and 7 p.m.[43] One report noted that the
regular play ended around 10 p.m., followed by comedy or comic opera until
midnight, when the theater was required to close. The paper noted, "Many
ladies and gentlemen, principally visitors from the Eastern States, attend
these unique performance and find themselves amply repaid by the novelty
of the scene."[44] The availability of two matinees and an evening show, along
with diverse content designated for each, explains how viewers such as Ah
Quin could freely enter and exit the theater from noon to midnight, enjoying
a variety of enticing programs.

   One other important social aspect distinguished the fourth Chinese theater: it was built after the Qing government established a consulate in San
Francisco, therefore benefiting from more official representation and diplomatic relations. The following year, several months after vetoing Congress's
proposed Chinese Restriction Act, President Rutherford B. Hayes made a
public visit to the new theater on Washington Street, where he and his party

stayed for an hour, accompanied by interpreters who explained the plays.[45] Chinese theater would also gain more official representation from the Chinese consul general in San Francisco. During the Chinese New Year of 1881, the vice consul, Lee Young, "called, in company with the Vice Consul, upon the Chief of Police and understood that permission was given that the play might go on without interruption until 2 o'clock AM during Chinese New Year."[46]

Despite these positive developments, the political and social environment was worsening for the Chinese community. In 1878 California decided to convene a state constitutional convention; a third of the 152 elected delegates were Workingmen's Party members. In March 1879, the California constitution was amended and ratified. Article 19 of the constitution sought to deter Chinese from immigrating to California; no private corporation could employ Chinese workers, nor could Chinese engage in public employment; it declared that all Chinese must be removed.

> No corporation now existing or hereafter formed under the laws of this State, shall, after the adoption of this Constitution, employ directly or indirectly, in any capacity, any Chinese or Mongolian. The Legislature shall pass such laws as may be necessary to enforce this provision.
>
> The Legislature shall delegate all necessary power to the incorporated cities and towns of this State for the removal of Chinese without the limits of such cities and towns, or for their location within prescribed portions of those limits, and it shall also provide the necessary legislation to prohibit the introduction into this State of Chinese after the adoption of this Constitution.[47]

This was the zenith of Kearneyism. The Workingmen's Party was gaining power, and advocates of immigration restriction succeeded in making it a popular agenda item. Earlier that year, the US Senate passed the Fifteen Passenger Bill, seeking to limit the number of Chinese passengers permitted on any ship arriving in the United States to fifteen. Facing strong objection from the Chinese minister and lobbyists, President Hayes vetoed the bill, citing the Burlingame Treaty. Instead, he initiated a renegotiation of the treaty, requesting Chinese consent to restrictions on immigration. These negotiations culminated in the Angell Treaty in 1880.

The fourth theater concluded the third phase of the development of Chinese opera theater in California; it also marked the end of the growth of commercial Chinese theater in nineteenth-century San Francisco. As the newest theater, Donn Quai Yuen was a place of sparkling energy and significant creativity and proved to be a powerhouse in the 1880s and the early nineties. It also became the most remembered theater name for future generations in

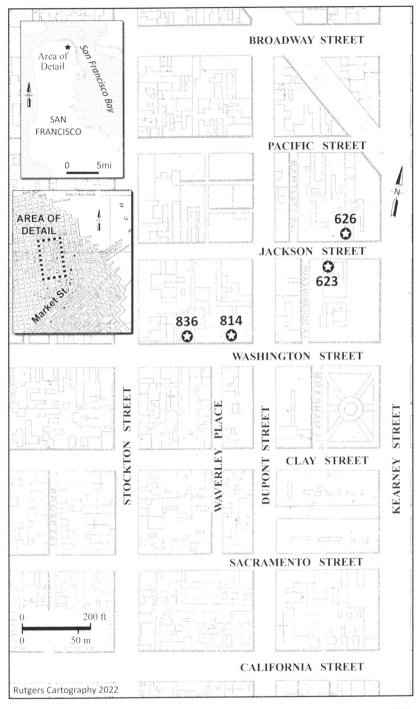

FIGURE 6.7 Map of the four Chinese theaters in San Francisco, 1879.
Michael Siegel, Rutgers Cartography, 2022.

the Chinese community, in memoir, anecdote, community legend, and even in the occasional written history of Chinese theater in San Francisco.

Figure 6.7 shows the locations of the four Chinese theaters established between 1868 and 1879 in San Francisco. As previously mentioned, during the peak of this period, the first three theaters operated concurrently from December 1877 to July 1879. Then they merged, and the fourth theater was established. Collectively they played a central place in the Chinatown community and connected to everyday life in San Francisco. Their success not only drew visitors from afar, but also attracted Chinese opera performers from other countries or continents. In 1881, the *Era* in London printed a lengthy report of a visit to San Francisco's Chinese theater, discussing the stage action of the leads and plot twists, as well as the orchestra's eight musicians.[48] The same year, the actress Chow Chi arrived in San Francisco from Australia, claiming to be "the only one outside of China"; another actress, Guia T. Mot, arrived from Cuba, after playing engagements in Havana.[49] With its vibrant Chinese theaters, San Francisco's potential as the primary hub of the transnational network of Cantonese opera performance began to emerge.

CHAPTER 7

Contesting Chinese Exclusion Laws
In re Ho King

Since its first arrival in 1852, Chinese theater had been the public face of the Chinese community in California. Thus, when anti-Chinese laws were passed by Congress in the 1880s and began to be enforced, Chinese theaters and actors were obvious targets. They unexpectedly became one of the first groups to contest the legislation. A series of laws restricting Chinese immigration beginning in 1882 resulted in detentions, interrogations and arrests. Because of the image, reputation, and visibility of Chinese theaters, immigration cases involving Chinese actors received widespread news coverage, at times making a spectacle of the court proceedings. As a prominent cultural institution, Chinese theater played a unique role in the public's perception and the community's contestation of the restriction of the Chinese immigration.

The Chinese Restriction Act (1882)

On May 6, 1882, Congress passed a bill to "execute certain treaty stipulations relating to Chinese," known at the time as the Chinese Restriction Act (later commonly referred to as the Chinese Exclusion Act). Signed into law by President Chester Arthur, it banned Chinese laborers from entering the United States for ten years. This bill had been the subject of both domestic and international negotiations for several years amid increasing anti-Chinese agitation at the national level. Its passing eventually reduced the power of the 1868 Burlingame Treaty, which had protected the rights of Chinese immigrants.

To reinforce US trade interests with China, the Burlingame Treaty had been signed in 1868. It promised the Chinese the right to free immigration and travel within the United States and the protection of Chinese citizens in the United States under the most-favored-nation principle, and vice versa. The treaty had the ultimate role in guarding the rights of Chinese in America. But under pressure of anti-Chinese sentiment, in 1880 China agreed to the Angell Treaty, which reversed course partly by recognizing the power of the US government to regulate, limit, or suspend labor immigration from China. This laid the diplomatic groundwork for the Restriction Act. In 1881 the bill was debated in the Congress and modified before it headed to President Arthur's desk in 1882. Anticipating the bill's inevitable passing and the hardship ahead, Chinese immigration grew exponentially from 5,802 (1880) and 11,890 (1881) to 39,570 (1882).[1] When the Restriction Act became law, it had the dubious distinction of being the first and only exception to the rule of open immigration to the United States. The law had a general negative effect on the immigration of Chinese at large. As the historian Beth Lew-Williams noted succinctly, "Anti-Chinese advocates had long maintained that the Chinese could never become American, and now federal laws helped make it so."[2]

The new legislation took effect on August 4, 1882. Collectors at all the ports had received prior instructions from the Treasury Department to begin its enforcement. On arrival in San Francisco, Chinese passengers were taken to the Customs House for interrogation and generally treated as laborers unless they had certificates issued by the Chinese government or could prove otherwise.[3] By early August, a Chinese sailor was stopped at the port, and Chinese sailors became the first group to test the application of the new law.[4] One such case was brought before the Circuit Court in San Francisco on August 23, concerning the sailor Ah Sing. A steamship contracted Ah Sing to sail to Australia and back. The ship left San Francisco before the Restriction Act went into effect, but on returning to the city, Ah Sing was denied entry. Many other Chinese sailors in similar situations, or who traveled between American ports, encountered similar problems. At the end of August, Judges Stephen Field and Ogden Hoffman ruled that under the circumstances, the Chinese sailors should be entitled to enter.[5]

Chinese actors tested the application of the Restriction Act almost immediately as well, placing Chinese theater in the immigration limelight. The first rejection of Chinese actors arriving from Panama was reported on August 26. The *Los Angeles Herald* reported:

> Complaint from Chinese Legation. Washington, Aug. 26—A member of the Chinese Legation visited the State Department today and informed Acting Secretary Davis that a party of Chinese play actors from Panama had been denied permission to land at San Francisco. Secretary Davis called upon Secretary Folger in reference to the matter. The result was that Secretary Folger telegraphed the Collector of Customs at San Francisco that the Department did not regard play actors as laborers within the meaning

of the Chinese act and suggested that the facts in the case might bring it within the late decision of Judge Fields, that the law did not apply to the Chinese who had shipped before the passage of the act.[6]

That the Chinese consul general intervened through diplomatic channels caused alarm among anti-Chinese proponents, even though the consul general merely sought to ensure that application of the Restriction Act stayed within its scope. In its report, the *San Francisco Examiner* interpreted the news in a headline as "Nullifying the Chinese Act."[7] The *Cincinnati Commercial*, the *Boston Herald*, and other newspapers criticized the Secretary of the Treasury for failing to protect American actors from "Chinese cheap actors."[8] Furthermore, they questioned the legitimacy of Chinese theatrical troupes. The *Examiner* speculated, "It is said that all Chinese actors (?) due on the next steamer are all provided with wardrobes to denote their calling, and it is hinted that these same wardrobes will be made to perform duty for all similar consignments, it being a very easy matter to send the wardrobes back to China by the said steamer."[9] Anti-Chinese sentiment fueled such insinuations of fraud in the reportage, but the newspaper was correct about the lack of uniform enforcement. "Washington gives the Collector the widest discretion in the matter and allows him to act in accordance with his own interpretation of the law."[10] In a prompt response, the deputy collector of the Port of San Francisco reassured the public of his commitment to strictly enforcing the Restriction Act, noting that the city "is now overstocked with" Chinese actors.[11] This notion of excess was the trope typically used to justify excluding Chinese.[12] Among these discussions, the often-revered Chinese opera costumes were given a surprising new role in the accusation of a possible "fraudulent scheme," namely, as the de facto evidence to prove nonlaborer status.

By September 11, 1882, the *Examiner* had painted Chinese theater as a significant loophole in the immigration law. "Considerable stir has been created in Chinese theatrical circles by the rumor that a shipload of Chinese actors were [sic] on the way from China armed with many technicalities, and who think themselves fully competent to get around the law." The paper concluded with a stern warning: "These [Chinese] theater people who are here can rest assured that these new importations, should they come, will be treated as laborers by the Customhouse, and will doubtless find that the trip from the ship to the shore, even though only ten feet away, will occupy them pretty near ten years before they reach terra firma."[13] These fantastical imaginings about and accusations of Chinese actors further fueled anti-Chinese anxiety. Although the Treasury Department reaffirmed that the new law must not violate the Angell Treaty's protection of nonlaborers, public opinion did not change. The public expected the Restriction Act to erect barriers against all Chinese immigrants, not merely laborers. In October, Chinese theaters and actors were again made targets. In a piece entitled "Chinese Actors Coming," the *Examiner* warned that Chinese tried to evade the Restriction Act by disguising themselves as actors. Even if they were legitimate, they were not "professional artists," but merely equipped with "a semblance of a wardrobe in order to establish their claim." Implying that a more stringent solution would be coming, it quoted the words of the Collector of Customs: "The matter would be taken up before the United States Court."[14]

In re Ho King

Indeed, at the same time that hysteria and obloquy circulated in the media, a case concerning a Chinese actor was brought to court and tried promptly. It would set precedents for the interpretation of the rights of not just Chinese actors but all nonlaborer Chinese. The case was heard by the United States District Court for the District of Oregon.[15]

On November 25, 1882, the actor Ho King boarded a steamer at the port of Hong Kong, traveling to Honolulu via Victoria, British Columbia and Portland, Oregon. The ship got to Portland on January 9, 1883, where its ship captain forbade Ho King to land on the basis of the Restriction Act. (Any ship captain allowing Chinese laborers to land would be fined five hundred dollars per laborer and possibly jailed for up to a year. Thus, the captain diligently enforced the law.) But since the Restriction Act was aimed specifically at laborers, it raised the question of whether an actor was a laborer and therefore subject to the restriction. Because he was an actor, Ho King's case immediately got the attention of the Chinese community in Portland. In two days, Chinese merchants petitioned for a writ of habeas corpus. Ho King's counsel argued that since he was "an actor or theatrical performer by occupation or profession," the Restriction Act did not apply to him, nor should he need "a certificate from the Chinese government showing his right to land in the United States, as is required by Section 6 of the act." (Ho King's original destination was Honolulu, so he did not acquire a certificate for entering the United States.)

Judge Matthew P. Deady, who had upheld the rights of Chinese on many occasions, ruled for Ho King and allowed him to land. On January 11, 1883, Ho King was released on bail in the sum of five thousand dollars. The bond was furnished by two wealthy Chinese merchants, Sid Bock and Ho Shut.[16] On the evening of January 12, Ho King performed at the Chinese theater in Portland, attracting a large crowd. It was a celebratory evening because of the legal victory of Ho King's release and the enchanting debut of fresh talent. The local newspaper the *Morning Oregonian* reported the jubilant mood: "The Chinese theater was crowded last night to its greatest capacity with the elite of Chinatown who were anxious to witness the performance of Ho King, the actor harbeas corpused from on bond the C. T. Hook, and allowed to go at large under $5000 bail in order that he might make his first appearance there."[17]

Judge Deady's final decision in In re Ho King on January 15 was published in full in the *Morning Oregonian*.[18] The judge noted that the case hinged on two questions. On the first, whether Ho King could be classified as a laborer, he wrote: "A Chinese actor engaged in dramatic representations upon the stage of a Chinese theater seems as far removed from such competition as it is possible for a person to be." The second question was whether a certificate was required. The judge wrote that as long as the Chinese person could establish proof of nonlabor status, "the certificate . . . was not the only competent evidence that a Chinese person is not a laborer." The decision showed a commitment to the ethos of equal rights and justice. As Judge Deady wrote, "Indeed, the fact of being compelled to make proof of his condition or character at all is a burden and inconvenience upon the Chinese coming to the United States which is not required by any other immigrant or visitor coming to this country."

Widely reported and referenced, In re Ho King confirmed that an actor was not a "laborer" and that a certificate was not the only competent evidence to support nonlaborer status. Newspapers immediately decried the possibility of competition, even though Chinese actors were never deemed a threat to the American labor force. The *New York Herald* wrote: "Now let the protectionists put a heavy tariff duty on them in order that our own stars and stock actors may be duly protected against these cheap Asiatic professionals."[19] The *Global* in Canada opined, "It will not be surprising if a great demand from the Chinese theatres in San Francisco is suddenly developed and a whole cargoes of 'actors' landed on the Pacific Slope."[20] In court, however, the case was used as precedent almost immediately, from state supreme courts to federal district courts.[21] Later it would be cited most significantly in an important US Supreme Court case, *Lau Ow Bew v. United States*, which applied the Ho King precedent to approve the reentry of a Portland Chinese merchant who had returned from China but did not have a section 6 certificate.[22] The far-reaching significance of the In re Ho King decision extended well into the twentieth century and beyond the US territory.[23]

In re Ho King was an immediate victory for Chinese theaters. In unambiguous language, the ruling ensured the admission of Chinese actors: "In this case the fact that King belongs to the privileged class is established in the judgment of the court by the admission that he is an actor, of which there is not a particle of doubt." At the same time, however, the case also was taken up by anti-Chinese proponents as evidence of the weak power of the 1882 Restriction Act to reduce Chinese immigration and deepened their resolve to amend the bill. The 1882 Restriction Act allowed laborers and merchants already resident in the United States to leave the country and return, if they had the proper certification. In 1884, Congress passed amendments that tightened the certification process for returning Chinese laborers, requiring the certificates to include more personal information and to be more precise, to be issued only by the federal government, and to constitute the only proof of residence.

In the meantime, the Restriction Act continued to cast a shadow over, and erect barriers to, the immigration of Chinese actors and theatrical troupes, who were routinely sent to the Customs House for investigation like all other Chinese passengers. The fear and distrust (continuing after In re Ho King) caused the Chinese to have little faith in passing through the gate unscathed. In October 1883, two actors were caught trying to pose as merchants with traders' certificates issued by the Chinese government. Their real profession as artists was revealed in a casual exchange with an interpreter.[24] Ironically, since Chinese theater was the public face of the community, a tentative respectability associated with Chinese actors came to the rescue. A reporter noted, "There was no doubt in the mind of Surveyor Morton that these two men came here to be actors. Both wore costly silk robes. They manifested more intelligence than most of their fellow passengers. When it came out that they were actors they were not at all abashed."[25] The unflinching courage of the actors faced with the threat of denied entry epitomized the ability of Chinese theater to counteract America's racist gaze successfully. Put differently, the powerful and dignified presence of Chinese performers on stage extended beyond the confines of theaters to combat and debunk the usual perception of inferiority associated with Chinese immigrants. The exquisite quality of their wardrobes also elevated their status in public opinion.

Still, whether or not they won in court, such reports of Chinese actors' cases created suspicion, diminished their and Chinese theater's legitimacy, and reinforced racial stereotypes. In August 1884, newspapers across the country printed the report of a fanciful scene in the court of Judge Ogden Hoffman in San Francisco involving four Chinese actors. The report satirized both the judge, who was known for treating Chinese as equal before the law, and Chinese theaters, noting that each actor demonstrated the falsetto and acrobatic movements expected of Chinese opera performers before the judge to prove his identity as an actor, and was subsequently released.[26] Another theatrical performance in the circuit court before Judge Myron Sabin was reported, involving an actor who, en route to Victoria, sought admission to land for an engagement at the Grand Chinese Theatre.[27] These news reports dramatized the predicament of the Chinese actors for a good laugh. These "minstrelized" accounts recycled Chinese theatrical stereotypes, making light of the severe and punishing effects of the Chinese exclusion laws. These commentators used what Jennifer Stoever called the "sonic color line" to racialize Chinese immigrants and enhance the "normalcy" of cultural citizenship in

America.[28] Such reports were willful caricatures of Chinese opera. However, in both cases, Chinese opera actors turned the racialized sonic stereotype on its head to successfully abort attempts to bar them from entry.

Mistaken Identities and Identity Papers

Racial anxiety over Chinese actors and theaters was in itself evidence of the prosperity and business success of Chinese theaters. The exclusionists lamented the large number of Chinese actors in San Francisco. Aside from the usual complaints about excess, their impression might have been derived from the theaters' frequent, elaborate attractions, as well as the high-profile visitors such as the British author Oscar Wilde, British royalty such as the marquess of Lorne and Princess Louise, the Swedish prima donna Christina Nilsson, and the highly regarded Hungarian soprano Etelka Gerster.[29] In addition to frequent newspaper reports on Chinese theaters, magazines offered portraits of Chinese theaters in feature articles and drawings (to be discussed in later chapters). In other words, Chinese theater had a very public presence in the social life of San Francisco, which intensified interest in accusations against Chinese actors. Unfortunately, the public nature of theatrical performance also meant that Chinese actors suspected of evading the new immigration law did not have the option of hiding, at least not in the long run.

In November 1884, a high-profile immigration case involving another Chinese actor became a complete spectacle in San Francisco for two months. The case concerned the famous female impersonator Hong Gee Cheong, who was recruited from China.[30] When the ship approached the port, the actor, fearing that he would face difficulty without a certificate, vanished from the ship and became wanted by the police. Later it was revealed that he had walked off the ship by disguising himself as a ship's crew member, and then went into hiding. After three weeks, thinking it was safe, the Chinese theater on Jackson Street announced his debut with large placards posted around town. His considerable fame stirred up much excited anticipation in Chinese community. He was reportedly the second-best actor in China and received an annual salary of three thousand dollars. Audiences lined up well before the performance to see this famous actor. The *Daily Alta California* described the debut in colorful terms:

> The boxes were occupied by the high Chinese dignitaries, headed by the Consul-General and staff and the mercantile crème de la crème of Washington, Dupont and Jackson streets. When the star appeared, in gorgeous robes of purple silk and costly fur, he met with an ovation such as was never before accorded one of his profession in the country. His acting fully justified the high encomiums that had preceded him across the water, and his success was assured from the moment he appeared on the stage.[31]

Tipped off by an anonymous letter, however, the police arrested Hong during the performance. The *Examiner* wrote: "The theater was packed from wall to wall and the galleries were jammed full of Chinese. The new actor had been extensively advertised, and all who could afford to pay thirty-five cents went to see him. . . . A riot threatened."[32] Indeed, the arrest caused a significant commotion at the crowded theater. Many major San Francisco newspapers reported the police tactics and maneuvers in making the arrest, with sensational headlines such as "A Clever Capture: A High-Priced Chinese Actor Arrested on the Stage by Deputy Marshals—Almost a Riot," "Strategy, Me Boy," or "A Strategic Seizure."[33] The arrested man was out on five thousand dollars' bail with Dr. Li Po Tai as surety. Dr. Li had been one of the sponsors for the second theater, which had opened in 1874 (see chap. 4). However, it was later determined that the captured man was not the real Hong Gee Cheong, but an actor who had already been performing in San Francisco for two years.[34] Humiliated by the blunder, the police arrested the real Hong. Both Hong and his proxy were brought before the commissioner of the US Circuit Court for California, Lorenzo Sawyer; after hearing the arguments, Sawyer dismissed the case. Despite pressure from the press and the public, Sawyer, together with Judge Ogden Hoffman of the Northern District, and the Circuit Court Judge Matthew P. Deady, were well known for their belief that "their judicial duty required them to interpret the Restriction Acts in light of the treaty with China" and sought to hear Chinese habeas corpus cases with judicial fairness.[35] Therefore, Sawyer's decision was hardly surprising. Yet, with the suspense and mistaken identity, as well as theater, actors, a police chief, Chinese dignitaries, and a judge, this case had all the ingredients of a drama. The news was constantly updated. With their tabloid-style narrative, however, the reports did nothing to advance Chinese actors' rights to legitimate entry as nonlaborers. Rather, they elaborated on racial stereotypes of Chinese as devious and cunning.

Consequentially, the Hong case challenged the legality of the arrest. An attorney for both actors argued that since this was a criminal prosecution brought by the district attorney, the burden of proof was on the government. And if no such evidence could be provided, the Chinese actors should be discharged. The *Daily Evening Bulletin* reproduced the exchange at the hearing:

> Counsel for actors—I move for the discharge of the prisoner. This is a criminal prosecution and the Government must make a case that the prisoner is unlawfully in this country. His confession that he had no certificate when he landed (made to Mr. Vrooman) does not prove that he had none.
>
> Mr. Cook—According to this construction as many Chinese can come from Victoria to the United States as may wish and when found here that would be the end of it. A man is innocent until he is proved guilty. The man

told Mr. Vrooman that he had no certificate. I will leave this case under advisement of the Commissioner.

Commissioner Sawyer—If you (Mr. Cook) honestly believe that you can produce any more evidence that this man is unlawfully in the country, and believe that there is testimony on which to hold him, I will hold him; otherwise not.

Mr. Cook—Because we cannot prove that he was searched, and that it was thus found that he had no certificate.[36]

This and other challenges to the scope of immigration restrictions angered the anti-Chinese proponents. They prompted calls to mandate Chinese individuals to carry certificates of identity in the United States. Two months after this court decision, the same newspaper printed a column calling the attention of Congress to the "difficulty of establishing Chinese identity . . . recently illustrated," citing the mistaken identity of the two Chinese actors as examples.[37] Indeed, with the drama of Hong Gee Cheong and false identity playing out in public, the confusion hardened the resolve of exclusionists to call for identity papers. These calls gained traction, eventually leading to passage of the Geary Act in 1892, requiring all Chinese in the United States to carry identification papers, the most devastating blow to the Chinese community.

"The Chinese Drama," an article in the *Rochester Democrat and Chronicle* at the end of 1885, revealed the general perception that Chinese actors and theaters largely evaded the Restriction Act:

The Dan Sang Fung, Loak Sang Fung, and other like establishments of this city [have] been stocked with talented members of the profession, and there is little difficulty in forming companies consisting of from thirty to fifty actors for the amusement of the host of theatergoers in the Chinese quarter. The salaries paid to the players vary from $10 to $40 a week, while such an actor as the great Tony Hoy commands as high a rate of remuneration as $3,000 a year. Evading the restriction act as "students" or "professionals," the players find no difficulty in reaching these shores, and a steamer rarely crosses the Pacific that it does not bear hither or thither a number of these worthy exponents of the Chinese drama.[38]

During the early years of the Restriction Act, even though the law did not target Chinese actors, it nevertheless cast suspicion on them, sowing doubt about their integrity through false accusations of fraudulence. It created the notion of Chinese as essentially illegitimate. As Mae Ngai noted insightfully, "illegal alienage is not a natural or fixed condition but the product of positive law."[39] Falsehoods about illegal Chinese circulated widely, and demand for more stringent restrictions on Chinese immigration was mounting.

In 1888, the Scott Act, another amendment to the Restriction Act, tightened the restrictions further by invalidating the certificates that the US government had issued to returning laborers before their departure to China. In effect, the Scott Act extended the immigration ban to all Chinese laborers, whether or not they held residency in the United States. About thirty thousand Chinese laborers who had temporarily left the United States for China were now refused reentry. It declared void the thirty thousand returned certificates issued to those Chinese who had temporarily left the country.[40] The most significant blow, however, came in 1892, when the US Congress passed the Geary Act. It extended the Restriction Act for an additional ten years and required Chinese laborers in the United States to register with the Internal Revenue Service within a year and to carry certificates of residence. Those caught not carrying the certificates would be sentenced to hard labor and deportation. The law also shifted the burden of proof from the government to the individual such that if charged with illegal status, a Chinese immigrant must prove his right to remain in the country. With these additional restrictions, the Geary Act effectively extended border control to domestic control, exposing all Chinese residents to inquiries and interrogations.

This began a dark age for the Chinese community. The Chinese Consolidated Benevolent Association (CCBA), previously known as Six Companies but formally renamed by the San Francisco consul general in 1882, tried to combat the legislation by enlisting the help of the Chinese legation to exert diplomatic pressure. They employed lawyers to challenge the law in court with a test case that went all the way to the US Supreme Court. Most important, the CCBA urged the Chinese resident community to resist the new law by not registering.[41] This act of civil disobedience put Chinese laborers at risk of arrest and deportation without opportunity for bail.

Despite court successes and the difficulty of government enforcement (due to both the large number of Chinese laborers and the immense expense of deportating them), the CCBA's efforts failed. Police raids of Chinatown resulted in the arrest and deportation of hundreds of unregistered Chinese laborers. The impact on Chinese theaters was immense. The police raids diminished daily activities in the community to a minimum. Different community forces arose as the position of the CCBA was weakened by its inability to protect the laborers; tong wars grew exponentially during this decade. ("Tong" refers to organizations or secret societies formed among Chinese immigrants for support and protection. Friction between different tongs caused battles.) Chinese theaters began a serious decline as the century drew to a close. Riots and purges became frequent, demonstrating the success with which, as Robert Tsai notes succinctly, "popular sovereignty [had] been used to license massive acts of inhumanity and inequality."[42]

Nevertheless, for most of the 1880s and early 1890s, In re Ho King gave Chinese theaters a period of significant protection during which they continued to thrive. Two months after that ruling in early 1883, a popular and entrepreneurial-minded actor, Loo Chin Goon, arrived in Philadelphia to expand Chinese theater to the East Coast. He was interviewed by a newspaper reporter, who wrote: "He declined to say anything about the anti-Chinese law, except that he was pleased to see that Celestial actors are free to come and go at their will, they being professional gentlemen, not laborers. He intends to make this country his home."[43] Loo Chin Goon's answer revealed his relief at the temporary reprieve, a sentiment shared by all Chinese theaters at the time. As the Chinese community surrendered to the fate of being the only group in the United States stripped of the right of free immigration, mobilizing cultural engagement became the only means to redress their tarnished reputation. The continuing effort to ensure and expand the circuit of Chinese theater was intended not only to boost business but also to sustain respectability. Such pursuit of respectability, embodied by Loo Chin Goon's presence in Philadelphia, would soon be taken up as cultural advocacy by a contemporary advocate, Wong Chin Foo, to be discussed in chapter 10.

In the early days of the Restriction Act, Chinese actors vigorously contested the law, and several consequential court rulings shielded them from its application. Thus, immigration control did not hinder the operation of Chinese theaters in the early 1880s. This period was essential to the grounding of Chinese theaters both in San Francisco and elsewhere in North America, although it could not prevent the turmoil that arose in the community as a result of the exclusion laws. Predictably, the Chinese population in America dropped by 42,437 between 1882 and 1900.[44] Later, as legislation continued to tighten control of Chinese immigrants both at the border and in the interior of the country, the restrictions eventually stifled the community, closed the pipeline for Chinese actors, and adversely affected the operations of Chinese theaters.[45]

CHAPTER 8

Star Power and the Chinese American Theater

Despite the setback of the Restriction Act, Chinese theaters in San Francisco thrived in the 1880s. The theaters drew large crowds night after night. They fiercely competed for top performers to outshine rival theaters, and popular actors angled for greater success, expanding their reach. Paradoxically, even as the Workingmen's Party made the Chinese community in San Francisco a target, Chinese theaters remained highly desirable tourist destinations, with a growing list of eminent visitors. Neither animosity nor stringent laws seeking to restrict Chinese immigration could stop the development and attraction of Chinese theaters for most of this decade.

The popularity of Chinese theaters was reflected in the frequency of newspaper reports, commentaries in travelogues, and feature articles in magazines. In addition to their high visibility and prominence as entertainment, they were also financially impressive. In February 1881, a New Orleans newspaper, the *Times-Picayune*, reported of San Francisco: "What causes the Caucasian managers to groan and look black is the fact that the Chinese theatres of this city, of which there are three, took in the sum of $110,000 during the last sixteen months. These theatres are institutions of no small importance in Chinatown."[1]

Rivalry and Competition

In the Chinese theater business, a complicated relationship existed among a host of interested parties: landowners, theater proprietors, booking agents, sponsoring merchants, theatrical troupe and company managers, actors, and musicians, as well as huiguan and other patrons or community organizations. Business rivalries resulted in disputes, frequent litigation, and even physical damage to the theaters. The *Daily Alta California* reported an incident of arson at the Donn Quai Yuen theater at the beginning of 1880.

It reflected the complicated involvement of several parties in the theater business:

> The troubles that led to the attempt, Tuesday night, to fire the building of the Chinese Grand Theatre Company on Washington street, by throwing phosphorous balls about the place, are as follows: Some time ago, Chung Yung and Man Tong, comprising the Quon Yet Tong Theatrical Company, went to China and expended $9000 in engaging for two years and bringing to this city two star theatrical performers named Long Chuck and Tong Long. When they returned to this city they found the Chinese theatrical business here concentrated under the name of the Wing Tie Ping Company, on Jackson street. With the $9,000 star actors on their hands, they sought a field for them. Finally they arranged to sublet them for two years to the Wing Tie Ping Company for $16,000 to be paid cash down. Of this amount, all but $2,625.50 has been paid. Since the making of the bargain above, an opposition company, the Grand, has opened. Recently the Wing Tie Ping Company failed, it is claimed, fraudulently, and with intent to avoid payment of certain debts, including the balance due on the star actors. Tuesday afternoon they reopened and gave the first performance after the failure, and the Quon Yet Tong people sued out a writ of injunction against the Wing Tie Ping Company to prevent either of the star actors from performing that night. The Wing Tie Ping people suddenly conceived the idea that the Grand Company had been instrumental in inducing the Quon Yet Tongs to obtain the order of injunction, and sent their emissaries to fire the Grand building in retaliation. They also discharged the injunction, and are to be arrested for contempt of court.[2]

The Grand Company noted here was Donn Quai Yuen, a newcomer that became the city's fourth Chinese theater when it opened in October 1879. Its appearance contested the monopoly of Wing Tie Ping, which by then was the sole representative of the venerable Chinese theaters in town. As the rivalry between the Donn Quai Yuen and Wing Tie Ping theaters escalated, a newly arrived troupe and its actors were drawn into the situation. For nearly a week, the arson incident and dispute were reported. (Even Ah Quin made reference to the incident, as discussed in the epilogue.) However, the story was very confusing, and contradictory accounts abounded. In contrast to the *Daily Alta California*'s account above, the *Chronicle*'s version portrayed the Wing Tie Ping company as the victim, tricked into paying an exorbitant amount, whereas the *Examiner* depicted the fire as Wing Tie Ping's desperate move to sabotage the success of a rival theater.[3] Clearly, the events were more complicated than these claims. After its manager, Chen Tuck Sain, and seven others were bailed out, Wing Tie Ping put out a public notice firmly denying the arson charges.

In China, the hardships for actors and troupes caused by the intense competition among theaters could be mitigated by professional guilds such as

Jiqing Gongsuo, but such an intermediary system did not appear to be established in North America at this time, despite the publication referring to it in 1875 (see discussion of the *Oriental* advertisement in chap. 5). As a result, theatrical troupes were in a particularly vulnerable position, caught in the rivalry among theaters. Often, however, the community itself settled the discord. On March 17, the *Daily Alta California* printed the following notice from the Superior Court: "(Judge Cary)—Chuy Fin, Man Tong vs. Chin Yulp, and Sam See Sing and the Wing Tie Ping Company, action on an injunction—On stipulation of counsel, cause dismissed and discontinued."[4]

This, for sure, would not be the last injunction to be litigated in court between Chinese theaters and their performers. Throughout the next two decades, the theaters would bring injunctions to stop their performers from appearing on the stages of their rivals. The continuing competition would at times escalate into malicious acts. The fighting and retaliation would even cause riots at Chinese theaters. Luckily for the audiences, these incidents were few and far between and did not severely affect the theater performances.

Star Power of Leading Actors:
A Painting and Loo Chin Goon

The arson incident that involved the Quon Yet Tong theatrical company, the Donn Quai Yuen theater, and the Wing Tie Ping theater illustrates the elevated status of star actors. The growing reputation of San Francisco's Chinese theaters and the high demand for performers had enticed more stellar performers from China. Undoubtedly, Long Chuck and Tong Long, at the center of the above injunction, came for such promising prospects.

Star actors were prime attractions, highly praised, and the accolades both fueled their power and elevated their salaries. At the end of 1879, it was the star actor-manager, Ti Gar Sing, who famously led the way in challenging the monopoly of Wing Tie Ping by starting a new theater. Earlier, several Chinese actors garnered nationwide attention for their impressive salaries, including Leong Yow of the Royal Chinese Theater, who was paid $6,700 in February 1879, and a leading actor of a new troupe arriving at Look Sun Fung, who was paid $7,000 in October 1878. In February 1882, Ung Yen, a comedian and chief actor of the company, was paid $5,000 a year, and in November 1883, the leading female impersonator, Bung Ah Soo, was paid $6,000 in annual salary.[5]

Newspapers were eager to report the high salaries received by Chinese actors. But what were the actors like and how were they regarded? Two examples illustrate the unprecedented prominence of star actors around this time: The first is a remarkable painting, and the second is the media attention paid to an actor's eastward venture.

A striking attestation of the power of a star actor was provided by a painting by Theodore Wores, shown in figure 8.1. It also appeared as a wood engraving

"1708 The Entry"—Chinese Theatre, San Francisco. *Taber* Ph[...]

FIGURE 8.1 Theodore Wores. *The Entry*. Photograph by Taler Photo Studio. Courtesy California History Room, California State Library, Sacramento.

in an 1884 article in *Century Illustrated Magazine* by Henry Burden McDowell. (The artist, Theodore Wores, and the significance of the painting are discussed further in chapter 9.) This painting recalls the actors in the Hong Kong photographer Lai Fong's portraits (see chap. 6). McDowell gave a detailed account of the impressive presence of the actor. After describing the costumes of the other opera performers, McDowell went on:

> But the most distinctive of all these costumes is the general's. In his headdress are five dragons rampant, and on the flap in front a lion's mouth. In time of action his sleeves are rolled up, and his loins are girded with a sash and rosette of light-blue silk. An enormous butterfly laps over and partly covers the sidepieces that protect his thighs. His boots are high-soled and add much to his stature. Two long feathers sweep from his helmet behind. As a symbol of power he wears four flags on his back, and as a token of strength a cockade of black silk on his forehead.[6]

This vivid description referred to a full-page image that faithfully reproduces the portrait by Theodore Wores for McDowell's essay. Titled *The Entry*, this painting shows an actor in a striking pose, revealing his position at his first appearance of the evening. In battle armor and platform shoes, the actor's dignified pose conveys the magisterial presence of a general. His piercing gaze suggested self-possession and confidence. Worn over the abdomen, the tiger-head design was a powerful symbol on stage, "an apotropaic image," notes the art historian April Liu. Such panels often were "completely filled with shiny gold couching swirling around brass and mirrored discs."[7] It is also seen in Lai Fong's actor portraits (see figs. 5.2a and 5.2b). Although the materials of the armor are hard to confirm from this black and white image, the use of extensive ornaments of brass, mirror, fur, and silk on such armor was typical and are faithfully rendered in the rich textures of the painting. The actor's headdress was similarly ornate, its coronet filled with circlets and jewels. Its pheasant feathers, two to three feet long, enhanced the general's every stage movement. Such headdress feathers, as noted in chapter 5, often became expressive tools as well, manipulated in different ways according to the dramatic situation to express anger, intense thought, or strong emotion. Typically, the pheasant feathers designated the high rank of the general.

McDowell explains the important duties of a leading actor in his description of performance practice:

> There is no stage manager. When a new play is to be produced, the author, who is generally also an actor, superintends the rehearsals as well as the performance. The cast is written down in a book and hung up in a conspicuous place in the greenroom. No parts are given out; the author merely tells the actor in a general way what he is to do, and that is all. The "cues," however, are written out, as well as the important sentences. A Chinese

actor, therefore, must be a man of intelligence, good education, and ready wit.[8]

"Middle-aged warrior" was the leading role type in Cantonese opera of the nineteenth century, the protagonist of many famous traditional operas. The most respected performer in the troupe, the actors in this role type were masters of martial arts and possessed solid singing skills. McDowell's article further illustrates the extent of the leading actors' responsibilities: they were involved in all aspects of the productions. Little wonder then that they demanded the highest salaries among all performers and were the main draw for the audience.[9] This portrait of a Chinese actor was a significant visual representation of the mastery of such a performer and was widely circulated. We will return to Wores's painting in a fuller historical context in the next chapter.

In another example of the prominence of star actors, Loo Chin Goon attracted much attention from the news media in March 1883 when he arrived on the East Coast from San Francisco. He was described as the "most famous and popular actor that ever delighted a Chinese audience in San Francisco." For a brief time, his name appeared widely, from the *Times-Picayune* (New Orleans) to the *St. Louis Post-Dispatch* to the *New York Times* to the *Buffalo Evening News,* and *Hong Kong Daily Press*.[10] He was reported on even in American ethnic newspapers (German) as well as news outlets in Europe.[11] All presented Loo Chin Goon as a resolute spokesperson for the importance of Chinese theater: its valuable and legitimate place in American entertainment, and its place on the East Coast. According to these reports, Loo Chin Goon had been recruited to San Francisco in 1879 by the Six Companies (later the Chinese Consolidated Benevolent Association) to perform at a theater on Jackson Street. He was regarded as one of the best, receiving a yearly salary of five thousand dollars as well as a percentage of the theater's profits. After three years in San Francisco, the forty-one-year-old actor traveled by train to Philadelphia to expand his career by opening a Chinese theater on the East Coast. On March 14, 1883, he arrived at Philadelphia's Broad Street Station on the Chicago Express train. There, he was received by a delegation of local Chinese as well as reporters, the latter of whom gave this description: "Goon is a large, powerfully built man, and wears spectacles. . . . He has a rich full voice and speaks very fair English."[12] The reception was led by So Yun Lee, reported as Loo's cousin and a successful businessman in Philadelphia.

In interviews, Loo Chin Goon was emphatic about the superiority of Chinese theater. "Goon has a great regard for the drama of his native country, and . . . [gave] glowing compliments to some of the 'one hundred plays of Yuen.'" On his arrival in Philadelphia, a group of reporters boarded the train to meet him, one of whom described the formidable actor: "He came East in a private car, just as he had been told [that] Salvini and Bernhardt [had] traveled east."[13] The reporter was referring to Tommaso Salvini, a famous Italian tragedian of Shakespeare plays, and Sarah Bernhardt, a much celebrated French actress; both had astoundingly successful American tours. In comparing Loo Chin Goon to Salvini and Bernhardt, the reporter noted Loo Chin Goon's self-regard. The reporter also mentioned his interest in English-language drama; Loo attended the celebrated actor John McCullough's famous play *Virginius* "and praised the performance very much, but he [was] of the opinion that the play [was] much inferior to a Chinese drama of the same kind."[14]

Several reports noted, "He intends to make this country his home," a phrase that recurred in many shortened syndications.[15] This pronouncement was particularly newsworthy because it conveyed an affiliation that was largely at odds with the popular image of Chinese as sojourners. It put him in a position not dissimilar to that of the well-established Chinese merchants in Philadelphia, who must have invited the reporters to join them in receiving Loo Chin Goon at the train station. To cultivate momentum for Chinese theater, the enterprising actor portrayed himself as a professional and impresario. In interviews, Loo Chin Goon laid out his plan for establishing a theater in New York, bringing a group of about a dozen performers from China. The *Daily Evening Bulletin*, coolly watching the hype from San Francisco, printed the same news report but with a different headline: "Loo Chin Goon: Eastern Gossip on Chinese Theatrical—A Subject New to Philadelphia, but Rather Old for San Francisco."[16] The paper sneered at the fuss made over something that it considered ordinary or even routine.

It was unclear whether Loo Chin Goon was generally known among the Chinese on the East Coast. But Wong Ching Foo, the editor of *Chinese America*, acknowledged that "he was an actor, and would undoubtedly create a sensation in America. . . . I will be glad to see Loo Chin Goon and will advocate the theater."[17] Indeed, the actor and the editor soon collaborated, translating a Chinese drama that they compared to the epics of Homer, Dante, and Goethe.[18] As we will discuss in chapter 10, Wong soon took up Chinese theater as one of his causes.

Both the impressive portrait and description of a Chinese actor and the sensation created by Loo Chin Goon reflect the significance of Chinese actors. They not only represented the prosperity of Chinese theaters in North America but also were emblematic of a kind of celebrity culture. The stardom of Chinese actors exerted a new kind of magnetic power that had not been seen before in the pages of American newspapers. In important ways, they paved the way for Chinese theaters to gain respectability as a legitimate form of art. Star actors both underscored and restored Chinese theater's image of integrity, challenging the denigrating image pushed by anti-Chinese sentiment and the Chinese Restriction Act.

Two Theaters: Dan Shan Feng and Donn Quai Yuen

Many documents indicate that four Chinese theaters presented shows concurrently in San Francisco in the 1880s or even into the 1890s. In addition to casual newspaper reports, from 1880 to 1891, *Langley's San Francisco City Directory* listed four Chinese theaters in its "Amusements" section: 623 Jackson Street; 626 Jackson Street; 814 Washington Street; and 836 Washington Street. Only in 1892 did this directory's listing reduce the number of Chinese theaters to two: 814 Washington Street and 623 Jackson Street. But city directories probably were not regularly updated. It is quite likely that long before 1892 these two theaters were the only ones in regular operation. As early as 1886, a newspaper noted that the Royal Chinese Theatre (626 Jackson Street, the first of the two Jackson Street theaters) had been converted into a large lodging house.[19] Also as early as 1883, the *Strangers' Guide to San Francisco and Vicinity* listed only two theaters. Indeed, the community maintained two Chinese theaters, named 丹桂院, Donn Quai Yuen (Grand Chinese Theater, Dan Gui Yuan) at 814 Washington Street; and 丹山鳳, Dan Shan Feng at 623 Jackson Street.[20] Dupont Street divided Chinatown into the upper (north) and the lower (south) sides. Accordingly, the community referred to Dan Shan Feng as the "upper troupe" (*shangbian* Ban 上邊班), and Donn Quai Yuen as the "lower troupe" (*xiabian* Ban 下邊班).[21] Figure 8.2 is a map that shows their positions in relation to one another.

Many contemporaneous pictures and drawings of these two theaters survive today, providing some visual clues about them. The most distinguishing features were the shape of the alcoves for the orchestra and the distinctive decorations for the two backstage doors. Other aspects of the interiors were renovated and changed over time; changes included landscape paintings, plaques of the theater names, valences, and drapery. The following briefly summarizes the physical characteristics of the two theaters.

Dan Shan Feng (Chinese Theatre, 丹山鳳), 623 Jackson Street

Dan Shan Feng was built in 1874. It was the second Chinese theater to appear on Jackson Street (south side) and had the backing of the famous doctor Li Po Tai. The theater seated 1,200 to 1,600. The stage was 49 by 15 feet, and the frontage of the theater was 80 by 40 feet. It might have undergone many changes. Figure 8.3 shows a photograph of the interior of the theater (see also fig. 9.9). The stage was distinguished by a crescent alcove at the center, above which is a rectangular wood railing of similar width that was a shrine for worship. On its two sides were the two *hudu* doors. The rectangular transom windows above the doors had ornate gilt

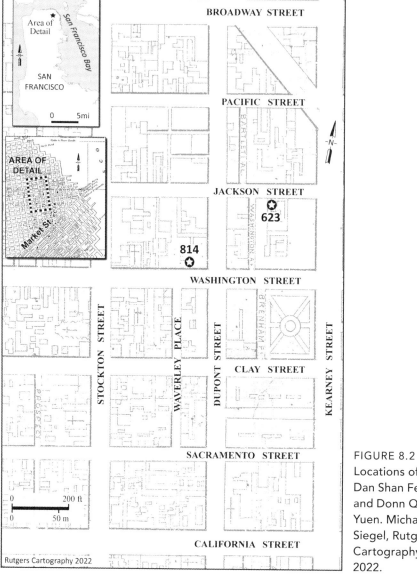

FIGURE 8.2 Locations of Dan Shan Feng and Donn Quai Yuen. Michael Siegel, Rutgers Cartography, 2022.

wooden carvings. This classical Chinese wood carving continued inside the top corners of the door frames. Scrolls of Chinese calligraphy, typically perpendicular, hung on the wall symmetrical to the stage doors. The photograph shows that this stage was also adorned with lanterns, various display objects, and a cloth banner across the top, on which is written the phrase "New Tune Composes Ode to Peace." It encapsulates the essence

288. Stage - Chinese Theater

FIGURE 8.3 Dan Shan Feng Theatre, 623 Jackson Street. Courtesy Bancroft Library, University of California, Berkeley.

of Chinese opera theater: the belief that dedicated theatrical efforts could bring auspiciousness to the community.

Donn Quai Yuen (Grand Chinese Theatre, Dan Gui Yuan, Tan Kwai Yuen 丹桂院), 816 or 814 Washington Street

Donn Quai Yuen was built in 1879, the fourth Chinese theater and the second to appear on Washington Street. The call for its construction was led by the famous actor Ti Gar Sing. Seating 2,600, the theater building was 95 feet deep with a 52-foot frontage and a 35-foot ceiling. It was a three-story building, the largest Chinese theater at the time (see fig. 8.4, as well as fig. 6.6).[22] The stage was distinguished by a rectangular alcove at the center, above which was a large space decorated with a round clock and a horizonal plaque with the romanization of the theater's Chinese name in Cantonese, Donn Quai Yuen. High above was a carved wooden grille similar in dimensions to the rectangular alcove below. On both sides of the alcove were *hudu* doors with round tops. Above those were cloud- or winglike decorations with an eclipse at the center. At one time, above the doors were a symmetrical pair of landscape murals. In this photo, a cloth banner with four Chinese characters also hung above the wooden plaque with the theater name, across the

FIGURE 8.4 Donn Quai Yuen Theatre, 816 Washington Street. Courtesy Bancroft Library, University of California, Berkeley.

backdrop of the stage. It reads "Noble Aspirations, Elegant Sound," a classic verse denoting integrity and fineness that was the theater's motto.

The two theaters' rivalry intensified as they competed for star performers and spectacles. Therefore, the stages were modified from time to time with additions and decorations. But clearly the newer theater, Donn Quai Yuen, was significantly larger and could accommodate larger crowds and grander presentations. In the 1905 Chinese Directory published by Horn Hong & Co., two theaters are listed: the Grand Theater 丹桂戲院 (Dan Gun Theater) at 816 Washington Street, and the Chinese Theater 昇平戲院 (Shang Ping Theater) at 623 Jackson Street.[23]

Chinese American Theaters and Performers

Chinese theaters' long history in San Francisco gave rise to their new designation as "Chinese American theater." This term appeared in the first of a series of three prominent articles on Chinese theater in the *San Francisco Examiner*. On November 19, 1882, an extensive article reported about the

Jackson Street theater, Dan Shan Feng. Its insightful description of linguistic identity is noteworthy:

> An actor for the Chinese-American theater is required to possess qualifications hardly requisite in the mother country. He must absolutely descend from the pure Chinese to the patois commonly in use in Canton, Hongkong [*sic*] and San Francisco. A Chinaman who has been in this country for a year or two learns to speak in a dialect peculiar to San Francisco; and, to be understood by all, the actor must conform to the rule. It does not differ materially from the usual Chinese dialect used in the large cities, but then the intonation is different.[24]

By bringing attention to both the route of circulation and a distinctive linguistic practice in San Francisco's Chinese theaters, the anonymous writer recognized its identity as Chinese American, rather than simply Chinese.[25] In other words, by noting the linguistic uniqueness of the Chinese community in San Francisco, this writer underscored the significance of the locality (San Francisco) of Chinese American theater. Indeed, the community comprised Guangdong immigrants speaking a range of different dialects, the most prominent of which were the Siyi (aka Taishanese), Guangzhou, and Zhongshan dialects.[26] In their daily lives, as well as in their cultural expression, the inhabitants of the Chinese community forged a mutual linguistic understanding that was distinctive and unique to this demographic, which the writer referred to as "a dialect peculiar to San Francisco." This article both recognized and ascribed a Chinese American identity to Chinese theater. Considering that this was the thirtieth year since Chinese theatrical troupes had first arrived in San Francisco, such an acknowledgment in a mainstream American newspaper, even in passing, was symbolically significant.

It was fitting that this article was also comprehensive in its discussion of the theater's actors and other personnel at the Dan Shan Feng theater. Table 8.1 is a summary of the twenty-three members of the theater described in the article. A few redundancies and contradictions make this list not fully reliable, but it nevertheless gives a picture of the theater. Female impersonators were the most valuable personnel. There were ten of them, and they received the highest pay. Taken as a whole, the list reflected a large operation with significant expenses.

The article focused on depicting three role types: female roles, comic roles and young male scholar roles. The writer closely observed the twenty-seven-year-old actor Bung Ah Soo, the graceful leading female impersonator who was the star of the theater. The actor's residence reflected a comfortable, cross-cultural domestic existence, as well as his eminent status at the theater. It was an apartment with four rooms, furnished in half-American, half-Chinese fashion. The writer's description of the actor getting ready for

TABLE 8.1 Personnel of Dan Shan Feng

Name	Role	Annual Salary	Age
Bung Ah Soo	Leading lady	$6,000	
Ho Leong	Comedienne	$3,200	27
Ah Po	Heavy lead	$3,600	
Ah Lum	Leading man (emperor, mandarin)	$3,600	
Fook Sing	Second leading man (also treasurer and heavy villain)	$3,200	
Ho Leong	Character old man [sic]	$3,000	
Goong Geock Boe	First old man	$3,200	
Mo Sung Hoang		$2,500	
Ah Kee (Ah Ching?)	Young woman (comedy, lady, soubrette)	$2,200	30
Ah Chow	Young mothers (wife of Ah Hong)	$1,500	30
Ah Hong	Young girls (husband of Ah Chow)	$1,500	
Toby Ho	First comedian	$1,200	
Ah Foo	Juvenile ladies	$1,600	
Moo Song Tin	Comedian	$1,500	
Die Kay	Second heavy and treasurer of the company	$1,200	
Goong Boe	Old woman (audience favorite)	$1,500	66
Ah Lie	First juvenile man (princes and lovers)	$1,500	
Ah Chey	Juvenile man	$1,500	
Suey Ting	Second old woman	$600	
Chung Ting	Character old woman	$800	
Suey Ting	Utility woman	$600	
Taing Yon Kit	Utility	$500	
Ty Fook	Utility (mask of black and white, always heavy black mustache)	$500	
Twelve servants			
Eight-man orchestra			
Chinese fiddle	Leader	$800	
Seven musicians	Each at $600	$600	

Source: Based on *San Francisco Examiner*, November 19, 1882.

a performance provides details about the meticulous steps and sequence of preparations, as well as assistance from the actor's wife:

> He first put on the shoes, richly embroidered in gold; then the underskirt, made of dark-blue satin cut in long tabs reaching to the floor, richly embroidered with flowers. After this he made up his face, which consisted in rubbing on lots of white powder, then, with a hare's foot, rubbing on his

cheeks and eyelids a quantity of Chinese vermilion. After that, he prepared to don the woman's wig, which was fraught with considerable difficulty. His queue was tightly wound into a knot by his wife and secured with a long pin to the back of his head. He then tightly placed a band around his head just above his forehead, and fastened at the back above his neck. A wig, already dressed according to the Chinese fashion, was then placed on his head and fastened with pins to the head. After this he donned a rich robe of light-green damask, edged with dark-blue satin, and, seating himself, he was ready for his evening's work.

Ah Soo's professional, confident, and dignified presence left a deep impression on the writer. Noting Ah Soo's pedigree (his father and grandfather were both actors), the writer praised him as a performer who "has already amassed a handsome competency."

The article then turned to comedians, another important asset to the theater. One of the principal functions of theaters was to provide comic relief for the audience. Two actors, Goong Bee and Toby Ho, were most popular.

The favorite of the company with the audience is Goong Bee, a man of about 66 years of age, who plays the ugly old woman, and who has been on the stage for fifty years. . . . The prime favorite of the company, however, is Toby Ho, first comedian. His province is to make the people laugh. . . . His appearance is a signal for a laugh, and before he has entered into any length in his absurd gesticulations and gyrations, he is heartily laughed at.

Laughter was a staple of engaging a popular audience, and farce and slapstick rose in the comedians' performance. The superb Toby Ho (or Toby Hoy) was indeed a celebrated comedian much admired by the community. He was also part owner of the house.[27] When he passed away three years later, the community lamented the loss and the theater managers gave him a respectful funeral.[28] The author was observant about the many role types and distinctive characteristics of the performers, including the appearance and grace of young male role types, even though they were generally less significant on the Cantonese opera stage at the time. And lest there be any question of the seriousness of the performing profession, the writer noted the strict rule for the actors: "Actors are required to be in the building, whether employed in the evening's performance or not, and frequently the comedian or heavy man is called on to perform a role at short notice." This observation revealed that Chinese theaters, which typically gave daily performances with different programs, maintained rigorous and highly disciplined troupes.

With perceptive insight, the writer also made keen observations about the opera costumes, in an effort to decode the symbolic meaning of colors and designs. Table 8.2 summarizes these observations. (A later article in the newspaper's series discussed the meaning of color and spectacle.)

TABLE 8.2 Characteristics of Costumes According to Role Types

Role type	Costume characteristics
Old men	Plain satin robes without gold, silver, or embroidery
Young men (princes, lovers and youthful heroes)	Long robes of the delicate shades of pink, blue, green, lavender, lilac and gray; the vestments are richly covered with bright embroidery, with only an edge of gold
Emperors, judges, mandarins	Robes of richer, deeper colors
Emperor	A special scarlet robe almost covered with golden embroidery, with tiny flags of the same color projecting from the robe at the front and back

Source: Based on *San Francisco Examiner*, November 19, 1882.

A Wooden Boat on Stage

The vibrant popularity of the theater was partly due to its innovations on stage. In December 1882, Dan Shan Feng theater turned to realism by using stage props and mechanical effects. It was the first appearance of a boat on Chinese stage. The news of the grand spectacle—a real boat—was received with skepticism as well as great anticipation in the community. The boat was created with "the mechanical genius of the stage carpenter and the artistic talent of the scene painter," reported the *Examiner* in the second of the series of articles.[29]

Sailing on a boat pushed by waves of raging water was an important scenario in Cantonese opera and appeared in many opera plots. Typically, the scene relied on actors' use of footwork and body movements to express the gentle or stormy motion of the waves. This artistic imitation of sailing was a main attraction. Thus, the novelty of using a real wooden boat on stage gave the convention a new twist. In this play, the star actor Ah Soo (spelled Ah Sue here, aka Bung Ah Soo) was featured with a boat (a junk) crossing the Yang Tse Kiang (Yangtze River). Given the convention of minimalist stage setting in Chinese theater, where one desk and two chairs are used to represent and symbolize a variety of locations and situations, the announcement that a boat would appear on stage was probably stunning, even incongruous, to the audience. Yet to the newspaper writer, the effect was extraordinary for its elaborate and experimental design. The *Examiner* wrote of the innovative scene:

> The curtains of the doorway on the right side of the stage parted and the junk walked in. In the bow of the vessel was Ah Sue, the celebrated actor, and in the stern another Chinaman, who also personated a woman. The junk was about eight feet long by four high, and was carried as the horsemen in burlesque scenes carry their steeds. The heads of the actors touched the roof of the junk, which was ablaze with candles and brilliant with tinsel

and paint. A piece of blue cloth with white dashes hung from the sides of the junk and partially covered the feet of the actors as they walked around. The naval constructor [*sic*] of the theater accompanied the actors on the stage and kept well in front of the orchestra so that the audience could see and admire him. . . . [H]e managed to have the junk outdo in agility anything ever seen on the waters of the Yang Tse Kiang. She bobbed up and down at the end of every verse of Ah Sue's song like a spavined streetcar horse, and twisted around as if the colic was working in her vitals. At every movement the theater roared with delight and amazement, and the waters of the Yang Tse Kiang, so as to leave their feet unobstructed, and with the naval constructor in close tow scooted back to the greenroom, the sensation reached its climax.[30]

As the leading actor of the theater, Ah Soo (aka Ah Sue) was the mastermind behind this radical innovation, a special spectacle for the audience. It was the first of such maneuvers that theatergoers had seen on the stage of a Chinese theater in San Francisco, according to the report. The evening was full of realism; the article noted other unusual stage props, such as a bed. Undoubtedly, this theatrical innovation was influenced by the stage productions of American theater, especially the work of David Belasco, who was in San Francisco during this time and was gaining attention for his realism in theatrical performance. Dan Shan Feng's presentation was, however, different. The "static form" of realism—that is, the props—was incorporated into the opera's traditional choreography to portray the rise-and-fall motion of a boat under sail. The combination of innovation with tradition at Dan Shan Feng embodied the spirit of Chinese American theater.

A Grand Presentation of *The Joint Investiture of a Prime Minister of Six Warlords*

In the third article of the series, the *Examiner* reporter returned to Dan Shan Feng for a new production of *Six Warlords* and again gave a very detailed description of the opera's grandeur. The writer commended Dan Shan Feng theater for being "the most progressive of all [Chinese theaters]. . . . It was there that stage properties were first introduced; there hobby horses first delighted a Chinese audience; there the wonderful property boat and the equally wonderful property bridge struck awe and amazement to the Chinese soul." The article discussed further the theater's new acquisitions and its penchant for innovations. Of the newly arrived wardrobe, the author wrote:

The greatest variety was in the head gear. Hats and helmets of every conceivable shape could be seen. . . . There were six grand square affairs for the six Emperors; a dozen enormous helmets surrounded by erecting fox tails for the twelve great warriors; helmets shaped like pyramids, all blazed with

gold lace and rich embroidery; helmets of black wicker work [. . .] for the
Chinese policeman; helmets of papier mâché, helmets of brass, helmets of
padded silk, and in fact, helmets of every material from cloth to crockery.
The adornments of many of these helmets were a strange mixture of the
styles of two countries—the cheap brass bound looking glass buttons of
Brunmagem side by side with quaint devices in soapstone and mother of
pearl.[31]

Six Warlords was popular; its frequent appearance had already made it familiar to many in white American society. The opera's role as a ritual offering was
only part of the reason. It also was a fantastic showpiece. The magnificent
display and the parade of performers established a victorious and triumphant mood. The opera begins with a formal meeting of the kings of the six
countries, a meeting of their six marshals, and then a scene of persuasion.
This scene is followed by a dance performed by two maidens, as well as a
parade of prop horses, large palace lanterns, and palace fans. After Su Qin
is presented with the prime minister's seal, more acrobatic maneuvers are
performed by soldiers and martial artists. A lively opening with minimal
singing, it mobilizes actors of all the roles in the theater company—as many
as forty to eighty—and has the symbolic meaning of presenting the full cast
in a walkthrough of the stage.

This 1883 report depicted the splendid scene. The performance featured
a hundred-member troupe in glamorous new costumes, as well as unusual
stage props such as a bridge, a horse, and a large, embroidered sunshade. If
the report is to be believed, the orchestra was enlarged with extra instruments as well:

> The Chinese orchestra last night at the Tang San Foon [*sic*] Theater was a
> vastly superior affair to the common run of Chinese orchestras. Three drum
> players with metal drums . . . three pipe players with metal pipes in tone the
> exact counterpoint of a Scotch bagpipe, one bass drum and an enormous
> pair of brass cymbals fully four feet in circumference had been added to
> strengthen the show, besides three most expert blowers of conch shells.

The number of musicians was significantly larger than the usual seven-
member orchestra. The *Examiner*'s report included a list of sixteen actors
and their roles in this opera, among whom was Toby Ho. With Toby Ho
leading the show, the use of innovative stage props—a California police club,
a hobbyhorse—added a new dimension to this familiar, conventional opera
and provided comic relief for the audience. The performance began as the
audience would expect but soon moved on to slapstick.

> The [emperors] marched on first just to give a sort of walkaround and
> show themselves to the audience. They were all dressed in the most gor-
> geous satin robes, reaching to the ground. On a body of true satin scrolls,

arabesques and all kinds of devices were richly embroidered with real gold thread and embossed with floss silk. Crimson, blue, yellow, green and gold were the predominating colors, and the effect was really superb. With the six emperors came two women, richly dressed.

The Emperor, as soon as installed, took his seat at a table in the middle of the stage and the coronation festivities commenced. Half a dozen policemen clad in black robes, red silk sashes and wicker hats entered first. Among them was Toby Ho, the great Chinese comedian, who convulsed the audience with laughter by exhibiting a regular California policeman's club . . . [as well as] great warriors clad in gorgeous robes and armed with huge swords. These swashbucklers gave a sort of dance, and sang a song illustrative of their retirement from politics consequent on the peaceful consolidation of the empire. Then came half a dozen women mounted on hobbyhorses. The huge cymbals clanked loudly as they entered. Toby Ho and his police gave a sort of a sword drill, clashing their clubs to the rhythm of the orchestra.

The next set was a grand tableau, played by the full strength of the company, 100 strong, including supers, and displaying all the new wardrobe. Such a pageant was never seen on any stage before. In the center were two little Chinese girls named Ah Hoe and Ah Moy, beautifully dressed in silken robes, and literally bowed down with the weight of the gold earrings, bracelets and other trinkets they wore. Around them were grouped the hobby horses and half a dozen women holding embroidered silk sunshades of huge proportion over the heads of the six Emperors. Then came the tumblers, in fantastic attire, and the warriors, police, soldiers, citizens and supes, until the stage was so packed that one could scarcely move. A space was cleared, however, and servants entered bearing rich presents for the wise man, Ah Lin, and the Emperors. The band played, the warriors danced a species of breakdown at the end of which the whole force left the stage to give place to the counselor.

For several weeks, noted the reporter, the community had been struck with awe and amazement by innovation after innovation at the Jackson Street theater, but with the grand display of *Six Warlords* the theater reached a pinnacle of extravagance that was emulated many times throughout the decade. The theater created a world of fantasy and beauty in significant contrast to the bleak political reality of the Chinese Restriction Act, a major blow to Chinese immigration and a threat to the existence of the Chinese American community.

Visitors and Audiences

The increased popularity of Chinese theater was apparent in the growing number of lengthy reports and articles about it. If, as the British paper *The Era* noted, unlike European visitors, Americans were influenced by the prevailing antagonism to the Chinese, and thus generally avoided exploring San Francisco's Chinese quarter, Chinese theater was an exception.[32] In 1883, a group of conventiongoers from Boston attended two different theaters on consecutive nights. They explained, "We should not have another chance to go to a Chinese theatre till we visited San Francisco again."[33]

A visitor from Philadelphia also appreciated Chinese theater, noting, "I have never heard anything more melancholy than the sounds which reached us." The report went on to give a vivid description of scenes of rescue, chase, sacrifice, battle, ordination of a priest, and cajolery for forgiveness, among others.[34] The famous Swedish diva Christina Nilsson attended a Chinese theater in 1882 during her San Francisco visit. Amazed by the falsetto, she proclaimed, "I never heard anything quite so lofty as that." The reporter wrote, "she adjusted her voice to its highest pitch and tried softly to measure notes with the Mongolian artist. 'I can't reach it,' she said: 'it is too high for me.'"[35] A famous Hungarian opera singer, Etelka Gerster, was invited by the Austro-Hungarian consul to visit a Chinese theater in 1883, "where a special play was produced in honor of the fair diva."[36]

An *Omaha Daily Bee* reporter joined a *San Francisco Star* writer who asked a friend, an influential Chinese merchant, for the free use of his private box at the Donn Quai Yuen theater on Washington Street. The writer gave a full description of both the coveted space and the stage:

> Attached to the balcony on the right-hand side, facing the stage, are four private boxes, each capable of holding six or eight persons; and two proscenium boxes overlooking the stage and holding a like number of people. Directly opposite the balcony and proscenium boxes there is a compartment corresponding in size to the entire boxes on the right hand sides specially set apart for the Chinese women who frequent the theater. On the night of our visit there this compartment was completely crowded with the fair sex, and in fact, so it is every night. The theater is lit up by a few gas jets, which are so distributed as to cast an even light over the whole scene. . . . [Onstage was] the name 'Don Quai Yuen' in electrical vibrating letters as a centerpiece.[37]

As a form of cultural connection, Chinese theater was enjoyed by the elite class and by other artists. Oscar Wilde made a visit during his lecture trip to San Francisco in 1882. Luigi Arditi, the Italian composer and conductor of the Havana Opera Company, was treated by the Bohemian Club members to special stage seats in a Chinese theater.[38]

In 1885, the Dan Shan Feng theater on Jackson Street was damaged by fire. After a turnaround, its reopening brought new attention. The *Chronicle*'s reporter visited the theater and wrote a long article, noting that "San Francisco had better opportunities of studying the Chinese drama than the people of any other American city."[39] He observed that the theater was well staffed with a full cast, such as crowd-pleasing comedians, highly skilled and eloquent middle-aged warriors, and female impersonators in costumes of "silks, laces, solid gold, pearl, tortoise shell and ivory ornaments, as well as the glossiest of headdresses and tiniest of sandals." On the initial information from an interpreter, the reporter wrote that the leading man at the theater, Mung Qua Choy, was "at the present one of the greatest actors in Chinatown. . . . He has assumed the place of that paragon in his profession, the highly esteemed and much-lamented Toby Hoy, who died about a month ago, and whose equal existed nowhere, not even in China." But later, the reporter got a more candid assessment of Mung Qua Choy from the interpreter: "He had been engaged at one playhouse and then another without giving much satisfaction. His acting would not compare with that of his illustrious predecessor and the patrons of the establishment took no pains to conceal their disappointment." Translating the words of a super, the interpreter added, "By and by Mung will go back to China."[40] The comment revealed by inference that, if a Chinese actor was popular, developing a performing career in America was a viable path. However, Mung Qua Choy was deemed not successful enough to establish himself in the United States. It led to a rare insight about Chinese audiences' discriminating taste, as described by the reporter:

> Chinese audiences are more critical, or, at least, more outspoken in their criticisms than are white theater goers. While making little if any demonstration when they are particularly pleased, they take no pains to conceal their disgust with what is not strictly *au fait*, and a bad actor on the Chinese stage feels less at home than do many of our pompous ranters and scene chewers. . . . Hissing is never heard, but the long drawn and far more effective "Ugh! Ugh!" resounds through the theater, and the subject of these expressions of disapproval is often compelled to leave the stage, very fortunate if he succeeds in dodging the soda-water bottles, bits of cane, and decaying fruit which are aimed at his retreating form.[41]

This observation sheds light on the theatergoing experience in Chinatown. Chinese audiences were not monolithic or indifferent, as most reports portrayed them, but rather had varied interests and different levels of appreciation of opera. Indeed, the tastes and interests of the Chinese audiences shaped the repertoire at their theaters. They were active, rather than passive, participants in theatrical culture.

A detailed description of a comic opera, *Sam Wang and the Pigs*, came from the pen of a playwright and theatrical manager in London, Howard Paul. In an 1885 essay for the *Illustrated Sporting and Dramatic News*, he wrote: "When last in San Francisco I was a regular attendant of the Theatre in China Town, and the manager, who spoke excellent English … enlightened me a little on the subject of the Chinese drama."[42] With an interpreter's help, Paul explained the story of *Sam Wang and the Pigs* (or *The Dim Pig-Seller*), a long-popular Cantonese opera known for its convoluted and twisted plot. The basic story leaves much room for improvisation and comic banter. It is a humorous story. A country bumpkin is sent by his wife to sell a pig at the market. He falls in with sharpers who swindle him out of his pig. Since his emptyhandedness is sure to anger his wife, a sharper pities him and teaches him ways of parrying the punishment, including boxing moves. At home, the irate wife punishes him and ties him to a post by the road. In the traditional story, he is freed after managing to fool and tie up a priest in his place.[43] The version given in Paul's essay has a complex ending, with the addition of a hunchback—which he notes is "a standard character in Chinese farce"—and a case of mistaken identity. It ends with the wife realizing the virtue and cleverness of her husband and forgiving him. With brilliant comedians, this opera was a favorite at the theater. The essay provides a vivid picture of this kind of humorous performance at the theater.

Chinese Actors on American Theater Stages, and Vice Versa

Given the attraction of Chinese theater, it is not surprising that Chinese actors began to be hired by American theaters for Chinese-themed theatrical and musical performances, a quick-growing trend that one author called "the latest Eastern craze."[44] In September 1885, the Bush Street theater in San Francisco led the way in its production of a burlesque version of *The Mikado*, proudly reporting that "a genuine Chinese actor, Ah Gow, took part." It was a weeklong run that unfortunately included a scene making fun of Chinese theater. As the *Examiner* reported, "A scene on the stage of a Chinese theater is imitated with comical faithfulness, Charley Reed's prancing about in the headdress and embroideries of the leading actor, while Alphonso, painted and bedizened, assumes the falsetto of the leading lady."[45] In this performance, Chinese theater was minstrelized with direct mockery. Still more abhorrent, however, was the appearance of yellowface actors portraying Chinese servants in contemporaneous plays such as *My Partner* (1879), which had already reinscribed racial stereotypes on the American stage.[46] Despite the mocking scene, Ah Gow's stage presence might have challenged the use of yellowface performers in American popular entertainment.

It came into notable vogue for Western dramas to include a Chinese role for comic purposes. In 1887, the Chinese actor Ah Wung Sing was lauded for his role in a play called *The Golden Giant*. As the *Omaha Bee* commented, "The only English speaking Chinese actor on the American stage in the part of a

California Chinese servant. . . . [H]e has made an artistic success, and come in regularly for his share of applause."[47] This was no small feat, considering that characters portrayed as artistic usually were reserved for actors who were English, Anglo-Saxons, or North Europeans (and their descendants)."[48] By performing in this play, the twenty-nine-year-old Ah Wung Sing became a member of the acting company led by the playwright-actor-manager McKee Rankin, which was touring the country. The *Indianapolis Journal* wrote of its performance at the new English's Opera House in that city: "The play is one of much interest, and . . . the different members of the company are equal to the requirements, including a novelty in the acting business in the form of a real Chinaman, Ah Wung Sing, who personates a Chinese servant."[49] The play added the Chinese role of Jim Lung as servant, Rankin's biographer explained, "because it had become obligatory for western drama to have a Chinese character, . . . where they were objects of merriment and comicality."[50] *The Golden Giant* met with considerable success, from the Grand Opera House in San Francisco to the Fifth Avenue Theatre in New York. News reports noted emphatically that Rankin's company included "a Chinaman from the Chinese Theater in San Francisco."[51] Later, according to news reports, when the company crossed over to Canada, it had to pay a fifty-dollar (Canadian) "duty"—actually a head tax—for Ah Wung Sing.[52] In 1885, in response to anti-Chinese sentiment, the Canadian government had passed a law stipulating that all Chinese entering Canada must pay fifty dollars as head tax.

As Chinese actors began appearing regularly on American theater stages, impresarios also tried to bring non-Chinese performers to Chinese theaters that typically had a large audience. In 1886, the *Chronicle* reported the engagement of white acrobats, jugglers, trapeze artists, and other entertainers to perform at the Donn Quai Yuen theater.[53] As primary cultural institutions in the community, Chinese theaters became a bridge to and a link of cultural exchanges, both unilateral and bilateral.

At century's end, a visitor from England strolled into a Chinese theater. He made evenhanded, acute observations, listening with keen curiosity. Most important, he captured the joy of the theater.

> From floor to roof it was filled with Chinamen, except one gallery, well screened off, which held, I believe, the Chinese ladies. There was but little talking: every one seemed interested in the play, except a few ragged children who were running about, some on the stage near us, and some behind it. A few of the men were smoking, including some of the actors not, for the time, taking part in the scene. About a dozen of musicians filled the back of the stage, and were playing continuously, except during the comparatively rare intervals of spoken dialogue on the part of the actors. Their music was exceedingly interesting, in spite of its monotony. It was all minor; the air,

repeated with little or no variation, being neither sad nor merry, reminding one distantly of some brisk Irish melody. It contained, I think, a subject and answer, each expressed in a few phrases, and written in a mode to which our minor seemed the nearest approach, but different from it in a way I could not grasp, though I tried very hard. A single violin led; there was no proper alto or tenor part, but a weird accompaniment, made by striking sticks of different lengths, which emit short sounds of determinate and high pitch; and by a sort of kettledrum, a triangle, and a pair of large brass cymbals. These last were not used all through, but to emphasize some special interesting part of the dialogue, or at the close of what perhaps corresponds to an act. . . . The audience evidently followed everything very closely, and now and then interrupted this very even performance, with roars of laughter. Everywhere I saw intelligent and beaming faces.[54]

The English writer, as a newcomer to the genre of Cantonese opera, was perceptive in grasping its sonic characteristics. What he heard as "a subject and answer" refers to the couplets in Cantonese opera arias that are set to pairs of closely connected musical phrases, the so-called upper and lower phrases.[55] His depiction of sticks creating "short sounds of determinate and high pitch," and the drum and large brass cymbals used to "emphasize special interesting parts of dialogue" reflected a comprehension of the function of percussion accompaniment in Chinese opera. Most important, he seemed to enjoy the opera along with other audience members.

CHAPTER 9

Picturesque Chinese Theater

The prosperous Chinese theater scene was a significant attraction not only to the Chinese community but to the population at large, whether they were born and raised in San Francisco, had moved to the city like the Chinese themselves, or were simply temporary visitors. In its fourth decade, Chinese theater became an essential part of the city's cultural life. Writers and journalists began to treat Chinese theater as a subject of study during its height in the1880s, making repeat visits to performances and learning the conventions of the opera genres. They were joined by artists and photographers who also sought to capture the people and scenes of the Chinese quarter with their cameras and paint brushes, almost all of whom did so with the help of Chinese assistants or apprentices. These texts and images produced a substantial, sometimes knowledgeable, representation of Chinese theaters for those who lived elsewhere. They appeared in magazines published in New York and books published as far away as London.[1] Artworks were bought by collectors on the East Coast or in Great Britain; postcards or photo prints circulated beyond California. As authoritative accounts and portrayals, these textual and visual studies documented the Chinese theaters of San Francisco in an unprecedented way. In this chapter, my goals are to establish a sense of how these depictions reflected the theaters, to retrieve, whenever possible, from these images and words something of the life and spirit of these theaters, and to decipher traces of their agencies in the images and words. In addition, I will consider how this textual and visual attention to Chinese theaters in the fourth decade constituted part of the larger cultural and social milieu inside and outside of Chinatown, including the wider, transoceanic manifestations.

Chinese Theater and the Bohemian Club

In the last quarter of the nineteenth century, San Francisco saw an immense growth of newspapers and magazines, as well as social and cultural groups.[2] As we will see below, for one group in particular, the Bohemian Club, the Chinese quarter made possible their exploration of the city's visual and sonic distinctiveness as part of their cultural investment. Chinese theaters were something for city dwellers, writers, and artists to ponder, whether or not they had empathy for the Chinese people. If for white laborers and politicians, Chinatown was a political target, for aspiring white writers, journalist, painters, and musicians, it was far more complicated. As the historian Raymond Rast notes, "They recast Chinatown as a vital preserve of authentic, premodern culture, conveniently if curiously located amidst the swirl of modernity."[3] By this time, Chinatown was physically located within the twelve-block area bounded by California and Stockton Streets, Broadway, and Kearny Street, close to the busiest part of the city. It attracted writers such as Catherine Baldwin, who visited "the quarter at various hours of the day . . . in order to experience and describe the pleasures of a stroll through Chinatown."[4] Cultural institutions such as Chinese theaters were fertile grounds for their artistic ambitions, as they allowed the writers to break from social constraints and "experience the 'real life' in its full intensity."[5] Thus, Chinese theaters participated in the development of cultural and creative activities in nineteenth-century San Francisco.

The Bohemian Club was formed in 1872 by a group of journalists and writers in a newspaper editorial room. They were soon joined by artists and patrons of the arts. Located close to Chinatown, the club became a social haven for those who were "connected professionally with literature, art, music, the drama, and those who, by reason of their love or appreciation of these objects, may be deemed eligible," as noted in the club bylaws.[6] The club's membership expanded over time and by 1879 boasted nearly five hundred "of the brightest and wittiest minds in the metropolis connected with letters, music and art, either professionally or by taste."[7] The art historian Anthony Lee provides a vivid description of their activities:

> Its original members were committed to fostering camaraderie between men of the arts and nurturing their artistic ambitions. They rented rooms on Sacramento Street near Kearney, the southeast corner of Chinatown, and made the place not only a meeting room but more famously an informal theater for "jinks"—brief though sometimes intricate plays that were partly dramatic but mostly satiric, based on wordplay and overwrought classical allusions. . . . The jinks soon became more regular (monthly) and often more elaborate. The plays became more complex, fully scripted with stage directions; the acting parts expanded; and the props and costumes soon

seemed more fit for a small stage than a rented room near Chinatown. The artist members began producing sketches, watercolors, and oil paintings to be included in the plays, or sometimes simply to announce them; and the club itself began to amass this collection of art and ephemera whose value quickly became considerable.[8]

The club's monthly High Jinks (entertainments) as well as its annual festivals of literary, dramatic, and musical productions, turned into prominent cultural events. One such production by two members, Templeton Crocker and Joseph Redding, eventually became a Chinese-themed American opera. Well-connected in the elite world of social dignitaries, several of its members were also appointed by the US government as representatives to China.[9] The Bohemian Club exemplified the unique cultural connection between San Francisco's Chinese theater and the city's art scene in the last quarter of the nineteenth century. Although only one artist discussed in this chapter, Theodore Wores, was a known active member of the club, a similar cultural milieu formed the backdrop for contemporary pursuits among writers, authors and artists in the city.[10] The significant relationship between the Bohemian Club and Chinese theaters will be discussed further later in this chapter, particularly in connection with Theodore Wores, who played a crucial role in the nineteenth century's most significant essay on Chinese theater in America.

Three Essays on Chinese Theaters

For their depictions of Chinese theater, the writers George Hamlin Fitch and Henry Burden McDowell and the painter Theodore Wores stood out. Their essays and artworks became important documents of San Francisco's Chinese theaters during the early 1880s. A decade later, a third writer, Rev. Frederic J. Masters provided a lengthy essay about Chinese theaters, based on his extensive missionary work. Unlike general reportage, these essays were close studies. It is notable that McDowell's essay demonstrated considerable engagement with San Francisco's Chinese theater at its height, whereas Masters's essay documented the decline.

These writers were not alone in depicting Chinese theaters in writing; as a major attraction in San Francisco, the theaters were the subject of many commentaries in travelogues and tour guides.[11] Two examples, both published in 1882, were most significant in length. In *Through America: Or, Nine Months in the United States*, the Englishman Walter Gore Marshall wrote of his visit to San Francisco on June 14, 1878. He offered twenty pages on Chinatown, of which five pages concerned the theater.[12] And in *America Revisited: From the Bay of New York to the Gulf of Mexico, and from Lake Michigan to the Pacific*, the famous English writer-journalist George Augustus Sala described his extended visit between November 1879 and April 1880.[13] His thirty-page chapter on Chinese theater was mostly tongue in cheek, as if he were in a contest with other writers on how best to make a caricature out of the Chinese theater experience. Like Marshall and Sala, many authors were temporary visitors to the city; most never returned. As travel literature, these accounts ranged from memoir to humorous writing. They were not explorations or studies. For quite a number of the authors, arrogance, ignorance and racial hatred filled the pages, and reactions to the theaters went little beyond outlandish descriptions and a tone of shocked disapproval. In particular, Sala considered it a sport to ridicule the music and singing of Chinese theater, an attitude which, due to his fame as a writer, worked to shape general perceptions of Chinese theaters.

In contrast, the three San Francisco writers were either local or made an extended residency in the city and were considered Californians in their time. They all contributed to the fourth phase of Chinese theater's development in the form of "sonic ethnology." Their essays were written from knowledge of the city and the Chinese quarter; their descriptions of Chinese theater reflected their exploration of, though not necessarily fondness for, its practices and conventions. Among the three, Fitch made clear his dislike of the music and his low opinion of both the theaters and the Chinese people. Nevertheless, they endeavored to observe, describe, and document. Their essays all appeared in East Coast publications, the first two articles in *Century Magazine* and the third in *Chautauquan Monthly*. Considered together, they also show the evolution of the use of visual media: Fitch depicted the picturesque theater with no help from illustrations; McDowell prominently incorporated wood engravings commissioned for his essay; and Masters used photographs. To the extent that these texts have long constituted the basis of today's understanding of nineteenth-century Chinese theater in San Francisco, as well as discourse about it, their historical significance is unmistakable. Furthermore, placing these essays in a larger context leads to further understanding of the ways in which Chinese theater became part of the texture of American society.

George H. Fitch, "In a Chinese Theater," *Century Illustrated Magazine*, June 1882

When he wrote this essay, George Hamlin Fitch (1852–1925) was at the beginning of a long and notable career as a writer and literary editor for the *San Francisco Chronicle* (1880–1915). This four-page article was written shortly after the very public rivalry between the Donn Quai Yuen and Dan Shan Feng theaters, which Fitch summarizes briefly in the opening. The article then focuses exclusively on the fourth theater, Donn Quai Yuen (also known as the Grand Theatre) on Washington Street, offering detailed descriptions ranging from physical structure to operation. He noted that the theater opened at 2 p.m. every day with short farces and comedies for audiences comprising primarily women and children, and again at 7 p.m. with regular evening performances. The theater had a jewelry and watch shop at the front, and a side entrance over which was a sign in gilt letters, "Grand Theatre," with a foot-tall Chinese version in four characters. From there, a few steps led up to the entry to the auditorium, shielded by a heavy cloth. The interior was a moderate-sized amphitheater with a slanted ground floor, a balcony, two narrow galleries, and private boxes. One of the private boxes was reserved for women and children. Fitch describes a fully packed house (he estimates three thousand) on a Saturday night, depicting a lively and fluid atmosphere in the theater: "There is continual conversation among the audience in a low tone, and continual restlessness among those standing at the rear of the room, while two streams of incoming and outgoing patrons keep pouring through the narrow doorway."[14] Spectators also stood on both sides of the stage, an enthusiastic crowd that needed to be forced back at times to ensure sufficient stage space. The green room was half filled with large, iron-banded trunks and rows of costumes and robes, their heavy silk and satin embroidered with beads. The walls were adorned with gilt and spangles, while elaborate headdresses and helmets hung from pegs. Fitch's description of the seven-member orchestra stemmed from a Western perspective: a fiddle player accompanied the singing and switched to cymbals as needed; a percussionist used a mallet to strike a brass gong suspended on a wire cord at the level of his head; another percussionist played on a drum made of wood; a third percussionist played drumsticks on a smaller disk of burnished brass; and three players performed on banjolike instruments, switching to hornlike instruments occasionally.

Noting that Chinese dramas often centered on the quarrels of dignitaries, Fitch focused on a description of *The Dragon Disputing Pearls* based on his observations:

> [T]he scene opens on the household of an Emperor, who is blessed with two wives. Each spouse represents a favored province that has shared in the honors and rewards of the royal choice. Each wife has borne a son, but to the son by the first wife belongs the inheritance of the throne. The fierce jealousy between the partisans of the two wives is communicated to the two brothers, and in a quarrel the younger slays his elder brother, throws the body into the river, and gives out the report of an accidental drowning. The truth of this domestic tragedy reaches the ears of the Emperor. He summons the younger wife and her son. In the mother's presence he kills her boy, but not before she has bruised his forehead in her struggle to save the youth. Injury to the Emperor's person is a capital offense, and

the wife escapes death only by declaring that she is with a child. A short time after she gives birth to a boy. The Emperor has a great desire to get possession of this infant heir to the throne. He succeeds in palming off a spurious infant on the nurse. The mother detects the fraud, ascertains where the genuine child is hidden, dons male attire, and at the head of an armed force (six "supers") marches to the province and demands her child. A long parley is held with the governor of the province, but when the imperial flag is shown, this functionary delivers up the infant, and the militant mother returns in triumph. The Emperor is struck with her ability, recognizes the child as his heir, and peace broods over the imperial household.[15]

Not surprisingly, this opera made ample use of Cantonese opera's popular tactic of suspense. The plot had multiple twists, incorporating familiar tropes such as partisans' petty fights, a stolen infant, a woman disguised as a man, and an awe-inspiring emperor awakening to his fault. Fitch took special note of the effectiveness of the crossdressing episode and praised the leading actor's balance of masterful martial movement and the comic element.

> [The audience's] enjoyment was elicited by the disguise of the mother in man's attire. When she stroked her long false beard, several of the spectators laughed heartily, while a ripple of smiles passed over the stolid faces of others. The roles of the two wives were played by Chinese men with fine soprano voices. One was a skillful actor, and imitated many peculiar feminine traits and gestures with much nicety. The leading man, who was brought over from Peking, and whose salary is $10,000 a year, has a face brim-full of fun. He succeeds in leavening with a comic element some of the heavy plays, and his command of all the stage "business" is consummate. When engaged in combat with a foe he whirls about like a spinning dervish, crosses long spears with marvelous rapidity, and, at the end, accompanies his triumph song with a jig that would do credit to the burnt-cork brethren.[16]

Although he did not use the term, the amusing effect of the double gender-crossing—that is, the irony of a male actor performing a female character who is disguised as a man—was not lost on Fitch. He praised the skilled performance again in a later essay in *The Cosmopolitan*: "The actors, of course, are all men, and the cleverest work is done by those that personate women."[17] Although he made clear his dislike of the music and the opera conventions, his close observations nevertheless conveyed the emotional dimensions of the dramatic performance. For example, he described a scene he watched from the backstage: "Suddenly, an actor bursts in, there is a wailing cry from the man at the stage door, the guards file upon the stage, with the [leading tragedian] hero at their head, and a moment after we hear his strong, resonant voice, between the crashes of cymbals, breathing threats of vengeance against his foes."[18] Another example of the wide range of emotion and powerful expression brought the scene to life for the readers:

> Defiance is hurled against an adversary to the full power of the speaker's voice, his distended eye and ferocious frown typify the workings of inward rage; his mouth betrays a capacity undreamed of at a casual glance. . . . But though he may disappear in a whirlwind of wrath, his face showing demoniac rage and his voice husky with strident bellowing, he will come back in a few moments with a placid smile on his flat face, gay, jaunty, debonair.[19]

As one of the first full-length essays on San Francisco's Chinese theater, Fitch's article in *Century Magazine* was widely reported in the news. Clearly, in addition to its vivid descriptions, this article's popularity was also largely due to readers' interest in the early stage of the fourth phase of Chinese theater's development. This article is a prime example of "sonic ethnology." Published in New York, it satisfied curiosity and sated the appetite for news about the famed Chinese theater scene on the nation's Pacific Coast. With such success, it is not surprising that *Century Illustrated Magazine* printed another article on Chinese theater two years later by yet another California newspaperman, this time almost five times the length of Fitch's article and with ample illustrations.

Henry Burden McDowell, "The Chinese Theater," *Century Illustrated Magazine*, November 1884

Henry Burden McDowell (1857–1928) arrived in San Francisco in the 1870s with his father, Irvin McDowell, a famous Union general who later retired from the army and served as the city's parks commissioner. As discussed in chapter 6, in September 1879 General McDowell hosted the former president Ulysses S. Grant in San Francisco on his return from Asia, where the decision was made to receive the delegate of the San Francisco Chinese consul with an official meeting and a visit to a Chinese theater. With a pedigree and a family fortune, as well as artistic ambition, the young McDowell developed a reputation for literary and theatrical interests. In 1879, although he was an integral part of the city's high society through his father, McDowell also was a staff writer for the *San Francisco Examiner*; wrote for the *Overland Monthly, Argonaut,* and *Daily Alta California*; and cofounded a weekly paper called the *Ingleside*, which lasted a year and closed after serious debt.[20] As a reporter for the *Examiner*, he quite likely contributed to the series of articles on Chinese theater published there from November 1881 to January 1882, which are discussed in chapter 8. His own first theatrical endeavor in San Francisco was *Wedded by Fate*, a play he cowrote with a Bohemian Club member, Edward Field. It premiered in 1881 at the city's Baldwin Theatre, managed by the famed impresario Thomas Maguire, whose advertisement noted that "the houses [are] crowded nightly with the elite of the city."[21] The play of five acts and six tableaux was directed by the then little-known David Belasco.[22] At the end of 1884, shortly after the publication of this article, McDowell leased the Oakland Theatre, ambitious to produce plays that would feature renowned actors and scenery painters, and a full orchestra.[23] His eighteen-page essay on the city's Chinese theaters is the most comprehensive of the period; its significance was noted widely by his contemporaries. Like the first essay discussed in this chapter, numerous newspaper reports drew attention to the article's publication. The article included fifteen illustrations, and the prose was inextricably linked to the powerful visual representations. We will discuss first the remarkable illustrations.

A. Theodore Wores and His Illustrations

The significant collaboration in this article of "decidedly popular interest" did not escape the attention of the *Daily Evening Bulletin*, which in complimenting the article noted, "The article is from the pen of Henry B. McDowell. The credit for clever illustrations belongs to Theodore Wores and Kenyon Cox."[24] Wores was the primary illustrator; following this successful collaboration, he and McDowell produced another article together in 1892.[25] Promising artists of the time were engaged for the illustrations, so the quality of the artwork was very high. As a whole, these fifteen illustrations gave a poignant presentation of Chinese theaters and actors, in stark contrast to both the panoramic views in the 1870s by Joseph Becker and the Reverend Samuel Manning, and the sensational depictions with racialized features by Ogden and Yeager in 1878 discussed in earlier chapters. Rather, Wores and Cox were generous with the gestures and physical characteristics of the performers and distinctive elements of the theaters. Their close studies provided informative, vivid, often witty portrayals of theater life.

The large number of artists involved in the illustrations is shown in table 9.1. Not all the artists and engravers are identified in the essay, so the list is incomplete. Nevertheless, it shows the complexity of the illustrations and the key roles of Cox and Wores. In what follows, I will first discuss the three images by Cox and then consider in greater length the significance of Wores as a painter and a Bohemian Club member, as well as his seven works for this article.

The New York-based painter Kenyon Cox did not set foot in San Francisco to render this artwork. Like many illustrators of his time, Cox worked in his New York studio to make these engravings after pictures. Trained in Philadelphia and Paris, he made a large number of wood engravings for magazines to support himself as a painter. Later he was selected as one of the

TABLE 9.1 Henry Burden McDowell, "The Chinese Theater," Artists

Title	Artist	Engraver	Source
The guard of the goddess of mercy		Kenyon Cox	
A hunter		Kenyon Cox	
A painted-face king		Kenyon Cox	
Two princes playing checkers		Kenyon Cox	
A candy seller	Theodor Wores	Anon.	after painting
In the women's gallery	Theodor Wores	Anon.	after painting
Makeup	Theodor Wores	Anon.	after painting
An entrance	Theodor Wores	Harry Davidson	after painting
A pirate	Theodor Wores	Not legible	
A god of thunder	Theodor Wores	Khayman	
The eclipse	Theodor Wores	Anon.	
Exterior of Washington Street Theatre		Stephens	
Post-office		Stephens	
Box-office		Stephens	
Interior of Jackson Street Theatre, morning		Anon.	

America painters featured in the 1889 Paris Universal Exposition. Balancing geometry with realism, Cox had a firm control of line, shape, light and dark, mass, volume, and texture. His engravings faithfully depict several role types, with witty and lighthearted portrayals of characters. "The guard of the goddess of mercy" (fig. 9.1) is a young warrior in armor with a comic expression. "A hunter" (fig. 9.2) is the *gongjiao* role type, a white-bearded man of lower social status. "A painted-face king" (fig. 9.3) is an *erhuamian* role type, a hot-tempered, virile man whose face paint reflects his fiery character. And "Two princes playing checkers" (not shown here) features one civic role of a scholarly type and another performer with a sophisticated headpiece more typical of a female character than a scholar. Sitting across from each other, their focus is on the checkers game on the table. A master of clear lines and concise composition, Cox created in these engravings close studies of vivid characters on the stage, both their visual appearance and their characteristic spirit. With skilled observation, he captured the mood and artistic flair of these performers.[26] Though simple in their composition, Cox's engravings marked a significant departure from earlier or contemporary illustrations of Chinese performers, where emphasis on facial or other physical features was

THE GUARD OF THE GODDESS OF MERCY.

FIGURE 9.1 Kenyon Cox. "The Guard of the Goddess of Mercy." Wood engraving. In Henry Burden McDowell, "The Chinese Theater," *Century Illustrated Monthly Magazine* 29, no. 3, November 1884.

A HUNTER.

FIGURE 9.2 Kenyon Cox. "A Hunter." Wood engraving. In McDowell, "The Chinese Theater," *Century Illustrated Monthly Magazine.*

A PAINTED-FACE KING.

FIGURE 9.3 Kenyon Cox. "A Painted-Face King," Wood engraving. In McDowell, "The Chinese Theater," *Century Illustrated Monthly Magazine.*

inevitably inserted by engravers for a more sinister version than the original drawing, such as the illustrations in both Sala's and Marshall's 1882 books.[27] Rather, Cox's realistic engravings of Chinese actors point to a new trend of artistic representation of Chinatown figures, which would continue to be developed by other artists. What's more, his engravings capture the distinctive characteristics of the role types, for example, the subdued and humble *gongjiao* role of the hunter and the resolute, awe-inspiring *erhuamian* in the painted-face king.

Like Cox, Theodore Wores provided illustrations for McDowell's text, but most likely he was also centrally involved in the writing of this article. In order to fully understand this painter's role, we must make a detour to consider how Wores acquired his reputation and the significance of the painting *The Entry*, which we have already discussed in chapter 8 (see fig. 8.1). This California native attracted attention for his series of Chinatown-themed paintings in the 1880s. Although many credited his focus on Chinese topics to his previous training in European art schools, one source placed the beginning of his interest in Chinese themes prior to that trip.[28] By his own account, Wores grew up walking daily through the Chinese quarter between his father's hat shop and home. Abroad, he received training at the Royal Art Academy in Munich and traveled to Italy, eventually returning to San Francisco in August 1881.[29] His first major work on a Chinese theme, *The Chinese Fishmonger*, was exhibited at the San Francisco Art Association in November 1881. With its fine treatment of dark tones, strong highlights, and animated expression, the painting immediately caught the attention of reviewers and was later sold by New York's prominent art gallery M. Knoedler & Co. The *Californian* wrote admiringly, "In the unique Chinese world, which preserves its Orientalism intact among us, he has found a fresh and picturesque subject."[30] The following October, when California's Governor Leland Stanford hosted a farewell dinner for General Irvin McDowell and Sir Thomas Hesketh, the latter bought Wores' painting *A Shop in Chinatown* for $1,250.[31] Following these successes, the art world watched with anticipation for Wores's next work on a Chinese theme. In February 1883, Wores moved his studio to Montgomery Street, as noted by a reporter, "where he designs to pursue his studies of Chinese subjects in the adjacent Mongol quarter. He intends to begin on a picture of the interior of a Chinese theater, where the figures will be life-size and the rich material of their dress permit the artist to treat texture, which he excels in representing."[32] His portrayal of the splendor of Chinese theater was eagerly awaited.

Three months after moving, Wores's progress on a painting called *Chinese Actor* was reported. "The costume and figure are finished, and the stage accessories and red-paper legends are now engrossing the artist's attention."[33] The painting was completed in July and was destined, after a brief exhibition, for

Goupil & Cie., a prominent Paris art dealer with a branch in New York City.[34]
In a detailed description of the painting, the reporter Philip Shirley noted,
"The robes and headdress, with its long, curving feathers, which form the
costume of the large figure in the foreground, are painted with fine artistic
fidelity to texture and color—the crude, strange, barbaric hues of Chinese
richness. The face of the actor is also of the higher type of the race than that
usually seen about the streets."[35]

The power of the painting is also an appreciation of the musical scene, as
shown in another major work, *Chinese Musicians*, which Wores produced
in spring 1884. This work drew attention from collectors such as "Messrs.
Yungling and Helm of New York and Sir Thomas Hesketh and Lord Rosebery of England," according to a *Chronicle* reporter.[36] Indeed, the critically
acclaimed *Chinese Musicians* was bought by Lord Rosebery and sent to
London.[37] It featured a drummer, a fiddler, and a lutenist, the last of whom
appeared in several other paintings as well.[38]

In its time, Wores's *Chinese Actor* was a celebrated work. It was photographed by the Isaiah West Taber studio, a prominent San Francisco photographer, and the photo print was circulated by both the painter and the
photographer (see Fig. 8.1). Retitled "The entry," the photograph is today
collected in many archives, one of which includes an inscription to the wife
of the famous San Francisco publisher of the *Chronicle*: "To Mrs. de Young,
with compliments of Theo Wores."[39] Although the original painting's location remains unknown, the photograph shows its complexity.[40] However, his
rise to fame in the intense atmosphere of anti-Chinese sentiment meant that
critics either rushed to reassure the public that they were not actually sympathetic to the Chinese or that they questioned the aesthetics of the congenial
image. In other words, it was a difficult sale. Wores's success with Chinese
themes was read through the lens of the nation's racial politics. In 1884,
Chinese Actor was included in the Fifty-fifth Exhibition of the Pennsylvania
Academy at Philadelphia, which received his artistry well: "Theodore Wores
has a striking full-length figure, 'Chinese Actor,' full of color and remarkably
well painted."[41] The price of painting was set high at $1,500.[42] But a comment
in *The American* showed the reviewer's bewilderment at its incongruence
with racial stereotypes:

> Mr. Theodore Wores' "The Chinese actor. Scene in the Chinese Theatre,
> San Francisco" (no. 238) is interesting as a study of character which is still
> strange to us, and which probably possessed for Americans few elements
> of permanent interest, but the picture is painted in a masterly way, and the
> subject is at least unhackneyed and unconventional. The strange impas-
> siveness of both the actor and the musicians so inconsistent with Western
> ideas of what constitutes dramatic interest, but eminently characteristic
> of the Orientals, has been admirably rendered.[43]

Embracing a beautiful painting of a dignified Chinese performer was probably too risky for American collectors, even in the art world. Luckily, this brilliant painting was not buried in oblivion. More than a year after its completion, an engraving of the magnificent *Chinese Actor* appeared, retitled "An Entrance," in McDowell's November 1884 essay for *Century Illustrated Magazine*. With the public's high regard for his work, Wores's illustrations also brought attention to the article. (Fig. 9.4 shows the wood engraving version in the article, whereas Fig. 8.1 is a photograph of the original painting.)[44] In many ways McDowell's article was intrinsically linked to the art and literary world that had shown such a strong interest in the picturesque Chinese theaters.

Wores's paintings unveiled an important dimension about the attraction of Chinese theater. If the novelty, most notably his faithful and sympathetic

FIGURE 9.4
Harry Davidson. "An Entrance." Wood engraving after Theodore Wores. In McDowell, "The Chinese Theater," *Century Illustrated Monthly Magazine*.

AN ENTRANCE.

VOL. XXIX.—5.

portrayal of Chinese actors and theaters, hindered the acceptance of his work by a certain faction of society, it was also the key factor in his success. The engraving of "An Entrance" was the only full-page picture in the article and was a clear focal point. It was expertly made by the *Century Illustrated Magazine*'s leading engraver, Harry Davidson. In the backdrop of "An Entrance," we can see traces of both theaters: Dan Shan Feng (the crescent stage design and a plaque bearing its Chinese name) and Donn Quai Yuen (the sculpted a dragon and waterspout above the door frame). Wores combined these elements to convey the theatrical atmosphere.[45] The composite may not be true to either theater, but the image reflects how a visitor or writer absorbed the richness of the spectacle at both venues.

All of Wores's artwork for McDowell's article is rich in detail and context. Whereas Cox's engravings of the performers eliminated the background to focus on the characters, in most of Wores' illustrations, a rich background constituted a crucial part of the story they told. "A Candy Seller" (fig. 9.5) shows a vendor balancing a round tray full of snacks on his shoulder while handling a transaction by handing an item to an audience member seated

A CANDY-
SELLER.

FIGURE 9.5 "A Candy Seller." Wood engraving after Theodore Wores. In McDowell, "The Chinese Theater," *Century Illustrated Monthly Magazine.*

in a row of wooden chairs. Such a tray, according to Fitch, contained "many compartments filled with oranges, limes, nuts, sweetmeats, bits of sugarcane, and peanuts."[46] Facing away from the stage, the peddler, in traditional Chinese trousers and shoes, tilts his body to deliver the candy, his routine act and casual stance in sharp contrast to the expansive gestures of the performers on stage, lightly sketched at the center of the picture. The audience member is distracted by the hand in front of his face, a clear divergence from the rows of attentive audience mesmerized by the performance. The depth of the theater is marked by perspective, formed by rows of audience members' heads and the straight lines of the gallery on the right, and by the variety of shapes depicted in the frame. From a small corner of the theater, a sense of spaciousness is conveyed in vivid detail.

"In the Women's Gallery" (fig. 9.6) depicts a group of nine audience members in the partitioned gallery for women and children to the right of the stage. A Chinese sign on the back wall notes clearly, "Separation of man and woman, please." On the left side of the picture, two ladies appear engaged by the stage happenings. Their high social status, and that of the two girls next to them clutching the railing, is made apparent by their dresses, ring, bracelets, and earrings. McDowell described the women's gallery as "picturesque with many colored handkerchiefs of flaming gold, blue, green, and yellow."[47] Accompanying the two ladies and the girls are an older maid and a wet nurse. There are several rows in the gallery, shown by the lines behind

IN THE WOMEN'S GALLERY.

FIGURE 9.6 "In the Women's Gallery." Wood engraving after Theodore Wores. In McDowell, "The Chinese Theater," *Century Illustrated Monthly Magazine*.

the family, as well as a single figure receding into the background. The attraction of the show is made clear by the absorbed expressions of the ladies and girls. Meanwhile, the central importance of theatergoing as a family routine is vividly portrayed by the interaction between the concerned maid and the wet nurse, busy with a needy infant and a toddler clinging to her, all behind the well-dressed ladies and girls engrossed by the stage. Wores's painting shows the mixture of desire, duty, and emotion circulating in this corner of a Chinese theater.

"Making Up" (fig. 9.7) captures a rare scene backstage, where an actor is applying face paint. The actor portraying a sturdy character, likely *erhuamian*, is half dressed for the stage, with only his inner garments on, and is in the

FIGURE 9.7 "Make Up." Wood engraving after Theodore Wores. In McDowell, "The Chinese Theater," *Century Illustrated Monthly Magazine.*

MAKING UP.

process of applying paint to his face, which already has pronounced shapes and lines. One hand firmly holds the paintbrush; the other holds out a mirror. Both gestures accentuate the actor's command of his professional skills. In front of him are a collection of paintbrushes in a box, while scattered at his feet is some of his gear—wardrobe trunk, stool, instrument, headdress, jar—showing the typical disarray of a dressing room as a performer prepares for the stage. Various vertical and horizontal items hanging from the ceiling or on the wall add to the sense of a crowded space and bustling mood. Because the face painting conveys the symbolism of a brusque and volatile character, the shapes and colors are quite dramatic. Wores also painted this man's complete transformation into his character as "A Pirate" (fig. 9.8). The outlines of the face painting in the dressing-room scene now appear in finished form: the white circles above the eyebrows and around the eyes, the white nose, the curved lines around the outer contours of the cheeks,

FIGURE 9.8 "A Pirate." Wood engraving after Theodore Wores. In McDowell, "The Chinese Theater," *Century Illustrated Monthly Magazine.*

A PIRATE.

and the downward-turning lips. The fervent character of this forceful role type is enhanced by his weapon, a long stick held confidently in one arm. This portrait without background was a quick study, as was another actor portrait, "A God of Thunder" (not reproduced) as well as the eclipse symbol that ended the article. Wores's artistic attention to Chinese theater reveals his close analysis of these everyday figures and activities and his masterful depiction of their theatrical spirit.

One cannot help but wonder about the role Wores played in McDowell's writing of this comprehensive essay. Could the painter and the writer have joined forces in the effort to communicate authoritative knowledge about Chinese theater, each rendering his observations in a different medium? Could McDowell's discussion of the leading actor be a kind of collaboration with Wores's painting? Did the periods of their extended studies of Chinese theater overlap? We do not know for sure. As noted above, in February 1883 Wores moved close to Chinatown with the intention "to begin on a picture of the interior of a Chinese theater." These pictures, therefore, could well represent the culmination of those months of studies, portraying the interior of a Chinese theater in both its glamour and its everyday activity.

Four more wood engravings in the article have a more ambiguous author-ship, either vaguely marked as "Stephens" or illegible. But they directly cor-respond to the text in the essay and keenly convey the daily life of the theater. "Interior of Jackson Street Theater, Morning" (fig. 9.9) confirms our previous

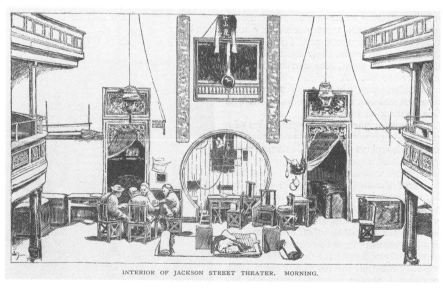

INTERIOR OF JACKSON STREET THEATER. MORNING.

FIGURE 9.9 "Interior of Jackson Street Theater, Morning." Wood engraving. In McDowell, "The Chinese Theater," *Century Illustrated Monthly Magazine*.

discussion about the distinctive features of the stage, with the circular alcove and the theater name in Chinese characters, Dan Shan Feng, at the very top. (See also Dan Shan Feng in fig. 8.3.) But instead of a theatrical presentation, it shows the mundane daily routine, with the carpet or sleeping gear rolled up at the center of the stage, chairs scattered around, the curtains of the back-stage doors pushed aside, and four men gathering around a table, conducting business or playing some sort of game. And "Exterior of Washington Street Theatre" (Figure 9.10) shows a plaque with the Chinese characters with the name of the Washington Street theater, Donn Quai Yuen, and in smaller English letters underneath, "The Grand Theatre." Behind its half-open door, a stairway leads up to the theater; off to the side, a storefront displays its wares. The horizontal lines of the theater on the side of the street, with a

EXTERIOR OF WASHINGTON STREET THEATER.

FIGURE 9.10 "Exterior of Washington Street." Wood engraving. In McDowell, "The Chinese Theater," *Century Illustrated Monthly Magazine.*

significant gradient, reveal the distinctive steep hills of the city. The two small drawings annexed to the picture are interesting as well. One shows a box office with small windows and Chinese signage: "Prosperity upon watching/ seeing." The other one, labeled "post-office," shows a stack of posts affixed to a column, the top of which reads, "Chen Lin, must return home immediately." McDowell explained, "The 'post-office,' a high pillar supporting the roof of the theater, is being frequently consulted. By the last advices, one Ma Chung is informed that his 'wife is sick' and that he 'must come home immediately."[48] The wood engraving as a whole reveals the functions of the theater: not only entertainment but also dissemination of messages from home or within the larger Chinese community. In this public space of large gatherings, someone would have been available to read posts for illiterate members of the audience. These pictures provided a glimpse of the crucial role of Chinese theaters as community spaces with multiple purposes. The inclusion of these candid illustrations shows the writer's keen sense of the theater as a living space as well as a performing space.[49]

In his panoramic 1870 drawing (Fig. 4.1), Joseph Becker emphasized the width of the theater with sweeping perspective, framing the stage at the far end with actors whose expressions are barely visible. He used the rows of spectators in the pit and the galleries to project the depth of the theater, accentuating the liveliness of the space with the interaction of audience members in the foreground and presenting the interior of the theater with proportion and structure. Similarly, published in 1876, Rev. Samuel Manning's depiction of a Chinese theater (Fig. 4.12) also included an array of attentive viewers to convey the sense of the width of the theater space, where the hatted audience in the foreground is effectively animated by their straining necks. In these two illustrations, the most prominent part of the theater spectacle is the audience, rather than what is happening on the stage; the actors' gestures and positions are rendered as backdrops. In their 1884 illustrations, however, Wores and his associates vividly portrayed the Chinese actors and connected them to the detailed descriptions in McDowell's essay.

B. McDowell's Discourse on Chinese Drama

McDowell's essay added information and analysis to the visual representation of Chinese theaters. Interested in both the theater and the mythology of Chinese culture, McDowell discoursed on Chinese folk religion, dramaturgy, and theatrical practice. His discussion of the conventions of Chinese opera performance relied on both the knowledge he had gathered of Chinese theater and his own extended viewing experiences. The earnest effort, however, did not save him from misconstruing some conventions. Even his misreadings enhanced the theater experience rather than diminishing it, for him and his readers, at least. And for the most part, his keen observations amounted to an indispensable record of performance practice at these theaters in the 1880s.

McDowell begins the essay by describing his attendance at a special performance honoring several deities. He discussed four ritual performances: Eight Immortals Offering Longevity; Peach Banquet for Queen Mother of the West; The Goddess of Mercy-Guanyin, Monkey King, and Four Kings of Sea; and God of Cash. McDowell probably imagined parts of the plots, dialogue, and choreography, but the essence of the Chinese legends came through. McDowell noted the central importance of deities in the theaters. He wrote that a box above the backdrop of the stage "is the means by which the patron Joss . . . can at once witness and preside over the performance." In a footnote he depicted an important scene related to the ritual function of the theater within the community:

> The Joss of one of the six companies in San Francisco was asked the other day, on the occasion of his birthday, which theater he preferred to attend, the Washington or the Jackson street. The sticks were thrown up. They came down on their flat side. The Joss had pronounced for the Jackson street establishment. He accordingly was carried through the streets of San Francisco with great pomp and placed upon the receiving altar.[50]

Though written in a humorous tone, this footnote attests to the importance of Chinese theater in the community and how opera performance constituted a prominent form of worship. It also explains the wooden railings at the top of the back wall of the stage in both theaters, making clear their function as altars. Deities also figured in McDowell's discussion of ticket prices in local practice. He explained that in southern China, because troupes were typically hired by wealthy patrons to perform for auspicious reasons—bringing blessings, evoking good fortune, and creating an uplifting atmosphere in temples or other public spaces—commoners did not have to pay.[51] In San Francisco, all audience members had to pay, but the low price of five cents for the last hour of the performance meant that everyone could enjoy the theater.

Since "pantomime" was how American audiences understood the stage movement of Chinese theater, it is not surprising that McDowell drew attention to it, as well as to other distinctive performance practices in dialect, plot outline, and improvisation, all of which were common in nineteenth-century Cantonese opera:

> For all the characters in the drama, except perhaps the comedian, who may, to save his joke from falling flat, occasionally drop into the vernacular, speak a dialect unfamiliar to the mass of the audience. . . . To correctly read these [theatrical] conventions, and thus get some little idea of the real meaning of a Chinese play, calls for more than an ordinary exercise of mental effort and intellectual sympathy. . . . A man who throws his leg into

the air on the Chinese stage is supposed to be mounted on horseback; but this should not be taken as a realistic act, but only as a conventional sign to which the spectator must add his imagination. . . . A change of scene on the Chinese stage is indicated in two ways. If the change takes place from one part of the house to another, the characters of the play indicate their entrance into another room by means of pantomime; the comedian sometimes going so far as to stumble over the imaginary threshold. If, however, the change is total, and does not admit of being acted out, it is suggested conventionally by the whole dramatis personae walking rapidly three times around the stage. . . . Most of the Chinese acting plays are, like those of the early Italian stage, the merest "outlines," the dialogue in most cases being left almost entirely to the spontaneous improvisation of the actors. Yet, strange enough, the conversations do not seem to lose much by the process, and appear quite as pointed and confined to the action as if they had been committed to memory.[52]

As noted earlier, Cantonese opera was performed is the *zhongzhou* (Central Dialect) dialect, which was different from the dialects spoken in San Francisco's Chinese community. Thus appreciation of the stage was a complex and acculturated activity that involved learning to "read" the conventions. The opera's reliance on plotline, scenario, improvisation, and stock characters recalled for McDowell the Italian commedia dell'arte of the sixteenth to the eighteenth centuries. In Cantonese opera, performers all mastered conventional scenarios, so even with only plotlines, their performances were well grounded in the same tradition.

From the recurring themes about scholarly success and history in the plots, McDowell commented insightfully on Chinese society's value system and historical legends as reflected in its theater:

Hardly a play is performed that some allusion or other is not made to a scholar's having received, or being about to receive, the first degree at the imperial examination. . . . In the minds of the Chinese, every play is conceived to be an intercepted portion of the history of China. This conception is as important as it is subtle; for only on such an hypothesis can be explained the frequent appearance and reappearance of the Emperor and his court, and the constant, if intermittent, conflict of the imperial troops with barbarians and with rebellious subjects. . . . The epic strain in the Chinese drama makes one play quite susceptible of being run into another, and has thus led to the popular error that Chinese plays are of inordinate length.[53]

At heart a student of theater, McDowell was keen to find the similarities between Chinese theater and Western tradition. He devised a systematic approach to explain Chinese opera conventions as he knew them, listing seven different plot types. The seven categories were likely drawn from knowledge of the conventions he gained from Chinese informants, as well as from his observations of performances and his own theorization of Chinese dramaturgy.

I. Historical Play or Tragedy
II. Comedy
III. Platonic-love Play
IV. Court Play
V. Chivalry Play
VI. Persecution Play
VII. Merit-rewarded Play

For McDowell, this taxonomy was a tool to decipher the wide-ranging variety of repertoire shown in the theaters. He grouped the last three types as "melodrama," in his opinion a lower artistic form. Of its psychological appeal, he wrote dismissively, "[I]t is precisely the inartistic, improbable character of the melodrama that makes it popular with its votaries; for, to a downtrodden and unhappy people, who have long given up the hope of substantial justice in real life, an agreeable improbability will always be preferable to a disagreeable truth about the stage." An interpretive logic stemming from English drama tradition, it probably was relatable to his readers, but also was quite pertinent to the opera convention.

McDowell's astute understanding of role types, on the other hand, allowed him to make connections between the two cultural traditions, such as the following depiction of the warrior role type:

> The conventional hero of the [Chivalry Play] is always a painted-face military character, who, like the knight-errant of medieval Europe, goes about doing good, in spite of the consequences. Though his motives are good, however, his methods are impulsive; the dramatic interest, therefore, is sustained by the trouble that these methods create, both for himself and his friends; and poetic justice is ultimately satisfied by the triumph of these methods at the end.[54]

The painted-face character is illustrated in Cox's drawing of the "Painted-Face King" (see fig. 9.3). In addition, McDowell appreciated the plot twists and characters of Cantonese opera, praising "its ingenuity of plot and strength of characterization." His understanding of the role types was considerable. To help his readers fully comprehend Chinese theater, McDowell also provided a systematic classification of role types in civil and martial operas.

A translated Dan Shan Feng theater playbill featuring *Che Young Kwong Builds a Ship That Sails on Land* was reproduced in the essay. Noting that spectacular operas typically drew large crowds on Saturdays, McDowell described the major attraction of the Dragon and Peacock ship, the appearance of actresses, and the movement of a cloud ballet. What he described was a conventional Cantonese opera based on a story about Emperor Yang of Sui (Young Kwong), who enjoyed extravagance and often conscripted laborers for massive construction projects. He was fond of traveling on water and had an imperial ship sufficiently large and luxurious to serve as a floating palace. When he desired to travel to Youngzhou—even though there was no waterway and travel by land was necessary—he insisted on bringing the imperial ship anyhow. He demanded that the roads be spread with soybeans and that beautiful girls be summoned to pull his ship, so the floating palace could sail on land. From McDowell's description, the Dan Shan Feng theater's production of this opera made an extraordinarily grand spectacle out of the emperor's extravagant boat, as well as his indulgence in elaborate entertainment with dancing, singing, and appearances by young girls. The article also revealed the theater's novel use of sophisticated stage props, rather than conventional chairs and tables, as well as employing actresses rather than all-male troupes. The description here echoes the 1883 article "A Walking Junk: The Great Dramatic Sensation of Chinatown," one of the three lengthy articles on Chinese theater published in the *Examiner* (see chap. 8).[55] They confirmed that during the 1880s, Chinese theaters in San Francisco broke from opera conventions of symbolism and fostered innovative ideas.

C. Impact on Theater Arts

Echoing Wores's meticulous paintings, McDowell's observations of Chinese theater and performance were thorough. His writing had considerable influence on his contemporaries in a variety of ways. The American ethnologist Frank Hamilton Cushing, who was known for his pioneer studies of the Indigenous Zuni people of New Mexico, incorporated McDowell's work in his comparative studies of Chinese theater and Zuni mythic drama. In 1887, Cushing spent time exploring Chinese theater in San Francisco, accompanied by McDowell and Kate Field, a noted journalist and playwright.[56] A lengthy article published in the *Examiner*, "The Mythic Drama: Cushing Compares the Chinese Theater with the Ka-Ka of the Zuni—The Sacred Masks—An American Ethnologist Makes a Discovery of Great Scientific Importance," relied heavily on McDowell's studies and reproduced two illustrations from his article, Wores's "A God of Thunder" and Cox's "A Painted-Face King."[57]

Less than a month after the November 1884 publication of McDowell's article, a New York correspondent for the *Daily Alta California* pointed out that it had created a strong interest in Chinese theater, and business plans for bringing Chinese theater to the East Coast were underway.

> Something Decidedly New: I have lately learned of an entirely new theatrical scheme which will probably soon be undertaken by an Eastern agent,

who makes almost annual trips to San Francisco. For the present I have promised to withhold his name. Harry [*sic*] McDowell's very able article on the "Chinese Stage and Drama," so well illustrated by Wores, which appeared in the November *Century*, awakened considerable interest on that subject in the East, and it is the intention of my managerial friend to take advantage of the same. It is his idea to bring East the entire theatrical company from one of the San Francisco Chinese theatres, with their entire outfit of costumes and stage paraphernalia, and play them in the principal Eastern theatres, remaining in no city more than a week and frequently only two or three nights. He would engage a first-class interpreter to explain the meaning of the play as it progressed, and also a company of expert tumblers and athletes. The enterprise would require very little advertising on his part, for its novelty would advertise itself, and it would arouse an extraordinary curiosity.[58]

This positive news report about Chinese theater reflected the elevated understanding of Chinese theater in the mid-1880s. Indeed, as anticipated, a Chinese theater would appear in New York City five years later. McDowell's in-depth article, with its vivid and inspired illustrations, deepened understanding of Chinese theater and pushed it to greater acceptance by mainstream America. His informative essay was also widely used by students of theater as a source of knowledge about Chinese theater and inspiration.

The impulse that led McDowell to examine Chinese theater so closely not only reflected his literary and artistic ambitions but also stemmed from his desire to challenge his own inherited culture. It recalled a similar impulse expressed in the *Boston Daily Globe* article "The Demand for a Chinese Theatre in Boson" published in 1877 (see chap. 5). Indeed, the growing interest in and knowledge of Chinese theater fueled a radical set of ideals, creative forces, and modes of expression, all of which broke with convention and pointed to, as the historian Daniel Joseph Singal calls it, the beginning of modernism at the end of nineteenth century.[59] As a dramaturge, McDowell leased Oakland Theater shortly after the publication of this successful essay, and engaged actors, scene painters, and musicians for a production. After his father passed away, he returned to the East Coast and embarked on the Theatre of Arts and Letters, which he helped found in 1891. It was a subscription theater for literary plays; its trustees included the actor Edwin Booth, the director Eugene Presbrey, and the playwright Augustus Thomas, among others. The object of the theater was to present "plays of real artistic value" in order to alter the current condition of theaters that produced "broad farces, vulgar comedies, coarse melodramas." Another objective was to "foster dramatic authorship in this country," according to the New York–based *Werner's Magazine*.[60] As an early organization in the independent theater movement, the Theatre of Arts and Letters had a high profile, supported by social elites.

It performed in New York and Boston and was reviewed widely. Although it was short lived, it remains historically significant. The famous theater critic Kenneth Mcgowan noted, "By a terrific effort the history of the rebel theatre in the United States can be forced back to 1892 and the abortive Theatre of Arts and Letters."[61]

The reception history of McDowell's comprehensive article reflected its impact across both the Atlantic and the Pacific Oceans. Almost immediately after its publication, London's *Illustrated Sporting and Dramatic News* noted, "A paper upon the Chinese Theater in San Francisco, by H. B. McDowell, is curious and interesting; it gives a much clearer notion than has been conveyed in anything which we have read on the subject hitherto, of the real methods and form of the Chinese drama."[62]

Theodore Wores was a very active Bohemian Club member, producing for the club many pictures of its High Jinks as well as a portrait of Oscar Wilde, who visited in 1882. Wores's exploration of Chinese theater closely matched the general interests of the club members, whose musical, theatrical and artistic endeavors often drew from the Chinese quarter. With a membership of five hundred in 1884, it held literary and musical meetings on the last Saturday evening of each month, for the "promotion of social and intellectual intercourse between journalists and other writers, artists, actors, and musicians, professionals and amateur."[63] The club's president, Joseph Redding, would present his first play on a Chinese theme, *Shy-Shy*, at one of the club's High Jinks (1891). The all-male Bohemian Grove productions were elaborate, specially written plays with extensive orchestral, choral, and solo vocal music that were performed annually by Bohemian Club members. *The Land of Happiness*, a Grove play by Redding and another member, Charles Templeton Crocker, was produced in 1917 in the Bohemian Grove. It was expanded and published as a Chinese-themed opera, *Fay-Yen-Fah*, which premiered in Monte Carlo in 1925.[64]

The wide circulation of the photograph of Wores's "Chinese Actor" also established a new model of representation. A photograph of another Chinese actor appeared in an 1888 article on San Francisco as part of the *Pacific Bank Handbook of California*, which also included photographs of the residence of Charles Crocker, a view of San Francisco from the residence of Governor Leland Stanford, the Palace Hotel, and other places of interest.[65] The original photo by Carleton Watkins that was used by the publication is shown as figure 9.11.[66] Photographs, rather than artistic wood engravings, were now the norm for magazine illustrations, as the next section will show.

In the background of the photograph of the actor in the young warrior costume, we can see various musical instruments. Bowed stringed instruments, such as an *erxian*, hang on the wall, and a *yueqin* is hung between the windows, below which is a *shagu* (drum) on a wooden stand.

FIGURE 9.11 Carleton Watkins. *Chinese Actor.* Photograph.
Courtesy of the J. Paul Getty Museum, Los Angeles.

Frederic J. Masters, D.D., "The Chinese Drama," *Chautauquan Monthly*, April–September 1895

Published in 1895, while the Chinese community was suffering under the harsh restrictions of the Geary Act, Rev. Frederic J. Masters's article depicts Chinese theater in a different light from the previous two authors.[67] Masters joined the Wesleyan Missionary Society in the 1870s, was stationed in southern China, and in 1885 arrived in San Francisco to serve as superintendent of the Pacific Coast Chinese mission.[68] A prolific writer, he supplemented the ministry stipend by publishing a series of articles on San Francisco's Chinese community.[69] The topics ranged from temple to highbinders (gangsters) to theater. Nine pages in length, "The Chinese Drama" contains many observations comparing the theater in its golden days with its more recent decline. With his language ability and his proximity to Chinese theaters (his Methodist Episcopal Mission House was located at 916 Washington Street), Masters was able to connect actors' romanized names with Chinese characters noted by some Chinese sources.[70] Just as important, though, his narrative reflects the circulation of knowledge resulting from nineteenthth-century missionary work, sinology, and transoceanic commerce.

As a missionary in San Francisco, Masters was familiar with the bleakness of Chinese life under the Geary Act, and his report on the Chinese theater scene conveyed that reality. Although Donn Quai Yuen remained in operation on Washington Street, as did the Jackson Street theater (now named Po Hing), they were open during alternate weeks due to the dwindling community, according to Masters. Theater proprietors rented their buildings, furniture, and wardrobes to other Chinese theatrical companies for ten dollars a month and worked out the division of the proceeds. The size of the companies was also reduced to only thirty members, making it impossible to produce grand historical plays. Masters noted the stratification of social classes. There were two tiers in the galleries for women and children—one for married women of the poorer class or second wives of merchants, and the other for the demi-mondaines with their colorful clothes and makeup. The boxes had curtains and were reserved for merchants and their first wives. Ticket prices still decreased as the evening went on, but were higher than before: twenty-five cents for the whole evening, fifteen cents after two hours, and ten cents for the last hour of the show.

During difficult times, worship of deities became even more important. Masters noted, "About ten feet above the stage is a little temple containing the images of Tam Kung Ye and Wah Kung, the god of fire." Ritual offerings remained central to the theaters' role, which district associations typically sponsored for $150 or $200 per night. The significant presence and vibrant presentation of the ritual offering, in addition to appeasing the deities, must have been a source of comfort for the community in this sorrowful time.

> The tutelary god of the clan or association, [is] carried in state to the theater amid salvos of gongs and firecrackers. A warm fur coat protects Joss' delicate constitution from the chill night winds when the weather is cold. . . . [It] is the commonest thing in China for a town or village to express thanksgiving to the gods for a good harvest or deliverance from pestilence, flood, or fire, by subscribing for a theatrical show to be held in their honor in a *matshed* erected in the temple yard.[71]

During Masters's mission in China, he was located in Foshan, a city with a prominent history of Cantonese opera.[72] However, instead of discussing the regional genres of Chinese opera, Masters relied on general sinology and wrote about the literary history of Chinese drama. References to famous figures in the Tang, Yuan and Ming dynasties abounded, such as the opera-loving Emperor Ming of Tang and the revered *Story of Pipa* by Tang Xianzu.

Similarly, with his description of the play *The Mender of Cracked Chinaware*, Masters brought a transoceanic network of knowledge to bear on his report of San Francisco theater. The English translation of the play, also known as *Pu Kang*, had a long history of circulation in missionary periodicals, travelogues, and sinology literature. It was included as an example of Chinese burlettas in the 1848 book by the missionary and sinologist Samuel Wells Williams, an 1838 report of the Hong Kong merchant William C. Hunter, and an 1849 book by the British vice consul in Hong Kong, Henry Charles Sirr.[73] Each of these widely diverse writers noted that this play was an example from which to draw certain conclusions about Chinese society. The inclusion of this opera in this essay, therefore, placed Chinese theater in the larger colonial knowledge.

The most significant contribution of Masters's essay is the information about performers. He meticulously recorded some performers' names and their salaries, suggesting the presence of several prominent Cantonese opera performers of the time (table 9.2). This list shows a significant disparity in compensation, and it echoes the famed top salary of ten thousand dollars reported by George H. Fitch a decade earlier. In reality, as Masters acknowledged, due to the hard times and the decline of Chinese theater, performers actually received only a fraction of these salaries. Nevertheless, the report shows the hierarchy of theater performers, as well as the appearance of actresses on stage.

Six photographs accompanied Masters's article: two of actresses, three of actors, and one of the theater interiors. Interesting in themselves, they also marked a significant step forward in the discourse on Chinese theater in America. The plain photographs with full-length portraits of performers were not as animated as the artistic wood engravings by Cox or the paintings by Wores, but they were important for another reason. Four of the portrait photographs were captioned with the romanized names of the performers— the first documents to link Chinese performers' names with their images.

TABLE 9.2 Salaries of Chinese Actors According to Masters, "The Chinese Drama"

Name	Role	Annual Salary in US Currency Unless Otherwise Noted and Possible Chinese Name
Cheong Kam Tong	proprietor of Washington Street Theatre	張錦棠 (Zhang Jintang)
Leung Chuck	lead singer	靓卓 (Liang Zhuo) $10,000
Pang Nga Su	comedian	崩牙蘇 (Bengya Su) $1,600 for 3 months in Portland
Pock-marked Hoh	tragedian	$8,000
Mrs. Ah Moy	star player of Doonn Quay Yuen, a married woman	$1,800
Tak Bing	female role, fa dan	$5,000
Lee San	principal comedian	$1,500
Soo Ho Tai	tragedian	$2,000
Anon.	fiend, manshang	$1,000
Anon.	musician (7)	$500

These photographs were a vast improvement on the faceless names in earlier reports and census data and the anonymous faces in drawings, postcards, and photographs. They signaled a major shift from considering Chinese performers merely as a type to recognizing them as individuals with distinctiveness, agency, and identity.

Just as significant was the photograph of the interior of Donn Quai Yuen on Washington Street (fig. 9.12). This was the first publication of a photograph of the theater, showing a well-appointed theatrical space. Landscape paintings decorate the panels of the railing along the galleries and the private boxes on both sides. The stage has many nice amenities: a carpeted floor, tables and chairs covered with drapery of embroidered cloth, an upstage wall adorned with two large landscape paintings. The rectangular alcove for the orchestra is decorated with an embroidered valance and gilt carvings; the two backstage doors have embroidered curtains as well as the symbol of an eclipse above the door frames, as discussed in McDowell's article. The position and placement of furniture on the stage suggests a court scene, with a mandarin presiding behind a table at the center, probably consulting with a prominent official sitting to his left. A lower-level attendant stands to the right of the mandarin. Two more figures sitting on each side of them appear to be of lesser importance.[74] Needless to say, pictorial representations of Chinese theaters had come a long

THE TAN KWAI YUEN THEATER, SAN FRANCISCO.

FIGURE 9.12 Donn Quai Yuen Theater. Photograph. In Frederic J. Masters, "The Chinese Drama," *Chautauquan* 21, no. 4 (July 1895).

way, from the receded and flattened image of a stage in Joseph Becker's 1870 drawing to this full and detailed photograph of a highly decorated stage. In other words, the Chinese stage was no longer the background of the ethnic scene of Chinese community but spotlighted here as a platform for the performing arts. The tables and chairs covered with opulent textiles resemble those in figure 5.2b, photographed by Lai Fong in Hong Kong. Incongruent with the stage scene, however, is the inclusion of two Caucasian men lounging against columns at the two sides of the stage. It is unclear why they were in the picture. Were they police officers? Their casual posture and apparent detachment from the stage scene reminded readers of the predicament of Chinese theater a decade into the Chinese Exclusion Act era.

Masters's essay, interwoven with a significant amount of colonial knowledge about Chinese drama, helps provide a vantage point for us to consider the homegrown perspectives on Chinese theater in San Francisco by writers and artists such as Fitch, McDowell, and Wores. Intimately connected to the local networks of art, literature, and theater, they viewed Chinese theater as an exciting, even dazzling, dramatic space, and took on the task of "translating" it and capturing its spirit for others. They approached the study of Chinese theater with respect for its long tradition and by personally experiencing its wonders. Their repeated visits to watch performances, and their search for answers and interpretations from theater insiders, were themselves a local and spatial negotiation of the cultural scene in the city. From the streets of the Chinese quarter and the stairs of the Chinese theaters, which bore their footprints, they produced a knowledgeable and vivid, though at times misconstrued, representation of Chinese theater. They participated in and unveiled the life of Chinese theater, leading the readers through dramatic performances, distinctive character types, and theatrical spaces with their narratives and illustrations. Their on-the-ground reports and first-person observations documented in sympathetic detail the story of Chinese theater in America.

In this respect, Wores's remarkable illustration of the "Candy Seller" was unique (fig. 9.5). It is a portrayal of the Chinese audience's perspective. In the pit (where only Chinese sat), amid the other Chinese spectators as well as peddlers weaving among the rows of seats, the man takes a moment from watching the performance to get snacks, supplied by the diligent peddler. It was an enjoyable time at the theater. This everydayness, shown in the nonchalance of the illustration, attested to the vibrancy of both the theater and the community. In contrast to the usual focus on the stage, the performers, or the anonymous rows of audience members merely creating perspective, this picture gave agency to one member of the audience, depicting the sense of pleasure the theater provided. It gave readers a glimpse of the theatergoing experience of the Chinese community. The theatergoer could almost be Ah Quin, the worker who spent hours and hours in the theaters.

CHAPTER 10

Civil Rights, Owning Glamour, and Sonic Ethnology

In spite of his impressive presence, the actor Loo Chin Goon's 1883 plan to bring Chinese theater from San Francisco to the East Coast did not succeed (see chap. 8). Yet his highly publicized arrival in Philadelphia was neither insignificant nor inconsequential. The enthusiasm and attention he received reflected the American public's growing fascination with Chinese theaters, thanks to their vibrant presence in California. People elsewhere in the country were eager to establish similar cultural institutions. McDowell's 1884 article also sparked a significant level of interest, as evidenced by the commentary of a theatergoer in the *Indianapolis Journal*: "The characters [of the Chinese theater] were almost the identical ones represented in H. B. McDowell's article. . . . [F]rom my hasty view of the performance and the characters, I judge this article is a pretty faithful description."[1] The interest in Chinese theater was further fueled by the American public's fascination with the 1889 Paris Universal Exposition, marking the height of the fourth phase in the development of Chinese theater in the United States—sonic ethnology.

Through Loo Chin Goon's arrival, an unexpected link between the theatrical initiative and the civil rights cause of Chinese Americans was established. His grand entrance motivated a Chinese American civil rights leader in New York City to champion and advocate Chinese theater and engaging in public discourse about Chinese drama. This leader was Wong Chin Foo.

Chinese Theater and Civil Rights Advocacy

Born in Shandong Province, northern China, Wong Chin Foo (王清福, 1847–1898) was baptized and came to the United States in 1867. After several years of study, he went back to China but returned to America in 1873, acquired US citizenship, and began his work as an advocate for Chinese in America. He was well regarded by the American reading public. In 1878, an

Illinois poster for his lecture "Buddhism and Confucianism" read, "Wong Chin Foo! The Illustrious Oriental Orator, in Full National Costume, in his Famous Discourse."[2] He later settled in New York in 1883 and founded the *Chinese American*, the city's first Chinese-language newspaper. The aim, he explained, was "to supply the long felt want of our countrymen." The paper coined the term "Chinese American," introduced it into the public consciousness, and charted out this newly defined identity. By this time, he was a frequent contributor to English newspapers and periodicals with poems, sketches, and articles about Chinese culture, serving as a counterforce to the anti-Chinese voice that gripped the nation. The *Journalist*, a New York magazine devoted to newspapers, authors, artists, and publishers, stood with Wong Chin Foo against his adversary:

> The best answer to the anti-Chinese argument, if such it may be styled, is the mere contrast between Wong [Chin Foo] and the leading Chinese of this city, educated, courteous, orderly and gentle, and Kearney and his heelers, ignorant, vulgar, dirty and lawbreaking. There is unlimited room in this country for the former; there should be none for the latter.[3]

Thus it was not surprising that when the opera actor Loo Chin Goon announced in Philadelphia his plan to establish Chinese theater in New York, reporters turned to Wong Chin Foo for his opinion. With his usual optimism, Wong noted, "I believe in the American stage, and it would now be distinguished at Chinese representations."[4] So inspired and enthusiastic was Wong that shortly after he began speaking of the translation of a Chinese play, *The Loyal Slave*, a drama that he claimed was the equivalent of Homer's *Iliad* and *Odyssey* for Chinese literature.[5] The translation was to be made for the first appearance of Loo Chin Goon on the East Coast.[6] Thus began Wong Chin Foo's association with and advocacy for Chinese theater.

Although Wong Chin Foo had paid no attention previously to Chinese theaters, he quickly took up the initiative, building on the momentum created by Loo Chin Goon's fame and the general enthusiasm. Wong felt that theater arts, an expression of Chinese civilization, was a source of pride for the Chinese community.[7] It suited his civil rights agenda well. Besides, art could change hearts more easily than speeches. Wong began advocating for establishing Chinese theater as a medium to enhance understanding of Chinese art and culture. He proceeded to provide authoritative accounts of theatrical conventions to educate non-Chinese and sought financial support to establish a Chinese theater. The latter he began almost immediately. In August 1883, the *Elkhart Daily Review* reported:

> Wong Ching [*sic*] Foo, editor of the Chinese American, is now in negotiation with the manager of the company of Chinese actors . . . in San Francisco with the object of bringing them to this city at an early date. A company of twenty stockholders will be formed in this city, each member of which will

subscribe $500. This is to defray the expense of the troop and the engaging of a theater for the production of the Chinese drama. Wong Ching Foo is to be manager. The actors will most likely remain here for about three weeks. If suitable arrangements can be agreed upon they will leave California early in Sep for this city.[8]

Wong's vision was grand: ten thousand dollars in capital and a troupe of seventy-five members. This lofty goal was unsurprising for a man of ideals, who had long since cut his queue and declared his devotion to bridging the cultural and racial divide.[9] He planned to lecture before each performance to enhance the general population's appreciation. He also intended to take the troupe to other cities, from Boston to St. Louis. Advocacy for Chinese theater was soon incorporated into his lectures educating Americans about the Chinese with the aim of reducing prejudice against them. He did not succeed, however, at least not right away. Wong kept up his efforts. Additional initiatives in Chinese theaters in 1884 and 1886 did not yield successful results, either. It was a difficult task. As the historian John Tchen pointed out, "the practice of non-Chinese representing Chinese in American commercial and political venues was already firmly rooted in New York City's community culture."[10] Charles T. Parsloe's yellowface performance of Ah Sin was a notable example. It did not help that, as Esther Kim Lee notes poignantly, "nonwhites were seen as lacking the emotional and physical capacity to be professional actors."[11] Nevertheless, Wong's public pursuit shone a spotlight on Chinese theater for its virtuous import and artistic value. Despite the lack of immediate success, his theater idea remained under public discussion.

Meanwhile, US legislation restricting Chinese immigration grew still more stringent, making it even more difficult for his proposal to gain traction. In 1887, a writer for the *Oswego Daily Palladium* commented on the improbability of the theater idea: "For some time Wong Chin Foo . . . has been agitating the subject of a Chinese theater. . . . The main difficulty is importing the company. . . . on account of the stringency of the laws relating to Chinese immigration."[12] Wong was undeterred. Like many outspoken Chinese before him, such as Norman Assing in 1852, he used the weight of culture to combat anti-Chinese sentiment. To this end, he penned some of his most famous and polemical writings during this time. Wong wrote the famous piece "Why Am I a Heathen?" in 1887, delineating the virtues of "heathenism" (a stand-in for Chineseness) while exposing the flaws of Western civilization.[13] His essays dispelled readers' misconceptions about Chinese culture.[14] They also rendered the Chinese community legible to curious readers by translating the names of Chinese food items and explained their uses and by discussing the significance of the proverbs displayed on the walls in stores and restaurants. This approach was the same kind of cultural intervention that he envisioned for Chinese theater.

Swentien Lok Royal Chinese Dramatic Company 順天樂

In June 1889, Wong Chin Foo's dream was realized. A Chinese theatrical troupe was presented in New York: Swentien Lok Royal Chinese dramatic company performed at the Windsor Theater.[15] Wong's aim of establishing a Chinese theater was accomplished with the help of funds from Tom Lee, other New York Chinese merchants, and merchants on the West Coast.[16]

With a guarantee of sixteen thousand dollars for the season, a group of Chinese performers who had just finished a five-month engagement in Portland canceled their plan of traveling to San Francisco and left for New York.[17] The *Oregonian* reported the troupe's imminent departure with a cautionary note, since the arrangement was very much pending.[18] Yet the news of a Chinese troupe's eastward trip quickly gained a lot of attention from around the country.[19] The idea that Chinese theater was no longer exclusive to the Pacific region was newsworthy. On its way to New York, the troupe's size increased from the original twenty to fifty performers. It first performed at the Falls City Opera House in Spokane, Washington, for a week and then passed through Helena, Montana, in early May.[20]

Negotiations with Helena's famed Ming's Opera House fell through, so the company continued east. When the troupe passed through St. Paul, Minneapolis, its manager, Wing Ping, gave an interview, from which the reporter painted a rather positive picture of the troupe, introducing its repertoire and performers.[21]

In Chicago, the troupe had a two-week engagement at the Madison Street Theater. The excitement it generated was palpable. The *Chicago Daily Tribune* reported, "All the Chinamen in town were present. . . . Nothing so fashionable has ever happened in the Chinese world of Chicago. There was also a sprinkling of American artists come to study the costumes, men of letters to catch the dialogue, musicians to study the native orchestra."[22] The long article detailed the plots and stage actions of the opera, accompanied by five simple sketches of scenes.

The Chicago *Daily Inter Ocean*, a newspaper that appealed to an upscale and affluent readership, published a lengthy quote from Lee Kay, a former Portland Chinese merchant and manager of the troupe. He sought to affirm the status of Chinese actors by underscoring their exclusivity and that of Chinese theater by emphasizing its exquisiteness and high morals. The paper seemed to endorse the legitimacy of the Chinese theater business by quoting his words:

> We expect to get some white men interested in Chinese theatricals, and believe we shall succeed in making Chinese theaters a regular feature in the larger cities where most of our people live. Several men of prominence and means in New York and San Francisco have recognized that there is

money in such an undertaking. . . . It was decided to make our first appearance here. . . . There will be a performance each night next week, except on
Thursday, when we can't get the theater, and performances each afternoon
and evening the following week. Our plays are all founded upon historical
and mythological incidents, and costumes used are exact copies, in every
detail, of the dress of such periods as they represent. They are made from
costumes exhibited in our museums, and are very costly. The hangings,
draperies, and other stage decorations we have are also very expensive.[23]

This language resonated with that of Wong Chin Foo, linking the costumes
to aesthetic objects in art museums. Meanwhile, the same article quoted
another Chinese merchant who spoke of Chinese theater's superiority: "'O—
h,' declared Sam May, with a long drawn sigh of satisfaction. 'I'd rather pay
$10 to see them play once than 10 cents to see a circus twice.'" Such rhetoric
sought to underscore Chinese theater's legitimacy and set it apart from the
spectacles of acrobats, clowns, sideshow curiosities, and massive menageries
that was made popular among the middle class by traveling circuses such as
Phineas T. Barnum's "Greatest Show on Earth."

High-class plays needed to be performed in a legitimate theater.[24] The
Madison Street Theater (later the Chicago Opera House) was home to the
Chicago Opera Company, whose eleven-week run of *The Mikado* in the spring
of 1886 drew large crowds.[25] The extreme popularity of *The Mikado*—touted
as "an entirely new and original Japanese opera"—might have prompted the
organizers to consider positively the possibility of an appetite for Chinese
opera in this city. A reporter wrote about the Chinese troupe's performance
of *Sen Gong Shang* and called its protagonist the "Cleopatra of the east," while
another reporter highlighted military scenes.[26] Despite the high praise and
promise of substance, however, the experiment in Chinese theater did not
last.[27] Nevertheless, both the troupe manager's and local Chinese merchants'
words were taken seriously by the newspapers.

After its moderate success in Chicago, the troupe continued east and
arrived in Philadelphia, where it began performing at Jacob's Lyceum Theater in June.[28] Here the theatrical company took the name Swentien Lok,
which was spelled in a variety of ways in newspapers ("Song Ting Lok,"
"Shun T'In Lok," "Shun Ting Lok"). Their arrival on the East Coast sparked
significant interest and garnered special attention. The *New York Herald*
gave them the headline "Chinese Actors in Quaker Town," evoking a percep-
tual dissonance with the juxtaposition of the two incongruent groups.[29] The
Boston Daily Globe reassured its readers, "The plays are centuries old, and
the times and people represented in them are those of the remote past."[30] It
also noted, however, the effect of racial prejudice: "[M]any of the proprietors
here refuse to lease, fearing that such action might tend to create a prejudice
against their houses." A new law, the Scott Act, had just been signed into

law by President Grover Cleveland in October 1888, which furthered the exclusionist agenda by prohibiting Chinese laborers overseas from returning to the United States.[31] Anti-Chinese legislation had an impact on cultural production; could the troupe's reputation weather it?

Eventually the troupe was able to lease the Windsor Theatre.[32] The fifty members of the troupe and over a hundred pieces of luggage reached New York on June 21, preparing for their premiere on the 24th. The *New York Amusement Gazette* sighed with relief: "The much talked of troupe of Chinese actors have arrived at last."[33] The *New York Herald* printed a long article, "Chinese Drama in New York," providing details about the troupe.[34] Advertisements also appeared in the *Gazette* and other newspapers. The theater seated eighteen hundred, and the ticket prices ranged widely: $15 (box), $1 (orchestra), $.75 (balcony), and $.50 (gallery). The high ticket prices were noted by the press, since the theater's tickets usually ran from $6 to $.25.[35] Although the show was priced for the elite, affordable tickets also kept it accessible to the average person. To mark the significant moment, Chinese business leaders gave their employees a half day off for the opening night. Urging its readers to attend, the *New York Times* noted the opportunity for an ethnographic work: "[I]t is expected that a large number will take advantage of the opportunity to study the manners and customs of China."[36]

Wong Chin Foo and his cohort promoted the troupe through myriad New York newspapers and magazines. Two days prior to the opening, the *New York Herald* printed an article titled "Just Like in Pekin," which included a synopsis of the three-act opera as well as the cast list of three principals and thirteen other actors.[37] The preview was remarkable for its normality. It was reported in the regular format of a detailed theatrical preview, rather than featured articles of ethnic enclaves or the curiosity, that constituted a notable recognition of the Chinese theater's legitimacy. It was most definitely not the kind of coverage that commonly greeted Chinese theaters in San Francisco.

The opening night was packed, including about two hundred white audience members. To enhance appreciation of the troupe's artistry, much effort was put into familiarizing the audience via printed materials. For opening night, an English program with a synopsis and cast list was provided to the audience. The program was *The Loyal Slave,* (*Shee Long Tan Mo*) 四郎探母, a classic that Wong Chin Foo had endeavored to translate. Its success was noted widely by the media.[38] From the number of positive reviews and detailed reports on the troupe's performance, it was clear that Wong Chin Foo's cultural interventions to counter the negative reception of Chinese theater had had a positive effect. The public would be introduced to the history and plays of Chinese theater through a series of articles.

Figure 10.1 reproduces the advertisements in the *Sun* of June 21, 24, and 25, showing the opera title and the addition of two matinee performances.

FIGURE 10.1 Advertisement for Swentien Lok, the *Sun*, June 21, 24, 25, 1889.

Five days later, the synopsis and cast list for another play, the comedy *A Dark Conspiracy*, was printed in the *New York Herald*, depicting the story of Tartars and a plan to seize power from the emperor with the help of a Tartar princess.[39] A week later the *New York Tribune* advertised the lively comedy *Yalan Sells a Pig*.[40] A host of detailed articles about the troupe appeared in various newspapers, including one about the troupe's principal actors attending an American show at the Broadway Theatre.[41] An *Allentown Critic* article noted that Chinese had established a regular theater in New York and explained that the actors' income was enhanced by the convention of "the audience throwing money on the stage as a kind of practical applause for effective work." It also quoted Chinese audience members who valued serious plays and detested vulgarity in entertainment:

> Moy Shing, a New York merchant, says in this regard: "Our favorite dramas are historical or legendary in character. We would never stand such American productions as I have seen or read about in this city. Any one of immorality or indelicacy would ruin the playwright, the manager and the actor alike. In fact, we go so far as to discountenance vulgarity and all forms of low or even poor life."[42]

Printing such admonitory statements by Chinese interlocutors was a characteristic part of sympathetic reports about Chinese theater after Swentien Lok's New York performances, distinguishing it from denigrating stereotypes of racialized Chinese in skits, variety shows, or plays. By underscoring the significant moral purpose in its theatrical tradition, the Chinese community pointedly challenged the moral crusade against the Chinese.

The memory of Chinese troupe's appearance in New York City thirty-six years earlier had not completely faded. The *Boston Globe* raised an eyebrow when the *New York Herald* claimed that this was the first time a Chinese theater had appeared in the city.[43] The *Globe* was referring to the Tong Fook Tong troupe's performance at New York's Niblo's Garden in 1853 (see chap. 1).[44] In comparing the two appearances, one may ask what difference those thirty-six years made. New York City's Chinese community had changed in two important ways. Now there was an abundance of wealthy Chinese merchants who were eager to foot the bill to "guarantee" and promote theatrical engagements. There was also a stronger demand for the entertainment among the established and still growing Chinese population in the New York area. According to the sponsor Tom Lee, the gross receipts for the two-week performance were $3,500.[45] Still, the high theater rental fee was not sustainable. After finishing the two-week engagement, the troupe returned to the Windsor Theatre for a week on July 29. Encouraged by its success there, the troupe extended its run by moving to a smaller theater at 113 Bowery for two months before moving again to 12 Pell Street.[46] For the time being, Chinese theatrical entertainment established a continuous presence in New York and became integrated into the city's daily cultural life. Swentien Lok achieved a degree of success, even if limited, that had not been attainable by the Tong Hook Tong troupe three decades earlier.

Portrayals in Magazines

The presence of Swentien Lok in Manhattan drew the attention of many prominent magazines in New York. Their portrayals of the troupe varied in tone and perspective. An article with an illustration was given half a page in *Frank Leslie's Illustrated Newspaper*. It depicted the community's elation at the arrival of this theatrical company: "Great, flaming-red posters have illuminated the entire Chinese quarter."[47] The illustration reproduced the troupe's large poster in Chinese characters, incidentally providing the Chinese characters of the troupe: 順天樂. (The troupe's name appeared in the 1875 Jiqing Gongsuo List; see fig. 5.1a.) Yet the picture was loaded with visual cues that conveyed contradictory narratives. The focal point was innocuous: the large Chinese poster announcing the theatrical troupe and the opening date, with a group of men at the center engrossed in reading it, all of which suggest the authenticity and significance of the event to the community. However, the illustration was also plagued by the 1880s' predominantly negative visual narrative of Chinese life—the opium den. The depiction of an improbable site for smoking opium in the upper right corner gives a sense of impropriety to the scene. This is reinforced by many other visual cues. The half-hidden figures in the darkness of door frames suggesting secretiveness; the exaggerated, sinister facial features; the long queues on one man in the foreground and wrapped around the head of another man in the center; the pensive men with fans and pipes; the crowded storefront—all of these combines to form a narrative of shadiness. This illustration is a sharp contrast to the majestic warrior and the other colorful characters in the Wores and Cox illustrations in the *Century* magazine's 1884 article (see chap. 9). Betraying its xenophobic anxiety, the *Frank Leslie* illustration vilifies the cultural event of a "Chinese theater." Could it be that for the publication's staff, the omission of conventional racial markers at the height of anti-Chinese agitation was unthinkable? Was it obligatory? Was showcasing racial stereotypes a selling point for this magazine? Perhaps such sensationalized illustrations suited the trend then. Indeed, from 1883 to 1887, negative visual depictions of Chinese men abounded in newspapers and magazines, as such illustrations proliferated

FIGURE 10.2 "The Introduction of the Chinese Drama in New York City—Scene in the Chinese Quarter: Reading the Announcement of the Play." *Frank Leslie's Illustrated Newspaper*, June 29, 1889.

with the advancement of printing technology. Many illustrated magazines such as *Frank Leslie's Illustrated Weekly*, the *Wasp, Harper's Weekly*, and the *Police Gazette* either visualized opium usage as a foreign curiosity to entertain Americans or connected it to salacious, anti-Chinese sentiment.[48] Here, the Chinese opium den both blurs the distinction between political cartoons and illustrated news, and provides emotional space for a deep-seated aversion to the Chinese. This drawing, together with the commentary, sent mixed messages to readers: alluring novelty and lurking danger. Such a disparaging notion associated with the Chinese was what Wong Chin Foo eagerly campaigned against. As we will see below, he mobilized his connections to ensure a positive public image of Chinese theatrical troupes.

In sharp contrast, a marvelous image and an essay on Chinese opera costumes appeared a month later in *Harper's Bazaar* by William E. S. Fales, an associate of Wong Chin Foo.[49] Fales wrote lengthy articles about Swentien Lok for two prominent New York magazines.[50] His piece for *Harper's Bazaar*, a New York weekly magazine, published in the July 27, 1889 issue, was the first of its kind.

Harper's Bazaar catered to women in the middle and upper classes, showcasing fashions from Europe, particularly France and Germany. The issue's cover featured the image of a Chinese opera diva, captioned "Tartar Emperor's Daughter," referring to an opera performed by Swentien Lok. It shows a female character in the wardrobe and headdress of a warrior, completed with flags and a pair of long pheasant feathers. This was the first time the image of a female Chinese opera character appeared on the cover of an American magazine. Not simply a static portrait, this image is animated by the performer's delicate gestures and motion. The performer holds the tip of one pheasant feather in the left hand, forming a circle imbued with tension. The image, by William Allen Rogers, is enlivened by two performing musicians and an actor of the *erhuamian* general type in the background.[51] With a slight smile and tilted head, this glamorous Chinese diva joins the usual drawings of European women in the latest fashions on the cover of *Harper's Bazaar*.[52]

In the accompanying article, Fales provided a study of the sophisticated and spectacular costumes. He began by underscoring of the significance of the Tang dynasty, the historical context of the opera.[53] The opera costumes were "faithful copies of what was worn" during the Tang period, he noted. His detailed descriptions were true to the magazine's reputation as a leading authority on fashion. Fales meticulously describes the fabric, color, design, and materials, making vivid the costumes' ingenious artisanship and opulence and providing expert explanations of how they enhance the performers' stage movements:

> The material of the robe is a coarse, strong silk of a dark blue color, which is entirely covered with embroidery of almost startling brilliancy. The chief

decorations are huge dragons in gold bullion, in which the metal thread is laid on in spirals, and fastened to the cloth below with fine gold wire. The wings, tail, legs, claws, teeth, and eyes of these dragons are picked out with threads of silver and scarlet, ultramarine and snow-white silk thread. Around the dragons and touching them at every point are leaves, vines, and flowers worked in silk floss, and these in turn are environed by grotesque but graceful patches filled with silk of the brightest hue. The side panels,

FIGURE 10.3 William Allen Rogers. "Tartar Emperor's Daughter." *Harper's Bazaar,* July 27, 1889.

which are very bouffant, are made to resemble tiger-skin, and at first sight seem to be of that beautiful fur. In dancing, the feet alone are displayed, the legs being covered with baggy Zouave trousers of grayish satin which almost touch the slippers. . . . To the shoulders are attached four small square flags, two on each side, of a dark brown, with relieved characters in black-red, old-gold, and indigo gray.

In vivid detail, the essay's examination of the material, tapestry, and embroidery deepened readers' understanding of the craftmanship and materials of the opera costumes. It bridged and mediated the social gap between the Chinese dramatic troupe and New York's upscale society, which already was familiar with the reputation of silk in China's trade. Fales also paid close attention to the headgear:

With the hair three different styles of singular ornamentation are employed. One consists of round pompons in bright colors attached to thin ebony rods, which are inserted in the coif. A second is of peacock feathers, arranged in a circle around the head so as to form a vivid halo. The third and most remarkable consists of the two long tail feathers of the Chinese pheasants. These are long willowy plumes, from five to nine feet in length and less than an inch in width, of a bright sepia, with scattered markings of old-gold. These are inserted in the back hair at an angle about 30 degrees out of the horizontal, and make two sweeping curves.[54]

The dress and headgear are accurately rendered by the staff artist William A. Rogers in his image of the princess on the cover. It depicts Chinese theater in the mode of grace, delicacy, and cultural civilization. The image negotiates the boundary between race and ethnicity, mediated primarily in aesthetic terms. Through Fales's text, the exquisite beautiful costumes became knowable as well.

This article responded ingeniously to the public craze over Chinese opera costumes as exemplified in a news report that was syndicated in over thirty newspapers in 1888: "One of the dresses of the outfit of a Chinese dramatic company, purchased for an opera in New York, contains over 4,000,000 stitches."[55] Fales's detailed article on Chinese opera costume was, in a seemingly pragmatic way, a guide to "owning the glamour." This glamour, however, was not regressive or passive but rather took the form of aesthetic authority. The cover image's caption, "Tartar Emperor's Daughter," appealed to those with an interest in ancient Asian royalty or civilizations. Together, Rogers's cover image and Fales's detailed article were a packaged representation of glamour whose referent—Chinese theater—was nearly forgotten.[56]

For a different audience, Fales provided an analysis of the dramatic craft of the actors. His other article on the Swentien Lok troupe appeared in the June 29, 1889 issue of *Harper's Weekly*. "The Chinese Mimes," was a dramatic review of Chinese theater that provided details about the troupe's cast, including the female impersonator, Tak-A-Wing; the leading male actor, Moo Sung Jee; and eight other actors.

> Minor female parts are taken by boys and youths; important ones by a class of actors who have no counterpart in the American dramatic world. Of this class the present company has a notable representative in Tak-A-Wing, who has long been considered a star of the greatest magnitude. His voice is a treble, both on and off the stage, has become permanent rather than falsetto in character. . . . [H]e reproduces the actions and manners which Oriental etiquette forces upon the sex with a fidelity which is remarkable. Of the actors who assume male parts, Moo Sung Jee is the most celebrated and popular. His roles may be fitly compared with those made familiar by Frank Mayo in D'Artagnan and Nordeck. He has an agreeable voice, a good stage presence and thorough knowledge of his arts. . . . Of the other members of the company, Tzung Yung, who plays pathetic "old men," Lee Yuen in royal characters, Chow Loon Yin and Woy Soon Wo as warriors and statesmen, Li Shi Dau as a ghost, genius, or demon, all deserve especial mention.[57]

Attending to the details of the actors' vocal quality, movements, and distinctive role types, the article addresses the substance of the performance. The comparison of Moo Sung Jee to Frank Mayo, an American actor of heroic and idealistic protagonist roles, also made him relatable to the readers. Furthermore, Fales names the Chinese actors and considers them professionals with serious craftsmanship rather than representing an ethnic type. Fales endows respectability on Chinese theatrical troupes in these articles, a trait seldom seen in American public discourse. From this perspective Chinese theater could absorb this new image, aligning with Wong Chin Foo's vision, and appeal to more American middleclass audiences.

The news of this troupe quickly crossed the Atlantic, where the London magazine *The Stage* gave an account of the troupe's eastward tour.[58] In addition, as a sign of Wong Chin Foo and his cohort's success in advocacy, the theatrical troupe had many more sympathetic ears among its East Coast audience. Shortly after the opening performance, a writer with the *Philadelphia Inquirer* reflected on Chinese theater in comparative terms, noting, "The plays now being given in New York are in many respects similar to those we are accustomed to seeing. They have something of the spirit of the old Greek tragedies and many of the characteristics of the Shakespearean dramas. . . . Their acting is rather unique. . . . [W]hen proper allowances are made it is found that they have reached a high state of perfection in their art."[59] The writer also quoted words of praise from the actress Sarah Bernhardt to underscore the sophisticated artistry of Chinese theater.

Many times Wong Chin Foo had been a fierce critic, openly challenging his viciously anti-Chinese opponent Denis Kearney. He also did not spare those who denigrated Chinese theater with their racialized negative reception.

In July 1889 he demonstrated the righteousness of his cause in a public letter chastising readers who all too often assumed a negative attitude toward cultures different from their own:

> [These] and countless other peculiarities puzzled the Caucasian's brain, simply because they cannot be brought to appreciate them, and because they were brought up differently. When my American friends criticized the Chinese theatrical troupe I immediately appreciate their position. Heaven . . . has given not only to every race a way of salvation spiritually, but . . . has given them a way of enjoying life while that lasts. I think the greatest happiness we have is the variety of sights, ideas, peculiarities, the more astonishing the better.[60]

Wong interrogated common stereotypes, questioned their biased underpinning, and appealed to the reader's sense of equity. His article was unflinching and remarkable for its time, especially because a legal challenge to the Scott Act had reached the Supreme Court in the spring of 1889. In May the court upheld the law (*Chae Chan Ping v. United States*, 130 US 581).[61] Wong Chin Foo's remarks on Chinese theater accompanied his continuing advocacy for civil rights in the midst of this setback, underscoring the cultural significance of Chinese theater. The sense of respectability he espoused ushered Chinese theater into a new era on the East Coast.

The 1889 Paris Universal Exposition and Sonic Ethnology

Despite the considerable geographical distance, the East Coast's experience of Chinese theater in June and July of 1889 couldn't help but be influenced by the concurrent Paris Universal Exposition, which ran from May 6 to October 31 of the same year. The Exposition attracted 30 million visitors, including a significant number of American delegates and news correspondents. It was a "measuring rod for the relative status of American and European" accomplishment.[62] Furthermore, it offered the guests not only an education in world achievements "but the illusion of 'authentic' encounters with other cultures," as the musicologist Annegret Fauser notes.[63] The Paris Exposition evoked fresh interest in Chinese theater, now under the ethnological lens. Although the Exposition's Chinese pavilion was modest, a group from Saigon in French Indochina presented the Théâtre Annamite (Annamite Theater), which showcased *hát tuồng*, a style of classical Vietnamese opera. This genre drew inspiration from Chinese opera, featuring similar costumes, face painting, stage movements, role types, and accompanying instruments.[64] Opened on June 5, the Annamite Theater was immensely successful.[65] Yet the reaction to the music in popular media was rather negative.[66] This attitude prompted a leading London journal, the *Musical World*, to publish a lead article on June 29, sharply criticizing European prejudice "in dealing with a subject of such interest to all students of comparative musical science. . . . It displays a complete inability to alter the critical standpoint, or to depolarize habitual convictions, two things which must be accomplished by anyone who undertakes to assess these performances [of Annamite Theater] at their true value."[67] The journal's reasoning echoed Wong Chin Foo's critical tone in his article of July 10.

Although the popular press ridiculed the music of the Annamite Theater, others responded differently to the exhibition. For a series of articles in the influential French music journal *Le Ménestrel*, the French musicologist Julien Tiersot studied and transcribed seven melodies into Western notation.[68] The staff notation accompanied his article in an effort to render audible the perception of non-Western music. Tiersot's approach aimed to pique musical and ethnographic curiosity, reflecting a trend described by the musicologist Jan Pasler as "sonic anthropology."[69] In the late nineteenth and early twentieth centuries, such notation of non-Western music, Pasler noted, "was often driven by the desire to understand racial origins and racial distinctions."[70] To align with the prevalent use of "ethnology" in 19th-century America, I will refer to the concept as "sonic ethnology." [71]

In the United States, news articles about the Paris Exposition kept the American public abreast of news about this largest world's fair. Two illustrations of the Annamite Theater actors, accompanying the article "The Parisian Wonder: The Great Exposition Appears to Be a Brilliant Success," were widely syndicated in papers from New Jersey to North Dakota.[72] Their Chinese-opera-style costumes naturally invited comparisons: the two long pheasant tail feathers, the headdresses, long robes, and armor. A prominent newspaper in Kansas astutely drew a direct comparison. A headline, "Chinese Actors" calls attention to the page's primary theme, which contained two articles, each occupying two full columns. The first, "Have Established a Regular Theater in New York," was an article about the Swentien Lok troupe in New York with line drawings of a Chinese actor and the manager.[73] The next article bore the familiar title "The Parisian Wonder: The Great Exposition Appears to be a Brilliant Success," featuring a drawing of the Annamite Theater actors. The ethnological field of the Paris Exposition was symbolically extended to encompass New York's Chinese theater. To put it differently, the pairing of these two events in this newspaper reflected how the editor conceptualized them together. Thus the Chinese troupe in New York was drawn unwittingly into the French exhibitions—"the crowning glory of anthropology."[74] The Exposition prompted a gradual shift of attitude toward Chinese theaters in the United States as a whole. More important, this shift in public attitude also accompanied, even contributed to, the positive development of long-term Chinese theater on the Atlantic coast.

The name of Swentien Lok disappeared from the news after October 1889, yet many of its troupe members remained in New York. Chinese actors became part of the urban cultural landscape. Numerous subsequent reports announced the impending opening of a Chinese theater in New York, a cause furthered by Wong Chin Foo's ongoing advocacy.[75] The East Coast was on the rise as a desirable destination for Chinese troupes. A performing network crossing the continent was emerging. In this process, Chinese performers gained new mobility and agency.[76] In addition to New York, Boston too had its Chinese theater by September 1890.

The American Folk-Lore Society in Boston

The quintessential example of the sonic ethnology phase was a special 1891 Chinese theater event in Boston under the auspices of the American Folklore Society (founded in 1888–89). This event was recorded in the society's own *Journal of American Folklore*.[77] Despite being newly established, the society had a keen interest in researching ethnic communities in the United States. Stewart Culin, one of its founders, published a book in 1887 titled *China In America: A Study in the Social Life of the Chinese in the Eastern Cities of the United States*, based on his close study of the Chinese community in Philadelphia. The book's widespread distribution to numerous individuals and organizations, along with the enthusiastic reception, is evident in a sizable scrapbook of acknowledgments housed at the Brooklyn Museum archive.[78] Despite the government's intensified anti-Chinese policy, a distinctly different atmosphere surrounded this occasion in Boston.

A week before the event, the *Boston Daily Adviser* ran a preview with the headline: "The Chinese Theatre: To Be Visited by Boston's Literati and '400.'" The reference to the "400," was a newly coined term for socially elite New Yorkers.[79] The distinguished Bostonian attendees included the poet and polymath Dr. Oliver Wendell Holmes, the novelist and editor of the *Atlantic Monthly* William Dean Howells, and the abolitionist Col. Thomas Wentworth Higginson, among others.

"The activity of the Boston Association has been considerable. Some pleasant features have been in order to give variety to the study in which the members are interested," noted a member.[80] Three days prior to the show, the *Boston Globe* published a statement that betrayed some reservations but nonetheless praised the open-mindedness of Bostonians in giving Chinese theater a fair consideration:

> Though somewhat smile-provoking, it is none the less credible to Boston culture that the very best of dramatic and literary critics in town have determined to give the Celestials a fair show, and the rush for tickets is said to be unprecedented.... [S]ome of the members of the American Folk

Lore Society, under whose auspices the coming performances are to be given, boldly proclaim their judgement that these Chinese representations will compare favorably with any now in the state. Everybody who comes to this country has a right to be heard, and to be rated for what he is worth in whatever he attempts to do. . . . [This] is really a stroke of true democracy.[81]

Many newspapers reported on the remarkable event, which involved two hundred guests.[82] In the *Boston Globe,* the news article was prominently placed on the front page, running across three columns, nearly half of the page, with several illustrations (see fig. 10.4).

Two unusual aspects mark this distinctive report. First is the transcription into Western notation of a folk song, "Mo li hua," with the caption "Tune That Reached Their Hearts."[83] The staff notation was a nod to the kind of sonic ethnology exemplified by Tiersot's musical transcription, discussed above. Here, it lent credibility to this article, befitting a Bostonian high-society affair. An 1889 travelogue by Lee Meriwether also printed transcriptions of "airs" for his report about San Francisco's Chinese theater.[84] However, most relevant in both cases is less what the transcriptions revealed than that they actually were made. As Jann Pasler insightfully notes, "neither translation nor transcription need to be 'exact' for the song to fulfill its function as a sign of race."[85] That the *Boston Globe* featured it on the front page underscored its visual significance.

Equally significant were the drawings accompanying the article. Two smaller sketches of prominent Bostonians showed the men in suits and the women in hats, face veils, and fur, all visual codes of high society. They were uncommon instances of illustrations depicting distinguished Caucasian audiences at a Chinese theater performance, even though a great many of them attended and recorded their visits. Other distinguished Caucasians attended various Chinese theater performances (such as the presidents or musicians noted in previous chapters), but no visual documentation of their visits exist. The names of several prominent people appear under these sketch portraits, as well as in numerous other news reports, depicting the genteel class seeking literary inspiration, as well as examining ethnological snippets, such as tales, myths, customs, rites, and so on.[86] The article showed that members of high society had great regard for this representation of Chinese civilization.

Rather than adhering to racialized visual codes, three drawings of Chinese performers onstage aligned with general standards of visual presentation applied to non-Chinese subjects. Spanning two newspaper columns, the largest and primary drawing provides a front view of three Chinese performers on stage, captioned "The Prima Donna Playing on Yung Kung," with the orchestra musicians half visible in the background. The prima donna, facing

Dr. Holmes Occupied Seat of Honor.

"Day of the Great Circus" a Big Success.

Jolly Devotees of Thespis in Harrison Avenue Temple.

THE PRIMA DONNA PLAYING ON YUNG KUNG.

FROM the fashionable luncheon hour on til 2 o'clock yesterday afternoon the tide of fashion set not toward any of the usual haunts of fashion, though fashion haunts queer places sometimes, but toward a Harrison av. basement, which, by the creation of a platform, and the placing of rows of settees, has been converted into a theatre.

Carriage load after carriage load of occupants, all "fair" and largely feminine, drifted up the old stone steps that did duty in Harrison avenue's palmy days before a small residence, but which now lead the way into a disreputable, dirty eatery, past the respectful young American to whom society most

COL. HIGGINSON, DR. HOLMES, MR. HOWELLS.

show its talismanic ticket, and then is allowed to retain it as a souvenir of the occasion; then through a door, down four or five perfectly dark and narrow steps, under a dirty "portiere," and behold the eyes, for entrance to which on this particular day, at this particular hour, the respectable day, the respectable day...

[column of faded text]

MRS. JACK GARDNER.

[column of faded text]

the pleasure syndicate of the actors, who accustomed to hand-clapping.

And for an encore?

"Annie Rooney" with variations.

LOVE SCENE.

The stage setting, as has been indicated, is of the most meagre description...

[column of faded text]

GENERAL MORNING STAR DRESS FOR YON KING.

And again he appeared in a dress with rectangular plates, covered with mother-of-pearl scales, a novel combination with the rich hues of the embroideries. A curious feature of the makeup of the older men is the beard, which is a long...

FIGURE 10.4 "Boston's Chinese Opera Boom." *Boston Globe*, February 9, 1891.

the audience, plays a *yangqin* (a kind of dulcimer) with two thin mallets or hammers as part of the character's featured performance. The journalist described the enthusiastic reception of the performance, referring to the folk song and highlighting the contrast in the sweet vocal timbre of the song and the rest of the opera.

> The scene of the opera that elicited the warmest applause represented this queen at her yung tum [*sic*], a glorified zither, upon which she played and sung, sometimes accompanied by her two maids. The song of the "Jasmine Flower," the words and translation and music of which are appended, showed a wider range and sweeter quality of voice than the recitatives of which most of the opera consisted.[87]

This eye-catching drawing conveyed the stance of the newspaper, whereby the staff artist compressed the complex social event and ethnic presentation into a series of respectable images. The wardrobes, headdresses, and heavily embroidered covering draped over the table all suggest the colorful opulence of the costumes and tapestries. The aura of the theater presented here, as well as the fine portrayal of the female role onstage, recall the glamour of the *Harper's Bazaar* cover (see fig. 10.3). The image is inviting, beckoning the readers to join the social elite in the enjoyment of the spectacle and music. A smaller illustration portrays two performers in a fight scene, adding an extra dimension to the acting in the theater. The writer discusses this in a thoughtful commentary and complemented the skillfulness of the actor.

This remarkable written report renders Chinese performers legible in theatrical art, rather than mere stereotypes. From the descriptions readers could gain some understanding of the stage action, as well as some nuances of the acting and performance. This type of respect and acceptance of legitimacy was a victory, albeit small, for Chinese theaters, one that Wong Chin Foo was aiming for with his advocacy of Chinese theater as a high art.

Abby Langdon Alger, the American Folk-Lore Society's vice president added, "[T]he performances of the Chinese company are somewhat in line with our work, which is in part the observation of the customs of different peoples."[88] This one-hundred-member society, in the second year of its existence, viewed Chinese theater as fitting within its construction of the subjects and aesthetics of ethnographical examination. The tickets and programs were printed on red paper and orange paper, with silver spangles. A noteworthy event for its contemporaries, the Folk-Lore Society's visit to Chinese theater highlighted its ethnographic lens. It led the trend, as a writer for *Buffalo Courier* noted: "If the 'intellectual few' of Boston's best society, including Mr. Howells can get enjoyment out of the tom-tom, and the one-stringed fiddle, we cannot see why it is not fitting that we show an equal interest in Chinese drama."[89]

Gradually Chinese theater in the United States emerged into the spotlight with a fresh kind of legitimacy. It should be noted that Henry Burden McDowell's 1884 article was an important contribution in this regard. Lengthy excerpts from the article were widely syndicated, nationwide and beyond.[90] In the last two decades of the nineteenth century, Chinese theaters began to branch out widely in United States. On the West Coast, Los Angeles established its Chinese theater by 1884; Portland had had Chinese theaters since 1880.[91] Now two cities on the Atlantic Coast had also joined. The popularity of this theatrical art attracted the attention not only of the media but also of ambitious Chinese theater managers. Herman Cook was one of them. While passing through Pittsburgh on his way to Boston, he told a reporter for the *Pittsburgh Press* in October 1890,

> I am in the theatrical business, but it is a different departure from the usual order. I have now in operation in San Francisco a Chinese theater, in Chinese regulation style. It has been now for some time and is proving a decided hit. Thus far I have met with complete success, and unless something unforeseen arises, like it has in a number of such ventures in regard to the Chinese, there is no reason why it should not be permanent. It is now my intention to establish similar places of amusement in Chicago, Philadelphia, New York and Boston, and in time make a regular chain of them across the continent. I am on my way to Boston to consult with friends upon the matter as to the most advisable course to follow.[92]

This vision, though strictly business, aligned with Wong Chin Foo's, who, in charting the path to a distinctive Chinese American identity, saw in Chinese theater an ideal representation of the culture and public face of the community. In 1891, after securing sponsorship, a location, and performers, he applied for a license to open a Chinese theater on Doyer Street in New York's Chinatown. It was declined. Indignant, he told a reporter, "[T]he Hebrews and the Germans are permitted to give performances, and I think the Chinese ought to be granted the same privilege."[93] In 1893 he founded the Chinese Equal Rights League. In March of the same year, the permanent Chinese Theater on Doyer street finally opened, under management by the dashing merchant Chu Fong.[94] A full-fledged operation, the theater had elaborate costumes with impressive embroidery and brass filigree and was staffed with thirty actors (recruited from Cuba, Vancouver, and elsewhere), and a stage director. The theater opened its doors with an inaugural performance of *Six Warlords*, formally establishing its residency in the location.[95] Forty years after its first performance in San Francisco, Chinese opera culture had reached the East Coast with an established Chinese theater. Situated in the heart of lower Manhattan, in close proximity to Chatham Square and the bustle of everyday activities, the theater's resonant melodies of Cantonese opera reverberated daily, weaving a captivating spell that enveloped the Chinese community night after night for the next decade.[96] A featured article by Wong Chin Foo about the theater in the *New York Herald* included illustrations of both performing Chinese actors on stage and musicians of the orchestra, as well as a vendor, refreshment and buying audience, echoing Theodore Wores's drawing in McDowell's 1884 *Century Illustrated* article (see fig. 9.5).[97]

Epilogue

Golden-leaved Chrysanthemum 金葉菊

In 1880, Ah Quin logged seventy-five visits to Chinese theaters before leaving for San Diego in October. At the start of that year, Wing Tie Ping and Gee Quon Yung were the mainstays of Chinese theaters, according to his diary. Ah Quin often referred to the latter, just opened the previous October, as the "new theater." However, he witnessed the opening of two more new theaters before he left the city: Hing Kig Chung in May (sometimes Hing Gag Tung, or H. G. T.) and Dan San Feng in October.[1] During his twenty-three-month stay in San Francisco, Ah Quin's diary recorded no fewer than seven different names for Chinese theaters, which speaks volumes about the fluidity of the rapidly changing Cantonese opera scene in San Francisco. (A chronology of theater names can be found in Appendix A.)

In many respects, Ah Quin was an average theatergoer for his time. As his diary reveals, theater was a part of the community's social fabric and daily life, and theatergoing was closely connected to social rituals. For example, Chinese Lunar New Year's Eve is the most important day for family reunions. Traditionally, the whole family would return home, gather for dinner in celebration, and stay up to see the new year in, the festivities often culminating in fireworks to welcome an auspicious start to the year. In southern China, opera troupes took a respite from performing, and theaters were closed on that day. However, it was different in San Francisco. Most Chinese in the community could not be with their families on the other side of the Pacific, so the bustling activities at the Chinese theater played a crucial role in providing the spirit of family and the celebration of the start of a new season and new vitality. On the morning of Chinese New Year's Eve in 1880, Ah Quin finished work at 10 and visited several friends in town, after which he spent the afternoon at the W. T. P. (Wing Tie Ping) theater until 3 p.m., had supper, tea, and auspicious candy with more friends, and then went to G. Q. Y. (Gee Quon Yung) theater at 6 p.m. for an evening of performance and festivity. Unfortunately, the show ended abruptly at 11:30, because the theater's gas lighting suddenly went out. "I think the bad man turn it [off]," Ah Quin wrote, disappointed.[2] "Rain is begin [sic] to fall," he continued, "home walk alone till in bed 1:30. [sic]" The state of loneliness and dispiritedness was exacerbated by the dark, wet night. On this day of family reunion, the theater was his, and many others,' surrogate family.

Ah Quin's sense of belonging was enhanced by the heightened enjoyment that theatergoers experienced together. The theater was a part of city life, which included gathering with people, playing cards, writing letters for friends, exploring business opportunities, and going to the barbershop, as well as attending various social and religious events. It was interconnected with the activities of everyday life. Theatrical events, therefore, were community affairs—including fandom. In March, Ah Quin heard from street chatter that a fire had been set at G. Q. Y. in an attempt to stop the performance of the renowned actor with the name "新蘇" (Ah Sue), who had just arrived from China. (This incident is discussed in chap. 8.) Ah Quin followed the frenzied crowd to catch a glimpse of the star. His first attempt was thwarted, but he succeeded on the second try, at a matinee. The community's fervor for this star was clear. A celebrated performer, Ah Sue was a leading actor of female roles. Two years later, the *Examiner* would write (referring to him as "Bung Ah Soo") that he earned a salary of six thousand dollars per annum and enjoyed an apartment furnished in a "half-American and half-Chinese fashion of elegance."[3] He wowed the audience with his unprecedented performance in a large wooden vessel on stage. The whole community turned out to watch him leading this innovation of realism (see chap. 8). The passion for opera and opera stars offered community members an escape from the mundane and from the hostility of a racist society; it provided a form of relationality in which they could feel accepted and seen and could recognize their collectivity.[4] Companionship was deepened in such a shared theater experience. During this year, it was increasingly common for Ah Quin to be joined on his theater visits by coworkers and to walk home together after the shows. Furthermore, he deftly combined his theatergoing with activities that would seem to be at the opposite end of the social spectrum. As his commitment to Christianity grew, more than a third of his theater visits in 1880 were preceded by activities at one of the three Christian organizations—the Presbyterian church, the Chinese mission school led by Otis Gibson, and Fok Yam Tang (the Chinese gospel house). There he would attend prayers and sermons, meet new pastors, sing hymns, and participate in Bible studies. Once, Ah Quin also brought both Chinese and American guests at a church wedding ceremony to see Chinese theater.[5] For him, these social activities constituted the urban space's everyday rhythm. Located centrally in the community, Chinese theaters offered what Jacek Blaszkiewicz calls "porous socialization," where audiences moved freely in and out of the theater spaces while engaged in a range of social and personal activities.[6]

Aside from mentioning *Six Warlords*, Ah Quin's diary reveals little about the operas he saw at the theaters. However, one notable exception offers a glimpse of his theatrical experience. In May 1880, the new theater group H. G. T. (Hing Gag Tung) came on the scene. Following its opening, Ah Quin's theater visits increased. For several days he attended only the new troupe but was lured back to G. Q. Y. (Gee Quon Yung, aka Donn Quai Yuen) on June 3. He wrote in the diary that day:

> the[n] dine 6:15, then go Town in Pre. church rest in cel. 1 hour then in De Yow barber shop to comb my hair, in G. Q. Y. see Di Ca Sing do Kin Yip Oak. he be the first one Lam Yap 月 Ca 嬌, then home in bed at just 12:30.[7]

> [I finished my work for dinner at 6:15. Then I went to town to the Presbyterian Church to rest in the cellar for an hour. Afterward, I went to the barber shop of De Yow to have my hair combed. Then I went to G. Q. Y. to see the actor Di Ca Sing perform the opera *Kin Yip Oak*. He played the first Lam Yap Ca 月嬌. After the opera, I went home and was in bed by 12:30.]

The performance must have left a strong impression, since Ah Quin included many details about the evening in his diary: the actor's name, and most unusual, the opera title and the female protagonist's name, with the Chinese characters for the latter (fig. E.1). *Kin Yip Oak* is the Taishan/Cantonese pronunciation of the classic Cantonese opera *Golden-leaved Chrysanthemum*

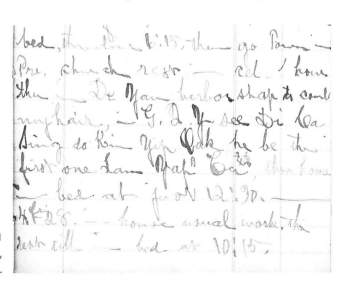

FIGURE E.1
Ah Quin, Diary,
June 3, 1880.

(金葉菊). That the famous actor Di Ca Sing performed the female protagonist, Lam Yap Ca (Lin Yuejiao, 林月嬌) must have been a true treat. Of all the different operas that Ah Quin went to see at the theaters, this one and *Luk Quok* (*Six Warlords*) were the only ones he named.

The named actor, Di Ca Sing, was the celebrated 大家勝 (Dajia Sheng), whose name had been spelled Ti Gar Sing the previous October in both American newspapers and Ah Quin's diary. As a renowned actor, he led the effort to establish the fourth Chinese theater in San Francisco (see chap. 6).

The classic opera *Golden-leaved Chrysanthemum* revolves around a melodramatic story with a female protagonist.[8] A statesman's son, Zhang Yinglin 張應麟, presents a golden-leaved chrysanthemum as a token of engagement to his fellow statesman's daughter, Lin Yuejiao. However, a villain who covets Yuejiao's beauty lures Yinglin to Plum Blossom Mountain Stream and kills him. The ghostly apparition of Yinglin shocks his mother to death. Yuejiao sings a long lament to convey her deep sorrow. To pay for the funeral expenses of her mother-in-law, they are forced to sell their young son, Guifang 桂芳. With the help of others, Guifang is sent to the capital, where Yuejiao's friend helps him with his studies, and he earns first place on the national exam. Eventually, on the son's triumphant return, mother and son are reunited, and the villain is brought to justice for his misdeeds.

Ti Gar Sing's performance of the sentimental female protagonist must have evoked sympathy in his audiences. *Golden-leaved Chrysanthemum* had a unique place in Cantonese opera, known for its heart-wrenching scenes whose emotive monologues and sentimental songs invariably moved audiences to tears. A Cantonese colloquial saying goes, "If you want to tear up, go see *Golden-leaved Chrysanthemum*."[9] The opera's melancholy aroused special feeling in Ah Quin as well, if his handwriting of the romanized name of the female protagonist is an indication. The letters for "Lam Yap Ca" are written in strong, thick, and well-shaped pen strokes, in contrast to the surrounding thinner, quicker pen strokes for other words. Another affectionate gesture is the two small Chinese ideograms added to the protagonist's feminine given names: 月 (moon) and 嬌 (delicate and charming). These two characters suggest intimate and gentle feeling. The sorrowful scenes and music of the opera made for a somber evening, particularly poignant for Ah Quin, a filial son who worried that he would not be able to see his parents again and who had been sending letters or money to his mother every few months.[10]

Chinese theaters, centrally located in the community, offered opera repertoire that attracted a full spectrum of audiences. The emotional, aesthetic, and social impact of these operas on the community was immense. Many of them, such as *Golden-leaved Chrysanthemum*, held personal significance for audiences. Thus the musical space of Chinese theater was deeply woven into the history of the city. The prevalence of Cantonese opera culture meant the permeation of the operas' sound and symbolic significance throughout the community, from sonorities to visual images, from street humor to social justice, and from satire to melodrama. The melodies and sonic gestures lingered in the ear, inspiring nostalgic longing and aesthetic imagination. Theatrical culture boosted social power and agency.

As a classic opera, *Golden-leaved Chrysanthemum* was among the earliest titles recorded by Victor Records for the Chinese music series on its Monarch label (fig. E.2). It was recorded in 1903 in North America, either in Philadelphia or San Francisco, with the aim of targeting the Chinese community.[11] Between August 1902 and August 1903, a total of thirty-two Chinese titles were recorded in San Francisco and Philadelphia. They were issued in 164 discs as a part of the Monarch 10-inch series by the Victor Talking Machine Company in the United States.[12] Unfortunately, few of these recordings have survived; finding one that matched this nineteenth-century Chinese immigrant's description seemed impossible. Amazingly, however, several Monarch Record discs of *Golden-leaved Chrysanthemum* have been identified; one has been shared on YouTube, providing an opportunity to hear the sound of Cantonese opera as played in Chinese theaters in North America during that period. This recording is the closest we have today that "remembers" the early sonority of Cantonese opera in San Francisco's Chinese theaters.[13] A partial transcription of this recording is provided in appendix B.

Connecting the opera mentioned in Ah Quin's diary in 1880 with the sound of the opera recorded in North America in 1903 holds a special significance

FIGURE E.2 Record label of *Golden-leaved Chrysanthemum*, Victor Monarch Record, 1885.

for me, despite the twenty-year gap between them. The registry of sound vibrations etched into that disc provides for the ear what heretofore could only be imagined. Because the textual evidence in the diary places the opera in North America, the storage of the sound of this opera, performed in the United States—a form of technical memory—on the Victor Monarch recording allows us, however partially, to engage the history of Chinese theater as a sonic-material event.[14] It provides the opportunity to forge an intimate, aural relationship with that history. The material existence of this sound does more than simply provide historical evidence. It also counters nineteenth-century prejudice about Chinese theater.

Listening Practice: Sound, Erasure, and Archive

In narrating the musical life of Chinese immigrants in the nineteenth-century United States, one of the most difficult challenges is its sound. Cantonese opera underwent significant changes during the twentieth century, such that even though lyrics of classic verses and scripts of traditional Cantonese opera survive, their relation to the performance practice of the nineteenth century remained little known. This left very limited sources for scholars to fully grasp the performance and even the repertoire of Chinese theater in the North America of the nineteenth century.

The lack of historical sources for Cantonese opera is not, however, the primary problem. Erasure is—many types of erasure. The first type concerns the conceptual space to which Chinese immigrants were relegated in US society. As discussed earlier, anti-Chinese initiatives began to appear in California as early as 1852. Chinese immigrants were deemed inferior and therefore inconsequential—of no import to American life. Under frequent siege by anti-Chinese forces, many were harassed or driven out of their lodgings, and thus lacked living conditions conducive to preserving personal records of any cultural expression.[15] Obstacles to establishing family, such as the 1875 Page Act, which resulted in a drastic decrease in the immigration of Chinese women, further diminished the possibility of cultural traditions being passed down orally or retained in some fashion across generations. The scarcity of Chinese narratives and materials in institutional archives ironically corroborates their inconsequence in US history; this erasure was further cemented by their general invisibility in the history texts of American music.[16] On the rare occasions when Chinese theater was mentioned in these texts, it was with the reassurance that its existence was marginal, relevant only to an unimportant, ethnic enclave. Conceptually, therefore, the sonic presence of Chinese theater was largely erased from the history of the American musical landscape.

The second kind of erasure pertains to the practice of listening. In *The Race of Sound*, discussing the relationship between vocalizers and a process of listening, Nina Sun Eidsheim writes, "The voices heard are ultimately identified, recognized, and named by listeners at large." Later she adds, "The category of the listener . . . embodies the category of the originator of meaning." This practice of listening could lead to what she calls the "figure of sound framework," wherein the naming is limited, encultured, and maintained in systematic ways.[17] In their commentaries on Chinese theater in California, nineteenth-century American writers, reporters, and travelers were quick to label the theater music as noise. (Well-known examples such as J. D. Borthwick and the British writers George Augustus Sala and Walter Gore Marshall were discussed in chap. 9.) The falsetto vocal timbre of Chinese opera actors and the instrumental timbre of gongs and Chinese fiddles were regularly the subject of derision.[18] A Tennessee editor who visited San Francisco's Chinese theater wrote of the music in his newspaper, the *Columbia Herald*, using terms such as "grotesque," "bombastic," "infernal," "hideous," and "deafening." Identifying the music with categories such as "inhuman" and "barbaric," this writer erased the sound of Chinese theater.[19]

Ubiquitous and relentless, mockery of Chinese theater music had an enduring impact. Crass jokes and insults proliferated and quickly became a popular sport in travelogues and news reports in the nineteenth century. Examples abound, but one in particular epitomizes the mode of listening. On September 25, 1869, as the completion of the transcontinental railroad increased the flow of people and ideas, the *San Francisco Chronicle* printed a review of a performance the previous evening by the Chinese opera troupe Lung Quong Toy Company at the city's eighteen-hundred-seat Metropolitan Theatre.[20] Noting that the special performance attracted a large audience, it proceeded to use terms such as "tin shop," "quartz mills" and "enraged cat on the roof" to deride the music.[21] This commentary was syndicated in more than thirty newspapers over the next five years (1869–73) in the United States and Britain. It constituted an "enculturated listening" to the performance of this ninety-member opera troupe, recently recruited from China by the first Chinese theater on Jackson Street, which had a similar capacity to the Metropolitan Theatre.[22] Such ridicule consisted of a string of false and incongruous images piled up to an extreme degree, far beyond any ordinary reach of fantasy, whose effect was amplified by repetition. It operated as a means to "excite the passion of contempt," and was therefore eagerly grasped by many news outlets to gratify people's favorite propensity. "Ridicule," noted the nineteenth-century *Encyclopaedia Britannica*, is a subject not of reasoning but of "sense or taste."[23] Our sense of ridicule is not only the true test of ridicule but the only test of what is ridiculous. Appealing to the sensory—the ear—ridicule impresses on the imagination outlandish images of obstreperous and unruly noise, stripping the music of any humanity. Endless repetition established ridicule as the figure of sound, which traveled widely and constituted the public discourse about Chinese theater's sonic presence.

"Listening . . . is always already a critical performance—that is, a political act," Nina Eidsheim reminds us.[24] In an era when an anti-Chinese agenda grew from state politics to become a national political platform, this listening practice, attuned to anti-Chinese sentiment, operated as a mode of erasure and continued to work at effacement in insidious ways. To the extent that Chinese theater music was identified through the sensory capacity of the ear as noise and inhuman—which was then interpreted as the sound of the race—this mode of listening enforced a kind of racialization of Chinese sound. It could be adopted by anyone and everyone. The figure of sound, sadly, could also be internalized by the Chinese American community itself, even long after Chinese theaters were gone.

Due to the scarcity of Chinese-language narratives, these reviews and commentaries, as the most prominent contemporary written accounts of Chinese theaters in the nineteenth-century United States, form the primary archive. Excavating a legible account of the sonic history of Chinese theater from this archive is practically impossible. The listening practice, marked by a resistance to listening, resulted in a "non-history" of Chinese American sonic existence, for it "erases any conventional modality for writing an intelligible [musical] past," to borrow a famous phrase from Saidiya Hartman.[25] In other words, it is nearly impossible to disentangle the sound world of Chinese opera singers and musicians in the United States from the disparaging written commentaries of white spectators. These accounts became the frame in which the sonic presence was captured; the archives of newspapers unfortunately provide the only pathway through which one can enter the historical field. Even as I carefully read against the grain to resuscitate what I consider to be a lively music history of early Chinese immigrants, I am keenly aware that I run the risk of underscoring the authority of the archives, the weight of the yellowed historical documents, and the plentitude of their presence in electronic newspaper databases. Its imprint—the racialized listening practice—on our society is lasting, because the archives, as Katherine McKittrick informs us, "also structure and frame how we enter into the present and future in our writing."[26] The racialized listening practice of the nineteenth century established a ranking of musical sound and worth that has yet to be dismantled.

The practice of listening exemplified by crass jokes in fact *activated* the colonial order and *enacted* anti-Chinese sentiment as a form of erasure. Therefore, to write a counternarrative is to create a space for sonic imagination unconfined by the words of mockery. It is to enact other listening practices, an intent listening for the embodiment of enjoyment in the special theatrical space. In this book, I have enlisted the help of the visual—the photographs and the illustrations of Henry Burden McDowell's article—to facilitate a kind of listening for the embodiment of enjoyment (more on alternative listening practice below).

The third type of erasure of the sound of Chinese theater was imposed by legal sanction and enforced by police action. Objections to Chinese theaters were frequently expressed as noise complaints and petitions for city ordinances to address them. This was a form of hysteria about racial spatialization. As a result, from the 1860s to the 1880s, cities passed many types of criminal ordinances—relating to noise, nuisances, disturbing the peace, and so forth—to curb and silence the sound of Chinese theater. As discussed in previous chapters, musicians and performers were routinely arrested, charged, jailed, and fined simply for performing and making music; theaters were raided for failing to comply with ordinances. Arresting musicians and taking punitive action against them criminalized the musical performance and the space. Reports of such events accounted for a significant portion of news about Chinese theater.

In early 1880, at the same time that Ah Quin was enjoying daily opera performances at the W. T. P. and G. Q. Y. theaters in San Francisco, Sacramento had lively Cantonese opera performances as well, stirring much excitement. The three-hundred-seat Sacramento Theatre attracted attention from the beginning of the year, and in February it was offering two daily performances.[27] Yet enjoyment at this theater would be forced to stop in June. The *Sacramento Daily Union* reported the criminalization of the performance:

> On Saturday evening complaint was made to police headquarters against the Chinese theater, alleging it to be a nuisance on the ground of its ceaseless din and unearthly caterwaul during the greater portion of the night. It is the same troupe from San Francisco which played last winter, and Saturday evening was their opening night. Upon complaint being made officers Rider and Ferral disconcerted the Celestial menagerie by arresting eight of the players and taking them to the lockup, when they gave bonds and are waiting for permission from Judge Henry to complete the Choctaw dance and jimjam which was so unceremoniously squelched.[28]

Since the Chinese theater had obtained theater licenses from the state, county, and city, giving them the privilege and protection to operate, the performers were released. A week later the theater reopened, but again the actors and musicians were arrested, this time the whole troupe as well as the proprietor. At the police court it was declared that the "evidence introduced to prove the theater to be a nuisance showed that the noise from it has been so loud and of unusual character as to be heard distinctly at Second and K, and at Fifth and I streets."[29] On appeal, the superior court sustained the judgment of the lower court. On August 5, the *Sacramento Daily Union* reported the decision and printed the full decision of Judge Samuel C. Denson, parts of which are quoted below.

> The People vs. Ah Tim and Ah Luck—This is an appeal from a judgment of the Police Court of the City of Sacramento, imposing fines upon said defendants upon a verdict finding them guilty of disturbing the peace. The defendants are performers or actors in a Chinese theater, situated upon Third street in said city, and the noises complained of as constituting a disturbance were those made in the ordinary course of a performance in such theater. That the noises were loud and unusual and continued late into the night cannot be denied, in view of the evidence contained in the record; in fact, counsel upon the agreement virtually conceded that the acts proven constituted a misdemeanor, unless such a performance was legalized by the State and county license held by the proprietor of the theater. A license was duly issued by the proper officer to the proprietor of the establishment to conduct a theater. . . . The word "theater" is one having a well-understood meaning, and almost any person of ordinary intelligence would readily understand the implication of a permit to have a theater. . . . But the law does not authorize the conducting of a Chinese theater, but merely permits a license for a theater.[30]

The judge went further by grouping offensive sound with immoral or obscene exhibitions such as nudity, opining that a license for a theater issued under the law "is not intended, in any sense, as an indulgence." The practice of listening was key to this decision, as the judge explained:

> In this case the evidence shows that the performance complained of commenced at an early hour in the evening and continued till about midnight, and that during all that time there was a continual din and noise, composed of discordant sounds, such as fell harshly upon the ear and made uncomfortable all persons in the immediate vicinity.[31]

Using a form of "racialized listening," the judge identified both the disagreeable timbre and the auditory discomfort it caused as evidence of its criminality.[32] This criminalization through listening practice sanctioned erasure. Under the identification of unlawfulness, Chinese sound had no claim to legitimacy, nor did its musical space. The theater's music, categorized as nuisance and noise, was targeted for silencing and punished by the state. At the end of the 1880 newspaper report, the Sacramento writer cheered the judge's decision, noting that "[it] will no doubt put a final period to the Third-street Chinese theater, much to the satisfaction of the denizens of that vicinity."[33]

Racialization of timbre figured prominently in this listening practice. An 1869 ordinance passed by San Francisco's Board of Governors banned "beating upon a gong or gongs" (see fig. 4.9). The timbre of gongs came to represent Chineseness. Timbre was the key, as underscored by a satire in the *San Francisco Chronicle*: "The Chinese Theater has made one more step toward civilization, by substituting a fife and drum for the usually execrable din of their gongs and squeak-tubes."[34] In an act of erasure, it replaced the racialized timbres with others of perceived whiteness.[35]

For the inhabitants of the Chinese community, such acts of erasure were a regular part of daily life. On May 13, 1876, San Francisco's Chinese-language weekly paper *The Oriental* included, as usual, a news entry about recent arrests made by "green-clothes men," a reference to the policemen of the community (fig. E.3).

> In the previous week the green-clothes men made two arrests of cubic air violations, one with thirteen offenders and the other with ten offenders, all subjected to a 10-dollar fine or, if unaffordable, 5-day imprisonment. In addition, they also arrested sixty members of the Yao Tian Cai theatrical troupe, each agreed to a ten-dollar fine.[36]

No reason was given in the Chinese newspaper for the opera troupe members' arrest. None was needed. Between 1875 and 1877, the city's police carried out five largescale raids of Chinese theaters for violations of the nuisance ordinance. After paying the fines, the performers probably returned to the stage.[37] This report was a record of everyday harassment, as was the next item about new Chinese-exclusionary measures to be adopted by the city. Comprising only two lines buried in this four-page weekly, the reported act of sound erasure enforced by the green-clothes men was easily submerged within the unfolding of daily life for this early Chinese American community. It neither changed nor defined the community's Chinese livingness.

My own encounter with this newspaper page (during the very early stage of this book project) brought an important revelation, however. When I first spotted this small news item in *The Oriental*, my heart skipped a beat; the beautiful name of the opera troupe—Yao-Tian-Cai Xiban 堯天彩戲班—jumped out from the newspaper page and evoked an emotion—palpable joy. It was a rare moment of recognition after day-in, day-out work on the mountainous erasure in the archives. I knew it! Lively-sounding moments of Chinese theater—melancholy singing, melodious music, buoyant sonorities—were usually irrevocably absent or tied to mockery in the archives. Yet here, printed in beautiful Chinese characters, the proper name rejected the enclosure of the disciplinary act of the green-clothes men. The printing of its ideogram registered promises of the enchanting music of Chinese theater. It is untethered to the listening of white spectators. If, by not having the same access to alphabetic writing, Chinese theater was placed outside the sonic register of the most prominent archives, this ideogram in a contemporaneous Chinese newspaper evokes another listening practice, recalls and recognizes the mellifluous presence of the actors singing in the background of archival silence.

堯天彩戲班: The Troupe of "Vivacity of a Peaceful and Prosperous Time"

The troupe with the elegant name—it greeted me from the depths of the archives.[38] Even though these few Chinese characters for the theatrical troupe were embedded in news of big events or small trifles, current affairs, commerce, political news, shipping schedules, and so on that constituted the bulk of this four-page weekly newspaper, they gave me a glimpse of the joy and fun of theatergoing.

There are many ways to listen to sound erasures. Read against the grain, the archives full of sound erasures are themselves powerful evidence of the successful, resounding, resilient life of performance at Chinese theaters. For each sneering remark and derisive account of Chinese theater music in news reports and magazine articles, there was a vibrant and lively evening of opera performance. For each arrest of Chinese musicians for violating city ordinances by performing music, there was a full house of Chinese immigrants mesmerized by the magical world of opera performance. For each complaint

FIGURE E.3 From *The Oriental (Tangfan gongbao)*, May 13, 1878.

of noise brought before a city's governing board, there was an opera troupe offering a full-fledged production. The music of Chinese theater has its roots in a long and popular tradition, filled with fantastic and fanciful yet familiar legends and stories. After their release from the "green-clothes men," the performers readily returned to the stage, to the audience awaiting them. Indeed, the more fervent the attempts at sound erasure, the more prominent and successful Chinese theaters became in the urban space and the more significantly their sound permeated society. Listening to the listening practice, one realizes these acts of sound erasure signaled racial anxiety over the vibrancy of Chinese theaters—the sonic emblem of Chinese communities' prosperity.

For me, laying bare the ways naming arises in the process of listening, rather than from the sound itself, is crucial, as it informs critical analysis of the listening practice and helps create a space for the exploration and imagination of what is not named, or is misnamed—an insurgent listening practice, one might say. To quote the anthropologist Ann Stoler, such insurgent listening helps us to "cut across the strictures of archival production" and refigure "what makes up the archival terrain."[39] I found that writing a counternarrative against the so-called material truth of the archives means exactly this: creating a textual, visual, conceptual, and material space to imagine another type of listening practice and exploring ways of intent listening for the voices singing in the background all this time.

My own engagement with the archives has been significantly changed with this practice. During my research, reading account after account of derision and assault against the music of Chinese theaters has long taken an emotional toll. Such accounts lodged in the psyche and slipped into the subconscious. For a long time, I shied away from studying nineteenth-century Chinese American music history, as I dreaded encounters with these disparaging comments. I also assumed that it would be impossible to excavate a useful understanding of Chinese musical life from these racialized accounts. The incessant nuisance complaints and city ordinances—from Portland to Honolulu, from Oroville to San Francisco—and the ubiquitous, obligatory derision of Chinese sound in newspapers and travelogues—made me cringe and avert my eyes. Such accounts are signs of trauma and racializing violence that take emotional energy to address. I skipped paragraphs and entries where they popped up, rather than collecting them, not only because of the violence but also because I feared that they were evidence justifying the invisibility of the Chinese in American music history.

But examining listening practice opens an analytical space. Racialized listening practices refused legitimacy to Chinese American music history. The dynamics of race, through which timbre, sound, and melody in Chinese theater were supposedly heard in the nineteenth-century United States, framed the practice of listening, whose written accounts became the "material truth" with which one must contend in the archives. To the extent that such a listening practice constituted the norm, society internalized it to measure the sonic characteristics of Chinese theater. This racialized listening practice defined the sound of Chinese theater for not only contemporaries but also future generations.[40]

As Michel de Certeau notes, "The transformation of 'archivistic' activity is the point of departure and the condition for a new history."[41] There is a lot to learn about how to perform listening through erasure. We might begin with what Nina Eidsheim calls "pause."[42] To excavate the sound of Chinese theater in nineteenth-century California is, perhaps, to listen to—to interrupt—the sonic erasures in their different modalities and commit ourselves to what Saidiya Hartman describes as "listening for the unsaid, translating misconstrued words, and refashioning disfigured lives."[43] This importantly means that we must *pause* before quoting any mockery of the music of Chinese theater without interrogating what Jennifer Stoever calls the "sonic color line" that was entangled in such listening practice.[44] All too often, commentaries ridiculing the sound of Chinese opera theater were used as evidence, presented as legitimate archival material, to highlight the supposed "strangeness and unassimilability" of Chinese culture and people, instead of exposing the white listening practice.[45] "Pause," Eidsheim and Walden noted, can "cause the release of the figure of sound within which nineteenth-century Chinese immigrants had been locked."[46]

We can also listen to listening through close reading and transference. We have read closely Ah Quin's pen strokes in both cursive English letters and complex Chinese ideograms to consider how they might reveal the interiority of this theatergoer. We could also "listen" through his pen strokes for embodied enjoyment. As Andrea Bachner notes, the act of inscription (writing) concretizes the imaginaries, and reveals "how materiality and signification interact."[47] Through Ah Quin's handsome, thick pen strokes, we can imagine the force of Lam Yap Ca's melodious voices as well as the personal significance for Ah Quin. Through listening, the images of the auditoria of Chinese theaters could also conjure up the resonance of gongs filling the large space, or the gentle turns of vocal phrases accompanied by erxian "lingering as unbroken as the threads of silk" (餘音嫋嫋，不絕如縷), to use a beautiful expression in a Chinese poem.[48] Through the early audio recordings such as the Victor Monarch records, we can imagine how these sounds and verses summoned emotion, memory, and engagement. The theatricality and music of popular storytelling in Chinese theater weave together for the audience the deepest layers of their mental and emotional lives.[49] Through this listening to the listening, we can begin to paint a picture, however fragmented, of the sonic moments of Chinese theaters, from the vantage points of the inhabitants of the theaters.

Transpacific History of American Music

Moving from the experience of one person going to Chinese theater as part of his daily life to the transoceanic network in which this individual was embedded, this book delineates the processes that brought Chinese opera and the entire Chinese community to San Francisco in the mid-nineteenth century and explores how these processes are essential to understanding what constitutes a music history of Chinese America and what it stood for. It shows how Chinese theater became, and functioned as, the most prominent musical space in early Chinese communities, with Cantonese opera the dominant musical genre. Although Chinese theater is the focus, at a macro level this book is a study of the transpacific history of American music. I use the term *transpacific* because, in contrast to *transatlantic*, which has long been the focus of American music historiography, it captures the important movements, activities, and influx of people on that other shore. "Transpacific" does not refer to a static space or region but rather to the flow of culture, people, and capital in both directions across the Pacific Ocean.

In order to understand how the music of Asian America is situated in today's American society, we need to start with the transpacific history of American music. The Chinese were the largest group in the nineteenth-century transpacific migration to America. (According to the 1880 US Census, San Francisco had 21,745 Chinese, 45 Japanese and no other Asians.)[50] In California, vibrant transpacific soundscapes could be found in the communities the early Chinese immigrants established, both along the shore and in the interior of the state. This soundscape was embedded in what Elizabeth Sinn calls "multidirectional . . . multileveled, interactive, interpenetrating, overlapping, and interlinked [networks]."[51] The cultural production and cultural meaning of the transpacific network as reflected in the history of Chinese theater reveals a lot about the constructions, discourses, and fantasies that characterize transpacific history. Theater experience intersected with "all facets of [migrants'] existence, as passengers, consumers of material and cultural things, merchants, investors, laborers, fathers and husbands who provided for transnational families, supporters of hometown enterprises, givers and recipients of charity, and much more, and, underpinning all these, as human beings with hopes and fears, diverse interests, and many desires."[52] The making and doing of Chinese theater in North America created the transpacific historical soundscape of nineteenth-century America, which this book seeks to make legible.

If the study of transpacific soundscapes involves the act of listening through erasure and imagining what remains unsaid, it is crucial to acknowledge the role of language as a mediating force in shaping these soundscapes. Transpacific soundscapes are a register of linguistic instability and multiplicity that are inherently connected to musical genres, practices, signification, and more.

The issue of language is an important consideration that runs throughout this book as a determinant of musical genres beyond translation, as a bodily experience of belonging in the mode of the mother tongue, as a sounded expression of community, as a means for mutual understanding across dialects of southern China and stage dialect, and as a heuristic for understanding Chinese theater's "hypervisibility." These considerations reveal layers of meaning and the fluidity of multiple sensory and cultural imaginations and social belongings. Consideration of linguistic complexity is an important entry point into understanding the mediated sonic environment of the transpacific soundscape and the complex emplacement of Chinese theatres in North America. For early immigrants, the magic of Chinese theaters lay in the ways they constituted embodied experience; this embodiment was shaped by mediating linguistic differences, among other factors. The historical traces of this soundscape are hidden in archives that are very resistant to giving up those traces. This book endeavors to uncover traces of this history by finding ways to document and listen.

As I came near the completion of this book project, I was invited to give a lecture on this topic at a graduate seminar on "nation/national identities/nationalisms" at the University of Southern California.[53] After I finished the last slide, a student raised her hand. Noting that Chinese theater performed Cantonese opera, which is one of the many Chinese opera genres, she said that, coming from a Taiwanese-American family, she didn't feel like it was a part of her past. Yet she quickly added that she nevertheless felt connected to those who had been silenced and whose histories had been erased. This candid response was important, prompting me to reflect on my own journey with my first book. As a music theorist studying American ultramodern music of the 1930s, I stumbled on contemporaneous traces of Chinese theater in New York. Intrigued by the discovery, I pored over music reference books and explored music archives in major libraries across North America to search for the history of Chinese American music. Unfortunately, my attempts were unsuccessful, and not much was found. As a result, the project stalled. The lack of archival evidence implied that the history did not exist, even though I knew it did. But this archival absence fits with the stereotype of Asian immigrants as newcomers in the United States. The historical vacuum was the predicament of a transpacific history of American music. Later, after expanding the direction of my archival research, seeking out Chinese-language materials, and uncovering a treasure trove of documents in the Chinese Exclusion Files at the National Archives, I gathered a rich array of materials and wrote a book about Chinatown opera theater in the 1920s.[54] My personal journey shows that music studies in North America have neglected the transpacific voice, and archival absence in turn has silenced that history. The nineteenth-century listening practice that determined what constituted music led to the archiving of only certain sounds; transpacific music making was not among them. My continuing study of Chinese theater in North America is an attempt to address the lacuna of transpacific history in American music.

But I understand the dilemma of the Taiwanese American student. As Hua Hsu noted, "a variety of pasts and futures gather under the capacious sign of the transpacific."[55] How incongruous it was for the student to feel alienated listening to the unfamiliar genre of Cantonese opera, while at the same time feeling the warmth of familiarity from the Chinese language, characters, opera titles, historical legends, and even people, flashing through the slide presentation. Yet identifying with Chinese musical tradition is not a prerequisite for acknowledging its erasure, its significance for the early Chinese immigrant community, or its legitimacy as part of American music history. I would argue that ultimately, the music making of early Chinese immigrants, in this case Cantonese opera, belongs not only to the history of Chinese Americans but also to the Asian American soundscape, as well as the musical landscape and racial terrain of American history. Chinese opera troupes' transpacific movements in the nineteenth century are constituents of the American musical past in every sense, but they are not the only ones. Many more came after them, and we are beginning to learn about those, too. In recent years, the study of the musical space of Asian Pacific Islanders in the United States has grown significantly, foregrounding their musical practices, community building, varied music genres, and traditions, as well as how they negotiated music careers. For examples, Deborah Wong's work on Asian American jazz musicians and on Asian American taiko; Oliver Wong on Filipino American mobile disc jockey crews; Kevin Fellezs on Hawaiian slack-key guitar; and Mari Yoshihara on Asian American classical musicians, to name only a few.[56] These studies shed light on the music history and soundscape of the transpacific population, point to a broad array of music genres, and expand our imaginations to recall musical memories and images. There are multidirectional, multilayered, and multi-sited transpacific histories of American music that await our discovery and listening.

The Taiwanese American student is not alone. Her remark highlights the importance of considering the heterogeneity among different Asian American groups and, accordingly, the different senses of belonging and engagement. Lisa Lowe, in her influential 1996 work, *Immigrant Acts: On Asian American Cultural Politics* had brought our attention to the "heterogeneity, hybridity, and multiplicity" of Asian America. She urges us to "dialectically [engage] with the national formation of Asian Americans from the perspective of an international history and location," in order to "generate conceptions of collectivity that are neither regulated by notions of identity nor prescribed by aesthetic, psychoanalytic, and political modes of identification."[57] Recognizing the role of transpacific in American music history is an important way to combat the perception of Asian Americans as perpetual foreigners and "newcomers." To this end, knowledge production is the key. By documenting, narrating, and contextualizing the lively music scene of the Chinese community in different histories and locations and the historical processes they went through while participating in the nation building, and by hearing the thousands of footsteps of our transpacific ancestors, we make an important intervention in the historical erasure of their sound and the mockery and criminalization of their music and space. It also means feeling and listening with Asian American music making and acknowledging, as the art historian Marci Kwon notes, "the multiple and complex ways Asian Americans have lived, worked, created and imagined in relation to a world that seeks ever more devious ways to homogenize and dehumanize them."[58] To write the new American music history is to reconceptualize it by acknowledging the significance of its transpacific history.

Chronology of Chinese Theaters in San Francisco

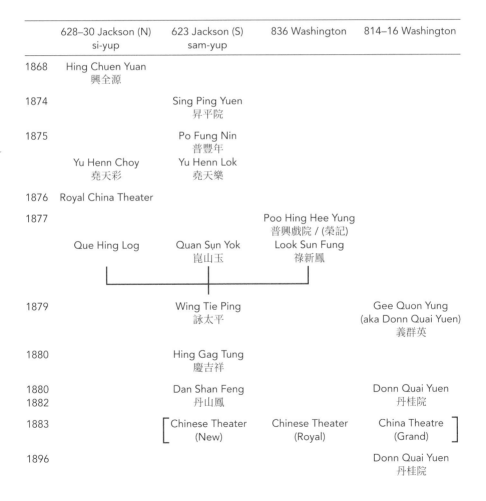

	628–30 Jackson (N) si-yup	623 Jackson (S) sam-yup	836 Washington	814–16 Washington
1868	Hing Chuen Yuan 興全源			
1874		Sing Ping Yuen 昇平院		
1875		Po Fung Nin 普豐年		
	Yu Henn Choy 堯天彩	Yu Henn Lok 堯天樂		
1876	Royal China Theater			
1877			Poo Hing Hee Yung 普興戲院 / (榮記)	
	Que Hing Log	Quan Sun Yok 崑山玉	Look Sun Fung 祿新鳳	
1879		Wing Tie Ping 詠太平		Gee Quon Yung (aka Donn Quai Yuen) 義群英
1880		Hing Gag Tung 慶吉祥		
1880 1882		Dan Shan Feng 丹山鳳		Donn Quai Yuen 丹桂院
1883	Chinese Theater (New)	Chinese Theater (Royal)	China Theatre (Grand)	
1896				Donn Quai Yuen 丹桂院

Stylistic Characteristics of Cantonese Opera and a Transcription of *Golden-leaved Chrysanthemum*

Cantonese opera, a genre with distinctive tradition and stylistic character-istics, is inextricably connected to the general history of Chinese opera (*xiqu* 戲曲). As spectacle, performance, and sound, Chinese opera is characterized by rich costumes, colorful painted faces, choreographic stage movements, powerful singing voices, heightened speech, fixed melodic types, and classic percussion gestures that punctuate the drama. Its repertoire has persisted through lively stage performance, produced in countless renditions by a great variety of regional genres. More than three hundred regional genres were recorded by the early twentieth century, many of which became integral to cultural practices and traditions of their regions.[1]

The early history of Cantonese opera is complex, with many prominent personalities and legends, such as Master Zhang Wu and the Li Wenmao Uprising, which have been addressed extensively in *The Rise of Cantonese Opera* by the historian Wing Chung Ng. The following is a quick survey of some essential stylistic characteristics.[2] In the second half of the nineteenth century—the period under consideration in this book—Cantonese opera was performed in a Mandarin-based language rather than Cantonese. Used only for performance, it was referred to by the Cantonese as "stage Mandarin" (戲棚官話). Also known as Central Dialect (中州音), stage Mandarin was developed through a gradual process of absorption of different dialect ele-ments from various, though primarily northern, regions. Descending from opera forms of other provinces, the music of Cantonese opera is based on two large tune families, *bangzi* (梆子) and *erhuang* (二黃), each of which has different aria types. An aria type is distinguished by structural features (mode, verse structure, linguistic tones, rhythm pattern, pitch hierarchy, melodic pat-tern, tempo, and voice type, the last of which dictates the register and hence the ending tones and tuning). In the nineteenth century, the official cast of

Cantonese opera troupes consisted of twelve role types, as documented by the opera's professional organization Jiqing Gongsuo (see chap. 5). (This tradition would be replaced by the simpler six role-type system in the twentieth century). The roles' vocal ranges, tessituras, timbres, and singing approaches also shape aria styles in important ways.

The accompaniment of Cantonese opera during this period comprised the following bowed and plucked stringed instruments and percussion instruments, with the occasional inclusion of wind instruments. The use of many large percussion instruments gave the genre a spirited character.

erxian 二弦, two-stringed fiddle with snakeskin-covered soundbox

sanxian 三弦, longnecked, fretless, three-stringed lute with snakeskin-covered sound box

zhutiqin 竹提琴, two-stringed fiddle with thin paulownia-wood soundboard

yueqin 月琴, short-necked, fretted, four-stringed moon lute with a round, hollow body

hengxiao 橫簫, wooden flute, also called *dezi*

gaobianluo 高邊鑼, large gong with a wide edge, suspended on a stand

dawenluo 大文鑼, large gong with a narrow edge, suspended on a stand or handheld

shagu 沙鼓, cone-shaped drum with a thick wood frame and a center hollow hole with a cover of thick leather

dabo 大钹, huge cymbals, 45–60 cm in diameter

Since the nineteenth century, Cantonese opera has established a core repertoire based on historical legends or the literary canon; it shared much of its repertoire with other regional genres of Chinese opera. They could be found among the lists of the "Eighteen Grand Operas" and the "New Eighteen Grand Paichang Operas." The famous opera *Pinggui Returning Home* (discussed in chap. 3) belongs to the former, while *Golden-leaved Chrysanthemum* (discussed in the epilogue) belongs to the latter. Toward the end of the nineteenth century, Cantonese opera began adopting more vernacular forms and developing repertoire based on popular *muyushu*, chapbooks or songbooks of popular narratives in the Cantonese vernaculars.

Ritual opera constituted an important part of Cantonese opera repertoire as a form of worship for specific purposes or sacred functions. These occasions included the celebration of holidays, festivals, and deities' birthdays; thanksgiving to deities or ghosts; the debut of a new troupe or theater; and other such events. Many were short playlets performed before the main repertoire. The most frequently seen title, *The Joint Investiture of a Prime Minister of Six Warlords*, is an important play for opening nights. It features a grand parade of the entire cast and an opportunity for a show of artistic strength with festive bustle. Other titles include *Sacrificial Offering to White Tiger*,

Birthday Greetings from Eight Immortals (performed as *Eight Genii* by Tong Hook Tong; see fig.1.3), *Dance of Promotion*, *The Heavenly Maiden Delivers a Son*, and *Sealing the Stage*. According to the Cantonese opera scholar Sau-yan Chan, "*White Tiger* is a solemn ritual reserved for initiating a piece of land that has never been used for building an opera stage; *Birthday Greetings* pays respect to the deities on behalf of the locals; *Promotion* and *Heavenly Maiden* both pray for prosperity and productivity; and *Sealing* closes the operatic series by thanking the deities and spirits."[3] From nineteenth-century reporters' descriptions of the performances in English-language publications, it is clear that these operas were performed regularly by the troupes in North America.

The following transcription from a 1903 recording provides a glimpse of the sonic presence of music performed inside Chinese theaters in nineteenth-century America. Figure B.1 is a transcription of the phonograph disc of an excerpt from the opera *Golden-leaved Chrysanthemum*. The opera is discussed in the Epilogue, where the synopsis is given. The music was recorded in North America, likely Philadelphia, and released on multiple discs on Victor's Monarch Records in 1903. This excerpt from the eighth disc, the only one currently available for this study, is transcribed here in Western staff notation. Notes in smaller size indicate the instrumental accompaniment. About three minutes in length, this disc contains an aria by a male character interspersed with sections from a female character, all sung in stage Mandarin. The lyrics are not fully recognizable in the recording, and no scripts could be found, making translation difficult. Thus, a general description will have to suffice. The aria involves the interaction between an older man (the *gongjiao* role type) and the female protagonist, Lin Yuejiao, who is inquiring about her husband, Zhang Yinglin. The man expresses his empathy, while Lin interjects with questions and laments about her misery. The gongjiao role type sings in a low voice; the actor typically performs the characters of loyal older servant or seneschal.

As for the music, the episode is sung in the *bangzi* tune type. Following the norm, rhymed couplets provide the basis for the structure of the arias, whose formal features include the number of words or syllables in a line (line length), the grouping of words, and patterns of linguistic tone and rhyme. This aria takes a moderate tempo that can be described as a 2/4 meter. The line length of the lyrics is ten words, grouped 3/3/2/2. In some lines, extra words are inserted as padding syllables to add interest or to improve the flow, but they do not interfere with the basic ten-word line length. The melody of each line follows the word grouping 3/3/2/2, so the lengths of the lines are similar. The aria of the male character comprises six couplets.

金葉菊
Golden-leaved Chrysanthemum

黃嘉恆記詞
Lyrics transcribed by Huang Jiaheng

雷采萍譯譜
Music transcribed by Lei Caiping

FIGURE B.1 Transcription of *Golden-leaved Chrysanthemum* from Victor Monarch Record 7218 H by Hueng Jiaheng and Lei Caiping.

FIGURE B.1 (continued)

FIGURE B.1 (continued)

FIGURE B.1 (continued)

Acknowledgments

Research and writing for this book has been supported by grants from the National Endowment for the Humanities, Rutgers University Research Council, and the Huntington Library Short-term Fellowship. The project began well before the support of a NEH Research Fellowship in 2020–2021, but that year of full immersion in research and writing was precious and critical to the project.

Katy Phillips at the San Diego History Center was a ray of light during the bleak time when travels and archive visits were unthinkable. I could not be more grateful for her generous and expert support. Some of the materials used for this book came from research done with the help of Hsihsi Chung at the Metuchen Public Library more than twenty years ago. Wing Chung Ng and Elizabeth Sinn kindly shared critical archival findings in early Chinese newspaper clippings. Ever since we first met in 2011, embarking together on a road trip to Marysville and Oroville, California he meticulously planned, David Lei has been a constant companion on this search for historical knowledge and always inspired me with his dedication, commitment, and vision for the performing arts of the Chinese American community.

I have relied on the expertise of the following colleagues, who kindly answered critical questions and specific inquiries that helped move the project along: Lauri Blunsom, Ho Chak Law, Chan Sau-yan, Fumitaka Yamauchi, Bell Yung, and Sai-Shing Yung. I am grateful for the help of the community of scholars and collectors of early recorded sound: Timothy Brooks, David Giovannoni, and Wei Xiaoshi, who collectively unlocked the mystery of the Chinese series in the Monarch Records of Victor Label; and Du Jun Min, whose generosity in sharing his personal collection of materials made it possible to recover some of the lost sounds. I am incredibly lucky to have received help from this community. It proved to be instrumental to this book, whose coverage encompasses the period prior to the commencement of the recording industry. Furthermore, I am deeply grateful to Chan Sau-yan for assisting with the transcription included in Appendix B, and to Hueng Jiaheng and Lei Caiping for their excellent work in the challenging task of transcribing an excerpt from what may be the earliest recording of *Golden-leaved Chrysanthemum*, made in 1902.

I have been fortunate to have the opportunity to present sections of the book to audiences in Asia, Europe, and North America over the years 2021 to 2023. I am grateful for the new friends I met on these occasions and the stimulating exchanges about issues addressed in this book. Their valuable feedback and insightful suggestions, whether in person or online, have sharpened the argument in the book and in some situations steered its direction as well. I am grateful for colleagues who invited me to speak at these seminars and colloquia at the following institutions and am happy to acknowledge them here: Interdisciplinary Histories Research Cluster, University of British Columbia; Hitchcock Institute for Studies in American Music, Brooklyn College; Music and Sound Studies Colloquium, Cornell University; Dalton School; Asian/Pacific Studies Institute, Duke University; Distinguished Lecture Series, Middle Tennessee State University; Techniques of Music Distinguished Scholars Lecture Series, The New School; Music Colloquium, University of Notre Dame; Asian American Lecture Series, Northern Illinois University; "Transpacific East Asia: Transformations and Trajectories in Sound and Music" Conference, University of Sheffield; Seminar on "Nation/National Identities/Nationalisms" University of South California; Tsou Lecture, Skidmore College; Colloquium Series in the Critical Music Studies, State University of New York, Stony Brook; Institute of Sinophone Studies, National Tsing Hua University; Center for Lingnan Musical Culture, Xinghai Conservatory of Music; and Museum of Chinese America, Washington, DC. I also appreciate the opportunity to participate in a collaborative research project at Universität Greifswald, entitled "The Operatic Canon as Cultural Heritage—Transformations and Fragmentations of a Global Repertoire," at Institut für Kirchenmusik und Musikwissenschaft. This collaboration provided distinctive perspectives from the lens of comparative study.

I am beyond grateful to Dean Hubbs and Hedy Law, who are always in my corner; their unflagging faith in the significance of the topic and trust in my ability to carry out this work have sustained me. For their friendship, and for insights on matters and ideas large and small, I thank my valuable interlocutors, Kofi Agawu, Hannah Chang, Mary Chapman, Nina Eidsheim, Joanna C. Lee, Mei Han, Judy Tsou, Emily Wang, Louisa Wei, Deborah Wong, and Zhang Wuyi. I also cherish the opportunity to have ongoing conversations with colleagues in Siniphone Studies: Howard Chiang, Shuh-mei Shih, and E. K. Tan. The completion of the manuscript coincides with my time as a fellow of "Voice: Sound, Technology, and Performance," an annual seminar at the Center for Cultural Analysis, Rutgers University. The rich conversation of this remarkable group of faculty, postdoc fellows, and graduate students was illuminating in many ways.

I thank the journal and online platform editors Andrea Bohlman, Todd Decker, Sara Haefeli and George Lipsitz for their invitations and help, which resulted in essays that appeared in various formats and reached more diverse, broader audiences. These invitations provided opportunities for me to reflect on the work in this book from different angles. Portions of these invited essays made their way into the epilogue of this book, where an address to a broader audience is needed. In particular, when I accepted the invitation from George Lipsitz, the editor of *Kalfou: A Journal of Comparative and Relational Ethnic Studies*, to write an essay for a printed symposium on Nina Eidsheim's *Race of Sound*, I did not foresee that the assignment would lead me to look deeply into a very personal issue—the erasure of the sound of Chinese theater in North America. The *Kalfou* essay is reworked as part of the epilogue of the book.

My much-treasured colleagues at Rutgers, Rebecca Cypess, Steven Kemper, Eduardo Herrera, and Jason Geary, have been incredibly supportive, for which I am very grateful. I am extremely fortunate to have my colleague Jacqueline Thaw as a collaborator. Her brilliant cover design for my first book set a high standard, and I am thrilled that she agreed to work with me again. I thank the Rutgers cartographer Michael Siegel for creating important maps so meticulously and Anqi Wang for her assistance with the glossary and bibliography, and for her diligence and enthusiasm. In 2023, I stepped into the role of editor-in-chief of *American Music*. I thank my editorial assistants, Rachel Horner and Dane-Michael Harrison, for being weekly interlocutors over the years, and for their vision and insight into what American music could be and what clarity in writing entails. I owe a big thanks to Yayoi Uno Everett and Wendy Heller for their dedicated friendship, intellectual companionship, and the numerous laughs, meals, and journeys we shared in various parts of the world.

My editor at the University of Illinois Press, Laurie Matheson, deserves special mention for the especially formative role she played. Her advice at several junctures in the writing of this book was critical, and her unwavering support and enthusiasm for this book in every one of our conversations was inspiring and joyful. I am grateful to Barbara Curialle and Jennifer Argo at the Press for their meticulous and superb work during the final stages of copy-editing and production. I am indebted to Gordon H. Chang, Patty

Howland, David McCarthy, and John Koegel for reading or editing different portions of the manuscript. The manuscript benefited especially from Patty, who not only lent her keen eye to the prose but also shared her expertise in law. Over the years, John has been extremely generous in sharing research materials and has always kept an eye out for Chinese theater when he is doing his research on Mexican American theater, and I cherish the precious time we spent together as Huntington Library fellows. I could not ask for a better comrade in the research of immigrant theaters.

Finally, I want to express my gratitude to my family, both here and in Taiwan. The unwavering love of my siblings has been my anchor. They have provided me with sage advice, artistic insight, and spiritual guidance. I am also thankful for the invaluable assistance of my daughter, Karen, a linguist who meticulously deciphered and transcribed pages of bilingual handwritten script from the nineteenth century. Without her intelligent and systematic approach, my understanding of Ah Quin's diary would not be the same. Erica and Isabel also contributed in numerous ways, from turning the sorting of research materials into a family game around the dinner table, to providing tech-savvy help on the images for this book with their artistic eyes, as well as lively conversations around the dinner table. I treasure all your vivaciousness, creative spirit, brilliance and good humor. Finally, I extend my deep gratitude to Nelson, who has stood by me lovingly through the highs and lows of this project, grounding me in all of its everydayness.

Notes

Prologue

1. Ah Quin Diary Collection, MS 209, San Diego History Center Document Collection. Ah Quin is the English name of Tom Chong-kwan (Tan Cong-kun, 譚聰坤, 1848–1916). Ah Quin is the Romanization of 阿坤. It should be pronounced as "ah-kwan" (in Cantonese) or as "a-kʹuən" (in International Phonetic Alphabet).

2. Ah Quin's diary has been the focus of the following studies: Susie Lan Cassel, "To Inscribe the Self Daily: The Discovery of the Ah Quin Diary," in *The Chinese in America* (Walnut Creek, CA: Alta Mira Press, 2002), 54–74; Yong Chen, "'China in America': The World of Ah Quin," in *Chinese San Francisco, 1850–1943: A Transpacific Community* (Stanford: Stanford University Press, 2000), 96–123; Yong Chen, "Remembering Ah Quin: A Century of Social Memory in a Chinese American Family," *Oral History Review* 27, no. 1 (Winter–Spring 2000): 57–80.

3. *Directory of Chinese Business Houses: San Francisco, Sacramento, Marysville, Portland, Stockton, San Jose, Virginia City, Nev.* (San Francisco: Wells Fargo and Co., 1878), digital copy available at Wells Fargo Archives (along with 1882 edition), https://history.wf.com/assets/pdf/publications/WFCA-1878-Chinese-Business-Directory.pdf.

4. Ah Quin, diary, December 12, 1878, Ah Quin Diary Collection, San Diego History Center, San Diego, CA.

5. Ah Quin, diary, December 7, 1878.

6. Ah Quin, diary, December 24, 1878. It is possible that *Six Warlords* was programmed for the festive occasion of Christmas Eve.

7. Yang Enshou, 楊恩壽, 坦園日記 [*Diary of Tan Garden*], April 12 and November 24, 1865 (Shanghai: Shanghai gu ji chu ban she, 1983), 114, 147.

8. In 1851 the number of arrivals was 2,716. Beth Lew-Williams, *The Chinese Must Go: Violence, Exclusion, and the Making of the Alien in America* (Cambridge, MA: Harvard University Press, 2018), 253–54.

9. Ah Quin, diary, October 26, 1879. It appears the tickets allowed reentry.

10. Zhang Yuanyuan 張圓圓, 《坦園日記》中的戲曲史料研究 [A Study on Historical Materials of Xiqu in Tanyuan Diary] (master's thesis, Shanxi Normal University, 2013), 33.

11. Samuel Weber, *Theatricality as Medium* (New York: Fordham University Press, 2004), 23.

12. Barbara E. Ward, "Not Merely Players: Drama, Art and Ritual in Traditional China," *Man* 14, no. 1 (1979): 34.

13. Ah Quin, diary, January 7, 1879; see also Andrew Griego, "Mayor of Chinatown: The Life of Ah Quin, Chinese Merchant and Railroad Builder of San Diego" (master's thesis, San Diego State University, 1979), 55.

14. His diary entry for February 6 noted taking the steamer at Black Point Cove to go up the shore and work for Captain Dyer; the February 19 entry noted his working at Angel Island.

15. Ah Quin, diary, February 27, 1879.

16. Ah Quin, diary, March 12, 1879.

17. A Chinese character is an ideogram composed of many strokes, with thirty-two different types of strokes. Each character is written out in adherence to the correct position, proportions, and order of the strokes. The number of types of strokes involved increases the complexity. Characters that have up to five or six strokes are considered simple. The three characters for Look Sun Fung are each composed of twelve to fourteen strokes.

18. Jing Tsu, *Kingdom of Characters: The Language Revolution That Made China Modern* (New York: Riverhead, 2022), xvi.

19. Tsu, *Kingdom of Characters*, xvi. This connection was important. Ah Quin retained a strong sense of filial responsibility to his parents in China. He prayed for them as well as sending money, which he did four separate times during 1879. The money added up to $51 (the equivalent of $1,602 in 2024). Yong Chen, *Chinese San Francisco*, chap. 4.

20. Ah Quin, diary entries, September 13 to October 10, 1879.

21. Ah Quin, diary, October 12, 1879. Although the choice of words here may seem mild, in Ah Quin's usage the word "happy" was an indication of a rather strong emotion. "Nice" was also rarely used.

22. Ah Quin, diary, November 19, 1879.

23. Ah Quin, diary, October 13, 1879.

24. Ah Quin, diary, June 10, 1879. He recorded the names of two performers: Kwai Fai Yun and Luing Chork.

25. The new theater opened with forty performers; Ah Quin made his first visit on December 28. Ah Quin, diary, December 28, 1884.

26. Virgil Kit Yiu Ho, "'Why Don't We Take Drama as Facts?'—Observations on Cantonese Opera in a Rural Setting," *Journal of the Royal Asiatic Society Hong Kong Branch* 53 (2013): 183–214, esp. 184.

27. Chen, *Chinese San Francisco*, 55. According to US censuses, San Francisco's population was 12,022 in 1870 and 21,745 in 1880. Chen notes that in 1860 over 75 percent of the adult population was between twenty and thirty-nine years of age, and less than 3 percent were above fifty years of age. In 1870, more than 68 percent

were between twenty and thirty-nine years old, and only 2 percent were above fifty years of age.

28. Katherine Meizel, "A Powerful Voice: Investigating Vocality and Identity," *Voice and Speech Review* 7, no. 1 (2011): 267–74.

29. Yeng Pway Ngon, *Costume*, trans. Jeremy Tang (London: Balestier Press, 2015), 123.

30. Siu Leung Li, *Cross-Dressing in Chinese Opera* (Hong Kong: Hong Kong University Press, 2003), 10. The complexity of this translation is also discussed by many others. See, for example, Daphne Pi-Wei Lei, *Alternative Chinese Opera in the Age of Globalization: Performing Zero* (London: Palgrave Macmillan, 2011), 8–11.

31. Cantonese opera is one of fourteen existing *xiqu* genres in China's Guangdong Province.

32. "Chinese Theater," *San Joaquin Republican*, August 21, 1852; "Chinese Dramatic Company," *Daily Alta California*, August 6, 1853; "Chinese Theatricals," *Daily Alta California*, October 20, 1852; "Another Celestial Concert," *Chico Record*, August 26, 1857. A writer also compared Chinese opera with Italian opera, "The Chinese Feast," *Sacramento Daily Union*, August 25, 1865. All references are in the California Digital Newspaper Collection, Center for Bibliographical Studies and Research, University of California, Riverside.

33. Patricia Sieber discusses how this nonconformity led to misunderstanding. Sieber, "Whither Theatricality? Toward Traditional Chinese Drama and Theater (*Xiqu*) as World Theater," *Journal of Chinese Literature and Culture* 9, no. 11 (April 2022): 225–55.

34. With a focus on theorizing intercultural encounters, rather than historical studies, Daphne Pi-Wei Lei suggests that American audiences attended Chinese theater either to confirm perceived notions of "real" Chinese theater based on Western plays such as *The Orphan of China* or to see a display of the "other" ethnicity, whereas the Chinese community used Chinese theater in a kind of self-fashioning. Together, they formed what she calls "Operatic China—an imagined community formed by Chinese, non-Chinese, and theatre in nineteenth-century California." This analysis positions Chinese theater as an "alien art form." See Lei, *Operatic China: Staging Chinese Identity Across the Pacific* (London: Palgrave, 2006), 85.

35. Michel de Certeau, *The Writing of History*, trans. Tom Cloney (New York: Columbia University Press, 1988), 75.

36. Toni Morrison, "Memory, Creation, and Fiction," and "The Source of Self-Regard," in *The Source of Self-Regard: Selected Essays, Speeches, and Meditations* (New York: Vintage, 2020), 304–21, 326–33, respectively.

37. Ann Laura Stoler, *Along the Archival Grain: Epistemic Anxiety and Colonial Commonsense* (Princeton, NJ: Princeton University Press, 2008), 47.

38. Lily Wong, "Transpacific—Transfiguring Asian North America and the Sinophonic in Jia Qing Wilson-Yang's *Small Beauty*," in *Keywords in Queer Sinophone Studies,* ed. Howard Chiang and Alvin K. Wong (New York: Routledge, 2020), 16–37.

39. This is a paraphrase of Maurice Wallace's original phrase for a different context in *King's Vibrato: Blackness, Modernism and the Sonic Life of Martin Luther King Jr.* (Durham, NC: Duke University Press, 2022), 8–9. See also a fuller argument in Nancy Yunha Rao, "From Chinatown Opera to *The First Emperor*: Racial Imagination, the Trope of 'Chinese Opera,' and New Hybridity," in *Opera in a Multicultural World: Coloniality, Culture, Performance,* edited by Mary Ingraham, Joseph K. So, and Roy Moodley (New York: Routledge, 2015), 50–67.

Introduction

1. The total Chinese population in the United States in 1860 was 34,933 and in 1890 was 107,488. See Sucheng Chan, *This Bittersweet Soil: The Chinese in California Agriculture, 1860–1910* (Berkeley: University of California Press, 1986), 43.

2. Maaike Bleeker, *Visuality in the Theatre: The Locus of Looking* (Basingstoke, UK: Palgrave Macmillan, 2008), 166.

3. The middle Ming dynasty saw the growing prominence of merchants in the Jiangnan area, which led to the prosperity of Chinese opera. This was evident in terms of increased patronage and the emergence of professional troupes, the refinement of tastes, and the transformation of opera tunes. See Hsiang-Chun Ko, 柯香君, 明代職業戲班研究 [A study of the theatrical troupes in the Ming Dynasty], 國文學誌 *Chinese Journal* 14 (June 1, 2007): 101–45.

4. Yu Xunqing, 俞洵慶. Quoted in Wing Chung Ng, *The Rise of Cantonese Opera: From Village Art to Global Phenomenon* (Urbana: University of Illinois Press, 2016), 23. I have adopted Ng's translation with small modifications.

5. For a detailed study of the actor Li Wenmao's involvement with the Taiping Rebellion and the aftermath, as well as the institutionalization of Cantonese opera in the late Qing, see Ng, *The Rise of Cantonese Opera*, 20–30.

6. Li Hsiao-t'I, *Opera, Society, and Politics in Modern China* (Cambridge, MA: Harvard University Press, 2019), 22.

7. Ng, *The Rise of Cantonese Opera*, 25–26.

8. Li, *Opera, Society, and Politics in Modern China*, 29.

9. Ng, *The Rise of Cantonese Opera*, 6, 25. Ng noted that by the end of the Qing, there were over thirty full-size opera troupes that each required a pair of red boats. The complexity of the performance venues and changes in Cantonese opera are beyond the scope of this survey. Further discussion of the performance venues can be found in Yu Yong 余勇. 明清時期粵劇的起源、形成和發展 [Cantonese opera in the Ming-Qing Period: origin, formation, and development] (Beijing: Zhongguo Xiju Chubanshe, 2009), 109–80.

10. Li, *Opera, Society, and Politics in Modern China*, 31.

11. Mae M. Ngai, *The Chinese Question: The Gold Rushes and Global Politics* (New York: Norton, 2021), 3. Mid-nineteenth-century British colonies included Canada, Australia, and New Zealand, as well as parts of India and Africa.

12. William Speer, February 8, 1855, 東涯新錄, *The Oriental*, quoted in Chen, *Chinese San Francisco*, 13.

13. Chen, *Chinese San Francisco*, 22. This view departs from the general assumption about Chinese migration. For further discussion, see Chen, *Chinese San*

Francisco, 11–23. Sue Fawn Chung also used oral histories to document that "clan leaders encouraged members to go abroad in order to contribute to the clan's general funds, which could be used to purchase land from destitute neighboring clans, thus enriching the clan coffers." In addition, "Self-financing was also popular among generational immigrants as one generation brought the next generation over in succession." See Chung, *Chinese in the Woods: Logging and Lumbering in the American West* (Urbana: University of Illinois Press, 2015), 26–27.

14. See Madeline Y. Hsu, "Chinese and American Collaborations through Educational Exchange during the Era of Exclusion, 1872–1955," *Pacific Historical Review* 83, no. 2 (2014): 318.

15. The gold rush also drew people from the eastern and southern United States, central Europe, Britain, Chile, Mexico, and elsewhere.

16. John E. Wills, "A Very Long Early Modern? Asia and Its Ocean, 1000–1850," in *Pacific America: Histories of Transoceanic Crossings,* ed. Lon Kurashige (Honolulu: University of Hawai'i Press, 2017), 16.

17. Elizabeth Sinn, *Pacific Crossing: California Gold, Chinese Migration, and the Making of Hong Kong* (Hong Kong: Hong Kong University Press, 2013), 3. It took an average of thirty-three days to sail from Hong Kong to San Francisco in 1852, an obvious advantage over the New York-to-San Francisco journey by way of Cape Horn, which took at least 115 days. See also Ngai, *The Chinese Question*, 19–26.

18. Lew-Williams, *Chinese Must Go*, 253. The arrival numbers were 11,085 in 1868; 14,994 in 1869; and 10,869 in 1870. This was the first large increase since 1854.

19. A travel route was established via San Francisco, Hong Kong, Yokohama, and Shanghai. See Robert A. Weinstein, "North from Panama, West to the Orient: The Pacific Mail Steamship Company, as Photographed by Carleton E. Watkins," *California History* 57, no. 1 (1978): 46–57. See also Lew-Williams, *The Chinese Must Go*, 253.

20. "San Francisco's thriving maritime trade transformed the Pacific from a peripheral trade zone to a nexus of world trade," Sinn, *Pacific Crossing,* 2.

21. This figure does not take into account those Chinese immigrants who departed the United States.

22. Sinn, *Pacific Crossing,* 54.

23. Yvonne Liao, "'Chinatown' and Global Operatic Knowledge," *Cambridge Opera Journal* 31, nos. 2–3 (2019): 280–90.

24. David Killingray, *"Introduction: Imperial Seas: Cultural Exchange and Commerce in the British Empire 1780–1900,"* in *Maritime Empires: British Imperial Maritime Trade in the Nineteenth Century*, ed. David Killingray, Margarette Lincoln, and Nigel Rigby (Woodbridge, UK: Boydell Press, 2004), 1.

25. Eric Odell Oakley, "Columbia at Sea: America Enters the Pacific, 1787–1793" (PhD diss., University of North Carolina, Greensboro, 2017), 396–409.

26. Sinn, *Pacific Crossing*, 45.

27. This list (of necessity, incomplete) was prepared by Selim E. Woodworth; a longer list appears in Sinn, *Pacific Crossing*, app. 2. The US naval officer Selim Edwin Woodworth (1815–1871) arrived in California in 1847, led the rescue of the Donner party shortly thereafter, and was elected for Monterey to the first California legislature in 1849 (which became the state legislature with California statehood

in 1850). He was also a member of the Committee of Vigilance and an early member of the California Pioneer Society. For Woodworth's role as a counselor to the Chinese, see Ngai, *The Chinese Question*, 50. This list identified sixty-nine Chinese arrivals from Macao, Hong Kong, Shanghai, and Whampoa (in Hong Kong), as well as one individual from Mazatlán, Mexico. See also "Chinese Emigration," *Daily Alta California*, August 13, 1852; and "The Chinese Emigration," *Daily Alta California*, May 10, 1852.

28. The *Bombay Calendar and Almanac* (Bombay: Times Office, 1941–42), 204, 225. See also *Lloyd's Register of Shipping 1852*, 156, https://archive.org/details/HECROS1852/page/n155/mode/2up.

29. Sinn, *Pacific Crossing*, 318.

30. "Memoranda," *Daily Alta California*, October 7, 1852.

31. *Sacramento Daily Union*, October 22, 1852; *Daily Alta California*, October 7, 1852; and *Daily Alta California*, October 8, 1852.

32. Misha Berson, *The San Francisco Stage: From Gold Rush to Golden Spike 1849–1869* (San Francisco: San Francisco Performing Arts Library and Museum (Journal Series no. 2, 1989).

33. John Koegel, "Non-English-Language Musical Theater in the United States," in *The Cambridge Companion to the Musical*, 3rd ed., ed. William A. Everett and Paul R. Laird, (Cambridge: Cambridge University Press, 2017), 21–50.

34. John Koegel, "What's in a Name? The Multiplicities of the Musical," in *The Routledge Companion to Musical Theatre*, ed. Laura MacDonald and Ryan Donovan (New York: Routledge, 2022), 503.

35. Sabine Haenni discusses the importance of considering how immigrant public cultures helped form urban commercial entertainment, rather than limiting immigrant theaters to their own enclaves. Sabine Haenni, *The Immigrant Scene: Ethnic Amusements in New York, 1880–1920* (Minneapolis: University of Minnesota Press, 2008), 6.

36. "The Spanish Theatre," *Daily Alta California*, July 21, 1853, quoted in John Koegel, "Mexican Music, Theater, and Circus at the Los Angeles Plaza, 1850–1900," in *De Nueva España a México: El universo musical mexicano entre centenarios, 1517–1917*, ed. Javier Marín López (Seville: Universidad Internacional de Andalucía, 2020), 47.

37. "The Chinese Must Go," *Buffalo Evening News*, August 21, 1883.

38. Him Mark Lai, "Historical Development of the Chinese Consolidated Benevolent Association/*Huiguan* System," *Chinese America: History and Perspectives* 1 (1987): 13–51.

39. Lai, "Historical Development."

40. *Boston Evening Transcript*, September 15, 1852.

41. Sylvia Sun Minnick, *Samfow: the San Joaquin Chinese Legacy* (Fresno: Panorama West Publishing, 1988), 13.

42. According to a study of the distribution of the Chinese population in California, in 1860, 91.2 percent (31,854) lived in mining regions and the Central Valley, compared with 7.8 percent (2,719) in San Francisco. A decade later, 62.4 percent

(30,758) still lived in mining regions and in the Central Valley. Chan, *This Bitter Sweet Soil*, 43.

43. Mae Ngai has discussed the difficulty in conducting research on the gold fields in California, due to the lack of official records during the early decades of the state's history. Ngai, *The Chinese Question*.

44. Ronald L. Davis, "They Played for Gold: Theater on the Mining Frontier," *Southwest Review* 51, no. 2 (1966): 172, 179. Davis reports that musicians could be paid sixteen dollars a night. One female organist accumulated four thousand dollars over a five-month period, a small fortune.

45. Ward, "Not Merely Players," esp. 29.

46. Ward uses the Chinese character *wang*, 旺, to explain this phenomenon, which she calls "magical significance" ("Not Merely Players," 29).

47. According to the 1870 US Census, the total population of Marysville, in Yuba County, was 5,677, of whom 1,484, or 26 percent of the population, were Chinese. Yuba County had a Chinese population of 63,250 (1870 US Census, Ancestry.com).

48. *Stockton Independent*, October 4, 1856; *Daily Evening Bulletin*, August 12, 1957.

49. 1880 US Census, United States Census Bureau, https://www.census.gov /programs-surveys/decennial-census/decade.1880.html#list-tab-693908974.

50. Berson, *The San Francisco Stage,* 15.

51. Miska Hauser, letter, April 15, 1853, in *The Letters of Miska Hauser 1853*, History of Music in San Francisco Series 3 (San Francisco: Works Progress Administration, Northern California, 1939), 41; "Coast News," *Marysville Daily Appeal*, September 14, 1880; "Lorne and Louise in Chinatown," *New York Times*, September 29, 1882; *Daily Alta California*, March 24, 1884; *Daily Evening Bulletin*, May 16, 1887; Gertrude Stanford in "A Chinese Theater Party," *San Francisco Examiner*, April 7, 1887.

52. The Bohemian Club was established in San Francisco during the 1870s by writers, artists, journalists, and some musicians, such as the guitarist-composer Manuel Y. Ferrer. After richer patrons joined, it became an elite private club. From its founding to the early twentieth century, the club offered performances open to the public, in public theaters, including excerpts from the Grove Plays (High Jinks).

53. Jann Pasler, "Sonic Anthropology in 1900: The Challenge of Transcribing Non-Western Music and Language," *Twentieth-Century Music* 11, no. 1 (2011): 7–36. For more discussion see Chapter 10.

54. Portland had a rather vibrant Chinese theatrical culture in the 1880s, and Los Angeles's Chinese theater endured for at least several decades. Regarding the Chinese in Victoria, British Columbia, see Karrie Marion Sebryk, "A History of Chinese Theatre in Victoria" (master's thesis, University of Victoria, 1993), 142; for Portland, see the *New York Herald Tribune*, September 2, 1880; for Los Angeles, see the *Los Angeles Herald*, October 25, 1884.

55. *Chinese-Language Business Directory and Lunar Calendar for 1905* (San Francisco: Horn Hong & Co., 1905), collected in W. H. Webber Chinese exclusion notebook, 1883–1916, mssHM 84094, Huntington Library, San Marino, CA.

56. Nancy Yunhwa Rao, *Chinatown Opera Theater in North America* (Urbana: University of Illinois Press, 2017).

57. Opera costuming was particularly known for its obfuscation of social strata during the Ming-Qing era. See Wu Jen-shu, 巫仁恕, 品味奢華：晚明的消費社會 與士大夫 [Taste of luxury: Consumer society and the scholar-literati circle in the Late Ming Dynasty] (Taipei: Academia Sinica, 2007), 137; and Rachel Silberstein, *A Fashionable Century: Textile Artistry and Commerce in the Late Qing* (Seattle: University of Washington Press, 2000), 155.

58. Yang Maojian 楊懋建, 夢華瑣簿 [*Random Thoughts of the Splendid Dream*], 1842, in Zhang Cixi 張次溪, ed., 清代燕都梨園史料 *Qing Dynasty Historical Material on the Theater in Beijing* (Beijing: Zhongguo xiju, 1988), 350. Here is the original Chinese: "其服飾豪侈，每登場金翠迷離，如七寶樓臺，令人不可逼視,雖京師歌 樓無其華靡." The translation is mine.

59. For Yang Enshou's description of Cantonese opera, see Yang, [Diary of Tan Garden], 116–84. Here is the original Chinese: 出宮粧天女凡七，各獻舞態，其宮粧 裏外異色，當場翻轉，睹之如彩雲萬道，彷彿天花亂落也. Steven Miles discusses how Yang Maojian jumped at the chance to watch Cantonese operas while in residence in Beiliu. See Steven B. Miles, "Where Diasporas Met: Hunanese, Cantonese, and the State in Late-Qing Guangxi," *Journal of Chinese History* 5 (2021): 263–84.

60. Masako Yoshida, "Trade Stories: Chinese Export Embroideries in the Metropolitan Museum," *Metropolitan Museum Journal* 49 (2014): 165–85, esp. 169.

61. Jean L. Kares, "Performance, Adaptation, Identity: Cantonese Opera Costumes in Vancouver, Canada," *Textile Society of America Symposium Proceedings* 978 (2016), 242–51, http://digitalcommons.unl.edu/tsaconf/978.

62. Rose Gouveneur Hoes, "Historical Costumes of Famous American Women," *Daughters of the American Revolution Magazine* 47, no. 5 (November 1915): 283–90, esp. 289.

63. *Republican Gazette*, April 27, 1888. This puff piece appeared in more than thirty newspapers around the country.

64. Phillip B. Zarrilli, "Toward a Phenomenological Model of the Actor's Embodied Modes of Experience," *Theatre Journal* 56, no. 4 (2004): 653–66, esp. 611. See also Helen Margaret Walter, "'On and Off the Stage': Costume, Dress, and Locating the Actor-Manager's Identity, 1870–1900," in *Performance Costume: New Perspectives and Methods*, ed. Sofia Pantouvaki and Peter McNeil (New York: Bloomsbury, 2021), 89–104.

65. Kares, "Performance, Adaptation, Identity," 248.

66. Anne Anlin Cheng, *Second Skin: Josephine Baker and the Modern Surface* (New York: Oxford University Press, 2011).

67. Sean Metzger, *Chinese Looks: Fashion, Performance, Race* (Bloomington: Indiana University Press, 2014), 7–8.

68. The film and media scholar Yiman Wang notes the Thai/Balinese influence on the costume as well. Email correspondence, February 10, 2024.

69. Anne Anlin Cheng provides a brilliant analysis of the scene in her book *Ornamentalism* (Oxford: Oxford University Press, 2019), 61–85. The complex scene and representation have received close scrutiny, but the connection to Chinese

theater is seldom noticed. The Chinese instrument, the *sanxian*, in the scene was often mistakenly called a *shamisen*, the Japanese stringed instrument, as seen in Cheng's analysis.

70. Sieber, "Whither Theatricality?" 231.

71. Sieber, "Whither Theatricality?" 232.

72. Cited in Pan Xiafeng, *The Stagecraft of Peking Opera* (Beijing: New World Press, 1995), 16–17.

73. Weber, *Theatricality as Medium*, 25.

74. Weber, *Theatricality as Medium, 28.*

75. Quoted in Siyuan Liu, *Transforming Tradition: The Reform of Chinese Theater in the 1950s and Early 1960s* (Ann Arbor: University of Michigan Press, 2021), 8–9.

76. "A Walking Junk: The Great Dramatic Sensation of Chinatown," *San Francisco Examiner,* December 4, 1882. See also ch. 8.

77. Quoted in Weber, *Theatricality as Medium, 24.*

Chapter 1. First Encounters

1. *California Senate Journal*, 3rd sess., January 7, 1852, 12–22 (quote on p. 15).

2. "Celebration of the Anniversary of Our National Independence," *Daily Alta California*, July 10, 1852.

3. The article "Chinese Celebration of the July 4th" was published in the *Hartford Daily Courant*, August 19, 1852; *Alexandria Gazette*, August 24, 1852; and *Portland Transcript*, August 28, 1852. This article underscored California's new status as the thirty-first US state.

4. "Celebration," *Daily Alta California*, October 31, 1850.

5. "City Intelligence," *Daily Alta California*, February 24, 1852.

6. "The Celestial at Home and Aboard," *Littell's Living Age*, no. 43 (August 14, 1852), 289–98, esp. 293.

7. Sinn, *Pacific Crossing*, 55.

8. *LeCount & Strong's City Directory for the Year 1854* (San Francisco: LeCount & Strong, 1854), 228. Norman Assing's life dates are unknown.

9. May-bo Ching, "A Preliminary Study of Theatres Built by Late Qing Cantonese Merchants," *Journal of Historical Science* 6 (2008): 101–12.

10. "Mission to the Chinese in California: Journal of William Speer," *Home and Foreign Record of the Presbyterian Church in the United States of America*, vol. 4 (1853), 214–15, quoted in Carl T. Smith, *Chinese Christians: Elites, Middlemen, and the Church in Hong Kong* (Hong Kong: Hong Kong University Press, 1985), 34–51.

11. D. J. MacGowan, "Chinese Guilds, or Chambers of Commerce and Trade Unions," *Journal of North-China Branch of the Royal Asiatic Society*, no. 21 (1886): 133–61, especially 135.

12. For more discussion, see Yucheng Qin, *The Diplomacy of Nationalism: The Six Companies and China's Policy toward Exclusion* (Honolulu: University of Hawai'i Press, 2009). Yong Chen identifies Yanghe as the largest huiguan. See Chen, *Chinese San Francisco*, 73.

13. Ngai, *The Chinese Question*, 85–87.

14. For further discussion see Ngai, *The Chinese Question*, chap. 4, "Bigler's Gambit."

15. Ngai, *The Chinese Question*, 105.

16. Hab Wa and Tong K. Achick [*sic*], "Letter of the Chinamen to His Excellency, Governor Bigler," *San Francisco Herald*, April 29, 1852; *Daily Alta California*, April 30, 1852.

17. Norman Assing, "To His Excellency Governor Bigler." *Daily Alta California*, May 5, 1852.

Despite their efforts, however, in May of that year California renewed the Foreign Miners' License Tax, which, as the *Daily Alta California* made clear, was "directed especially at Chinamen, South Sea Islanders, &c., and is not intended to apply to Europeans." *Daily Alta California*, May 1, 1852. Another long letter was written later in May; see Tong Achick [*sic*] and Chun Aching, "To His Excellency Governor Bigler from the Chinamen," in *An Analysis of the Chinese Question* (San Francisco: *San Francisco Herald*, 1852), 10–14.

18. "John Chinaman vs. John Bigler," *Daily Alta California*, August 28, 1852.

19. Early visual evidence of the presence of Chinese is found from Colorado to Idaho; for example, "Chinese New Year Parade," item ID 76-18-9, Idaho Historical Society, https://idahohistory.contentdm.oclc.org/digital/collection/p16281c01112 /id/431/rec/4.

20. Ngai, *The Chinese Question*, 49.

21. Charles J. McClain, Jr., "The Chinese Struggle for Civil Rights in Nineteenth Century America: The First Phase, 1850–1870," *California Law Review* 72, no. 4 (1984): 529–68.

22. *Fremont Weekly Freeman*, October 26, 1850.

23. *North China Herald*, December 28, 1850.

24. A lithographic print commemorating the event shows the winding line of the procession snaking from the bottom to the top of the image, even longer than that in the July 4 print. Separated from the procession, a group of Chinese is depicted off to one side, led by the large triangular flag of the Qing dynasty and a dignified man on horseback. The print reads, "Funeral procession of H. Clay [F]rancis. Died June 29, 1852. Aged 75 years. Born April 12, 1777. S. Francisco. Published and for sale by B. F. Butler [1852]." Printed Ephemera Collection, Library of Congress, https:// lccn.loc.gov/2021771252.

25. Qin, *The Diplomacy of Nationalism*, 26.

26. Sue Fawn Chung, *In Pursuit of Gold: Chinese American Miners and Merchants in the American West* (Urbana: University of Illinois Press, 2011), 19.

27. Red R. Myers, *Pintupi Country, Pintupi Self: Sentiment, Place, and Politics* (Washington, DC: Smithsonian Institution Press, 1991), 109.

28. "Chinese Play Actors," *Dwight's American Penny Magazine, and Family Newspaper*, 1, no. 32 (September 13, 1845), 497–99, HathiTrust. From a different perspective, Daphne Lei suggested that *The Orphan of China*, the English adaptation of a Chinese play performed on American stage in 1767, as well as the performances during the 1830s by the famous conjoined ("Siamese") twins Chang and Eng

constituted the American preconception of Chinese theater. See Daphne Pi-Wei Lei, *Operatic China: Staging Chinese Identity Across the Pacific* (London: Palgrave, 2006), 39–43.

29. "500 Chinese," *New York Herald*, September 5, 1852; "Chinese Theater," *San Joaquin Republican*, August 21, 1852 (reprinting a news item from *The San Francisco Daily Herald*).

30. "Pellegrini Opera Company at Adelphi Theater," *Daily Alta California*, February 12, 1851.

31. Ronald L. Davis, *A History of Opera in the America West* (Englewood Cliffs, NJ: Prentice-Hall, 1965), 85.

32. "A Chinese Theatre in San Francisco," *New-York Organ*, September 18, 1852. This was a reprint from an unidentified San Francisco paper.

33. For example, a recurring advertisement listed, "An entire invoice of Chinese goods, comprising extra rich heavy Canton embroidered white shawls; Fancy colored Shawls; Extra fine assorted colors Satins, etc." *Daily Alta California*, October 12, 1852.

34. The troupe performed in San Francisco, Sacramento, and in other parts of California, and then traveled eastward, performing in New Orleans, Philadelphia, Baltimore, New York, Boston, Cincinnati, and Canada. Several extensive descriptions of their program were printed in the *Times Picayune* (New Orleans), December 2–5, 1852. For the "Western Barnum," see *Boston Evening Transcript*, November 16, 1852; *Boston Globe* August 18, 1853.

35. *Theatrical Journal: Review of the Drama, Music, and Exhibitions* 14, no. 684 (January 1853), 23–23.

36. *Sacramento Daily Union*, October 20, 1852.

37. The *St. Louis Intelligencer*'s writer was a certain Crockett (likely Col. David Crockett, who moved to San Francisco in 1852). His report was quoted in "The Chinese Dramatic Troupes," *New York Herald*, December 24, 1852; and "Chinese Music," *Weekly National Intelligencer*, January 1, 1853.

38. "American Theatre," *Daily Alta California*, October 24, 1852.

39. Albert Benard de Russailh, quoted in Lawrence Estavan, *Theatre Buildings, Part 1. San Francisco Theatre Research* (San Francisco: Work Projects Administration, 1940), 61.

40. Estavan, *Theatre Buildings*, 60.

41. "The Chinese Dramatic Troupe," *New York Herald*, December 24, 1852.

42. Ward, "Not Merely Players," 29.

43. "Chinese Theatricals," *Daily Alta California*, October 20, 1852.

44. *Nevada Journal* (Nevada City, CA), October 22, 1852.

45. "The Chinese Dramatic Troupes," *New York Herald*, December 24, 1852.

46. See advertisements in *Daily Alta California*, October 18–24, 1852.

47. Adjustments appeared in the advertisements printed in the *Daily Alta California*: the admission prices were reduced on October 19; *My Neighbor's Wife* was added on October 20; An American farce was added on October 22; "Old standard," *Sacramento Daily Union*, October 22, 1852. "Feats of skills," *Daily Alta California*, October 20, 1852.

48. On August 28, 1852, *Daily Alta California* published the article "John China-man vs. John Bigler," praising Tong A-Chick and Norman Assing's rebuttal to the governor's denigrating remarks. See a report of the heated situation in "The Bigler-ian Government," *Daily Alta California*, October 28, 1852, 1.

49. It is not possible to identify all the titles of Chinese operas performed in nineteenth-century California, as they were advertised in English-language news-papers. Sometimes, the English translation of the title is too vague to trace back to its original Chinese.

50. This meant that Xu Ce had to sacrifice his own son, who was sent to be executed in place of Xue Jiao, because the empress had ordered Xue Jiao and his family to be executed.

51. May-bo Ching, "A Preliminary Study of the Theatres Built by Cantonese Merchants in the Late Qing," *Frontiers of History in China* 5, no. 2 (2010): 253–78.

52. The quote from the *Hong Kong Gazette* was included in a report of the *Sacramento Daily Union*, October 22, 1852.

53. Office for National Statistics, as discussed in Ian Webster, "The British Pound Has Lost 99.428% of Its Value," CPI Inflation Calculator, https://www.in2013dollars.com/uk/inflation/1852.

54. *Daily Alta California*, October 17, 1852.

55. Qin, *The Diplomacy of Nationalism*, 33.

56. Sinn, *Pacific Crossing*, 141.

57. Sinn, *Pacific Crossing*, 311.

58. "Chinese Mechanics," *Daily Alta California*, August 28, 1852.

59. Sinn, *Pacific Crossing*, 140.

60. Sinn, *Pacific Crossing*, 318. This is the conclusion I drew after a study of the timeline of the troupe's arrival, noted in general newspaper reports of the pertinent time.

61. *London Lloyd's List 1852*, June 14, 1852, July 17, 1852.

62. *Daily Alta California*, October 20, 1852.

63. The romanization of Chinese names presents some challenges. Norman Ass-ing is Yuan Sheng, 袁生; Tong Chick is probably Tong A-Chick, 唐亞植 (also known as Tang Tinggui 唐廷桂); Likeoon is likely Lee Kan (Li Gen), 李根. "Likoon" is the spelling used for Likeoon in John Kuo Wei Tchen, *New York Before Chinatown: Orientalism and the Shaping of American Culture, 1776–1882* (Baltimore: Johns Hopkins University Press, 2001), 86.

64. *San Diego Herald*, December 11, 1851.

65. Qin, *The Diplomacy of Nationalism*, 9.

66. "Grand Chinese Festival," *Daily Alta California*, October 30, 1852.

67. *Daily Alta California*, September 24, 1852.

68. In his November 11, 1852 journal entry, Rev. William Speer refuted the rumor about the opening of a Chinese temple, noting, "No [Chinese] temple yet exists in California." Speer, "Mission to the Chinese in California," 214. Therefore this temple, dedicated in December, might be the first. In addition, another article, "Chinese Dedication," on the construction of a Chinese temple, was reported else-where in January 1853; see as *Eastern Times*, January 6, 1853.

69. "Chinese Dedications," *Buffalo Morning Express*, December 21, 1852.

70. Quoted in Bell Yung, *Cantonese Opera: Performance as Creative Process* (Cambridge: Cambridge University Press, 1989), 35.

71. Titled "Chinese Buddhistic Worship in San Francisco," this is a letter sheet, a kind of stationery popular between 1849 and 1869. The textual description is part of the letter sheet. These letter sheets were typically 10 1/2 by 8 1/2 inches when folded in half. They had lithographed vignettes or small pictures on the front so the sender could share scenes of buildings of interest with friends or family. Many of them were expertly and beautifully drawn by famous artists. See Catherine Hoover and Robert Sawchuck, "'From the Place We Hear about . . .': A Descriptive Checklist of Pictorial Lithographs and Letter Sheets in the CHS Collection," *California Historical Quarterly* 56, no. 4 (1977/1978): 346–67.

72. Commercial theaters were later developments in southern China. See Ching, "A Preliminary Study of the Theatres Built by Cantonese Merchants."

73. This practice gave rise to the traditional name of the Cantonese opera stage, *xipeng*, which literally means "hut for drama." Not until the mid-1850s did Cantonese opera performances in China start to move from temporary bamboo sheds to purpose-built commercial theaters.

74. "The Chinese Theatre in San Francisco," *San Francisco Herald*, December 30, 1852, quoted in the *New York Herald*, January 31, 1853.

75. John David Borthwick, *Three Years in California* (Edinburgh: W. Blackwood and Sons, 1857), 76–77.

76. Lois Rodecape, "Celestial Drama in the Golden Hills: The Chinese Theatre in California, 1849–1869," *California Historical Society Quarterly* 23, no. 2 (1944): 102.

77. *The Golden Era*, quoted in Lois Rodecape Rather, "Chinese Theaters in America" (unpublished manuscript), San Francisco Performing Arts Library and Museum, 22.

78. *Pioneer and Democrat* (Olympia, WA), February 5, 1853.

79. "A Chinese Theatre," *Maine Farmer*, March 3, 1853.

80. "The Celestials in New York," *New York Herald*, June 29, 1853.

81. *Daily Alta California*, February 25, 1853.

82. *Daily Alta California*, February 25, 1853; *Sacramento Daily Union*, March 29, 1853; and *New York Herald*, April 28, 1853.

83. "The 'Tong Hook Tong,'" *New-York Daily Times*, April 27, 1853, quoting from the *San Francisco Journal*.

84. "Dramatic and Musical," *New-York Daily Times,* May 18, 1853.

85. "Curious Chinese Dramatic Entertainment," *New-York Daily Tribune,* May 21, 1853.

86. "Curious Chinese Dramatic Entertainment."

87. Gemotice, "The Chinese Opera, at Niblo's," *The Spirit of the Times: A Chronicle of the Turf, Agriculture, Field Sports, Literature and the Stage,* May 28, 1853.

88. "Dramatic and Musical," *New-York Daily Times*, May 18, 1853; "The Chinese Opera, at Niblo's," *New-York Daily Times,* May 23, 1853; "Chinese Entertainment," *Alexandria Gazette* (Alexandria, VA), May 24, 1853.

89. "Last Night of the Tong Hook Tong," *New York Herald,* May 26, 1853. The unfortunate situation was widely reported for the rest of the year. See "The

Celestials in New York," *New York Herald*, June 29, 1853. For a fuller study of Tong Hook Tong on the East Coast, see Tchen, *New York Before Chinatown*, 86–90.

90. Advertisement, *Daily Alta California*, December 25, 1852.

Chapter 2. Bringing Opera to the Mines and Railroad Chinese

1. "The Chinese Exodus," May 27 and "The fourth of July and Chinese Race," July 8, 1854, *Golden Hills' News* 金山日新録. The quote is from the July 8 issue. A digital reproduction of this May issue can be found at https://californiahistoricalsociety.org/blog/come-forward-as-friends-the-golden-hills-news/. California Historical Society, San Francisco. A digital production of the July issue can be found at the Beinecke Rare Book and Manuscript Library, https://collections.library.yale.edu/catalog/2036937.

2. *Golden Hills' News*, July 8, 1854.

3. Elmer Sandmeyer, *The Anti-Chinese Movement in California* (Urbana: University of Illinois Press, 1991), 27.

4. Sucheng Chan, "Chinese Livelihood in Rural California: The Impact of Economic Change, 1860–1880," in *Working People of California*, ed. Daniel Cornford (Berkeley: University of California Press, 1995), 59–60.

5. Thad M. Van Bueren, "Late-Nineteenth-Century Chinese Farm Workers in the California Mother Lode," *Historical Archaeology* 42, no. 3 (2008): 80–96.

6. Lew-Williams, *The Chinese Must Go*, 21.

7. Gordon H. Chang, *Ghosts of Gold Mountain: The Epic Story of the Chinese Who Built the Transcontinental Railroad* (Boston: Houghton Mifflin Harcourt, 2020), 43.

8. Sylvia Sun Minnick, *Samfow: The San Joaquin Chinese Legacy* (Fresno, CA: Panorama West Publishing, 1988), 9–11, 23.

9. Mark Kanazawa, "Immigration, Exclusion, and Taxation: Anti-Chinese Legislation in Gold Rush California," *Journal of Economic History* 65, no. 3 (2005): 783.

10. Jean Pfaelzer, *Driven Out: The Forgotten War Against Chinese Americans* (Berkeley: University of California Press, 2008), 36.

11. The Foreign Miners' Tax Act of 1850 was passed by the state of California and signed into law by Governor Peter Hardeman Burnett. It imposed a tax of twenty dollars per month on foreign miners. The law met with protests from Irish, English, Canadian, and German miners and was rewritten to exempt any miner who was a "free white person" or any miner who was eligible to become an American citizen. In 1851 John McDougal became the governor; he favored Chinese immigration, and the law was repealed. A new Foreign Miners' License Tax was introduced in 1852 under Governor John Bigler. The new tax was three dollars per month and was raised to four dollars a month the following year. In 1855, the legislature distinguished foreigners eligible from those ineligible for citizenship, raising the tax on ineligible foreigners (the Chinese) by two dollars per month. James J. Rawls and Richard J. Orsi, eds., *A Golden State: Mining and Economic Development in Gold Rush California* (Berkeley: University of California Press, 1999).

12. Pfaelzer, *Driven Out*, 32.

13. Pfaelzer, *Driven Out*, xix–xx.

14. Pfaelzer, *Driven Out*, 45.

15. Chan, "Chinese Livelihood in Rural California," 65. Chan focuses in particular on Sacramento, Yuba City, and San Joaquin, but also examines the rural area as a whole.

16. Chan, "Chinese Livelihood in Rural California," 63.

17. According to Kenneth Owens, "Under the federal government's Preemption Act of 1841, any settler who was head of a family, a single male, or a widow, and who was either a US citizen or had filed a declaration of intent to gain citizenship could establish a preemption claim to a quarter section (160 acres) of unoccupied public land." After California was made a possession of the United States in 1884, all lands that did not have a prior claim through Spanish or Mexican land grants became unsurveyed US public domain. Kenneth Owens, *Gold Rush Saints: California Mormons and the Great Rush for Riches* (Norman: University of Oklahoma Press, 2005), 112–14.

18. Chan, "Chinese Livelihood in Rural California," 65.

19. Pfaelzer, *Driven Out*, 43.

20. Kanazawa, "Immigration, Exclusion, and Taxation," 781.

21. US Federal Censuses, 1860 and 1870, Ancestry.com. According to the Report for California in the 1860 US Census, Chinese were the largest foreign-born population at 34,935, followed by the Irish at 33,147.

22. Their circulation can be traced from newspaper reports, which ranged from brief notices to lengthy reviews.

23. Edward W. Syle, diary, October 30, 1855, HM 83407, Huntington Library, San Marino, CA.

24. San Francisco was "Dai Fu" ("Big City"), and Marysville "San Fou" ("Third City"). Chan, "Chinese Livelihood in Rural California," 61.

25. "Sacramento, California," *American Journal of Education* 19 (1870), 118. The report also notes forty-five Chinese children under the age of twelve in Sacramento.

26. Minnick, *Samfow*, 13. The building was purchased for the use of the Sze Yup Association in 1851, but it is unclear when the opera performances were held in this space.

27. *Sacramento Daily Union*, May 8, 1855. The quote is from "Chinese Theatricals," *Sacramento Daily Union*, May 7, 1855.

28. "Chinese Theatricals," *Sacramento Daily Union*, May 23, 1855.

29. "Sacramento Theater. May 23d. One night only! Immense attraction! The Chinese Dramatic Company! Mountain wizard. The great rebellion!" [Sacramento: s.n., 1855], 15.5 × 6 in. RB 496506, Huntington Library, San Marino, CA.

30. The Cantonese opera *Shatuo Moving the Army* 沙陀班兵 consists of three well-known episodes, the last of which features Wong Een Chuang as a central figure. However, the description of this character in the broadside in figure 2.3 diverges from the conventional narrative. Such variations were not unusual: Cantonese opera plots were often flexible, incorporating stock elements from other operas.

31. Advertisement, *Sacramento Daily Union*, April 6–7, 1857.

32. "Celestial Theatricals," *Daily Alta California*, April 13, 1857.

33. "Celestial Theatricals," *Weekly Columbian* (Columbia, CA), May 2, 1857, 1; and "Chinese Theatricals in California," *Daily Evening Bulletin*, May 12, 1857.

34. "Chinese Theatricals in California."

35. "Chinese Theatricals," *Sacramento Daily Union*, June 24, 1857; "Shameful," *Sacramento Daily Union*, April 10, 1857.

36. *Daily Alta California*, May 11, 1857. "Celestial" is a derogatory word for a person of Chinese descent used frequently in the nineteenth century. It comes from a former term for China, the "Celestial Empire."

37. "Chinese Theatricals in California," *Daily Evening Bulletin*, May 12, 1857.

38. *Stockton Independent*, October 4, 1856; "Chinese Theatricals," *Daily Evening Bulletin*, October 8, 1856.

39. "Chinese Theatre," *Stockton Independent*, October 4, 1856.

40. "Celestial Theatricals," *Daily Alta California*, October 8, 1856.

41. Lew-Williams, *The Chinese Must Go*, 36.

42. "Chinese Theatre," *San Andreas Independent*, August 8, 1857.

43. It would cost $55,442 today.

44. "Mariposa," *San Joaquin Republican*, April 24, 1858. Unusually, the report also noted an actress in addition to the twenty-five actors.

45. "A Chinese Town Projected," *Placer Herald*, May 8, 1858; and "Chinamen in Mariposa," *Daily Alta California*, April 27, 1858.

46. Frank Marryat, "The Bar of a Gambling Saloon," in *Mountains and Molehills; Or, Recollections of a Burnt Journal* (New York: Harper and Brothers, 1855), 43, https://archive.org/details/mountainsmolehi100marr_1/page/n7/mode/2up. There are two versions of this famous image: one a color lithograph, and the other a black and white wood engraving.

47. Laura E. Ferguson, "Gateway City: The Makings and Meanings of San Francisco's 'Golden Gate,' 1846–1906" (PhD diss., University of Michigan, 2015), 58.

48. Hab and Tong, "Letter of the Chinamen."

49. See Marryat, *Mountains and Molehills*, 298. "Sansome Street, San Francisco, 1850" and "High and Dry" are held by the Crocker Arts Museum, San Francisco. See Borthwick, *Three Years in California*, 51 and 267.

50. Marryat, *Mountains and Molehills*, 33.

51. "Celestial Entertainment," *Oroville Daily Butte Record*, August 10, 1857.

52. "Another Celestial Concert," *Oroville Daily Butte Record*, August 26, 1857.

53. Advertisement, *Oroville Daily Butte Record*, August 10, 1857; and "Music, What Is Music," *Oroville Daily Butte Record*, August 6, 1857.

54. Advertisement, *Daily National Democrat* (Marysville), October 26, 1858; and *Nevada Democrat*, November 10, 1858.

55. *Sacramento Daily Union*, April 26, 1858; and *Daily Alta California*, April 27, 1858.

56. William B. Clark, *Gold Districts of California: California Gold Discovery to Statehood* (Sacramento: Department of Conservation, Division of Mines and Geology, 1998), 153, https://digitalcommons.law.ggu.edu/caldocs_agencies/257.

57. Quartz mining is the mining of gold from veins or ore bodies in place, as distinguished from placer mining, which is the process of extracting gold from stream bed (placer) deposits, especially by surface washing, dredging, or hydraulic mining.

58. Chang, *Ghosts of Gold Mountain*, 118.

59. "Chinese Theatricals," *Daily National Gazette* (Grass Valley), January 7, 1860.

60. "Chinese Theater," *Daily National Gazette*, December 31, 1859.

61. From the *Auburn Herald,* quoted in "Chinese Theater," *California Farmer and Journal of Useful Sciences*, August 10, 1855.

62. "Celestial Theatricals in the Mines," *Daily Alta California*, May 11, 1857.

63. *Mountain Democrat* (Placerville), November 27, 1858.

64. The Foreign Miners' Tax Act of 1850 was signed into law by California Governor Peter Hardeman Burnett. It imposed a tax of twenty dollars per month on foreign miners. After protests from Irish, English, Canadian, and German miners, the law was rewritten to exempt any miner who was a "free white person" or any miner who could become an American citizen. The Act was repealed in 1851. A new Foreign Miners' License Tax was introduced in 1852 under Governor John Bigler. The new tax was three dollars per month, and was raised to four dollars a month the following year. In 1855, the legislature distinguished foreigners eligible from those ineligible for citizenship, calling for the tax on ineligible foreigners (i.e., the Chinese) to increase by two dollars per month. This was particularly consequential, due to the large population of Chinese miners in the state: 10,648 in 1860. See also note 17.

65. "Chinese Theatre in El Dorado," *Daily Alta California,* February 23, 1859.

66. "Chinese Expulsion," *San Joaquin Republican*, April 7, 1855; *Amador Ledger-Dispatch* (Jackson), December 8, 1855; and "Against the Chinese," *Sacramento Daily Union*, March 10, 1859.

67. Randall Rohe, "Chinese Mining & Settlement at the Lava Beds, Ca.," *Mining History Journal* 3 (1996): 51–60.

68. *Marysville Daily Appeal*, May 6, 1874; Rohe, "Chinese Mining & Settlement."

69. *Weekly Butte Record*, June 6, 1874.

70. "Chinese Theatre," *Chico Record*, February 11, 1857; and *Weekly Butte Record*, February 21, 1857.

71. "Chinese Theater," *Morning Union* (Grass Valley), October 15, 1869.

72. "Anti-Coolie Association," *Morning Union*, September 21, 1869.

73. "Chinese Theatre," *Chico Record*, February 11, 1857.

74. Chang, *Ghosts of Gold Mountain*, 70.

75. Gordon H. Chang and Shelley Fisher Fishkin, eds. *The Chinese and the Iron Road: Building the Transcontinental Railroad* (Stanford: Stanford University Press, 2019), 10.

76. Chang, *Ghosts of Gold Mountain*, 72.

77. Chang, *Ghosts of Gold Mountain*, 72. Advertisement, "Notice to Rail Road, Turnpike and Mining Companies," *Placer Herald*, August, 29-September 12, 1963. Hung Wah's office was in Auburn.

78. William F. Chew, *Nameless Builders of the Transcontinental Railroad: The Chinese Workers of the Central Pacific Railroad* (Victoria, BC: Trafford, 2004), 37. Chew cites extant payroll records.

79. The numbers could be even larger, since most Chinese likely did not work for the entire duration of the construction. See Chinese Railroad Workers in North America Project, Stanford University, https://web.stanford.edu/group/chineserailroad/cgi-bin/website.

80. Lawrence Tom and Brian Tom, *Gold Country's Last Chinatown: Marysville, California* (Charleston, SC: History Press, 2020), 16.

81. Tom and Tom, *Gold Country's Last Chinatown*, 26. These figures differ slightly from the 1970 U.S. Census.

82. "Oroville Striking for the Humbolt Trade," *Marysville Daily Appeal*, September 14, 1862.

83. *Shasta Courier* (Redding), May 8, 1869.

84. *Albany* (OR) *Register*, November 27, 1869.

85. *Spirit of Jefferson* (Charles Town, WV), January 11, 1870.

86. *Idaho World* (Idaho City, Idaho Terr.), August 19, 1869.

87. "Railroads," *Shasta Courier*, December 4, 1869.

88. "Chinese Theatricals," *Marysville Daily Appeal*, October 13, 1869.

89. Carolyn Grattan Eichin, *From San Francisco Eastward: Victorian Theater in the American West* (Reno: University of Nevada Press, 2020), 19.

90. "Chinese Theater," *Marysville Daily Appeal,* October 17, 1869.

91. "Chinese Theater," *Marysville Daily Appeal,* September 8, 1868.

92. Advertisement, *Marysville Daily Appeal*, September 16, 1868.

93. "Chinese Theater," *Marysville Daily Appeal,* September 11, 1868.

94. "Chinese Theater," *Marysville Daily Appeal,* September 16, 1868.

95. "The Chinese Theater," *Marysville Daily Appeal,* September 19, 1868.

96. "Chinese Theater," *Marysville Daily Appeal,* October 15, 1869.

97. "The Chinese Theater," *Marysville Daily Appeal*, November 12, 1869.

98. Erin Bentley, *The Life of Drama* (New York: Atheneum, 1964), 244.

99. Clarence Caesar, "The Historical Demographic of Sacramento's Black Community, 1848–1900," *California History* 75, no. 3 (1996), 210. Sacramento had its National and Forest Theaters in the late 1850s, and its Metropolitan Theater and Academy of Music in the late 1860s.

100. "Shut Out," *Marysville Daily Appeal,* October 17, 1869.

101. "Another Moth," *Marysville Daily Appeal*, November 30, 1869.

102. *Sonoma Democrat* (Santa Rosa), December 18, 1869.

103. "Driven Away," *Marysville Daily Appeal,* December 11, 1869.

104. Advertisement, *Sacramento Daily Union*, December 24, 1869.

105. "Italian Opera," *Marysville Daily Appeal*, December 18, 1869; and "No Opera," *Marysville Daily Appeal*, December 29, 1869.

106. *San Francisco Chronicle*, December 30, 1869.

107. *Marysville Daily Appeal,* January 7 and 12, 1870.

108. *San Francisco Chronicle*, January 24, 1870; and *Daily Evening Bulletin*, January 13, 1870.

109. "Thirty Years Ago," *Marysville Daily Appeal*, January 12, 1900.

110. *Marysville Daily Appeal,* June 6, 1874. Both Oroville and Marysville continued to host Chinese theatrical troupes; see *Marysville Daily Appeal*, December 31, 1889 and February 28, 1898.

111. Kathryn Gin Lum, "Religion on the Road: How Chinese Migrants Adapted Popular Religion to an American Context," in *The Chinese and the Iron Road: Building the Transcontinental Railroad*, ed. Gordon H. Chang and Shelley Fisher Fishkin (Stanford: Stanford University Press, 2019), 159–78.

112. Sau Y. Chan, "Performance Context as a Molding Force: Photographic Documentation of Cantonese Opera in Hong Kong," *Visual Anthropology* 18, nos. 2–3 (2005): 167–98. The discussion in the following section is derived from Chan's article.

113. The exception would be when ritual opera involving religious taboos such as *Sacrificial Offering to the White Tiger* were performed to fend off evil spirits. Such ritual operas were performed for troupe members only and were not open to the public.

114. Chang, *Ghosts of Gold Mountain*, 118.

115. "Annual Chinese Festival," *Weekly Butte Record*, September 5, 1868.

116. "Chinese Theatrical Company," *Sacramento Daily Union*, September 30, 1868.

117. "Left Us," *Sacramento Daily Union*, December 25, 1868.

118. "Chinese Theatric Company," *Sacramento Daily Union*, January 13, 1869.

119. The steamer *Capital* was one of largest river steamships at the time, at 1,625 tons. *Stockton Independent*, December 8, 1869. For a state fair at Sacramento, the *Capital* arrived with six hundred passengers and seven hundred seventy tons of freight. *Daily Alta California*, September 16, 1868.

Chapter 3. Performing Chinese Opera in San Francisco

1. Hauser, letter, April 15, 1853, in *The Letters of Miska Hauser*, 41.

2. "Chinese Theatricals in San Francisco," *Saturday Evening Post,* June 28, 1856, citing the *California Chronicle*.

3. "Chinese Theatricals in San Francisco," *Saturday Evening Post*, June 28, 1856.

4. "The Chinese Drama in San Francisco: Characteristics of Chinese Theatricals—Review of *The Return of Sit Ping Quai*," *Daily Evening Bulletin*, December 6, 1856.

5. Advertisement, *Daily Alta California*, December 2, 1856.

6. *Colville's San Francisco Directory* (San Francisco: Monson, Valentine, & Co., 1857), 123.

7. Advertisement, *Wide West* (San Francisco), August 3, 1856, California Digital Newspaper Collection. The "Dutch act" was not Dutch at all but rather a pseudo-German accented dialect act in English, named after the American pronunciation of the noun "Deutsch" (German). Two of the most famous "Dutch act" performers were Gus William and J. K. Emmet. See John Koegel, "The Dutch Act": German American Theatrical and Literary Characterizations," in *Music in German Immigrant Theater: New York City, 1840–1940* (Rochester, NY: University of Rochester Press, 2009), 179–94.

8. *Daily Evening Bulletin*, December 20, 1856.

9. "The Chinese Drama in San Francisco: Characteristics of Chinese Theatricals—Review of *The Return of Sit Ping Quai*."

10. "Chinese Drama in San Francisco," *Daily Evening Bulletin*, December 6, 1856; and "The Chinese Drama in San Francisco: Resume of the Review of 'The Return of Sit Ping Quai,'" *Daily Evening Bulletin*, December 17, 1856.

11. "The Chinese Drama in San Francisco," *Daily Evening Bulletin*, December 17, 1856.

12. Gradually English-language melodramas could be said to incorporate some Chinese characteristics, such as Western dramas that included Chinese characters, or yellowface drama. "Yellowface" was the practice of non-Asian actors playing Asian-identified characters, using makeup and imitating their behavior.

13. "The Chinese Theatre," *Daily Alta California*, December 14, 1856. Candle grease was used together with pomade to stiffen the hair to create fashionable styles. For example, in the seventeenth century, military officers in England wore wigs that were greased and powdered. See Ruth Turner Wilcox, *Five Centuries of American Costume* (New York: Dover, 2004), 32.

14. Eichin, *From San Francisco Eastward*, chap. 2, esp. n. 112. Prostitution and gambling were significant components of social life in nineteenth-century California. Although journalists and reformers often pointed sensationalistically and with racist insinuations to Chinatown as a place rampant with vice and prostitution, California's many prostitution districts in towns and cities throughout the state served both non-Chinese and Chinese customers. Chinese brothel owners did not dominate this commercial enterprise, as shown by Eichin, who notes that an 1885 grand jury investigation in Marysville "found forty brothels in the city [. . .] ten of which were under Chinese operation" (Eichin, *From San Francisco Eastward*, 18).

15. San Andreas, *Daily Alta California*, October 8, 1856; *Daily Evening Bulletin*, October 7, 1856; *Stockton Independent*, October 4, 1856; and Dryton, *Volcano Weekly Ledger*, August 16, 1856.

16. Eichin, *From San Francisco Eastward*, 18. Also see Shauna Vey, *Childhood and Nineteenth-Century American Theatre: The Work of the Marsh Troupe of Juvenile Actors* (Carbondale: Southern Illinois University Press, 2015), 86.

17. Eichin, *From San Francisco Eastward*, 10.

18. "The Chinese Theatre," *Daily Evening Bulletin*, December 20, 1856; "Chinese Theatre," *Daily Evening Bulletin*, December 23, 1856; "The Chinese Theatre," *Daily Evening Bulletin*, February 3, 1857; and *Daily Alta California*, February 5, 1857.

19. "Chinese Theatricals in California," *Daily Evening Bulletin*, May 12, 1857.

20. Elmer Sandmeyer, *The Anti-Chinese Movement in California* (Urbana: Illinois University Press, 1939), 16. These numbers come from table 1.

21. This figure is based on Eichin, *From San Francisco Eastward*, 9, and on newspaper reports of the period.

22. "Burning of a Theatre," *San Joaquin Republican* (Stockton), June 4, 1858, California Digital Newspaper Collection.

23. *New York Clipper*, May 15, 1858.

24. Cantonese opera emerged from a gradual fusion of local genres with northern opera conventions. In the mid-nineteenth century, two types of troupes coexisted: those using the Central dialect and the other the Cantonese dialect (Ng, *Rise of Cantonese Opera*, 20).

25. This and the following routes are derived from the study of reports and advertisements in several newspapers between 1857 and 1859, especially the *Chico Record*, the *San Andres Independent*, the *Oroville Daily Butte Record*, the *Sacramento Daily Union*, the *Daily Evening Bulletin*, and the *Daily Alta California*.

26. Reports of Chinese theater performances at these locations appeared in the *Oroville Daily Butte Record*, August 6, 1857; the *San Andreas Independent*, August 8, 1857; the *Oroville Daily Butte Record*, August 10, 1857; the *Daily Evening Bulletin*, August 12, 1857; and the *Chico Record*, August 26, 1857.

27. *San Joaquin Republican*, April 24, 1858; *Sacramento Daily Union*, April 26, 1858; "Chinamen in Mariposa," *Daily Alta California*, April 27, 1858; and *Placer Herald* (Rocklin), May 29, 1858.

28. Lauren Clay describes a similar web of opera theaters in Paris and surrounding areas. Lauren R. Clay, *Stagestruck: The Business of Theater in Eighteenth-Century France and Its Colonies* (Ithaca, NY: Cornell University Press, 2013), 7.

29. Richard Crawford, *America's Musical Life: A History* (New York: Norton, 2001), 194.

30. *Hydraulic Press* (North San Juan), May 19, 1860, California Digital Newspaper Collection.

31. "An Evening at the Chinese Theatre," *Daily Evening Bulletin*, March 5, 1860. Another depiction of the theater, again written by Glaucus, was printed in the *New York Times* three weeks later. It appears to be a notice of the same performance, although the *Times* article is full of denigrating comments, a sharp contrast with the piece in *Bulletin*. "China in California," *New York Times*, March 28, 1860.

32. "China in California: The Chinese Opera," *New York Times*, March 28, 1860. This report nearly duplicated the article "An Evening at the Chinese Theatre" (see n. 32).

33. Henry G. Langley, comp., *San Francisco Directory* (San Francisco: Valentine & Co., 1860), 341. The entry reads, "Chinese Theater: Commercial near Kearny."

34. "Chinese Feast," *Sacramento Daily Union*, May 4, 1860, quoting *San Francisco Herald*, May 2, 1860.

35. *Daily Alta California*, May 12, 1860. What was meant by "objectionable features" is unclear.

36. "The Great Chinese Exhibitions," *Daily Alta California*, May 12, 1860.

37. "The Career of Maguire," *San Francisco Call*, January 22, 1896.

38. "The Chinese Performances This Evening," *Daily Alta California*, May 15, 1860.

39. "Opera House," *Daily Evening Bulletin*, May 15, 1860.

40. "Opera House," *Daily Evening Bulletin*, May 16, 1860.

41. Advertisements, *Daily Alta California* from March 3 to August 1860 and later. This store was then located at 166 Washington Street. In 1852, Tong A-Chick's letter to Gov. John Bigler noted that Chy Lung was a prominent merchant who had just arrived with "$10,000 in China goods, has sold out and returned for another cargo on the Challenge." Hab Wa and Tong K. Achick [*sic*], "Letter of the Chinamen to His Excellency, Governor Bigler." Chy Lung was also among the leading Chinese merchants whom James Rusling met in San Francisco: "large, dignified,

fine-looking . . . and a noted silk-factor." James F. Rusling, *Across America: Or, the Great West and the Pacific Coast* (New York: Sheldon & Company, 1874), 304. Judy Yung notes that the Chy Lung Bazaar—opened by Lai Chu-Chuen, who arrived in 1850—was Chinatown's first bazaar, "importing teas, opium, silk, lacquered goods and Chinese groceries." Lai passed away in 1869, but the store remained open until 1912. See Judy Yung, *San Francisco's Chinatown* (Arcadia Publishing, 2006), 19.

42. "Death of a Pioneer Chinese Merchant of San Francisco," *Daily Alta California*, September 1, 1868. Chy Lung had a significant role in San Francisco's Chinatown and established related firms in Shanghai, Canton, Hong Kong, and Yokohama. Elizabeth Sinn explores his business dealings in detail (Sinn, *Pacific Crossing*, chap. 2).

43. *Daily Alta California*, June 23, 1858.

44. *Chy Lung & Co.'s Store*, 1866, Chy Lung & Co.'s store, Chy Lung & Co. was listed in Wells Fargo's 1878 *Directory of Chinese Business Houses*, 5.

45. *Daily National Democrat* (Marysville), May 12, 1860; and advertisement, *Daily Evening Bulletin*, May 17, 1860.

46. Advertisement, *Daily Alta California*, May 20, 1860. The company was led by Maguire and William Saurin Lyster for 129 performances. George Martin, *Verdi at the Golden Gate: Opera and San Francisco in the Gold Rush Years* (Berkeley: University of California Press, 1993), 189–99.

47. Martin, *Verdi at the Golden Gate*, 3.

48. The bill did not pass. The *Trinity Journal* speculated that it was because another ban on Chinese immigration two years before was deemed unconstitutional. "Ninth District Court—April Term," *Trinity Journal* (Weaverville), April 14, 1860.

49. Eichin, *From San Francisco Eastward*.

50. "Chinese Immigrants," *Marysville Daily Appeal*, June 9, 1860.

51. "Chinese Arrivals," *Marysville Daily Appeal*, August 5, 1860.

52. Sebryk, "A History of Chinese Theatre in Victoria," 114–15.

53. Estavan, *Theatre Buildings*, 112–13, 195.

54. Advertisement, *Daily Alta California*, August 9–15, 1860; see also *San Francisco Herald* and *Daily Evening Bulletin* around the same dates.

55. "Chinese Theatricals," *Daily Evening Bulletin*, August 9, 1860.

56. Glenna Matthews, *The Golden State in the Civil War: Thomas Starr King, the Republican Party, and the Birth of Modern California* (Cambridge: Cambridge University Press, 2012), 4.

57. "Chinese Dramatic Troupe," *San Francisco Herald*, August 10, 1860.

58. Advertisement, *Daily Alta California*, August 9, 1860.

59. Advertisement, *Daily Alta California*, August 9, 1860.

60. "The Chinese Dramatic Troupe," *San Francisco Herald*, August 13, 1860.

61. Advertisement, *San Francisco Herald*, August 15, 1860; and "The Chinese Vaulters," *San Francisco Weekly Herald,* August 16, 1860.

62. Katherine Preston, "American Musical Theatre before the Twentieth Century," in *The Cambridge Companion to the Musical*, ed. William A. Everett and Paul R. Laird (Cambridge: Cambridge University Press, 2002), 31. See also Preston, *Opera on the Road: Traveling Opera Companies in the United States, 1825–1860* (Urbana: University of Illinois Press, 1993).

63. Langley, *San Francisco Directory*, 211.

64. Monika Trobits, "The Shadow of War in San Francisco," in *Antebellum and Civil War San Francisco: A Western Theater for Northern & Southern Politics* (Charleston, SC: History Press, 2014).

65. "The Drama of the Chinese Players," *San Jose Weekly Mercury*, December 26, 1861, California Digital Newspaper Collection, quoting *Folsom Telegraph*.

66. *Daily Alta California*, September 22, 1864.

67. "The Chinese Theatre, San Francisco," *Boston Investigator*, May 3, 1865.

68. "New Chinese Theatre," *San Francisco Examiner*, June 23, 1865.

69. Rusling, *Across America*, 308. Although Rusling's book was not published until 1874, it is an important document about the social life of the Chinese community in San Francisco in 1866 and 1867.

70. Eichin, *From San Francisco Eastward*, chap. 3.

71. Although little documentation about this theater is available, it is known that its actors went to work for the new theater in 1868. See "Row among the Chinese," *Daily Evening Bulletin*, January 31, 1868.

72. *Frank Leslie's Illustrated Newspaper*, June 29, 1867, 228–30.

73. "Paris Gossip," *Boston Post*, May 20, 1867.

74. "Musical and Dramatic Gossip," *New York Herald*, May 29, 1867; *New York Times*, June 20, 1867.

75. *Globe and Mail* (Toronto), June 25, 1867. A Chinese theater in London did not materialize. According to Ashley Thorpe, the first performance of Chinese opera in London was during the International Health Exhibition of 1884. See Thorpe, *Performing China on the London Stage: Chinese Opera and Global Power, 1759–2008* (London: Palgrave, 2016).

76. *Daily Alta California*, September 23, 1867.

77. *Daily Dramatic Chronicle* (San Francisco), January 25, 1868.

78. "Altamonte," "Celestial Entertainment," *Chicago Tribune*, October 15, 1867. The writer notes that this group was superior to the troupe at the Globe Theater. Interestingly, the report also includes a description of a Japanese troupe performing at the Metropolitan Theatre.

79. *Daily Dramatic Chronicle*, January 18, 1868. Fred Bert later became a manager of the California Theater, as well as Olympic Hall.

80. "Chinese Enterprise—New Theatre," *Daily Evening Bulletin*, November 20, 1867.

81. "Chinese Theatre," *San Francisco Examiner*, November 21, 1867.

82. *Daily Evening Bulletin*, November 20, 1867.

Chapter 4. Cultural Capital

1. *Weekly Arizona Miner* (Prescott), November 28, 1868. There were 975 new buildings in San Francisco, of which 240 were of brick construction.

2. *Bangor Daily Whig and Courier* (Maine), September 8, 1869; *Wisconsin State Journal* (Madison), September 9, 1869; and *Times-Democrat* (Charlotte, NC), September 12, 1869.

3. The Burlingame-Seward Treaty (1868) was a landmark treaty between Qing China and the United States. Anson Burlingame, the US minister to China (1861–67), was directed by Secretary of State William Seward to establish the United States' power in Asia, to gain access to profitable trading opportunities, and to foster the spread of Christianity in Asia. In 1868, however, Burlingame gave up his post as US representative and headed a Chinese diplomatic mission to the United States to assist the Chinese in their treaty negotiations with Seward. Expanding on the 1858 Treaty of Tianjin, the new treaty protected commerce conducted in Chinese ports and cities and established the right of China to appoint consuls to American port cities. It promised the Chinese the right to free immigration and travel within the United States, and allowed for the protection of Chinese citizens in the United States in accordance with the most-favored-nation principle. And the citizens of the two nations were given reciprocal access to education and schooling when living in the other country. All of these articles served to reinforce the principle of equality between the two nations.

4. "The Celestial Drama in San Francisco," *Chicago Daily Tribune*, December 10, 1867. In 1873, the lot size was noted as 68 feet, 3 inches by 137 feet, 3 inches. See *Daily Evening Bulletin*, August 1, 1873.

5. "Dedication of the New Chinese Theatre," *Daily Alta California*, January 24, 1868.

6. "Inauguration of the New Chinese Theatre, 'Hing Chuen Yuen,'" *Daily Alta California*, January 28, 1868. In 1866, the newspaper had covered the Burlingam-Van Valkenburgh farewell banquet extensively. The banquet, with sixty-two guests, was hosted by the "leading Chinese firms of the city—Tung Yee & Co., Chy Lung & Co., and Wing Wo Sang & Co." The bill of fare included three courses (each containing eight, nine, and ten dishes, respectively) and eight varieties of dessert, as well as wines and cigars. Between the second and third courses, Chy Lung spoke for all the hosts to present a toast through the translator Charles Carvalho. Over ten guests spoke of China with passionate goodwill. "Oriental Banquet in Honor of the American Ministers to China and Japan," *Daily Alta California*, June 2, 1866. Chy Lung & Co. and Wing Wo Sang & Co are listed in Wells Fargo's 1878 *Directory of Chinese Business Houses*, 5 and 42, respectively.

7. "Oriental Banquet," *Daily Alta California*, June 2, 1866, and "The Chinese Festivities," *Daily Evening Bulletin*, January 29, 1868. (This report includes a detailed description of the banquets.) Because it was the third day of the Chinese New Year, the inauguration doubled as a Chinese New Year celebration ("The Chinese New Year," *San Francisco Examiner*, January 28, 1868).

8. "Inauguration of the New Chinese Theatre," *Daily Alta California*, January 28, 1868.

9. "The Chinese Theatre in San Francisco: Grand Banquet a la Chinois," *Chicago Tribune,* February 22, 1868, quoting the *New York World*.

10. Correspondent, *Manchester Guardian*, September 27, 1869.

11. Correspondent, *Manchester Guardian*, September 27, 1869.

12. *Daily Alta California*, February 6, 1868.

13. "Chinese Theatre," *New York Times*, October 24, 1868, quoting the *San Francisco Times*; and "A Chinese Theater," *Detroit Free Press,* January 28, 1872.

14. "A Chinese Theatre in San Francisco," *Chicago Tribune*, July 13, 1869, quoting the *San Francisco Morning Call.*

15. In October 1869, Joseph Becker took one of the first cross-Rockies trains, traveling in a luxurious Pullman car from Omaha/Council Bluffs through to San Francisco (with a change of trains in Sacramento), visiting California for six weeks into the early part of 1870. Reminiscing later in his life, Becker discussed this special assignment and revealed that the decision to depict Chinese people was secretly planned by Frank Leslie as "a 'scoop' on [their] competitors." See Joseph Becker, "An Artist's Interesting Recollections of Leslie's Weekly," *Frank Leslie's Illustrated Newspaper*, December 14, 1905, 570.

16. "'The Coming Man,' A Splendid Supplementary Picture of the Interior of the Great Chinese Theatre in San Francisco," *Frank Leslie's Illustrated Newspaper*, April 30, 1870, 98.

17. Thomas W. Knox, "The Coming Man," *Frank Leslie's Illustrated Newspaper*, May 7, 1870, 121–22.

18. Erin Pauwels, "José María Mora and the Migrant Surround in American Portrait Photography," *Panorama: Journal of the Association of Historians of American Art* 6, no. 2 (2020), https://doi.org/10.24926/24716839.10613.

19. Lai Yong, unknown Chinese woman, Carl Mautz Collection of Carte-de-Visite Photographs Created by California Photographers, Beinecke Rare Book and Manuscript Library, Yale University, https://collections.library.yale.edu/catalog/2015087. Lai Yong was listed as Lai Yung, Photographer, in the 1878 *Wells Fargo Directory of Chinese Business Houses* at 743 Washington Street, San Francisco, 18. The Chinese name of the studio recorded in the directory is 黎墉影相油畫樓.

20. Chang, *Gold Mountain*, 50–51. For more on Lai Yong, see Anthony W. Lee, *Picturing Chinatown: Art and Orientalism in San Francisco* (Berkeley: University of California Press, 2001), 29–31.

21. Carleton Watkins, "Chinese Lady," c. 1870, print by I. W. Taber, http://www.getty.edu/art/collection/objects/81659/carleton-watkins-print-by-iw-taber-chinese-lady-american-about-1870/?dz=0.4134,0.4134,0.41. Watkins employed a Chinese darkroom assistant named Ah Fue, who may have provided him with access to the elite Chinese community located only a few blocks from his studio on Montgomery Street. See Peter E. Palmquist, *Carleton E. Watkins, Photographer of the American West* (Fort Worth: Amon Carter Museum of Western Art 1983), 55.

22. For further discussion of the role of the studio portrait during this time, see Jean Sagne, "All Kinds of Portraits: The Photographer's Studio," in *The New History of Photography*, ed. Michel Frizot (Cologne: Könemann, 1994), 102–30.

23. Knox, "The Coming Man," 121–22.

24. Mary M. Cronin and William E. Huntzicker, "Popular Chinese Images and 'The Coming Man' of 1870: Racial Representations of Chinese," *Journalism History* 38, no. 2 (2012): 87. The popularity of the travel issues of *Frank Leslie's Illustrated Newspaper* was reflected in a disclaimer printed with the series: "We have

no traveling agents. All persons representing themselves as such are imposters." *Frank Leslie's Illustrated Newspaper*, April 30, 1870, 98.

25. "The Coming Man," *San Francisco Chronicle*, May 10, 1870.

26. "Barnum: The Prince of the Showmen Again," *San Francisco Chronicle*, May 20, 1870.

27. "Fourth Day of the Bostonian Visitation," *San Francisco Chronicle*, June 5, 1870.

28. US Federal Census, 1870, Ancestry.com.

29. "The Yun Sing Ping Company," *Daily Alta California*, September 22, 1868. The paper noted about this new troupe: "The company is the largest which ever left China, and its arrival has created quite a sensation among the Celestials."

30. Advertisement, *Daily Alta California,* September 22–28, 1868; and advertisement, *Daily Alta California,* September 27, 1868.

31. *San Francisco Examiner,* January 12, 1869; and *Daily Alta California,* January 19, 1869. According to the news report, the theater paid $6,500 for theater licenses over eight years, and after erecting a new building paid a ground rent of $425 on a ten-year lease. However, one petition noted that the complaint was unfairly targeted at only the Globe Hotel theater.

32. *Daily Alta California*, September 23–25, 1869.

33. General George H. Thomas commanded the Division of the Pacific, with headquarters at San Francisco. "Amusements," *San Francisco Bulletin*, September 24, 1869.

34. *Daily Alta California*, February 8–11, 1870. The advertisement listed the Quon Soon Tong Company as purchasing the Son Son Fong Theatre Company.

35. "The Chinese Riot Yesterday," *Daily Alta California*, February 3, 1870.

36. *Daily Alta California*, May 28, 1870. It is unclear whether Quon Soon Tong stayed in one location or moved from Dupont Street to Commercial Street. The details of the swift change of ownership are murky. In any case, the New Idea Theatre (the old Union Theatre) was torn down in September 1871. *Daily Alta California*, September 12, 1871.

37. Advertisement, *San Francisco Chronicle,* July 14–16, 1870.

38. "The Chinese Invasion. They are coming, 900,000 more, Map of Chinatown: Having a Population of 25,000 Chinese, Together with a Key to the Places of Interest," compiled by H(enry) J(osiah) West, 1873 San Francisco, Digital Library, California Historical Society, https://digitallibrary .californiahistoricalsociety.org/object/3981?solr_nav%5Bid%5D=94a7a0847e144 99d1a19&solr_nav%5Bpage%5D=8&solr_nav%5Boffset%5D=23/.

39. "A Chinese Theatre in California," *The Era* (London), April 23, 1871.

40. *Abendpost*, quoted in "A Chinese Theater," *Pall Mall Gazette* (London), November 29, 1871. The reporter also noted the use of dialects: "The language used on the stage is different from the Chinese dialects spoken by the [Chinese] in San Francisco, though not sufficiently so to be unintelligible to them."

41. Jos[eph] M[.] Rothchild, "'The Heathen Chinee,' His Position, Haunts, and Peculiarities," *Israelite,* October 11, 1872. An interesting practice was also noted: "On the gas brackets we saw several slips of paper with Chinese characters written

upon them, and was told that in this way they informed Chinamen who were or expected to be present, that they were wanted elsewhere."

42. "Behind the Scenes of a Chinese Theatre," *New York Clipper*, April 26, 1873.

43. Advertisement, *Daily Alta California*, February 25, 1873.

44. "Chinese Theatricals," *Daily Evening Bulletin*, February 24, 1873.

45. Advertisement, "The Very Latest Novelty: The Imperial Chinese Theatrical Co.," *New York Clipper*, April 12, 1873.

46. The US census of 1870 recorded fourteen Chinese musicians in San Jose and four in Marysville.

47. The US census of 1870 recorded two Chinese theaters in San Francisco. See United States Federal Census, 1870, San Francisco, Sixth Ward, pp. 55–57 for the Sun Heen Lok Theater Company, and San Francisco, Fourth Ward, pp. 285–287 for the Yang Fung Theater.

48. United States Federal Census, 1870, San Francisco, Sixth Ward, concert room, p. 55; seven musicians, p. 217.

49. "Unjust," *Chico Record,* February 15, 1858.

50. "Board of Supervisors: Chinese Theater," *San Francisco Chronicle*, January 5, 1869.

51. "Board of Supervisors: Chinese Theater," *San Francisco Chronicle*, January 19, 1869.

52. "Local Intelligence, Board of Supervisors," *Daily Alta California*, January 19, 1869.

53. *Daily Evening Bulletin*, February 24, 1869.

54. "Board of Supervisors," *San Francisco Chronicle,* June 29, 1869.

55. San Francisco Municipal Reports, Fiscal Year 1871–72, Ending June 30, 1872, by San Francisco Board of Supervisors, p. 588, https://ia804701.us.archive.org/17/items/sanfranciscomuni71sanfrich/sanfranciscomuni71sanfrich.pdf.

56. "Police Arrests," *San Francisco Chronicle*, July 31, 1869.

57. *Daily Evening Bulletin,* August 5, 1869. See also "Police Court Record: Celestial Theatricals," *San Francisco Chronicle*, August 6, 1869.

58. "Police Court Record: Chinese Gongs and R. Beverly Cole," *San Francisco Chronicle*, August 13, 1869.

59. Hudson N. Janisch, "The Chinese, the Courts, and the Constitution: a Study of the Legal Issues Raised by Chinese Immigration to the United States, 1850–1902" (JSD diss., University of Chicago, 1971), 297–98.

60. *San Francisco Chronicle*, May 3, 1870.

61. "Chinese theatres," *Daily Alta California*, May 3, 1870.

62. *Daily Evening Bulletin*, May 24, 1870.

63. "Jottings about Town," *San Francisco Chronicle*, August 21, 1870.

64. "The Coming Man," *San Francisco Chronicle*, May 10, 1870.

65. *Daily Alta California,* December 8, 1872; and *San Francisco Chronicle,* December 20, 1872.

66. San Francisco Municipal Reports, Fiscal Year 1871–72, Ending June 30, 1872 by San Francisco Board of Supervisors, p. 154, https://ia804701.us.archive.org/17/items/sanfranciscomuni71sanfrich/sanfranciscomuni71sanfrich.pdf.

67. "Patronage has fallen off at the Chinese theater in California since the ordinance relating to the number of cubic feet of air necessary went into effect." *Bloomington Progress* (Indiana), January 22, 1873. *Indianapolis News*, July 1, 1873.

68. *Daily Evening Bulletin*, June 13, 1873.

69. "Real Estate," *Daily Evening Bulletin*, August 1, 1873. The theater was sold for $56,000.

70. In October 1871, violent disputes over the control of the prostitution business evolved into a mass lynching in Los Angles. A non-Asian mob about five hundred in number stormed the city's Chinatown. Fifteen Chinese immigrants were tortured and then hanged while a crowd of white Angelenos watched and even cheered. They also fatally shot three more, and destroyed Chinese American property.

71. "Successful Theatre Management," *Daily Evening Bulletin*, August 19, 1873.

72. "The Celestial Drama: An Exciting Scene during the Production of the Historical Piece at the Chinese Theatre," *Daily Evening Bulletin*, October 29, 1873.

73. "Chinese Theatres," *The Jeffersonian* (Jeffersontown, KY), January 29, 1874. The long report quotes from the *Morning Calls* and ends with doubt on the legitimacy of the theater: "The day may come when Hong Ting Huen may form a "side head" under the title of "Amusements" in the daily press. . . . But that day is at present a few centuries down the dim vista of futurity."

74. *San Francisco Chronicle*, June 22, 1874.

75. Advertisement, *Daily Alta California*, June 21–28, 1874.

76. "A Chinese Jubilee," *Daily Evening Bulletin*, June 27, 1874.

77. "A New Chinese Theater," *Daily Evening Bulletin*, April 3, 1874.

78. Tamara Venit Shelton, *Herbs and Roots: A History of Chinese Doctors in the American Medical Marketplace* (New Haven: Yale University Press, 2019), 78.

79. Samuel Williams, *The City of the Golden Gate: A Description of San Francisco in 1875* (San Francisco: Book Club of California, 1921), 21.

80. *San Francisco Chronicle*, June 4, 1869.

81. *Sacramento Daily Union*, August 19, 1872.

82. Him Mark Lai, *From Overseas Chinese to Chinese American* (從華僑到華人) (Hong Kong: Joint Publishing, 1992), 16. In addition to practicing medicine, Li Po Tai also invested in real estate quite successfully. "'Dr.' Li Po Tai Lining His Nest," *Charles D. Carter's Real Estate Circulars*, 4 no. 2 (December 1869).

83. "Changrong Yachu" was probably 803 Dupont Street, where Poo High Yuen & Co., Drugs (普泰源藥材蘇杭舖) was situated. See *1878 Directory of Chinese Business Houses: San Francisco, Sacramento, Marysville, Portland, Stockton, San Jose, Virginia City, Nev.* (Wells, Fargo & Co, 1878), 24.

84. "The Celestial Drama: A Glimpse at John Behind the Footlights," *San Francisco Chronicle*, June 22, 1874.

85. "A Chinese Jubilee," *Daily Evening Bulletin*, June 27, 1874; "A New Chinese Theater," *New York Times*, July 2, 1874; *North American and United States Gazette* (Philadelphia), July 10, 1874; and "A Chinese Theater," *Juniata Sentinel and Republican* (Mifflintown, Juniata Township, PA), August 5, 1874.

86. "A New Chinese Theater," *Daily Evening Bulletin*, April 3, 1874.

87. Samuel Manning, *American Pictures, Drawn with Pen and Pencil* (London: Religious Tract Society, 1875–1876), 101.

88. "Samuel Williams, for many years prominently identified with journalism on this coast," *Sacramento Daily Union*, July 2, 1881. "The City of the Golden Gate," *Scribners Monthly* 10, no. 3 (July 1, 1875): 276. The artist is not named. However, Manning frequently referred to *Scribners* in *American Pictures*. This illustration was reused by many other authors. Such practice was quite common. Another example is the reuse of the picture of the Chinese theater interior from "The Coming Man" (first printed in *Frank Leslie's Illustrated Newspaper* of 1870) in *Frank Leslie's Popular Monthly* in 1878, without attribution to the artist.

89. The practice of incorporating cow characters on stage as described here, as well as the possible repertoire, has not been corroborated by current studies.

90. Steven Platt, "The Military," in *China's Hidden Century: 1796–1912*, ed. Jessica Harrison-Hall and Julia Lovell (Seattle: University of Washington Press, 2023), 107–8.

91. "Roscius with a Pigtail: A Midnight Hour among the Chinese Actors," *San Francisco Chronicle*, August 30, 1874.

92. "A New Chinese Theatre," *New York Times*, July 2, 1874.

93. "Roscius with a Pigtail."

94. Advertisement, *Daily Evening Bulletin,* September 8–14, 1874.

95. "Petitions," *Daily Alta California*, September 15, 1874; Sang Kee, the manager of Sing Ping Yuen, was arrested. "Police Court," *Daily Evening Bulletin*, September 17, 1874. Of the sizes of the theater, other writers also estimated the capacity of 1,500 in each of these theaters. See G. B., Densmore, *The Chinese in California* (San Francisco, Pettit & Russ, 1880), 54–58.

96. "Orders and Resolutions," *Daily Evening Bulletin*, November 3, 1874.

97. *Daily Evening Bulletin*, December 12, 1874.

Chapter 5. Prosperity

1. The *San Francisco Chronicle*'s report of the number is quoted in "John Chinaman in San Francisco," *Scribner's Monthly* 12, no. 6 (October 1876): 862–72.

2. L. Eve Armentrout Ma, "The Big Business Ventures of Chinese in North America," in *The Chinese American Experience*, ed. Genny Lim (San Francisco: Chinese Historical Society of America and Chinese Culture Foundation, 1984), 102; Qin, *The Diplomacy of Nationalism*, 58.

3. Qin, *Diplomacy of Nationalism*, 58.

4. Ngai, *The Chinese Question*, 143.

5. Eric W. Fong and William T. Markham, "Anti-Chinese Politics in California in the 1870s: An Intercounty Analysis," *Sociological Perspectives* 45, no. 2 (2002), 183–210.

6. "Expel the Chinese and Bankrupt the State," *Daily Alta California*, February 23, 1859.

7. The first Chinese newspaper, *Golden Hills' News* 金山日新錄, was first published on April 22, 1854 in San Francisco, edited by the Reverend William Speer (1822–1904), a Presbyterian minister. It lasted a few months and was followed by

Tung-Ngai San-Luk [The Oriental], 東涯新錄, which was first published on January 4, 1855, edited by Rev. Speer and Lee Kan (a graduate of the Morrison School in Hong Kong). Both newspapers were mostly bilingual. Their publication schedule changed, at one point triweekly in Chinese and weekly in English. This schedule was later changed to weekly issues in Chinese and monthly versions in English. It lasted just two years, folding in 1857. In Sacramento, the *Chinese Daily News* was first published in December 1856, edited by a Chinese immigrant, Ze Too Yune. Publication stopped in 1858. Few Chinese newspapers were attempted again until the 1870s, when a number of titles began to appear. In 1874, the *San Francisco China News* 舊金山唐人新聞紙 was published by Bocardus and Gordon. On September 11, 1875, Chock Wong and J. Hoffman began a new weekly, *Tanfang Gongbao* (The Oriental) 唐番公報, published by Wah Kee. These early Chinese newspapers were written by hand with Chinese brush and ink, and the printing was via lithography on newspaper sheets. See Him Mark Lai, "Chinese-American Press," in *The Ethnic Press in the United States: A Historical Analysis and Handbook*, ed. Sally M. Miller (Westport, CT: Greenwood Press, 1987), 27–43.

8. Mai Xiaoxia 麥嘯霞. 廣東戲劇史略 [A brief history of opera theater in Guangdong], in 廣東文物 [Art and heritage in Guangdong], ed. Guangdong Wenwu Zhanlanhui 廣東文物展覽會, 3:8 (Hong Kong: Zhongguo Wenhua Xiejinhui, 1942), 791–835. A comparison of the cast list in table 5.1 with the list of famous historical performers in "A brief history of opera theater in Guangdong" shows at least ten prominent actors: young warrior Bengya Qi (崩牙啟); bearded warrior Shegong Rong (蛇公榮); Xinbiao (新標), and Xinhua (新華); young belle Dezai (德仔) and Dajia Bing (大家炳); comic role Shuishe Rong (水蛇容); young scholar Yaduo (亞鐸); young belle warrior Zhajiao Wen (札腳文).

9. Ng, *The Rise of Cantonese Opera*, 27.

10. According to Wing Chung Ng, "They ensured that qualified troupes were duly represented, each by its hung wooden plaque (*shuipai*), and that information about the principal members and their role-types, as well as the repertoires, were all ready for preliminary examination" (Ng, *The Rise of Cantonese Opera*, 26).

11. In Chinese dynasties, the "reign title" was the name by which the ruling emperor indicated and recorded the years of his rule. Japanese and Korean emperors adopted similar practices. The printing of cast lists of top troupes gradually would become a standard Cantonese opera practice in Guangzhou, appearing in the form of trade paper called *Zhen Lan Bao*, which continued well into the twentieth century. See Rao, *Chinatown Opera Theater*, 84–85.

12. The difference in spelling is a result of my use of Pinyin to romanize the names of Chinese troupes on the list and the American newspapers' use of Cantonese dialect for their romanization. More troupes on the list appeared in North America: for example, the seventh troupe, Shun Tian Le (Swin Tien Lo), appeared in New York City in 1889. Both the third and eighth troupes would appear within the next ten years in both New York and San Francisco.

13. Du served as a prefect in Guangdong from 1866 to 1880. He recorded that officials held elaborate banquets and private opera performances for special celebrations, and that the Pu Feng Nian troupe was a top choice for those occasions. Du himself hired this troupe in the spring of 1873, when officials proposed

to engage a troupe for the birthday celebration of his mother, despite the fact that he was a Zhejiang Province native, speaking a different dialect. See Zhiyong Chen, 陳志勇, "晚清嶺南官場演劇及禁戲-以《杜鳳治日記》為中心" [Official plays and prohibited plays in Lingnan in the late Qing dynasty—in the case of "Du Fengzhi's Diary"], *Journal of Sun-yat Sen University*, 中山大學學報, 1 (2017): 27–38.

14. Yu, *Cantonese Opera in the Ming-Qing Period*, 134.

15. Yu Henn Choy, which began performing in September 1874, was listed as a new troupe arriving from China (advertisement of New Royal Chinese Theatre, *Daily Evening Bulletin*, September 8, 1874).

16. List of 32 for the Chinese Educational Mission to study in the United States, *The Oriental*, November 27, 1875; list of 64 in the top place for the Imperial Provincial Military Examination for eastern Guangdong, *The Oriental*, January 1, 1876.

17. *The Oriental,* May 13, 1876.

18. *The Oriental,* January 1, 1876.

19. For example, Liu Boji zhu 劉伯驥, 美國華僑史 [History of the Chinese in the United States of America], (Taibei Shi: Xing zheng yuan qiao wu wei yuan hui: Zong fa xing suo Li ming wen hua shi ye gu fen you xian gong si, 1976), 112.

20. Lai Fong (1839–1890) was considered the best Chinese photographer in Hong Kong in the nineteenth century, as attested by a contemporary in 1907. See Jeffrey W. Cody and Frances Terpak, "Through a Foreign Glass: The Art and Science of Photography in Late Qing China," in *Brush and Shutter: Early Photography in China* (Los Angeles: Getty Research Institute, 2011), 61.

21. Figures 6.23, 6.26 are included in Terry Bennett, *History of Photography in China: Chinese Photographers 1844–1879* (London: Quaritch, 2013). See also https://gwulo.com/node/31857.

22. April Liu, *Divine Threads: The Visual and Material Culture of Cantonese Opera* (Vancouver: Figure 1 Publishing, 2019), 52.

23. Liu, *Divine Threads*, 52.

24. John Thomas, a Scottish photographer, published several photographs of Chinese actors in his *Illustrations of China and Its People: A Series of Two Hundred Photographs, with Letterpress Descriptive of the Places and People Represented*, 2. (London: Sampson Low, Marston, Low, and Searle, 1873).

25. Ng, *The Rise of Cantonese Opera*, 30.

26. The curfew was widely reported as being connected to the raid discussed in this section.

27. "Mongolian Theatricals: The Police Pounce upon Royal China," *San Francisco Chronicle*, October 25, 1875.

28. "Raid on Royal Chinese Theatre," *Daily Alta California*, October 25, 1875. A similar raid was reported in *The Oriental* on January 1, 1876.

29. "Disarming the Chinese," *San Francisco Chronicle*, December 27, 1875.

30. "A Terrible Accident at the Royal Chinese Theater," *Daily Alta California*, October 31, 1876.

31. "Panic in the Royal Chinese Theater," *New York Tribune*, November 14, 1876.

32. "A Day's Crimes," *San Francisco Chronicle*, March 14, 1877; "An Extra Act," *San Francisco Chronicle*, April 2, 1877.

33. *Panama Star & Herald*, July 11, 1877; and "Peruvian Sketches," *Daily Evening Bulletin*, February 17, 1876. A reference to "the Grand Chinese Theatre, with sounding of gongs, drums and smelling of opium from 7 to 11 o'clock every night" appears in "Jottings from Havana, Cuba," *New York Clipper*, February 17, 1877.

34. "The Heathen Drama," *San Francisco Chronicle*, July 22, 1877.

35. "Riot in San Francisco," *Sacramento Daily Union*, July 24, 1877.

36. Winfield Davis, *History of Political Conventions in California, 1849–1892* (Sacramento: California State Library, 1893), 368.

37. "Chinese Immigration," *Daily Evening Bulletin*, October 23, 1877.

38. Davis, *History of Political Conventions in California*, 371–72.

39. "Letter from California," *Baltimore Sun*, August 7, 1877.

40. *San Francisco Chronicle*, October 13, 1877. The report continues, "They are engaged at a uniform yearly salary of $1,500 each, with board, the whole company eating and sleeping in the theatre."

41. "Opening a New Chinese Theatre," *Daily Alta California*, December 5, 1877.

42. "Floating Facts," *Jewish Messenger* (New York), November 2, 1877.

43. The monetary figures here are from "Confucian Amusement," *San Francisco Examiner*, December 4, 1877. However, the *San Francisco Chronicle* listed a different set of figures: $650 for monthly rent and $75,000 for the land. See also "New Chinese Theatre," *San Francisco Chronicle*, October 13, 1877. This third theater was smaller than the first theater (70 by 160 feet); see chap. 4.

44. "Opening a New Chinese Theatre," *Daily Alta California*, December 5, 1877.

45. *Daily Evening Bulletin*, January 29, 1878.

46. *San Francisco Chronicle*, December 11, 1877; *San Francisco Examiner*, "Confucian Amusement," December 7, 1877.

47. *San Francisco Examiner*, December 7, 1877.

48. *San Francisco Chronicle*, July 16, 1870.

49. *Jeffersonian* (Stroudsburg, PA), January 19, 1874, quoting the *Morning Call*. "Side head" refers to a subject heading in the newspaper page.

50. Davis, *History of Political Conventions in California*, 375–76.

51. *Daily Evening Bulletin*, December 5, 1877.

52. "A Visit to the Chinese Quarter San Francisco," *Frank Leslie's Popular Monthly*, March 1878, 345–51, esp. 347.

53. Yong Chen, *Chinese San Francisco*, 94. Chen also drew this conclusion from the study of Ah Quin's diary.

54. Mrs. Frank Leslie, *California: A Pleasure Trip from Gotham to the Golden Gate, April, May, June 1877* (New York: G. W. Carleton & Co. Publishers, 1877).

55. "Character Sketches in San Francisco: An Evening in the Chinese Quarter," *Frank Leslie's Illustrated Newspaper*, August 24, 1878, 421–22.

56. The *shagu* (沙鼓), a sand drum, has a frame made of hard, thick wood, and looks like a cone-shaped bun. It is hollow with a hole slightly more than one inch in diameter in the center of the top, called the heart of the drum. The drum is covered with cowhide (or other animal skin), which is fastened with round-headed iron nails all around. The shape of the drum resembles the head of a monk, so it is also called "monk's head" and is played with a bamboo stick.

57. "Character Sketches in San Francisco: An Evening in the Chinese Quarter by H. Ogden and Walter Yeager," *Frank Leslie's Illustrated Newspaper*, August 24, 1878.

58. Today we have little knowledge about the purpose of this costume or practice.

59. Aladdin, "Feuilleton: The Demand for a Chinese Theatre in Boston, Some of Its Possibilities," *Boston Daily Globe,* December 23, 1877.

60. "The text was translated under the supervision of the interpreter of the Chinese Legation." "Berlin Is to Have a Chinese Play—Scenery, Dresses, and All," *Los Angeles Herald*, June 8, 1878.

Chapter 6. Education, Diplomacy Culture, and the Fourth Theater

1. "A Chinese Exhibition," *San Francisco Chronicle*, June 8, 1878.

2. "A Chinese Exhibition."

3. "The Chinese School Festival," *Daily Alta California*, June 8, 1878.

4. "The Chinese School Festival."

5. Both the seventh (1877) and ninth (1879) anniversary celebrations were held at the Missionary School House. Anniversary programs, Ethnic Studies Library, University of California, Berkeley, https://oac.cdlib.org/ark:/13030/hb196n97m9/?brand=oac4.

6. Gibson continued, "The proceeds of this anniversary, at twenty-five cents admission, after paying all expenses of the occasion, amounted to about $250," *Sixtieth Annual Report of the Missionary Society of the Methodist Episcopal Church for the Year 1878*, January 1879, 174.

7. "San Francisco, California," *American Journal of Education* 19 (1870), 118–19.

8. "Mongolian Music," *San Francisco Chronicle,* April 30, 1877; *Cincinnati Enquirer*, May 11, 1877.

9. "Mongolian Majesty: Enthusiastic Reception of the Chinese Embassy," *San Francisco Chronicle*, July 27, 1878.

10. "Why Have They Come?" *San Francisco Chronicle*, July 28, 1878.

11. Chen Lanbin, 陳蘭彬、 使美紀略 [Brief record of a mission to America], in 小方壺齋興地叢鈔 [Collected books on geography from the Xiaofanghu Studio] (Shanghai: Shuyitang, 1877–1894). Translation by the author.

12. This weekly paper, *The Review of the Times*, 萬國公報, was published by Young John Allen in Shanghai, vol. 9, p. 5459.

13. "Why Have They Come?" *San Francisco Chronicle*, July 28, 1878.

14. "The Imperial Embassy on Its Passage Through Chicago," *Chicago Tribune*, August 9, 1878.

15. "The Imperial Embassy on Its Passage Through Chicago."

16. "The Youngest Nation to the Oldest," *New York Herald*, July 27, 1878.

17. "The Chinese Ambassadors: Formal Recognition of Minister Chin Lun Pin and His Assistant by the President," *New York Times*, September 29, 1878.

18. "Trouble in Chinatown," *Daily Alta California*, October 19, 1878; "Celestial Amusements," *San Francisco Chronicle*, October 21, 1878; and "A Row in the New Chinese Theatre," *Daily Evening Bulletin*, October 21, 1878.

19. "A Novelty in Theatricals," *Daily Alta California*, November 12, 1878.

20. "Grand Opera Theatre," *Daily Alta California*, November 14, 1878.

21. "The Chinese Performers," *San Francisco Chronicle*, November 17, 1878.

22. Quon San Yok appeared in Ah Quin's diary of 1878 and 1879.

23. "A Chinese Actor in Trouble," *Daily Evening Bulletin*, February 6, 1879.

24. *Mattoon Gazette* (Illinois), March 28, 1879: "The rivalry between the two leading Chinese theatres in San Francisco is not less intense than that between two of our first-class theatres.... Thereupon the manager of the theatre they were about to quit locked them ... to persuade them to renew the contract."

25. "New Chinese Theater: Competition in the Theatrical Circles of Chinatown," *San Francisco Chronicle*, September 25, 1879. The "Yew Hin Look" noted here is a different romanization of "Que Hing Log," as noted by Ah Quin.

26. "The Celestials: Trouble in the Chinese Theatrical Professions," *San Francisco Chronicle*, June 21, 1879.

27. Advertisement of eighty performers at the Chinese Theatre," *Pacific Commercial Adviser*, September 6, 1879; and report of the Look Sun Fung company, *Pacific Commercial Advertiser*, September 20, 1879.

28. From the beginning of the publication of the *Hawaiian Almanac and Annual* in 1875, mentions of Chinese theater appeared regularly every year, though only as markers of location regarding stands for licensed carriages. See Thomas G. Thrum, *Hawaiian Almanac and Annual for 1875*, (Honolulu: Honolulu Star-Bulletin), 40. By 1898, Honolulu would have two Chinese theaters, according to a traveler. See Charles M. Taylor Jr., *Vacation Days in Hawaii and Japan* (Philadelphia: George W. Jacobs & Co., 1898), 76–77.

29. "New Chinese Theater: Competition in the Theatrical Circles of Chinatown," *San Francisco Chronicle*, September 25, 1879.

30. *East-West* 東西報, January 6, 1971.

31. "F. A. Bee and Chinese Meet with Former President Grant," *New York Times*, September 26, 1879, 1; Zhu Wei-bin and Jing Min 朱衛斌 敬敏, "論傅列秘對美國華僑的保護," [Research on Frederick Bee's protection of Chinese in America], 學術研究, *Academic Studies* 8 (2019):106–13.

32. John Russell Young, *Around the World with General Grant* 2, pt. 2 (New York: Subscription Book Department, American News Co., 1879), 629–30.

33. "Grant and Kearney," *New York Times*, September 27, 1879.

34. "A Chinese Banquet," *San Francisco Chronicle*, October 2, 1879.

35. "A Chinese Theater," *Detroit Free Press*, December 28, 1879.

36. "A New Chinese Theatre," *Daily Evening Bulletin*, October 11, 1879, reprinted in *New York Times*, October 27, 1879. The theater's iron-front construction and size were so impressive that it was also reported in the principal entertainment paper, the *New York Clipper*, October 11, 1879.

37. "A Chinese Theater," *Detroit Free Press*, December 28, 1879.

38. *Washington Post*, October 23, 1879.

39. Ah Quin, diary, October 13, 1879.

40. For another romanization of the theater, "Gee Quuen Yung" see "A Notable Event in Chinatown," *Daily Evening Bulletin*, October 13, 1879; "A New Chinese Theatre," *New York Times*, October 27, 1879; and "Donn Qui Yuen and Grand Theater: A Chinese Theater," *Detroit Free Press*, December 28, 1879.

41. *San Francisco Examiner*, March 10, 1880.

42. Ah Quin, diary, 1879.

43. "A Chinese Theater," *Detroit Free Press*, December 28, 1879.

44. "A Chinese Theater."

45. "The Movements of the Presidential Party Yesterday—A Visit to Chinatown," *Daily Alta California*, September 14, 1880.

46. *Daily Evening Bulletin*, January 31, 1881.

47. *Supplement to the Codes and Statutes of California*, ed. Theodore Henry Hittell, 3:39 (San Francisco: A. L. Bancroft, 1880). The laws enacting these provisions were swiftly struck down in federal courts that ruled they violated the Fourteenth Amendment's guarantee of equal protection. See 1878–1879 Constitutional Convention Working Papers, https://www.sos.ca.gov/archives/collections/constitutions/1879.

48. "Chinese Theater," *Era*, September 3, 1881.

49. "Chinese Actress," *Sacramento Daily Record-Union*, October 24, 1881; "A Chinese Actress," *The Sun* (New York), April 21, 1881; both in Chronicling America: Historic American Newspapers, Library of Congress, Washington, DC.

Chapter 7. Contesting Chinese Exclusion Laws

1. Beth Lew-Williams, "Before Restriction Became Exclusion: America's Experiment in Diplomatic Immigration Control," *Pacific Historical Review* 83, no. 1 (2014): 24–56 (esp. 52).

2. Beth Lew-Williams, *The Chinese Must Go*, 87.

3. As Section 6 of the Restriction Act noted, the Chinese government would issue certificates to nonlaborers to be used as prima facie evidence for the right to enter the United States.

4. "Chinese Passports," *San Francisco Examiner*, August 10, 1882; and *New York Times*, August 18, 1882.

5. "The Latest Chinese Case," *Sacramento Daily Record Union*, August 23, 1882; and "Chinese Play-Actor," *San Francisco Examiner*, August 30, 1882.

6. "Complaint from Chinese Legation," *Los Angeles Herald*, August 27, 1882. For an excellent discussion on the complexity in the execution of the 1882 Restriction Act see Beth Lew-Williams, *The Chinese Must Go*.

7. "Nullifying the Chinese Act," *San Francisco Examiner*, August 27, 1882.

8. "Chinese Cheap Actors," *Cincinnati Commercial*, August 27, 1882; "Chinese Actors," *Boston Herald*, August 27, 1882.

9. *San Francisco Examiner*, August 30, 1882. The question mark is in the original article.

10. "Chinese Play-Actors," *San Francisco Examiner*, August 30, 1882.

11. "The Chinese Actors," *San Francisco Examiner*, August 31, 1882.

12. See discussions about the use of "excess" as a rationale to limit Chinese theater in chapters 2 and 3 of Rao, *Chinatown Opera Theater*.

13. "Chinese Registration," *San Francisco Examiner*, September 11, 1882.

14. *San Francisco Examiner*, October 12, 1882.

15. In re Ho King, 14 Fed. Rep. 724. Jan. 15, 1883 United States District Court for the District of Oregon. https://cite.case.law/f/14/724/.

16. "The Restriction Law," *Morning Oregonian*, January 12, 1883.

17. "He Appeared," *Morning Oregonian*, January 13, 1883.

18. "Decision in U.S. District Court, Deady J," *Morning Oregonian*, January 23, 1883. Deady had a complicated career. He supported slavery and believed in racial hierarchy but issued numerous favorable decisions involving Chinese litigants. He showed sympathy for them, upholding their rights and protecting their safety according to his understanding of the rule of law. He also condemned anti-Chinese mobs.

19. "Free Trade in Chinese Actors," *New York Herald*, February 25, 1883.

20. "Notes and Comments," *Globe* (Toronto), February 28, 1883.

21. According to Lexis, In re Ho King was cited in thirteen cases between 1883 and 1935, ranging from state supreme courts to federal district courts and the US Supreme Court.

22. *Lau Ow Bew v. United States*, 144 U.S. 47 (1892), https://supreme.justia.com/cases/federal/us/144/47/.

23. It was applied in a Philippines case in 1903. See Josh Stenberg, "Xiqu in the Philippines: From Church Suppression to MegaMall Shows," *Journal of Chinese Overseas* 16, no. 1 (2020): 58–89.

24. "Canton Certificate: More Chinese Traders Arrive on the Tokio," *Daily Evening Bulletin*, October 24, 1883.

25. "Canton Certificate."

26. "A Circus in Court," *New York Times,* August 23, 1884, reprinted from the *San Francisco Call*, August 15, 1884.

27. "A California Court Scene," *Fairfield News and Herald* (Winnsboro, SC), June 25, 1884.

28. Jennifer Lynn Stoever, *The Sonic Color Line: Race and the Cultural Politics of Listening* (New York: New York University Press, 2016).

29. "Oscar Wilde," *Deseret News*, May 31, 1882; "Lorne and Louise in Chinatown," *New York Times*, September 29, 1882; "Nilsson in Chinatown: The Swedish Prima Donna Visits a Chinese Theatre, Restaurant and Hoss-House," *Boston Globe*, December 26, 1882; "Social Doing of Mme Gerster," *Daily Alta California*, March 24, 1884.

30. The actor's name appeared as "Hong Gee Cheong" in the *Daily Alta California* and as "Hoa Gee Chung" in the *San Francisco Chronicle* and *Examiner*.

31. "A Clever Capture: A High-Priced Chinese Actor Arrested," *Daily Alta California*, November 19, 1884.

32. "Strategy, My Boy," *San Francisco Examiner*, November 19, 1884.

33. "Strategy, My Boy"; "A Clever Capture"; and "A Strategic Seizure," *San Francisco Chronicle*, November 19, 1894.

34. "That Chinese Actor," *Daily Alta California*, November 20, 1884.

35. Christian G. Fritz, "A Nineteenth Century 'Habeas Corpus Mill': The Chinese before the Federal Courts in California," *American Journal of Legal History* 32, no. 4 (1988): 347–72 (quote on 349).

36. "Landed Chinese: The Celestial Actors before a Commissioner," *Daily Evening Bulletin,* December 22, 1884.

37. "Chinese Immigration: Necessity of Positive Identification to Prevent Fraud— Some Interesting Instances in Point," *Daily Evening Bulletin*, February 21, 1885.

38. "The Chinese Drama," *San Francisco Chronicle*, quoted in *Rochester Democrat & Chronicle*, August 26, 1885.

39. Mae M. Ngai, *Impossible Subjects: Illegal Aliens and the Making of Modern America* (Princeton, NJ: Princeton University Press, 2004), 6.

40. Robert L. Tsai, "Racial Purges," *Michigan Law Review* 118 (2020): 1148.

41. The Chinese consul general in San Francisco gave the Chinese name Jinshan zhonghua zong huiguan (金山中華會館 Chinese Association of San Francisco) to what had been known as Six Companies. The Chinese Consolidated Benevolent Association was the official English name.

42. Tsai, "Racial Purges," 1145. There were many anti-Chinese riots, expulsions, and massacres, including the Rock Springs massacre (1885), the Tacoma expulsion (1885), the Seattle expulsion (1886), the Truckee method (1886), and the San Jose Chinatown burning (1887), to name only a few.

43. "Chinese Actor: An Interesting Heathen," *Salt Lake Herald*, March 16, 1883.

44. Lew-Williams, *Chinese Must Go*, 223.

45. The effect of the tightened control of Chinese immigrants following the Chinese exclusion acts is discussed in chapters 2 and 3 of Rao, *Chinatown Opera Theater*.

Chapter 8. Star Power and the Chinese American Theater

1. *Times-Picayune*, February 27, 1881.

2. "The Chinese Theatre Trouble," *Daily Alta California*, March 11, 1880.

3. "An Uncrushed Tragedian," *San Francisco Chronicle*, March 13, 1880; "Chinese Caprices," *San Francisco Examiner*, March 10, 1880.

4. "Superior Court," *Daily Alta California,* March 17, 1880.

5. "The Chinese Drama," *San Francisco Chronicle*, February 27, 1882; *Buffalo Weekly Courier*, March 15, 1882.

6. Henry Burden McDowell, "The Chinese Theater," *Century Illustrated Monthly Magazine*, 19 (new ser. vol. 7) (November 1884), 27–44.

7. Liu, *Divine Threads*, 52.

8. McDowell, "The Chinese Theater," 42.

9. What McDowell describes here as a conspicuously placed book of the cast probably was intended to be used as part of the *tigang xi* practice. Cantonese opera of this time relied heavily on *tigang xi*, the practice of plot outline or synoptic form (similar to the *canovaccio* of seventeenth-century *commedia dell'arte*). A sheet of paper was posted backstage for the performers' reference. On the paper was a grid with squares indicating scenarios or formulas with defined patterns of conventional role types, arias, music, and so on. Performers were well trained in the conventional scenarios. See Rao, *Chinatown Opera Theater*, 88–91.

10. "Loo Chin Goon: A Chinese Tragedian Will Start a Theater in Philadel- phia," *St. Louis Post-Dispatch*, March 15, 1883; "A Chinese Tragedian," *Times Union* (Albany, NY), March 24, 1883; "A Famous Chinese Actor. Loo Chin Goon's Cordial Reception in Philadelphia," *New York Times*, March 15, 1883; "A Celestial Theater,"

Buffalo Evening News, March 22, 1883; "The Star Interviewed," *Buffalo Evening News*, March 23, 1883; "A Popular Chinese Actor," *Hong Kong Daily Press*, April 21, 1883; "A Famous Chinese Actor," *Times-Picayune* (New Orleans), March 21, 1883.

11. *Indiana Tribüne* (German-language), March 21, 1883. *Era* (London), April 28, 1883; *Northern Echo* (Darlington, County Durham, England), May 5, 1883.

12. "Loo Chin Goon: A Chinese Tragedian Will Start a Theater in Philadelphia," *St. Louis Post- Dispatch,* March 15, 1883.

13. Julius Chambers, "Walks and Talks," *Brooklyn Daily Eagle*, February 5, 1908.

14. "Chinese Actor: An Interesting Heathen," *Salt Lake Herald*, March 16, 1883.

15. "Chinese Actor: An Interesting Heathen"; "Eastern Dispatches," *Reno Evening Gazette*, March, 15, 1883; "A Chinese Actor," *Morning Appeal* (Carson City, NV), March 16, 1883.

16. "Loo Chin Goon," *Daily Evening Bulletin*, March 15, 1883.

17. "A Celestial Theater," *Buffalo Evening News*, March 22, 1883.

18. "Ku Lee Minoo," *The Critic*, March 17, 1883.

19. *Santa Cruz Sentinel,* February 17, 1886.

20. "There are two theatres—the Tan Sung Fung, 623 Jackson Street; and the Bow Wah Yiug, at 814 Washington Street. They are open every day from 2 o'clock p.m. until midnight. Price of admission fifty cents, boxes two dollars and a half." See William C. Disturnell, *Strangers' Guide to San Francisco and Vicinity* (San Francisco: W. C. Disurnell, 1883), 106. Ronald Riddle found that two theaters dominated throughout the 1880s; see Riddle, *Flying Dragons, Flowing Streams: Music in the Life of San Francisco's Chinese* (Westport, CT: Greenwood Press, 1983), 62.

21. Jufen Luozhu, 聚芬樓主, "金山掌故 [Old Tale of Gold Mountain]," 東西報 *East-West Weekly*, January 7, 1970, 18.

22. Riddle, *Flying Dragons, Flowing Streams*, 54.

23. See clipping of the directory in W. H. Webber, Chinese exclusion notebook, 1883–1916. HM 84094, Huntington Library.

24. "Chinese Actors: The Manner of Their Performance and What They Enact. Remuneration for Their Work," *San Francisco Examiner,* November 19, 1882.

25. Although not mentioned here, onstage Cantonese opera was sung in the formal Zhongzhou dialect instead of in colloquial dialects, a tradition from near the central area of mainland China, where stage dialogue was sung in Cantonese.

26. Chang Song-hing and Zhuang Chusheng, "Geographical Distribution of Guangdong Dialects: Their Linkage with Natural and Historical Geography," *Journal of Chinese Studies* 48 (2008): 407–23.

27. "A Walking Junk: The Great Dramatic Sensation of Chinatown," *San Francisco Examiner*, December 4, 1882.

28. "Last Sunday Toby Hoy, the Chinese comedian, died of consumption, and was buried Wednesday with great honors by the Jackson-street Theatre," *Daily Alta California*, June 19 1885; also see *Sacramento Daily Union*, June 19, 1885; *New York Times*, June 25, 1885; *San Francisco Chronicle*, August 14, 1885.

29. "A Walking Junk."

30. "A Walking Junk."

31. "The Six Emperors: A Grand Display of Oriental Magnificence, A New Play and New Wardrobe," *San Francisco Examiner*, January 8, 1883. See also Liang Pei Jin, 梁沛錦, 六國大封相 [Six Kings] (Hong Kong: Xiang Gang Shi Zheng Ju Gong Gong Tu Shu Guan, 1992).

32. *Era* (London), September 3, 1881.

33. "A Chinese Theatre, Scenes behind the Scenes at a Celestial Playhouse," *Boston Globe*, July 8, 1883.

34. M. D. Conway, "A Chinese Theatre: An interpreter Explains the True Inwardness of the Play," *Press Democrat* (Santa Rosa, CA), October 26, 1883. The byline of the report is "M. D. Conway in Philadelphia Times."

35. "Nilsson in Chinatown," *Boston Globe*, December 26, 1882.

36. "Social Doings of Mme. Gerster," *Daily Alta California*, March 24, 1884.

37. "Chinese 'Singsong': A Visit to 'Conn Quai Yuen' Theater in San Francisco," *Omaha Daily Bee*, April 12, 1884.

38. "Signore Arditi Visits the Chinese Theatre," *Daily Alta California*, March 22, 1885.

39. "Pagan Play Actors: The Chinese Drama and Its Votaries," *San Francisco Chronicle,* August 14, 1885.

40. "Pagan Play Actors."

41. "Pagan Play Actors."

42. Paul Howard, "Chinese Plays and Players," *Illustrated Sporting and Dramatic News*, December 5, 1885, 298.

43. This plot summary is taken from *Anthology of Cantonese Opera Synopses,* 粵劇劇目綱要 (Guangzhou: Zhongguo Xijujia Xiehui Guangdong Fenhui, 1961; Yangcheng Wanbao reprint ed., 2006).

44. *Daily Alta California,* September 27, 1885.

45. "Amusements: Bush-Street Theater," *San Francisco Examiner,* September 22, 1885.

46. Esther Kim Lee traced the theatrical origin of yellowface in America to European theater history, well before the 1850s. She "locates the origins of the [American] stage Chinaman in British pantomime traditions." In America, the ambiguous "legal status of Chinese laborers influenced the representation of Chinese characters" on stage. See *Made-Up Asians: Yellowface During the Exclusion Era* (Ann Arbor: University of Michigan Press, 2022), 19, 45.

47. *Omaha Bee*, November 13, 1887.

48. Richard Dyer, *White: Essays on Race and Culture* (London: Routledge, 1997), 12, quoted in Lee, *Made Up Asians*, 66.

49. "Amusements: 'The Golden Giant Mine' at English's," *Indianapolis Journal,* March 13, 1888.

50. David R. Beasley, *McKee Rankin and the Heyday of the American Theater* (Waterloo, ON: Wilfrid Laurier University Press, 2002), 241.

51. *Daily Wabash Express* (Terre Haute, IN), October 1886.

52. *Indianapolis Journal,* March 11, 1888; *Evening World*, October 11, 1887; Harrison Grey Fiske, ed., *New York Mirror Annual and Directory of the Theatrical Profession for 1888* (New York: New York Mirror), 28.

53. "A Pacific Invasion," *San Francisco Chronicle*, January 14, 1886.

54. Thomas Cunningham Porter, *Impressions of America* (London: C. A. Pearson, 1899), 147–49.

55. For a discussion of the phrase structure, see Rao, *Chinatown Opera Theater*, chap. 5.

Chapter 9. Picturesque Chinese Theater

1. In addition to those that will be discussed in this chapter, the articles in the nineteenth century also include Paul Frenzeny, "Chinese Theaters in San Francisco," *Harper's Weekly*, May 12, 1883, 296–97; Arthur Inkersley, "The Chinese Drama in California," *London Strand Magazine* 15, April 1898, 402–9; G. W. Lamplugh, "In a Chinese Theatre," *Macmillan's Magazine* 57, November 1887, 36–40. Articles published shortly after the turn of the century include E. M. Green, "The Chinese Theater," *Overland Monthly and Out West Magazine*, February 1903, 7–9; Stanley Scott, "The Chinese Drama in San Francisco," *English Illustrated Magazine*, February 1905, 483–88.

2. *Elite Directory for San Francisco and Oakland* (San Francisco: Argonaut Publishing Company, 1879) listed more than a dozen of social groups and clubs.

3. Raymond Rast, "The Cultural Politics of Tourism in San Francisco's Chinatown, 1882–1917," *Pacific Historical Review* 76, no. 1 (February 2007): 39.

4. Rast, "The Cultural Politics of Tourism," 38.

5. Rast, "The Cultural Politics of Tourism," 40.

6. *Bohemian Club: Certificate of Incorporation, Constitution, Bylaws and Rules, Officers, Committees and Members* (San Francisco: Bohemian Club, 1939).

7. *Elite Directory for San Francisco and Oakland*, 176.

8. Lee, *Picturing Chinatown*, 63.

9. One of its earliest members, Benjamin Parke Avery, an editor at the *Daily Evening Bulletin*, was appointed ambassador to China in 1874. Another prominent member, George T. Bromley, was appointed consul in Tian Tsin (Tianjin) in China in 1885. The Bohemian Club held a grand farewell party for Bromley and commissioned a painting by Theodore Wores of him in an elaborate Chinese opera warrior costume, titled *Bohemian Cathay*. See Robert Hoew Fletcher, ed., *The Annals of the Bohemian Club: Comprising Text and Pictures Furnished by Its Own Members* 2 (1880–87) (San Francisco: Bohemian Club, 1939), 149–51. Other Bohemian Club members who served as ministers to China included John F. Swift and J. Ross Browne. See *Annals of the Bohemian Club*, 149–56, 205.

10. Paul Frenzeny was another artist associated with the Bohemian Club who was deeply engaged with Chinatown and its theater. His work can be seen in *Chinatown Sketches: An Artist's Fascination with San Francisco's Chinese Quarter, 1874–1882* (San Francisco: Book Club of California, 2013).

11. Some examples include Rusling, *Across America*, 308–11; Benjamin E. Lloyd, *Lights and Shades in San Francisco* (San Francisco: A. L. Bancroft, 1876), 264–66; Helen Hunt Jackson, *Bits of Travel at Home* (Boston: Roberts Bros., 1878), 69–74;

Iza Duffus Hardy, *Between Two Oceans; or, Sketches of American Travel* (London: Hurst and Blackett, 1884), 164–66.

12. Walter Gore Marshall, *Through America; Or, Nine Months in the United States* (London: Sampson Low, Marston, Searle & Rivington, 1882), 297–301. On page 292 Marshall briefly describes how (unnamed) theater owners were alarmed by the recent parade of ten thousand members of the Workingmen's Party and limited their hours of operation. He also reprinted the two images "The All Night Supper in the Dressing Room of the Royal Theatre" (p. 298) and "Interior of the Royal Theatre during a Performance" (p. 300) from "Character Sketches in San Francisco: An Evening in the Chinese Quarter," *Frank Leslie's Illustrated Paper*, August 24, 1878, 421–22. Some details in the original images were omitted, and the facial features were more racialized.

13. George Augustus Sala, *America Revisited: From the Bay of New York to the Gulf of Mexico, and from Lake Michigan to the Pacific* (London: Vizetelly & Co., 1882), 474–86. This book reused the same 1878 images from *Frank Leslie's Illustrated Newspaper*, as well as several additional images. Sala's visit (circa November 1879 through April 1880) took place slightly later than Marshall's.

14. George H. Fitch, "In a Chinese Theater," *Century Illustrated Magazine* 114, no. 2 (June 1882), 190.

15. Accompanied by an American fluent in Chinese, Fitch gathered enough information to follow the opera's plot line.

16. Fitch, "In a Chinese Theater," 191–92.

17. George Fitch, "A Night in Chinatown," *The Cosmopolitan* 2 (February 1887), 354.

18. Fitch, "In a Chinese Theater," 191.

19. Fitch, "In a Chinese Theater," 192.

20. Henry McDowell's name appeared as early as 1876 along with those of San Francisco's mayor, the Board of Supervisors, railroad magnates such as Leland Stanford, and others in "The Last Rail," *Sacramento Daily Union*, September 5, 1876. He was also listed in the *Elite Directory for San Francisco and Oakland*, 121. McDowell listed "The Chinese Theater" and "The New Light upon the Chinese" as his most important articles in *Harvard College, Class of 1878, Secretary's Report, No. VI, 1908* (Cambridge, MA: Riverside Press, 1908), 63–64. Also see *Harvard College Class of 1878, Fiftieth Anniversary Report, 1878–1928* (Cambridge, MA: Riverside Press, 1928), 133.

21. Advertisement, *Daily Alta California*, January 22, 1881.

22. In its week-and-half-long run of performances, "all the town went to see it," according to "Dance and Drama," *The Californian*, 3, no. 5 (March 1881), 282–83. See also *Annals of the Bohemian Club, Volume 1, 1872–1880* (San Francisco: Bohemian Club, 1900), 110.

23. Of McDowell's play at the Oakland Theatre, a newspaper review noted a "first-class lot of actors, with scenery painted by Voegtlin, and a full orchestra, led by Mr. Charles Shultz, time out of mind the California Theater's music-maker," *Daily Alta California*, February 3, 1885. In 1893, after moving back to the East Coast,

Henry McDowell worked with the Theatre of Arts and Letters in New York, which featured experimental literary plays.

24. *Daily Evening Bulletin*, October 20, 1884; *Boston Daily,* October 22, 1884.

25. Henry Burden McDowell, "A New Light on the Chinese," *Harper's New Monthly Magazine* 86 (December 1892), 1–17 (with illustrations by Theodore Wores et al.).

26. In a letter to his mother dated May 27, 1884, Cox wrote: "I have worked like a horse all last week at arranging the exhibition of the Society of American Artists, and the week before that at some drawings of Chinese actors for the *Century*." See H. Wayne Morgan, *An Artist of the American Renaissance: The Letters of Kenyon Cox, 1883–1919* (Kent, OH: The Kent State University Press, 2014), 40.

27. Sala's and Marshall's books incorporated illustrations that were re-engravings of the two illustrations by Henry Alexander Ogden and Walter Yeager from *Frank Leslie's Illustrated Newspaper*, August 25, 1878, discussed in chapter 5. However, these reengraving were made more menacing than the originals by exaggerating the stereotypical racialized features.

28. "One of these [studies of the Chinese quarter] formed the basis for a painting which so pleased Lord Rosebery." In "California Art Gossip," *LSK The Art Amateur: A Monthly Journal Devoted to Art in the Household* 19, no. 1 (1888), 6.

29. The shop of Wores's father was located on Washington Street, between Montgomery and Kearny. For a detailed study of the early life of Theodore Wores, see California Art Research Project WPA Project 2874, vol. 10, ed. Gene Hailey, 91–153. https://digitalassets.lib.berkeley.edu/cara/ucb/text/Cara_Volume_10.pdf.

30. "Art and Artists," *Californian* 4, no. 24 (December 1881), 534–35.

31. *Sacramento Daily Union*, October 21, 1882.

32. *Sacramento Daily Union*, February 10, 1883.

33. *Sacramento Daily Union*, May 19, 1883.

34. *The Record-Union* (Sacramento), October 8, 1883. Goupil & Cie. was a prominent Paris art dealer with branches in several major cities.

35. *Sacramento Daily Union*, July 21, 1883.

36. "A genre painting, striking in originality and completeness. . . . Mr. Wores has for some years devoted himself almost entirely to Chinese subjects and with great success. But the public has seen but little of his work, as his pictures have always happened to be bought in the studio almost before they were finished. Messrs. Yungling and Helm of New York and Sir Thomas Hesketh and Lord Rosebery of England each own one or more of his Chinese pictures." "Art Notes," *San Francisco Chronicle*, April 6, 1884.

37. See the report of London exhibition, "Messrs. Dowdeswell's Gallery," *Morning Post* (London), July 12, 1889. See also Chad Mandeles, "Theodore Wores's Chinese Fishmonger in a Cosmopolitan Context," *American Art Journal* 16, no. 1 (1984): 65–75.

38. *San Francisco Call*, October 7, 1909. Wores continued painting Chinese themes, including *Interior of Chinese Restaurant* and *New Year's Day in San Francisco Chinatown*, among others. Years later, George Bernard Shaw would comment on a London exhibition of Wores's paintings: "The pictures have a certain

pre-Raphaelite sincerity and strength of colour." George Bernard Shaw, "Rousolff and Wores, 3 July 1889," in *Bibliographical Shaw, Including a Supplement to Bernard Shaw: A Bibliography by Dan H. Laurence*, ed. Fred D. Crawford and Dan H. Laurence (University Park: Pennsylvania State University Press, 2000), C601.

39. *Photograph of a Painting by Theodore Wores of a Standing Warrior with Musicians in the Background*, Digital Archive of Chinese Theater in California, Museum of Performance and Design, Performing Arts Library, San Francisco, http://www.oac.cdlib.org/ark:/13030/kt967nc8kb/?order=1.

40. The last known appearance of the painting (*Chinese Actor*) was in a gallery exhibit in Liverpool in 1892, "Sale of Pictures from the Continental Gallery," *Liverpool Mercury*, November 16, 1892.

41. *Philadelphia Inquirer*, October 30, 1884.

42. *Catalogue of the Fifty-fifth Annual Exhibition, Pennsylvania Academy of the Fine Arts* (Philadelphia, 1884), 21.

43. "Fifty-fifth Exhibition of the Pennsylvania Academny," *The American* 12, no. 222 (November 8, 1884), 75.

44. Although the difference is minute, the photograph version shows the particular artistry of Wores through the more genuine facial expression (in contrast to the rigid lines in the wood engraving), the strengths conveyed in the gestures of both hands (in contrast to the awkward left hand), and the ease in the postures of the instrumentalists. In contrast, the wood engraving accentuates the details of the costume.

45. In the backdrop of "An Entrance," Wores added an object of the sculptured element above the door frame from the stage of the Donn Quai Yuen Theater to the stage of Dan Shan Feng. From the photo of Donn Quai Yuen in figure 6.6, we can see the sculpted element but not much detail. In this image, the sculpted element appears to depict a dragon and a waterspout (part of the stage in Donn Quai Yuen).

46. Fitch, "In a Chinese Theater," 190.

47. McDowell, "The Chinese Theater," 28.

48. McDowell, "The Chinese Theater," 28.

49. The working relationship between McDowell and Wores must have been fruitful, because eight years later they collaborated again in a *Harper's New Monthly Magazine* article, "A New Light on the Chinese," which included engravings of ten paintings on Chinese themes by Wores. Some of these, such as "Chinese Musicians," "Chinese Shop," and "Chinese Maiden," were already well known and had been sold to collectors. See McDowell, "A New Light on the Chinese," 1–17.

50. McDowell, "The Chinese Theater," 31.

51. It was the convention in many regions of China to hire opera troupes to perform for the deities in an effort to appease them and receive their blessings and protection.

52. McDowell, "The Chinese Theater," 30–31.

53. McDowell, "The Chinese Theater," 32.

54. McDowell, "The Chinese Theater," 35.

55. "A Walking Junk: The Great Dramatic Sensation of Chinatown," *San Francisco Examiner*, December 4, 1882. We do not know whether the article's author and

McDowell depict the same performance. If they do not, these two performances nevertheless shared much in common.

56. "Interesting Discovery: Prof. Cushing Traces the Zuni Tongue to an Oriental Origin," *Sacramento Daily Union*, December 12, 1887.

57. "The Mythic Drama: Cushing Compares the Chinese Theater with the Ka-Ka of the Zuni," *San Francisco Examiner*, November 20, 1887. Cushing also wrote lengthy reports on Zuni Pueblo, New Mexico for *Century* magazine. See Frank Hamilton Cushing, "My Adventures in Zuñi," *Century Illustrated Magazine* 25, no. 2 (December 1882), 191–207; and 25, no. 4 (February 1883), 500–511. Cushing's comparative work on Zuni and Chinese drama is also documented in David R. Wilcox, "Anthropology in a Changing America: Interpreting the Chicago 'Triumph' of Frank Hamilton Cushing," in *Coming of Age in Chicago: The 1893 World's Fair and the Coalescence of American Anthropology*, ed. Curtis M. Hinsley and David Wilcox (Lincoln: University of Nebraska Press, 2015), 125–52.

58. "Something Decidedly New," *Daily Alta California*, December 4, 1884; this article was attributed to the correspondent "Modus," the pen name for Fritz Morris, a member of New York Press Club. Also see the discussion of Morris in *Daily Alta California*, October 22, 1884.

59. Daniel Joseph Singal, "Towards a Definition of American Modernism," *American Quarterly* 39, no. 1 (1987): 7–26.

60. "The Theatre of Arts and Letters," *Werner's Magazine* 15, no. 2 (1893), 38. *The Critic: A Weekly Review of Literature and the Arts* published substantial reviews of the organization's performances. See "Boston Letter," *The Critic*, no. 581 (April 8, 1893), 221–23; "The Drama: Miss Wilkins's 'Giles Corey' on the Stage," *The Critic*, no. 584 (April 29, 1893), 276–77.

61. Kenneth Mcgowan, "Little Theatre Backgrounds," *Theatre Arts Monthly* 8, no. 9 (September 1924), 579–96 (quote on p. 588). See also *Harvard College, Class of 1877, Seventh Report, June, 1917.* (Norwood, MA.: Plimpton Press, 1917), 161–63.

62. *Illustrated Sporting and Dramatic News*, November 1, 1884, 22, 567; pg. 163.

63. *Langley's San Francisco Directory* (San Francisco: Francis, Valentine & Co., 1884), 107.

64. *Annals of the Bohemian Club, Volume 1, 1872–1880*, 163. Since 1902, the Grove plays have been presented during the Bohemian Club summer encampments held at the private Bohemian Grove, near Gurneville in Sonoma County, north of San Francisco.

65. *Pacific Bank Handbook of California* (San Francisco: The Bank, 1888), 90–92.

66. Carleton Watkins (American, 1829–1916) was known for his studies of San Francisco's Chinatown in the 1870s and 1880s. As seen here, his portraits reveal a deep respect for the integrity of Chinese actors. It is assumed that through a Chinese darkroom assistant named Ah Fue, Watkins had access to the elite Chinese community, located only a few blocks from his studio on Montgomery Street.

67. Frederic J. Masters, "The Chinese Drama," *Chautauquan* 21, no. 4 (July 1895), 434–42.

68. Frederic Palmer Wells, *History of Barnet, Vermont From the Outbreak of the French and Indian War to Present Time* (Burlington, VT: Free Press Printing Co., 1923), 136.

69. Frederic J. Masters, "The Recent Disturbance in China," *Californian* 1, no. 2 (January 1892), 62–74; Masters, "Pagan Temples in San Francisco," *Californian* 2, no. 6 (November 1892): 227–41; Masters, "Among the Highbinders—An Account of Chinese Secret Societies," *Chinese Recorder and Missionary Journal*, 23, no. 6 (1892): 268–315.

70. By Chinese sources, I mean the *East-West Weekly*, discussed in chapter 8, as well as anecdotal accounts given elsewhere.

71. Masters, "The Chinese Drama," 437.

72. The *matshed*, a temporary structure, was a typical performing space for Cantonese opera that focused on worship of the deities. The practice continues today, but is little noted in North America.

73. Xiulu Wang, "History of Translation and Reception of the Chinese Folk Opera *Pu Kang* in the 19th Century," *Compilation and Translation Review* 13, no. 1 (2020): 39–70; Samuel W. Williams, *The Middle Kingdom*, vol. 1, *A Survey of the Geography, Government, Literature, Social Life, Arts, and History of the Chinese Empire and Its Inhabitants* (New York: Wiley and Putnam, 1848); William C. Hunter, "Remarks on the Chinese Theatre; with a Translation of a Farce, Entitled 'The Mender of Cracked Pots,'" *Chinese Repository* 6 (1838), 575–79; and Henry Charles Sirr, *China and the Chinese* (London: W. S. Orr & Company, 1849). A translation of the play was also published as "The Mender of Cracked Chinaware," *Chautauquan* 3 (June 1883), 503–5.

74. Notably, at the center right above a clock a plaque indicates the theater's formal English name, Donn Quai Yuen, although the photo was captioned with another romanization, "Tan Kwai Yuen Theater."

Chapter 10. Civil Rights, Owning Glamour, and Sonic Ethnology

1. A. W. Macy, "A Chinese Josshouse," *Indianapolis Journal*, December 7, 1884.

2. As a contemporary newspaper noted, "Mr. Wong Chin Foo's lectures for the past two years have created a universal excitement and comment by the Press of the United States." *Quincy Daily Herald* (Illinois), February 19, 1898.

3. *The Journalist* 6 no. 5 (October 22, 1887), 9.

4. "Chinese Actors," *Salt Lake Herald*, March 17, 1883.

5. *Evening Item* (Richmond, IN), April 11, 1883.

6. *Fort Wayne Daily Gazette*, March 25, 1883.

7. For further discussion, see Scott D. Seligman, *The First Chinese American: The Remarkable Life of Wong Chin Foo* (Hong Kong: Hong Kong University Press, 2013), 126–28.

8. "The Chinese Drama," *Elkhart Daily Review* (Indiana), August 29, 1883.

9. Wong Chin Foo told the *New York Tribune*: "I have an idea that will help each people to understand the other. I will establish the Chinese theatre in the United States for the presentation of the Chinese drama, the oldest in the world going back to the first stages of recorded history." *New York Tribune*, September 2, 1883.

10. Tchen, *New York Before Chinatown*, 283.

11. Esther Kim Lee notes that although Chinese performers were not difficult to find, playwrights and authors employed yellowface actors. See Lee, *Made-Up*

Asians, 55–56. Charles Parsloe excelled at the stage Chinaman role, particularly his performance of Wing Lee in *My Partner* (1879) by Bartley Theodore Campbell. See Sean Metzger, "Charles Parsloe's Chinese Fetish: An Example of Yellowface Performance in Nineteenth-Century American Melodrama," *Theatre Journal* 56, no. 4 (December 2004), 627–51. For more discussion of yellowface performance, see also Metzger, *Chinese Looks*; Krystyn R. Moon, *Yellowface: Creating the Chinese in American Popular Music and Performance, 1850s-1920s* (New Brunswick, NJ: Rutgers University Press, 2005); James S. Moy, *Marginal Sights: Staging the Chinese in America* (Iowa City: University of Iowa Press, 1993); Robert G. Lee, *Orientals: Asian Americans in Popular Culture* (Philadelphia: Temple University Press, 1999); Josephine Lee, *Oriental, Black, and White: The Formation of Racial Habits in American Theater* (Chapel Hill: University of North Carolina Press, 2022); and Ju Yon Kim, *The Racial Mundane: Asian American Performance and the Embodied Everyday* (New York: New York University Press, 2015).

12. *Oswego Daily Palladium* (New York), March 22, 1887.

13. Wong Chin Foo, "Why Am I a Heathen?" *North American Review* 145, no. 369 (August 1887), 169–79.

14. Wong Chin Foo, "The Chinese in New York," *Cosmopolitan* 5, no. 4 (August 1888), 297–311.

15. *San Francisco Examiner*, July 29, 1889; *Detroit Free Press*, October 13, 1889.

16. According to John Tchen, Tom Lee founded the Sam Hop Hui secret society as a kind of Chinese Masonic lodge, to which Wong Chin Foo also belonged. Tchen, *New York Before Chinatown*, 256.

17. "Going to New York," *San Francisco Chronicle*, October 22, 1889. A group of six merchants, led by Lee Bing, had leased a Chinese theater several months earlier, but the group's relationship with the group is unclear (*Portland Oregonian*, February 25, 1889). Chinese theater had been established in Portland since 1880. "A Chinese Company," *Daily Inter Ocean* (Chicago), May 14, 1889.

18. "A company of Chinese actors has been organized here to play through the East. It comprises twenty two members. . . . If properly billed and managed they will double play to big houses all through the East, but it is understood they have a Chinese advance agent, and have not been booked off any circuit. It is to be feared that like many another theatrical company, they will come to grief, and may perhaps count the loss from Chicago here." *Oregonian*, April 24, 1889.

19. According to a news report, a "Chinese theatrical troop [*sic*] has been organized at Portland, Or., to make a tour of the United States" (*Daily Evening Bulletin*, April 26, 1889). This news report was reprinted in more than ten newspapers, including the *Idaho Avalanche* (May 11), the *Boston Investigator* (May 15), and the *Bangor Daily Whig and Courier* (Maine), May 9, 1889.

20. "Chinese Dramatists" and Advertisement, *Morning Review* (Spokane Falls, Washington), April 25 and 26, 1889. The advertisement reads "Falls City Opera House: the Lee Toy Imperial Chinese Dramatic Company, from San Francisco, consisting of 35 members," *Bismarck Tribune* (North Dakota), April 28, 1889. The report notes, "Helena is all agog over a Chinese theatrical company which will visit the city May 9th . . . Such a novel company as this would draw a big house in Bismarck—in fact anywhere."

21. The St. Paul reporter was quoted in "Portland's Chinese Actors: They Are Corralled by a Reporter in St. Paul and Interviewed," *Oregonian*, June 7, 1889.

22. "Ke Chung Makes His Bow: The Chinese Actor Appears at a Chicago Theater," *Chicago Daily Tribune,* May 14, 1889. The engagement began on May 13.

23. "Flowery Kingdom Actors," *Daily Inter Ocean*, May 12, 1889.

24. Lawrence Levine, *Highbrow Lowbrow: The Emergence of Cultural Hierarchy in America* (Cambridge, MA: Harvard University Press, 1990), 76–77.

25. "Madison-street Theatre," *New York Clipper*, May 1, 1886. Chicago had its production of *The Mikado* in July1885. In January 1886, a Mikado Ball given by the department-store magnate Marshall Field was a great sensation as well. See Josephine Lee, *The Japan of Pure Invention: Gilbert and Sullivan's* "The Mikado" (Minneapolis: University of Minnesota Press, 2010).

26. "Seng Gong Shang War: Celestial Actors Amuse Benighted Barbarians with High Tragedy," *Daily Inter Ocean*, May 15, 1889; "Amusement: General Mention," *Daily Inter Ocean*, May 16, 1889.

27. Four years later, Chinese theater would be a major attraction at the 1893 Chicago World's Columbian Exhibition, through the efforts of Wah Mee Company. The repertoire performed included *The Six Kings* (*Chicago Daily Tribune* May 19, 1893, and September 24, 1893). Pictures of two actors, Ki Hing and Foke Sing, were included in a catalogue of the fair. See Frederick W. Putnam, *Portrait Types of the Midway Plaisance* (St Louis: N. D. Thompson Publishing Co., 1894), 100. Wong Chin Foo was also involved in this event. See Mae Ngai, "Transnationalism and the Transformation of the 'Other': Response to the Presidential Address," *American Quarterly* 57, no. 1 (2005): 59–65; Z. Serena Qiu, "In the Presence of Archival Fugitives: Chinese Women, Souvenir Images, and the 1893 Chicago World's Fair," *Panorama: Journal of the Association of Historians of American Art* 7, no. 1 (Spring 2021), https://doi.org/10.24926/24716839.11645.

28. "Chinese Actors in Quakertown," *New York Herald,* June 14, 1889.

29. "Chinese Actors in Quakertown."

30. "Howard's Gossip: Almond-Eyed Actors to Dazzle New York—Oriental Faith and Humor Embodied in Their Plays," *Boston Daily Globe*, June 13, 1889. The author of this article may have been Howard Malcolm Ticknor, a poet and critic active in theater-savvy Boston who wrote frequently for the *Globe*. See also Terry Alford, *Fortune's Fool: The Life of John Wilkes Booth* (New York: Oxford University Press, 2015), 132.

31. The Scott Act was written by the Pennsylvania congressman William Lawrence Scott. As a result, twenty thousand Chinese workers with return certificates were abruptly stranded outside the United States after they had been promised an exemption from the Exclusion laws.

32. New York had more than two dozen theaters. Considering the schedule, the success might be attributed to timing: the regular season was ending, and many people were leaving town for the summer. Between fourteen and seventeen of the twenty-four major performing venues that regularly advertised in the *New York Amusement Gazette* were closed during this time. See the weekly advertisements of *New York Amusement Gazette*, June 24-July 8, 1889.

33. *New York Amusement Gazette*, 12 no. 48 (June 24, 1889), 449.

34. "Chinese Drama in New York," *New York Herald,* June 17, 1889.

35. "'The Royal Slave,'" *Philadelphia Inquirer*, June 25, 1889; and "A Chinese Play with Chinese Actors," *Boston Journal*, June 25, 1889.

36. "Theatrical Gossip," *New York Times,* June 20, 1889.

37. "Just Like in Pekin," *New York Herald*, June 22, 1889.

38. *New York Amusement Gazette* 12, no. 50 (July 1, 1889), 456.

39. "'A Dark Conspiracy' in Chinese," *New York Herald*, June 29, 1889.

40. "A Lively Chinese Comedy," *New York Tribune*, July 6, 1889.

41. "Chinese Actors to See 'The Oolah," *New York Tribune*, July 9, 1889. Reflecting its interest and the newsworthiness of the event, the *Tribune* published daily reports on the troupe from July 5 to July 10.

42. "Chinese Actors: They Have Established a Regular Theater in New York," *Sunday Critic* (Allentown, PA), June 30, 1889.

43. "Chinese Drama in '49," *Boston Globe*, July 30, 1889.

44. For the troupe's activities and failure in New York, see Tchen, *New York Before Chinatown*, 73–92.

45. "Chinese Drama Didn't Pay," *Evening World* (New York), July 8, 1889.

46. *New York Amusement Gazette*, July 29-September 2, 1889. Swentien Lok performed in the theater at 113 Bowery from August 9 to September 30. See also "A number of Chinamen, encouraged by the success of the native company which lately appeared in that city, have formed a partnership to establish a permanent Chinese theater in New York." *Indianapolis News*, August 30, 1889. The paper named the theater "Lumtien Lok Company."

47. "Chinese Theatricals in New York," *Frank Leslie's Illustrated Newspaper*, June 29, 1889, 352. The opening date in Chinese characters in the illustration was given in the lunar calendar and translated as June 25, 1889. The article gives more detail: "The company which thus introduces the Chinese drama on New York boards is brought here at an expense of $20,000, and whether it will remain will depend upon the success which attends its representations. The cost of the experiment is paid by the Chinese merchants of this city, who have been in negotiation with the company for two or three years." The troupe's Chinese name, as shown in the illustration, clarifies the less legible characters in an earlier report's accompanying image: "Seng Gong Shang War," *Daily Inter Ocean*, May 15, 1889 (see n. 26).

48. Lorraine Dong, Philip P. Choy, and Marlon K. Hom, eds. *The Coming Man: 19th Century American Perceptions of the Chinese* (Seattle: University of Washington Press, 1995).

49. According to Wong Chin Foo's biographer, William E. S. Fales was a well-known Brooklyn attorney and did business with Chinese community. Earlier he also represented the theosophist Madame Helena Blavatsky. Wong might have become an attorney as a result of an apprenticeship to Fales. Seligman, *The First Chinese American,* 128.

50. Well acquainted with the Chinese community and the Chinese language, William E. S. Fales was later appointed a United States consul in Amoy, China. See Louis J. Beck, *New York's Chinatown: An Historical Presentation of Its People and Places* (New York: Bohemia Publishing Company, 1898), 298.

51. The illustrator William Allen Rogers was a staff artist at *Harper's Bazaar*. He was a prolific political cartoonist and later worked for the *New York Herald*. His work for *Harper's* included vivid artistic and pictorial illustrations for literary works. The other two *Harper's Bazaar* cover images he produced in 1889 accompanied the noted writer Marion Harland's article "Nota Bene," *Harper's Bazaar*, December 28, 1889, 954; and "Diogenes's Daughter," a poem by the American poet Will Carleton, August 24, 1889. These images were the first of several drawings he was commissioned to create for the covers of *Harper's Bazaar*.

52. This "Chinese Play" was the first cover drawing that Rogers did for *Bazaar*. His drawings were far more animated than the average cover images, which often depicted women's fashions for traveling, walking, different seasons, and so on. The magazine's other articles on Chinese fashion and women were not accompanied by illustrations.

53. William Fales, "The Chinese Play," *Harper's Bazaar* 22, no. 30 (July 27, 1889), 543.

54. Somehow Fales felt the need to retract his praise of the costumes, noting that the costumes were deficient in delicacy. See Fales, "The Chinese Play."

55. *Republican Gazette*, April 27, 1888.

56. Reflecting on Derrida's notion of language, Judith Brown writes, "Representation cannot be understood as having a referent that remains untouched by representation: referent and representation reflect, distort, and contaminate the other in an infinite and promiscuous dialectic that undoes and commits violence on any notion of a pure source or origin." See Judith Brown, *Glamour in Six Dimensions: Modernism and the Radiance of Form* (Ithaca, NY: Cornell University Press, 2009), 52.

57. William E. S. Fales, "The Chinese Mimes," *Harper's Weekly*, June 29, 1889, 528.

58. *The Stage* (London), August 2, 1889, 9.

59. "The Chinese Drama," *Philadelphia Inquirer*, July 3, 1889.

60. Wong Chin Foo, "He Didn't Understand: A Chinaman Answers Criticisms of the Chinese Drama," *Courier-Journal* (Louisville), July 10, 1889.

61. When the laborer Chae Chan Ping returned to the United States in 1888 after a trip to China, he was denied entry at the port of San Francisco. He challenged the denial, and the case reached the Supreme Court. The court rejected the challenge and upheld the federal government's power over immigration and Congress's authority to pass new legislation contradictory to international treaties. The case, *Chae Chan Ping v. United States*, or the Chinese Exclusion Case, was decided on May 13, 1889 in favor of the United States.

62. Mauricio Tenorio-Trillo, *Mexico at the World's Fairs: Crafting a Modern Nation* (Berkeley: University of California Press, 1996), 17. Merle Curti argues that the United States showcased "American power and greatness to the world" at world's fairs. American participation demonstrated the expansion of American patriotism and enterprise and provided a "measuring rod for the relative status of American and European" achievement. See Merle Curti, "America at the World Fairs, 1851–1893," *American Historical Review* 55, no. 4 (1950): 833–56.

63. Annegret Fauser, *Musical Encounters at the 1889 Paris World's Fair* (Rochester, NY: University of Rochester Press, 2005), 5.

64. See Jason Gibbs, "Spoken Theater, La Scène Tonkinoise, and the First Modern Vietnamese Songs," *Asian Music* 31, no. 2 (2000): 1–33; Colin Mackerras, "Theatre in Vietnam," *Asian Theatre Journal* 4, no. 1 (1987): 1–28; Fauser, *Musical Encounters*, 183–95. This region of central Vietnam was home to people with partial or full Chinese ancestry. At the 1889 Paris Exposition, Annamite theater made a strong impression on Debussy, who wrote of it in 1901: "In the Annamite theatre they present a sort of operatic embryo, influenced by China. . . . A small, furious clarinet is in charge of emotion; a tam-tam is the organizer of terror . . . and that's all! No purpose-built theatre, no hidden orchestra. Nothing but an instinctive need for art which has found an ingenious way of satisfying itself; not a trace of bad taste." Quoted in Roger Nichols, *The Life of Debussy* (Cambridge: Cambridge University Press, 1998), 57–58.

65. The Annamite Theater earned 230,000 franc in five months, and an estimated 480,000 people attended the theater. Fauser, *Musical Encounters*, 184.

66. According to Fauser, "Reading the general press gives the impression of the journalists entering a competition as to who could write the most outrageous condemnation." *Musical Encounters*, 189.

67. "Facts and Comments," *Musical World* 69, no. 1 (June 29, 1889), 409, quoted in Fauser, *Musical Encounters*, 190–91.

68. Fauser, *Musical Encounters*, 194–95. Julien Tiersot, "Promenades musicales à l'Exposition," *Le Ménestrel* 55, no. 25 (June 23, 1889): 195–96.

69. For further discussion about the ethnographic work of Julien Tiersot and his contemporaries, see Pasler, "Sonic Anthropology in 1900."

70. Pasler, "Sonic Anthropology in 1900."

71. *Ethnology* is used as a historical term in this context; it was well established and frequently used in late-nineteenth-century America. Prominent ethnologists included Frank Hamilton Cushing, who studied the Zuni Indians of New Mexico; and Stewart Culin, who studied Chinese in America and established the Department of Ethnology at the Brooklyn Museum in 1903. The federal Bureau of Ethnology published *Contributions to North American Ethnology* between 1877 and 1893; the Boston-based *Journal of American Ethnology and Archaeology* appeared between 1891 and 1908. Usage of the term increased precipitously in 1865, but its peak in 1893 was followed by a general decline. At the end of the nineteenth century, *anthropology* emerged as a more common term, but with a somewhat different meaning. During the twentieth century, *anthropology* became the prevalent term, and the notion of ethnology evolved and took on a different scope and meaning.

72. "The Parisian Wonder" and illustrations were published in newspapers between July 8 (*Plainfield Evening News*, New Jersey) to July 25 (*Wabash North Manchester Journal*, Indiana).

73. "Chinese Actors: They Have Established a Regular Theater in New York," and "The Parisian Wonder: The Great Exposition Appears to Be a Brilliant Success," *Wichita Daily Eagle*, July 21, 1889.

74. The contemporary American ethnologist Otis T. Mason considered the Paris Exhibition "the crowning glory of anthropology." See Otis T. Mason, "Anthropology

in Paris during the Exposition of 1889," *American Anthropologist* 3, no. 1 (1890): 27–36.

75. The *Pittsburg Dispatch* reported that Tom Lee had already sent $1,555 to his agent in San Francisco for expenses. "Chinese Actors in Trouble," *Pittsburg Dispatch*, October 13, 1889. The names of the actors were Sun Mun, Mo Sang Hing, and Mow Don Sun. A Po Nge Yee dramatic company was formed in 1890 in New York. A brick building on Pell Street was turned into a theater, and by 1892 a Chinese theater was established on Doyer Street. *Springfield Republican* (Massachusetts), June 22, 1890. "New Chinese Theatre: A Company Once More to Try the Venture in New York," *Boston Herald*, March 10, 1890; and *New York Clipper*, June 14, 1890.

76. World's fairs in the United States during the nineteenth century prominently featured Chinese theater. See David Samuel Tiedemann, "Britain and the United States at the World's Fairs, 1851–1893" (PhD diss., University College London, 2019). For Chinese theater at the 1893 Chicago World's Fair, see Ngai, "Transnationalism and the Transformation of the 'Other.'" Many other fairs featured Chinese theaters, such as the California Midwinter International Exposition (San Francisco, 1894); see Barbara Berglund, *Making San Francisco American: Cultural Frontiers in the Urban West, 1846–1906* (Lawrence: University Press of Kansas, 2007); a photo of performers onstage at the fair is available at the California State Library; Tennessee Centennial and International Exposition (1897); Cotton States and International Exposition (Atlanta, 1895); Trans-Mississippi Exposition (1898); National Export Exposition (Philadelphia, 1899); and several more fairs in the twentieth century. For further studies see Krystyn R. Moon, *Yellowface*, 80–82.

77. "Local Meetings and Other Notices," *Journal of American Folklore* 4 (1891): 183.

78. Stewart Culin, *China in America: A Study in the Social Life of the Chinese in the Eastern cities of the United States* (Philadelphia: Franklin Printing Co., 1887), Brooklyn Museum, Culin Archival Collection, Subseries 12.1: Scrapbooks on Chinese America.

79. "The Chinese Theatre: To Be Visited by Boston's Literati and '400,'" *Boston Daily Adviser*, February 7, 1891. The term "Four Hundred," coined by the high-society influencer Samuel Ward McAllister, referred to a particular group of New York social elites. The society matron Caroline Astor developed a list of four hundred socially acceptable New Yorkers from wealthy families, which was published in the *New York Times*. "The Only Four Hundred," *New York Times*, February 16, 1892.

80. Robert Lee J. Vance, "Folk-Lore Study in America," *Popular Science Monthly* 43 (September 1893), 586–98.

81. "Boston's Chinese Opera Boom," *Boston Globe*, February 9, 1891.

82. "The Chinese Drama in Boston," *Milwaukee Daily Sentinel*, February 17, 1891; "Celestial Actors: Boston Society People on Harrison Ave," *Boston Daily Advertiser*, February 13, 1891; "'Seeing' a Chinese Drama. Boston Social and Literary Celebrities Have an Idea That They Were 'Impressed,'" *New York Herald*, 13, 1891; "The Latest Boston Fad Chinese Theater on Harrison Avenue Haunted by the Brahmins," *Worcester Daily Spy*, February 13, 1891; "The Chinese Play: a Boston View of its Latest Fad," *Providence Journal*, February 22, 1891; Wilmot Atherton Brownell, "A

Celestial Theatre: Dramatic Arts Exemplified by Mongolians in Boston," *Providence Journal*, March 1, 1891

83. The existing source to date cannot confirm whether "Mo li hua" actually was performed. The song was known to be one of the tunes in musical boxes produced by a Swiss maker and would later be made famous in Puccini's *Turandot* (post., 1926). See W. Anthony Sheppard, "Puccini and the Music Boxes," *Journal of the Royal Musical Association* 140, no. 1 (2015): 41–92.

84. Lee Meriwether, *The Tramp at Home* (New York: Harper & Brothers, 1889), 188–91. Two airs were transcribed by a spectator whom Meriwether ran into: Maurice Arnold, an African American composer and a student of Antonín Dvořák. The music was a simple pentatonic melody in strophic form with unadorned piano accompaniment. It was a transcription of a performance by "Mr. Fong Fang on an instrument not unlike a zither." According to the report, San Francisco still had two Chinese theaters; the Grand Theatre was then named Po Wah Ying. Yuen Sing was the manger of the theater and also a female impersonator with an annual salary of six thousand dollars.

85. Pasler, "Sonic Anthropology in 1900," 10.

86. "Second Annual Meeting of the American Folk-Lore Society," *Journal of American Folklore* 4, no. 12 (1891): 1–12.

87. "Love of Lore. First Among Bostonians See the Play," *Boston Daily Globe*, February 13, 1891.

88. "The Chinese Theatre." Alger noted: "Americans who think the Chinese cannot act labor under a great mistake. To my mind the acting of this company will compare very favorably with most of that to which we are accustomed upon our own stage."

89. *Buffalo Courier*, March 1, 1891.

90. Furthermore, McDowell was a part of the Boston elite circle. Several figures attending the American Folk-Lore Society event were also closely connected to the initiatives of the American Theatre of Arts And Letters; Oliver Wendell Holmes accepted McDowell's invitation to become an honorary member in 1893, and William Dean Howells was anticipated to complete a play for it. "The Theatre of Arts and Letters," *Review of Reviews*, January 1893, 664.

91. The earliest known notice of a Chinese theater in Portland, Oregon is from 1880 (*New York Herald Tribune*, September 2, 1880) and in Los Angeles from 1884 ("A Chinese Theatre," *Los Angeles Times*, October 21, 1884).

92. "Catering to Chinese," *Pittsburgh Press*, October 29, 1890.

93. Seligman, *The First Chinese American*, 221.

94. Chu Fong was in the news often for various deals and for his noteworthy wedding. He was a member of the Wah Lung Import Company at 33 Mott Street. The theater on Doyer Street opened with thirty actors in March 1893. "Got a Good Start Last Night: The Play at the New Chinese Theater Will Last a Week," *New York Times*, March 25, 1893. Wong Chin Foo, however, wrote a long piece with four illustrations to introduce the play *Moy Leon Yuk*. See Wong Chin Foo, "Dramatic Art in Doyer's Street: Wong Chin Foo describes the Play now going on at the Chinese Theatre," *New York Herald*, April 1, 1993. An extensive discussion about Chu Fong can be found in Beck, *New York's Chinatown*, 262–66; and Mary Ting Yi Lui, *The*

Chinatown Trunk Mystery: Murder, Miscegenation, and Other Dangerous Encounters in Turn-of-the-Century New York City (Princeton, NJ: Princeton University Press, 2005), 35–37.

95. "Chinatown's New Theatre: Opens with the Drama of 'Look Quook; or, the Six Kings,'" *The World*, March 26, 1893. The opening of the new theater in New York might be related to the Chinese theater at the World's Columbian Exposition in Chicago, which opened around the same time. The details of this connection await further exploration.

96. The daily performances at the Chinese theater on Doyer Street were deemed in violation of the Sunday law, which forbade some or all activities on certain days, usually Sundays. Noting the theater's name, Po Yun Hen, the *Journal* reported that Chu Fong was arrested and failed to convince the authorities that the Sunday performance was sacred. "Divergent View of a Chinese Play," *Journal* (New York), March 20, 1896; "Chu Fong and His Play," *New York Times*, March 20, 1896.

97. Wong Chin Foo, "Dramatic Art in Doyers Street," *New York Herald*, April 16, 1893.

Epilogue

1. Hing Kig Chung: first mentioned in Ah Quin's diary on May 31, 1880 (also appeared as Hing Gag Tung, or H. G. T.); Dan San Feng: first mentioned on October 2, 1880.

2. Ah Quin, diary, February 9, 1880. Chinese New Year was February 10 in 1880.

3. "Chinese Actors The Manner of Their Performance and That They Enact," *San Francisco Examiner*, November, 19, 1882; "A Walking Junk," *San Francisco Examiner*, December 4, 1882.

4. Craig Jennex, "Diva Worship and the Sonic Search for Queer Utopia," in *Fan Identities and Practices in Context Dedicated to Music*, ed. by Mark Duffett (New York: Routlege, 2016), 45–61.

5. Ah Quin, diary, August 20, 1880. For a discussion of Ah Quin's religious activities, see Chen, *Chinese San Francisco*, 77–79.

6. The term "porous socialization" is borrowed from Jacek Blaszkiewicz, *Fanfare for a City Music and the Urban Imagination in Haussmann's Paris* (Berkeley: California University Press, 2023). Blaszkiewicz uses this term to describe the café culture of nineteenth-century Paris, in contrast to the more regulated theater spaces with boxes, stairs, and so on.

7. Ah Quin, diary, June 3, 1880.

8. The summary here is based on a synopsis printed on a Le Wan Nian theater playbill in San Francisco, July 30, 1923 (Him Mark Lai Collection, Ethnic Library, University of California, Berkeley). The basic plotline can have many variations, and this summary is different from that of the 1950s.

9. Li-Ming Luo, 羅澧銘, "新春佳節應時戲曲談 [Discussion on seasonal operas during the Spring Festival]," in 顧曲談 [On appreciating music], ed. by Zhu Shaozhang, 朱少璋 (Hong Kong: Joint Publishing Co., 2020), 19. This book also includes a full-length synopsis of *The Golden-leaved Chrysanthemum*.

10. For example, in addition to letter writing, Ah Quin has several notes about sending money to his mother: twenty dollars on October 2, 1879, ten dollars on January 13, 1880, and a five-dollar gold coin on May 15, 1880.

11. Du Jun Min, "The Development of Chinese Records to 1911," *Antique Phonograph News*, January-February 2008, https://www.capsnews.org/apn2008-1 .htm; Du Jun Min, "The Development of Chinese Records from the Qing Dynasty to 1918," *Antique Phonograph News*, January–February 2009, https://www .capsnews.org/apn2009-1.htm; *Encyclopedic Discography of Victor Recordings. Pre-Matrix Series [1900–37]*, comp. Ted Fagan and William R. Moran (Westport, CT: Greenwood Press, 1983). *The Golden-leaved Chrysanthemum* was recorded on twelve disks (nos. A-1874 to A-1885). I am indebted to Du Jun Min for his generosity in sharing his collection of four of these disks. The records of this title were available in San Francisco's Chinatown as shown in an advertisement for Shin Shung & Company in *Chung Sai Yat Bo* (San Francisco) 中西日報, June 5, 1903. Many thanks to Sai Shing Yung for help on information regarding this recording.

12. The series was so popular that many of these discs were reissued later on Victor's "Good Listening" label. *Golden-Leaved Chrysanthemum* (see fig. E.2) was such a reissue. This was an important trend. In 1903 the Edison Phonograph Company also recorded Chinese titles in California. The company sent its engineer and its best equipment from the factory in Orange, New Jersey, to California to make the recordings. Edison released nineteen Chinese titles on its Gold Moulded sublabel. A total of forty-six hard-wax cylinder records of these nineteen Chinese titles were released. To promote the records, Edison added a bilingual brochure in its catalogue of Records of Foreign Selections.

13. Unknown artists, "*Golden-leaved Chrysanthemum*," recorded 1902, 7218 H, 8th disc (part 8 of the performance), Victor Monarch Record, uploaded by Daniel Melvin, April 15, 2023. https://www.youtube.com/watch?v=dEjNf30J5FY&t=16s. A commenter notes that the number 1881 was crossed out and the number 7218 added.

14. The notion of sonic materiality discussed here draws from Dugal McKinnon, "Materiality: The Fabrication of Sound," in *Oxford Handbook of Sound Art*, ed. Jane Grant, John Matthias, and David Prior (New York: Oxford University Press, 2021), 273–286.

15. Pfaelzer, *Driven Out*.

16. For example, Chinese and Asian music are absent in Gilbert Chase's *America's Music: From the Pilgrims to the Present* (New York: McGraw-Hill, 1955; 3rd ed.: Urbana: University of Illinois Press, 1992). In a 2001 discussion of the absence of non-European ethnic traditions in US music history books by three authors (Charles Hamm, H. Wiley Hitchcock, and Chase), Richard Crawford concluded with equivocation: "The place of ethnic musical traditions in the United States remains uncertain." Richard Crawford, *America's Musical Life: A History* (New York: Norton, 2001), 782–84.

17. Nina Sun Eidsheim, *The Race of Sound: Listening, Timbre, and Vocality in African American Music* (Durham, NC: Duke University Press, 2019), 12, 21, 50.

18. This was not unique, of course. As early as 1852, Hector Berlioz responded to Chinese music by treating its vocal timbre as inhuman noise: "Imagine a series

of nasal, guttural, moaning, hideous tones, which I may without too great exaggeration compare to the sounds a dog makes after it stretches its limbs and yawns." Hector Berlioz, *Evenings with the Orchestra*, trans. and ed. Jacques Barzun (New York: Alfred A. Knopf, 1956), 247–48.

19. William B. Given, quoted in *Lancaster Intelligence*, "Scene in Chinatown," July 18, 1888. I have decided to refrain from giving complete quotes of these racist accounts so as to not give them more social currency.

20. For a discussion of the size of the theater, see *Daily National Democrat*, June 25, 1861; for the report, see *San Francisco Chronicle*, September 25, 1869. The troupe's name, Lung Quong Toy Company, appeared in an advertisement in *Daily Alta California*, September 23, 1869.

21. *San Francisco Chronicle*, September 25, 1869. The news item was syndicated in fifteen papers in Britain and sixteen in the United States. Its last appearance was in the *Vermont Journal*, September 20, 1873.

22. "Chinese Theatricals," *Marshall County Republican* (Plymouth, Indiana), August 5, 1869. This was Hing Chuen Yuan (aka Yu Henn Choy), the first of four prominent Chinese theaters built in San Francisco in the 1860s and 1870s (see also n. 23). Its opening in January 1868 was celebrated with festivities that included addresses by invited luminaries from judges to a police chief.

23. *Encyclopaedia Britannica; or, Dictionary of Arts, Sciences, and General Literature*, 7th ed., 19, no. 1 (Edinburgh: Adam and Charles Black, 1842), 239.

24. Eidsheim, *The Race of Sound*, 25.

25. Saidiya Hartman, *Lose Your Mother: A Journey along the Atlantic Slave Route* (New York: Farrar, Straus and Giroux, 2007), 31, quoted in Ketu H. Katrak, "'Stripping Women of Their Wombs': Active Witnessing of Performances of Violence," *Theatre Research International* 39, no. 1 (2014): 31–46.

26. Katherine McKittrick, *Dear Science and Other Stories* (Durham, NC: Duke University Press, 2021), 105.

27. "A Theater Not Often Noticed," *Sacramento Daily Union*, February 16, 1880.

28. "Chinese Theater Closed," *Sacramento Daily Union*, June 21, 1880.

29. "Trial of the Chinese Theater Cases," *Sacramento Daily Union*, July 2, 1880.

30. "Chinese Theater Case," *Sacramento Daily Union*, August 5, 1880.

31. "Chinese Theater Case."

32. Eidsheim, *The Race of Sound*, 26.

33. "Chinese Theater Case."

34. San Francisco Ordinance Order No. 884; *San Francisco Chronicle*, August 21, 1870 (see fig. 4.9).

35. In Portland, a Chinese theater was built in 1879 at 87 Second Street. It was frequently under attack for its hours and sound. When in 1881, the city council passed an ordinance prohibiting operation after midnight, the Chinese community protested. In the end, the Chinese "agreed to limit the number of musical instruments that lasted past midnight." According to Wong, by 1890 there were three Chinese theaters all on Second Street. See Marie Rose Wong, *Sweet Cakes, Long Journey: The Chinatowns of Portland, Oregon* (Seattle: Washington University Press, 2004), 223–24, 306.

36. *The Oriental*, May 13, 1876.

37. The Chinese theater in Sacramento not only reopened in October of the same year but also placed a prominent advertisement in the *Sacramento Daily Union*, boasting, "Chinese Theater will open Saturday, October 8th, and will continue until further notice, by an entire new company." *Sacramento Daily Union*, October 9–16, 1880.

38. 堯天彩戲班 was the name of several prominent Cantonese opera troupes in both the nineteenth century and the early twentieth century. It can be translated literally as "color of the time of national peace and prosperity during the Emperor Yao era," or more figuratively as "luminous and prosperous time."

39. Stoler, *Along the Archival Grain*, 34.

40. The continuing absence of Chinese opera theater in US music history textbooks speaks volumes. But the listening practice also manifested itself in other ways. For example, negative portrayals can have concrete and direct psychological effects. See Rao, *Chinatown Opera Theater in North America*, 8–9.

41. Michel de Certeau, *The Writing of History*, trans. Tom Cloney (New York: Columbia University Press, 1988), 75.

42. Eidsheim, *The Race of Sound*, 182.

43. Saidiya Hartman, "Venus in Two Acts," *Small Axe* 12, no. 2 (2008): 2–3.

44. Stoever, *The Sonic Color Line*.

45. For example, pages of quotes and paraphrases of mockery of Chinese music without critical analysis appeared often in discussions of Chinese theater in North America. It gives them weight and may have unintended effects.

46. Nina Eidsheim and Daniel Walden, "No Conclusions: Response to Symposium, August 16, 2021," *Kalfou: A Journal of Comparative and Relational Ethnic Studies* 9, no. 2 (2022): 357–58.

47. Andrea Bachner, *The Mark of Theory: Inscriptive Figures, Poststructuralist Prehistories* (New York: Fordham University, 2018), 4.

48. This verse was written by the Song dynasty poet Su Shi, "Former Ode on the Red Cliffs" (1082).

49. This expression is borrowed from Tom Gunning, "Foreword: The Same Old Tune, but with a Different Meaning," in Berthold Hoeckner, *Film, Music, Memory* (Chicago: University of Chicago Press, 2019), viii.

50. The 1880 US Census is quoted in Mina Yang, *California Polyphony: Ethnic Voices, Musical Crossroads* (Urbana: University of Illinois Press, 2008), 14. According to Yang, Japanese immigrants also saw themselves as racially compatible with white Americans and as superior to the Chinese. Whereas nearly three decades of anti-Chinese campaigns culminated in the Chinese Exclusion Act in 1882, the Japanese in San Francisco endured their first organized anti-Japanese campaign in 1892. For the anti-Japanese campaign see Eiichiro Azuma, "Japanese Immigrant Settler Colonialism in the U.S.-Mexican Borderlands and the U.S. Racial-Imperialist Politics of the Hemispheric 'Yellow Peril,'" *Pacific Historical Review* 83, no. 2 (2014): 259.

51. Elizabeth Sinn, "Pacific Ocean: Highway to Gold Mountain, 1850–1900," *Pacific Historical Review* 83, no. 2 (2014): 221.

52. Sinn, "Pacific Ocean."

53. The invitation was extended by Lisa Cooper Vest, associate professor of musicology, University Southern California. The class was a graduate seminar about nation/national identities/nationalisms. The students were assigned several of my articles to read, including the then newly published article that constitutes part of this epilogue, "Listening Practice and History: Sound, Erasure," Symposium on the Race of Sound by Nina Sun Eidsheim, *Kalfou: A Journal of Comparative and Relational Ethnic Studies* 8, no. 2: 307–17.

54. See Rao, *Chinatown Opera Theater*.

55. Hua Hsu, *A Floating Chinaman: Fantasy and Failure across the Pacific* (Cambridge, MA: Harvard University Press, 2016), 13.

56. Deborah Wong, *Speak It Louder: Asian Americans Making Music* (New York: Routledge, 2004); Deborah Wong, *Louder and Faster: Pain, Joy, and the Body Politic in Asian American Taiko* (Berkeley: University of California, 2019); Oliver Wong, *Legions of Boom: Filipino American Mobile Disc Jockey Crews in the San Francisco Bay Area* (Durham, NC: Duke University Press, 2015); Su Zheng, *Claiming Diaspora: Music, Transnationalism, and Cultural Politics in Asian/Chinese America* (New York: Oxford University Press, 2010); Kevin Fellezs, *Listen But Don't Ask Question: Hawaiian Slack Key Guitar Across the TransPacific* (Durham, NC: Duke University Press, 2019); Mari Yoshihara, *Musicians from a Different Shore: Asians and Asian Americans in Classical Music* (Philadelphia: Temple University Press, 2008); Grace Wang, *Soundtracks of Asian America: Navigating Race through Musical Performance* (Durham, NC: Duke University Press, 2015); Krystyn Moon, *Yellowface: Creating the Chinese in American Popular Music and Performance, 1850s-1920s* (New Brunswick, NJ: Rutgers University Press, 2004); Tamara Roberts, *Resounding Afro Asia: Interracial Music and the Politics of Collaboration* (New York: Oxford University Press, 2016). For a fuller bibliography, see "Asian American Music," *New Grove Dictionary of American Music*, 2nd ed., ed. Charles Garrett (New York: Oxford University Press, 2013), 1:220–32.

57. Lisa Lowe, *Immigrant Acts: On Asian American Cultural Politics.* (Durham, NC: Duke University Press, 1996), 35.

58. Marci Kwon, introduction to "Asian American Art, Pasts and Futures," *Panorama: Journal of the Association of Historians of American Art* 7, no. 1 (2021), https://doi.org/10.24926/24716839.11446.

Appendix B

1. This appendix aims to provide essential information about the genre in its nineteenth-century style and is a much-condensed version of chapters 4 and 5 of my book *Chinatown Opera Theater in North America*. More information can be found in those two chapters.

2. For a fuller discussion in English of the stylistic characteristics, see Bell Yung, *Cantonese Opera: Performance as Creative Process* (Cambridge: Cambridge University Press, 1989).

3. Sau-yan Chan, "Cantonese Opera," in the *Routledge Encyclopedia of Traditional Chinese Culture*, ed. Sin-wai Chan (New York: Routledge, 2019), 169–85, esp. 171–72.

Glossary

Personal Names, Company Names, and Other Terms

Ah Fong Studio	華芳照相館
Ah Fook Wing	(不詳戲院經理名)
Ah Quin (Tom Chong-kwan; Tan Cong-kun)	譚聰坤
Ah Sue	新蘇
Ah Wang	(不詳戲院經理名)
Ah Wung Sing	(不詳演員名)
Bengya Qi	崩牙啟
Chen Lanbin	陳蘭彬
Chen Shutang	陳樹棠
Cheong Kam Tong	張錦棠
Chy Lung & Co.	濟隆盛號
daai hei	大戲
Dajia Bing	大家炳
Dezai	德仔
Di Ca Sing (Dajia Sheng, see also Ti Gar Sing)	大家勝
Du Fengzhi	杜風治
erxian	二弦
Fok Yam Tang (the Chinese gospel house)	福音堂
Guangxu	光緒
Guifang	桂芳
gwongfu daai hei	廣府大戲
Ho King	(不詳演員名)
Hong Gee Cheong	(不詳演員名)
Huiguan	會館
huqin	胡琴
Jinshan zhonghua huiguan (Chinese Association of San Francisco)	金山中華會館
Jiqing Gongsuo	吉慶公所

Journey to the West	西遊記
Kun tune	昆曲
Lai Fong	黎芳
Lam Yap Ca (Lin Yuejiao)	林月嬌
Lee Kan	李根
Leung Chuck	靚卓
Li Po Tai	黎普泰
loh gu hei	鑼鼓戲
Mai Xiaoxia	麥嘯霞
Menghua Suobu	夢華瑣簿
Moo Sung Jee	(不詳演員名)
Mung Qua Choy	(不詳演員名)
Norman Assing (Yuan Sheng)	袁生
108 Outlaws at Mount Liang	水滸傳
Pang Nga Su	崩牙蘇
pipa	琵琶
Sam Yap (Sam Yup; Sanyi)	三邑
San Francisco China News	舊金山唐人新聞紙
sanxian	三弦
shagu	沙鼓
Shangbian Ban ("upper troupe")	上邊班
Shegong Rong	蛇公榮
Shengjia Luo	聲架羅
Shuishe Rong	水蛇容
Story of Three Kingdoms	三國演義
Su Qin	蘇秦
Sze Yap (Siyi; Si Yup)	四邑
Tak-A-Wing	(不詳演員名)
Tan Cong-kun	譚聰坤
Tan Qianchu	譚乾初
Tang Xianzu	湯顯祖
Tangfan Gongbao (*The Oriental*)	唐番公報
Tanyuan Riji (*Diary of Tan Garden*)	坦園日記
The Sam Yup Association	三邑會館
The Sze Yup Association	四邑會館
The Young Wo Association (Yanghe)	陽和會館
Ti Gar Sing (Dajia Sheng)	大家勝
tien sok	弦索
Tong A-chick (Tong Achick)	唐亞植, 唐廷桂
Wang Xiqi	王錫祺
Wing Wo Sang & Co	永和生號
Wong Chin Foo	王清福
Xi	戲
Xiabian Ban ("lower troupe")	下邊班
Xinbiao	新標
Xinhua	新華

Xiqu	戲曲
Yaduo	亞鐸
Yang Enshou	楊恩壽
Yang Mengjian	楊懋建
Yang Tse Kiang (Yangtze River)	揚子江
yangqin	揚琴
Yeng Pway Ngon	英培安
Yiyang tune	弋陽腔
yot kom	月琴
Yu Xunqing	俞洵慶
Zhajiao Wen	札腳文
Zhang Yanlin	張彥麟
Zhongshan dialect	中山音
Zhongzhou dialect	中州音

Opera Titles and Song Titles

Che Young Kwong Builds a Ship That Sails on Land	徐文廣陸地行舟
Eight Genii (Birthday Greetings from Eight Immortals)	八仙賀壽
Feng Siang	封相
Joint Investiture of a Prime Minister of Six Warlords (Six Kings)	六國封相
Kin Yip Oak (Golden-leaved Chrysanthemum)	金葉菊
Look Quok	六國
Mo Li Hua	茉莉花
Parting at Park-Kew (Farewell at Ba Bridge of Guan Gong and Cao Cao)	灞橋送別
Pinggui Returning Home (The Return of Sit Ping Quai)	平貴回窰
Pu Kang (The Mender of Cracked Chinaware)	補缸
Rising of the Lions, or Looking at the Pictures	舉獅觀圖
Royal Slave, Shee Long Tan Mo	四郎探母
Sam Kwok	三國
Shatuo Jiebing (Borrowing Soldiers: The Great Rebellion)	沙陀借兵
Sung Kong: The Robber Chief of the Laong Hills	宋江殺惜
Wenji Returning to Han	文姬歸漢
Yalan Sells a Pig (Yalan Trades Pigs; The Dim Pig-Seller; Sam Wang and the Pigs)	亞蘭賣豬

Theater and Troupe Names

Ak Ling Tong	(不詳戲班名)
Dan Shan Feng (Dan San Feng)	丹山鳳
Donn Quai Yuen (Donn Qui Yuen; Dan Gui Yuan; Dan Gun Theater)	丹桂院
Gao Tian Cai	高天彩
Gee Quuen Yung (Gee Quon Yung)	義群英

Hing Chuen Yuen (Hing Ching Yuen; Hing Chung Yuen)　興全源
Hing Gag Tung　慶吉祥
Hong Ting Yuen　(不詳戲班名)
Look Sun Fung (Look Sung Fung; Luck Shun Fun;
　　Look Sun Foong; Luk Suhn Fung)　祿新鳳
Lung Quong Toy　(不詳戲班名)
Po Fung Nin (Bo Fung Lin; Pu Fengnian)　普豐年
Po Nge Yee　(不詳戲班名)
Poo Hing Hee Yung (Yung Kee)　普興戲院 (榮記)
Quan Sun Yoke (Quan Sun Yok; Quon San Yok;
　　Kun Shanyu)　崑山玉
Que Hing Log (See also Yew Hin Look)　(possible 堯天樂)
Quon Soon Tong　(不詳戲班名)
San Nang Foo　(不詳戲班名)
San San Fong　(不詳戲班名)
Sheng Ping Theater　昇平戲院 (香港)
Sing Ping Yuen (Shang Ping Theater)　昇平院
Sing Song Fung　(不詳戲班名)
Swentien Lok (Song Ting Lok; Shun T'In Lok;
　　Shun Ting Lok; Shuntian Le)　順天樂
Tong Hook Tong (Hong Fook Tong; Hook Took Tong;
　　Hong Took Tong; Hook Tong Hook; Tung Hook Tong;
　　Tung Hong Took; Hook Took Tong; Tong Hong Tock;
　　Tong Kong Tong; Tong Hook Tung)　同福堂, 鴻福堂
Wing Tie Ping　詠太平
Yew Hin Look (Yu Henn Lok; Yao Tienle)　堯天樂
Yu Henn Choy (Yao Tian Cai)　堯天彩
Yu Sing Ping　(不詳戲班名)

Bibliography

Primary Sources

COLLECTIONS

Ah Quin Diary Collection, San Diego History Center, San Diego
American Antiquarian Society
Ancestry.com
Brooklyn Museum Archive
California Digital Newspaper Collection, University of California, Riverside
California Historical Society, San Francisco
Cornell Library, Special Collection
HathiTrust
Him Mark Lai Collection, Ethnic Library, University of California, Berkeley
Huntington Library, San Marino, CA
Illinois Digital Newspaper Collection
Chronicling America: Historic American Newspapers, Library of Congress
Library of Congress, National Jukebox: http://www.loc.gov/jukebox/
Library of Congress, Photograph Collection
New York City Municipal Archives
ProQuest Historical Newspapers
San Francisco City Directories Online
United States Federal Censuses
University of California, Berkeley, Bancroft Library
University of California, Los Angeles, Ethnomusicology Archive
University of California, Santa Barbara, Discography of American Historical Recordings
Wisconsin Historical Society

CHINESE NEWSPAPERS

The Oriental (Tang Fan Gong Bao) 唐番公報
The Oriental (Tung-Ngai San-Luk) 東涯新錄

San Francisco China News 舊金山唐人新聞紙
Chinese Serial 遐邇貫珍
The Review of the Times 萬國公報

ARTICLES AND BOOKS

"Altamonte," "Celestial Entertainment." *Chicago Tribune*, October 15, 1867, Chronicling America: History American Newspapers, Library of Congress.

Annals of the Bohemian Club, Volume 1, 1872–1880. San Francisco: Bohemian Club, 1900.

Assing, Norman. "To His Excellency Governor Bigler." *Daily Alta California*, May 5, 1852.

Beck, Louis J. *New York's Chinatown: An Historical Presentation of its People and Places*. New York: Bohemia Publishing Company, 1898.

Becker, Joseph. "'The Coming Man,' A Splendid Supplementary Picture of the Interior of the Great Chinese Theatre in San Francisco." *Frank Leslie's Illustrated Newspaper*, May 7, 1870.

——. "Entrance to Chinese Theatre, San Francisco." White gouache and graphite on toned paper, 9 in. × 6.5 in. Becker Collection, Boston College Libraries, https://beckercollection.bc.edu/items/show/1965.

Berlioz, Hector. *Evenings with the Orchestra*. Translated and edited by Jacques Barzun. New York: Alfred A. Knopf, 1956.

The Bohemian Club: Certificate of Incorporation, Constitution, Bylaws and Rules, Officers, Committees and Members. San Francisco: Bohemian Club, 1939.

Borthwick, John David. *Three Years in California*. Edinburgh: W. Blackwood and Sons, 1857.

Brewer, William H. *Up and Down California in 1860–1864: The Journal of William H. Brewer*, edited by Francis P. Farquhar. New Haven: Yale University Press, 1930.

California Senate Journal, 3rd session, 1852. San Francisco: G. Fitch & Co. and V. E. Geiger & Co., 1852.

Catalogue of the Fifty-fifth Annual Exhibition, Pennsylvania Academy of the Fine Arts. Philadelphia, 1884, https://babel.hathitrust.org/cgi/pt?id=uc1.a0011289279&seq=5.

"Celebration of the Anniversary of Our National Independence." *Daily Alta California*, July 10, 1852.

Chen Lanbin 陳蘭彬. 使美紀略 [Brief record of a mission to America]. In 小方壺齋輿地叢鈔十二帙 [Collected books on geography from the Xiaofanghu Studio], edited by Wang Xiqi 王錫祺. Hangzhou: Hangzhou Guji Shudian, 1891.

"Chinese Actors: The Manner of Their Performance and That They Enact." *Daily Examiner*, November, 19, 1882.

"Chinese Theater." *California Farmer and Journal of Useful Sciences*, August 10, 1855.

"Chinese Theatricals." *Daily National Gazette* (Grass Valley), January 7, 1860.

Chinese-Language Business Directory and Lunar Calendar for 1905. San Francisco: Horn Hong & Co., 1905. Collected in W. H. Webber Chinese exclusion notebook, 1883–1916, mssHM 84094. Huntington Library, San Marino, CA.

Cooke & Le Count, lithographers, *Celebration of the 4th, July, in San Francisco, Cal.*, ca. 1852, Special Collections, Bancroft Library, University of California, Berkeley, http://www.oac.cdlib.org/ark:/13030/hb18700149/?brand=oac4.

Culin, Stewart. *China in America: A Study in the Social Life of the Chinese in the Eastern Cities of the United States*. Philadelphia: Franklin Printing Co., 1887. Brooklyn Museum, Culin Archival Collection, Subseries 12.1: Scrapbooks on Chinese America.

Cushing, Frank Hamilton. "My Adventures in Zuñi." *Century Illustrated Magazine* 25, no. 2 (December 1882), 191–207; and 25, no. 4 (February 1883), 500–11.

Davis, Winfield. *History of Political Conventions in California, 1849–1892*. Sacramento: California State Library, 1893.

Directory of Chinese Business Houses: San Francisco, Sacramento, Marysville, Portland, Stockton, San Jose, Virginia City, Nev. San Francisco: Wells Fargo and Co., 1878. Digital copy available at Wells Fargo Archives (along with 1882 edition), https://history.wf.com/assets/pdf/publications/WFCA-1878-Chinese-Business-Directory.pdf.

Disturnell, William C. *Strangers' Guide to San Francisco and Vicinity*. San Francisco: W. C. Disturnell, 1883.

Elite Directory for San Francisco and Oakland. San Francisco: Argonaut Publishing Company, 1879.

Encyclopaedia Britannica; or, Dictionary of Arts, Sciences, and General Literature, 7th ed., 19, no. 1. Edinburgh: Adam and Charles Black, 1842.

Estavan, Lawrence, ed. *Theatre Buildings*. San Francisco Theatre Research 15, part 1. San Francisco: Work Projects Administration, Northern California, 1940.

"An Evening at the Chinese Theatre," *Daily Evening Bulletin*, March 5, 1860.

Fales, William E. S. "The Chinese Mimes." *Harper's Weekly* 30, no. 1679 (June 29, 1889), 528.

——. "The Chinese Play." *Harper's Bazaar* 22, no. 30 (July 27, 1889), 543.

Fiske, Harrison Grey, ed. *New York Mirror Annual and Directory of the Theatrical Profession for 1888*. New York: New York Mirror, 1888.

Fitch, George H. "In a Chinese Theater." *Century Illustrated Magazine* 114, no. 2 (June 1882), 189–92.

——. "A Night in Chinatown." *Cosmopolitan* 2 (February 1887), 349–58.

Fletcher, Robert Hoew, ed. *The Annals of the Bohemian Club: Comprising Text and Pictures Furnished by Its Own Members*, 2 (1880–1887). San Francisco: Bohemian Club, 1939.

Foo and Wing Herb Company. *The Science of Oriental Medicine: A Concise Discussion of Its Principles and Methods, Biographical Sketches of Its Leading Practitioners, and Its Treatment of Various Prevalent Diseases, Useful Information on Matters of Diet, Exercise, and Hygiene*. Los Angeles: G. Rice and Sons, 1897.

Frenzeny, Paul. *Chinatown Sketches: An Artist's Fascination with San Francisco's Chinese Quarter, 1874–1882*. San Francisco: Book Club of California, 2013.

——. "Chinese Theaters in San Francisco." *Harper's Weekly*, 27, no. 1377 (May 12, 1883), 296–97.

Green, E. M. "The Chinese Theater." *Overland Monthly and Out West Magazine*, February 1903, 7–9.

Hab Wa and Tong K. Achick [*sic*]. "Letter of the Chinamen to His Excellency, Governor Bigler." *San Francisco Herald*, April 29, 1852; *Daily Alta California*, April 30, 1852.

Hailey, Gene, ed. "Theodore Wores." In California Art Research Project WPA Project 2874, 10, 91–153, https://digitalassets.lib.berkeley.edu/cara/ucb/text/Cara_Volume_10.pdf.

Hardy, Iza Duffus. *Between Two Oceans; or, Sketches of American Travel*. London: Hurst and Blackett, 1884.

Harvard College, Class of 1877, Seventh Report, June 1917. Norwood, MA.: Plimpton Press, 1917.

Harvard College, Class of 1878, Fiftieth Anniversary Report, 1878–1928. Cambridge, MA: Riverside Press, 1928.

Harvard College, Class of 1878, Secretary's Report, No. VI, 1908. Cambridge, MA: Riverside Press, 1908.

Hauser, Miska. *The Letters of Miska Hauser, 1853*. Translated by Eric Benson, Donald Peel Cobb, and Horatio F. Stoll, Jr. History of Music Project 3. San Francisco: Works Progress Administration, Northern California, 1939.

Hunter, William C. "Remarks on the Chinese Theatre; with a Translation of a Farce, Entitled 'The Mender of Cracked Chinaware.'" *Chinese Repository* 6 (1838), 575–79.

Inkersley, Arthur. "The Chinese Drama in California." *London Strand Magazine* 15 (April 1898), 402–9.

Irwin, Will. "The Drama in Chinatown." E*verybody's Magazine*, 20, no. 6 (1909), 857–69.

Jackson, Helen Hunt. *Bits of Travel at Home*. Boston: Roberts Brothers, 1878.

"John Chinaman in San Francisco." *Scribner's Monthly*, 12, no. 6 (October 1876), 862–72.

Knox, Thomas W. "The Coming Man," *Frank Leslie's Illustrated Newspaper,* May 7, 1870, 121–22.

Lamplugh, G. W. "In a Chinese Theatre." *Macmillan's Magazine* 57 (November 1887), 36–40.

Langley's San Francisco Directory. San Francisco: Francis, Valentine & Co., 1858–99.

Leslie, Frank, Mrs. (Miriam). *California: A Pleasure Trip from Gotham to the Golden Gate, April, May, June 1877*. New York: G. W. Carleton & Co. Publishers, 1877.

Lloyd, Benjamin E. *Lights and Shades in San Francisco*. San Francisco: A. L. Bancroft, 1876.

MacGowan, D. J. "Chinese Guilds, or Chambers of Commerce and Trade Unions." *Journal of North-China Branch of the Royal Asiatic Society* 21 (1886): 133–61.

Manning, Samuel. *American Pictures, Drawn with Pen and Pencil*. London: Religious Tract Society, 1875–76.

Marryat, Frank. *Mountains and Molehills; Or, Recollections of a Burnt Journal*. New York: Harper & Brothers, 1855.

Marshall, Walter Gore. *Through America; Or, Nine Months in the United States*. London: Sampson Low, Marston, Searle & Rivington, 1882.

Mason, Otis T. "Anthropology in Paris during the Exposition of 1889." *American Anthropologist* 3, no. 1 (1890): 27–36.

Masters, Frederic J. "Among the Highbinders—An Account of Chinese Secret Societies." *Californian* 3 (1892), 314–25.

——. "The Chinese Drama." *Chautauquan* 21, no. 4 (July 1895): 434–42.

——. "Pagan Temples in San Francisco." *Californian* 2, no. 6 (November 1892), 227–41.

——. "The Recent Disturbance in China." *Californian* 1, no. 2 (January 1892), 62–74.

McDowell, Henry Burden. "The Chinese Theater." *Century Illustrated Monthly Magazine* (November 1884), 27–44.

——. "A New Light on the Chinese." *Harper's New Monthly Magazine* 86 (December 1892), 1–17 (with illustrations by Theodore Wores et al.).

Mcgowan, Kenneth. "Little Theatre Backgrounds." *Theatre Arts Monthly* 8 (September 1924): 579–96.

Meriwether, Lee. *The Tramp at Home*. New York: Harper & Brothers, 1889.

Mitchell, Louise D. "A Pencil Sketch of San Francisco." *Christian Work and Envagelist* 80, no. 2046 (May 5, 1906), 597–99.

Ng Poon Chew. "The Treatment of Exempted Classes of the Chinese in the U.S. (1908)." In *Chinese American Voices: From the Gold Rush to the Present*, edited by Judy Yung, Gordon H. Chang, and H. Mark Lai, 111–12. Berkeley: University of California Press, 2006.

Ogden, Henry Alexander, and Walter Yeager. "Character Sketches in San Francisco: An Evening in the Chinese Quarter." *Frank Leslie's Illustrated Newspaper*, August 24, 1878, 421–22.

Pacific Bank Handbook of California. San Francisco: The Bank, 1888.

Porter, Thomas Cunningham. *Impressions of America*. London: C. A. Pearson, 1899.

Richardson, Albert D. *Beyond the Mississippi: From the Great River to the Great Ocean; Life and Adventure on the Prairies, Mountains, and Pacific Coast*. Hartford, CT: American Publishing Company, 1867.

Rusling, James F. *Across America: Or, the Great West and the Pacific Coast*. New York: Sheldon & Company, 1874.

Sala, George Augustus. *America Revisited: From the Bay of New York to the Gulf of Mexico, and from Lake Michigan to the Pacific*. London: Vizetelly & Co., 1882.

Scott, Stanley. "The Chinese Drama in San Francisco." *English Illustrated Magazine*, February 1905, 483–88.

Sirr, Henry Charles. *China and the Chinese*. London: W. S. Orr & Company, 1849.

"The Six Emperors: A Grand Display of Oriental Magnificence, A New Play and New Wardrobe." *San Francisco Examiner*, January 8, 1883.

Sixtieth Annual Report of the Missionary Society of the Methodist Episcopal Church for the Year 1878. New York: Missionary Society, January 1879.

Speer, William. "Mission to the Chinese in California: Journal of William Speer." In *Home and Foreign Record of the Presbyterian Church in the United States of America*, 4 (1853), 212–15.

Supplement to the Codes and Statutes of California. Edited by Theodore Henry Hittell. 3:39. San Francisco: A. L. Bancroft, 1880.

Syle, Edward W. Diary, 1851–56. HM 83407, Huntington Library, San Marino, CA.

Tan Qianchu 譚乾初. 古巴雜記 [General description of Cuba]. In 小方壺齋與地叢鈔十二帙 [Collected books on geography from the Xiaofanghu Studio], edited by Wang Xiqi 王錫祺. Hangzhou: Hangzhou Guji Shudian, 1891.

Taylor, Benjamin Franklin. *Between the Gates*. Chicago: S. C. Griggs & Co., 1878.

Taylor, Charles M., Jr. *Vacation Days in Hawaii and Japan*. Philadelphia: George W. Jacobs & Co., 1898.

Thomas, John. *Illustrations of China and Its People: A Series of Two Hundred Photographs, with Letterpress Descriptive of the Places and People Represented*, Vol. 2. London: Sampson Low, Marston, Low, and Searle, 1873.

Thrum, Thomas G. *Hawaiian Almanac and Annual for 1875*. Honolulu: Honolulu Star-Bulletin.

Tiersot, Julien. "Promenades musicales à l'Exposition." *Le Ménestrel* 55, no. 25 (1889): 195–96.

Tong Achick [Tong A-Chick] and Chun Aching. "To His Excellency Governor Bigler from the Chinamen." In *An Analysis of the Chinese Question*. San Francisco: *San Francisco Herald*, 1852), 10–14.

Towle, Russell. *The Dutch Flat Chronicles, 1849–1906*. Dutch Flat, CA: Giant Gap Press, 1994.

Vance, Robert Lee J. "Folk-Lore Study in America." *Popular Science Monthly* 43 (1893), 586–98.

"A Visit to the Chinese Quarter San Francisco." *Frank Leslie's Popular Monthly*, March 1878, 345–51.

"A Walking Junk." *Daily Examiner*, December 4, 1882.

Wells, Frederic Palmer. *History of Barnet, Vermont From the Outbreak of the French and Indian War to Present Time*. Burlington: Free Press Printing Co., 1923.

Williams, Samuel. "The City of the Golden Gate." *Scribner's Monthly*, 10, no. 3, July 1, 1875, 266–85.

——. *The City of the Golden Gate: A Description of San Francisco in 1875*. San Francisco: Book Club of California, 1921.

——. *The Middle Kingdom: A Survey of the Geography, Government, Literature, Social Life, Arts, and History of the Chinese Empire and Its Inhabitants*. New York: Wiley and Putnam, 1848.

Wores, Theodore. "The Children of Chinatown in San Francisco." *St. Nicholas*, 23 (May 1896), 575–77.

Yang Enshou 楊恩壽. 坦園日記 [Diary of Tan Garden]. 1874–1891; reprint, Shanghai: Shanghai gu ji chu ban she, 1983.

Yang Maojian 楊懋建. 夢華瑣簿 [Random thoughts of the splendid dream], 1842. In 清代燕都梨園史料 [Qing dynasty historical materials on the theater in Beijing], edited by Zhang Cixi 張次溪. Beijing: Zhongguo xiju, 1988.

Young, John Russell. *Around the World with General Grant*. New York: Subscription Book Department, American News Co., 1879.

Zhang, Yinhuan 張蔭桓. 三洲日記 [Itinerary in three continents]. Jingdu: Yuedong xinguan, 1896.

Zhu Bing-tan 朱炳堂. 粵調歌曲精華 [Essence of Cantonese arias and songs]. San Francisco: Sun Tai Lok Co, 1926.

Secondary Sources

"Asian American Music." *New Grove Dictionary of American Music*, 2nd ed., edited by Charles Garrett. New York: Oxford University Press, 2013, 1:220–32.

Alford, Terry. *Fortune's Fool: The Life of John Wilkes Booth*. New York: Oxford University Press, 2015.

Anthology of Cantonese Opera Synopses, 粵劇劇目綱要. Guangzhou: Zhongguo xijujia xiehui guangdong fenhui, 1961; reprint: Yangcheng Wanbao, 2006.

Arkush, R. David, and Leo O. Lee, eds. *Land Without Ghosts: Chinese Impressions of America from the Mid-Nineteenth Century to the Present*. Berkeley: University of California Press, 1989.

Azuma, Eiichiro. "Japanese Immigrant Settler Colonialism in the U.S.–Mexican Borderlands and the U.S. Racial-Imperialist Politics of the Hemispheric 'Yellow Peril.'" *Pacific Historical Review* 83, no. 2 (2014): 255–76.

Bachner, Andrea. *The Mark of Theory: Inscriptive Figures, Poststructuralist Prehistories*. New York: Fordham University Press, 2018.

Beasley, David R. *McKee Rankin and the Heyday of the American Theater*. Waterloo, ON: Wilfrid Laurier University Press, 2002.

Bennett, Terry. *History of Photography in China: Chinese Photographers 1844–1879*. London: Quaritch, 2013.

Bentley, Erin. *The Life of Drama*. New York: Atheneum, 1964.

Berger, John. *Ways of Seeing*. London: Penguin Books, 1990.

Berglund, Barbara. *Making San Francisco American: Cultural Frontiers in the Urban West, 1846–1906*. Lawrence: University Press of Kansas, 2007.

Berson, Misha. *The San Francisco Stage from Gold Rush to Golden Spike, 1849–1869*. San Francisco: San Francisco Performing Arts Library and Museum (Journal Series no. 2), 1989.

———. "The San Francisco Stage from Golden Spike to Great Earthquake, 1869–1906." *San Francisco Performing Arts Library and Museum Journal* 4 (February 1992): entire issue.

Blaszkiewicz, Jacek. *Fanfare for a City: Music and the Urban Imagination in Haussmann's Paris*. Berkeley: University of California Press, 2023.

Bleeker, Maaike. *Visuality in the Theatre: The Locus of Looking*. Basingstoke, UK: Palgrave Macmillan, 2008.

Blodgett, Peter John. *Land of Golden Dreams: California in the Gold Rush Decade, 1848–1858*. Los Angeles: Huntington Library, 1999.

Bonner, Arthur. *Alas! What Brought Thee Hither? The Chinese in New York, 1800–1950*. Madison, NJ: Fairleigh Dickinson University Press, 1997.

Brown, Judith. *Glamour in Six Dimensions: Modernism and the Radiance of Form*. Ithaca, NY: Cornell University Press, 2009.

Broyles, Michael. "Immigrant, Folk, and Regional Musics in the Nineteenth Century." In *The Cambridge History of American Music*, edited by David Nicholls, 135–57. Cambridge: Cambridge University Press, 1998.

Bryant, Lei Ouyang. "Performing Race and Place in Asian America: Korean American Adoptees, Musical Theatre, and the Land of 10,000 Lakes." *Asian Music* 40, no. 1 (2009): 4–30.

Caesar, Clarence. "The Historical Demographic of Sacramento's Black Community, 1848–1900." *California History* 75, no. 3 (1996): 198–213.

Cassel, Susie Lan. "To Inscribe the Self Daily: The Discovery of the Ah Quin Diary." in *The Chinese in America*. Walnut Creek, CA: Alta Mira Press, 2002.

Certeau, Michel de. *The Practice of Everyday Life*. Translated by Steven Rendall. Berkeley: University of California Press, 1984.

——. *The Writing of History*. Translated by Tom Cloney. New York: Columbia University Press, 1988.

Chalmers, Claudine. *Paul Frenzeny's Chinatown Sketches: An Artist's Fascination with San Francisco's Chinese Quarter, 1874–1882*. San Francisco: Book Club of California, 2013.

Chan, Annette KeLee. "A Performance History of Cantonese Opera in San Francisco from the Gold Rush to the Earthquake." PhD diss., University of California, Davis, 1993.

Chan, Sau-yan. "Performance Context as a Molding Force: Photographic Documentation of Cantonese Opera in Hong Kong." *Visual Anthropology* 18, nos. 2–3 (2005): 167–98.

Chan, Sau-yan. "Cantonese Opera." In the *Routledge Encyclopedia of Traditional Chinese Culture*, edited by Sin-wai Chan, 169–85. New York: Routledge, 2019.

——. "Exploding the Belly: Improvisation in Cantonese Opera." In *In the Course of Performance: Studies in the World of Musical Improvisation*, edited by Bruno Nettl and Melinda Russell, 199–218. London and Chicago: University of Chicago Press, 1998.

Chan, Sucheng. *This Bittersweet Soil: The Chinese in California Agriculture, 1860–1910*. Berkeley: University of California Press, 1986.

——. "Chinese Livelihood in Rural California: The Impact of Economic Change, 1860–1880." In *Working People of California*, edited by Daniel Cornford, 57–75. Berkeley: University of California Press, 1995.

——, ed. *Chinese American Transnationalism: The Flow of People, Resources, and Ideas between China and America during the Exclusion Era*. Philadelphia: Temple University Press, 2005.

Chang, Dongshin. *Representing China on the Historical London Stage: From Orientalism to Intercultural Performance*. New York: Routledge, 2015.

Chang, Gordon H. *Ghosts of Gold Mountain: The Epic Story of the Chinese Who Built the Transcontinental Railroad*. Boston: Houghton Mifflin Harcourt, 2020.

Chang, Gordon H., and Shelley Fisher Fishkin, eds. *The Chinese and the Iron Road: Building the Transcontinental Railroad*. Stanford: Stanford University Press, 2019.

Chang, Gordon, Mark Johnson, and Paul Karlstrom, eds. *Asian American Art: A History, 1850–1970*. Palo Alto: Stanford University Press, 2008.

Chang, Kornel. "Enforcing Transnational White Solidarity: Asian Migration and the Formation of the U.S.–Canadian Boundary." *American Quarterly* 60, no. 3 (2008): 671–96.

——. *Pacific Connections: The Making of the U.S.–Canadian Borderlands*. Berkeley: University of California Press, 2012.

Chang, Ning Jennifer 張寧. 異國事物的轉譯：近代上海的跑馬、跑狗與回力球賽 [Cultural Translation: horse racing, greyhound racing, and jai alai in modern Shanghai]. Taipei: Academia Sinica, 2019.

Chang Song-hing and Zhuang Chusheng. "Geographical Distribution of Guangdong Dialects: Their Linkage with Natural and Historical Geography." *Journal of Chinese Studies* 48 (2008): 407–23.

Chase, Gilbert. *America's Music: From the Pilgrims to the Present*. New York: McGraw-Hill, 1955; 3rd ed.: Urbana: University Illinois Press, 1992.

Chen Feinong 陳非儂. 粵劇六十年 [Sixty years of Cantonese opera: Chan Feinong's memoir]. Edited by Ng Wing Chung and Chan Chak Lui. Hong Kong: Cantonese Opera Research Programme, Chinese University of Hong Kong, 2007.

Chen, Yong. *Chinese San Francisco, 1850–1943: A Transpacific Community*. Stanford: Stanford University Press, 2000.

——. "Remembering Ah Quin: A Century of Social Memory in a Chinese American Family." *Oral History Review* 27, no. 1 (2000): 57–80.

Chen Zhiyon 陳志勇. 晚清嶺南官場演劇及禁戲—以《杜鳳治日記》為中心 [Official plays and prohibited plays in Lingnan in the late Qing dynasty—in the case of "Du Fengzhi's Diary"], *Journal of Sun-yat Sen University*, 中山大學學報 1 (2017): 27–38.

Cheng, Anne Anlin. *Ornamentalism*. Oxford: Oxford University Press, 2019.

——. *Second Skin: Josephine Baker and the Modern Surface*. New York: Oxford University Press, 2011.

Chew, Ron. *Reflections of Seattle's Chinese Americans: The First 100 Years*. Seattle: University of Washington Press, 1994.

Chew, William F. *Nameless Builders of the Transcontinental Railroad: The Chinese Workers of the Central Pacific Railroad*. Victoria, BC: Trafford, 2004.

Chiang, Howard. *Transtopia in the Sinophone Pacific*. New York: Columbia University Press, 2021.

Chinese Railroad Workers in North America Project, Stanford University, https://web.stanford.edu/group/chineserailroad/cgi-bin/website.

Ching, May-bo. "Literary, Ethnic or Territorial Definitions of Guangdong Culture in the Late Qing and the Early Republic." In *Unity and Diversity: Local Cultures and Identities in China*, edited by Tao Tao Liu and David Faure, 51–66. Hong Kong: Hong Kong University Press, 1996.

——. "A Preliminary Study of the Theatres Built by Cantonese Merchants in the Late Qing." *Frontiers of History in China* 5, no. 2 (2010): 253–78.

Chinn, Thomas W. *Bridging the Pacific: San Francisco Chinatown and Its People*. San Francisco: Chinese Historical Society of America, 1989.

Chow, Rey. *Ethics After Idealism: Theory, Culture, Ethnicity, Reading*. Bloomington: Indiana University Press, 1998.

Chu, Peter, et al., eds. *Chinese Theaters in America*. Washington, DC: Bureau of Research and Publications, Federal Theater, California, Works Progress Administration (WPA), 1936.

Chung, Sue Fawn. *Chinese in the Woods: Logging and Lumbering in the American West*. Urbana: University of Illinois Press, 2015.

———. *In Pursuit of Gold: Chinese American Miners and Merchants in the American West*. Urbana: University of Illinois Press, 2011.

Clark, William B. *Gold Districts of California: California Gold Discovery to Statehood*. Sacramento: Department of Conservation, Division of Mines and Geology, 1998, https://digitalcommons.law.ggu.edu/caldocs_agencies/257.

Clay, Lauren R. *Stagestruck: The Business of Theater in Eighteenth-Century France and Its Colonies*. Ithaca, NY: Cornell University Press, 2013.

Cody, Jeffrey W., and Frances Terpak. "Through a Foreign Glass: The Art and Science of Photography in Late Qing China." In *Brush and Shutter: Early Photography in China*, 33–68. Los Angeles: Getty Research Institute, 2011.

Crawford, Richard. *America's Musical Life: A History*. New York: Norton, 2001.

———. *The American Musical Landscape: The Business of Musicianship from Billings to Gershwin*, updated ed. Berkeley: University of California Press, 2000.

Cronin, Mary M., and William E. Huntzicker. "Popular Chinese Images and 'The Coming Man' of 1870: Racial Representations of Chinese." *Journalism History* 38, no. 2 (2012): 86–89.

Curti, Merle. "America at the World's Fairs, 1851–1893." *American Historical Review* 55, no. 4 (1950): 833–56.

Davis, Ronald L. *A History of Opera in the America West*. Englewood Cliffs, NJ: Prentice-Hall, 1965.

———. "They Played for Gold: Theater on the Mining Frontier." *Southwest Review* 51, no. 2 (1966): 169–84.

Decker, Todd. "Race, Ethnicity, Performance." In *The Oxford Handbook of the American Musical*, edited by Raymond Knapp, Mitchell Morris, and Stacy Wolff, 197–209. New York: Oxford University Press, 2011.

Doggett, Anne. "'Strains from Flowery Land': Responses to Chinese Musical Activity in Mid-Nineteenth-Century Ballarat." *Context: Journal of Music Research* 33 (2008): 107–20.

Dong, Lorraine, Philip P. Choy, and Marlon K. Hom, eds. *The Coming Man: 19th Century American Perceptions of the Chinese*. Seattle: University of Washington Press, 1995.

Donovan, Brian. *White Slave Crusades: Race, Gender, and Anti-vice Activism, 1887–1917*. Urbana: University of Illinois Press, 2006.

Du Jun Min. "The Development of Chinese Records to 1911." *Antique Phonograph News*, January–February 2008, https://www.capsnews.org/apn2008-1.htm.

———. "The Development of Chinese Records from the Qing Dynasty to 1918." *Antique Phonograph News,* January–February 2009, https://www.capsnews.org/apn2009-1.htm.

Dunn, Geoffrey. *Chinatown Dreams: The Life and Photographs of George Lee*. Capitola, CA: Capitola Book Company, 2003.

Dyer, Richard. *White: Essays on Race and Culture*. London: Routledge, 1997.

Editorial Team of Overseas Chinese History, History Department, Fujian Normal University, comp. 福建師範大學歷史系華僑史編輯組, 晚清海外筆記選 [Selected notes about overseas in late Qing dynasty]. Beijing: Ocean Publisher, 1983.

Eichin, Carolyn Grattan. *From San Francisco Eastward: Victorian Theater in the American West*. Reno: University of Nevada Press, 2020.

Eidsheim, Nina. *The Race of Sound: Listening, Timbre, and Vocality in African American Music*. Durham, NC: Duke University Press, 2020.

——. *Sensing Sound: Singing and Listening as Vibrational Practice*. Durham, NC: Duke University Press, 2015.

Eidsheim, Nina, and Daniel Walden. "No Conclusions: Response to Symposium, August 16, 2021." *Kalfou: A Journal of Comparative and Relational Ethnic Studies* 9, no. 2 (2022): 353–71.

Encyclopedic Discography of Victor Recordings. Pre-Matrix Series (1900–37). Compiled by Ted Fagan and William R. Moran. Westport, CT: Greenwood Press, 1983.

Estavan, Lawrence. *Theatre Buildings, Part 1. San Francisco Theatre Research*. San Francisco: Works Progress Administration, 1940.

Farkas, Lani Ah Tye. *Bury My Bones in America: The Saga of a Chinese Family in California, 1852–1996—From San Francisco to the Sierra Gold Mines*. Nevada City, CA: Carl Mautz Publishing, 1998.

Fauser, Annegret. *Musical Encounters at the 1889 Paris World's Fair*. Rochester, NY: University of Rochester Press, 2005.

Fellezs, Kevin. *Listen But Don't Ask Question: Hawaiian Slack Key Guitar Across the TransPacific*. Durham, NC: Duke University Press, 2019.

Ferguson, Laura E. "Gateway City: The Makings and Meanings of San Francisco's 'Golden Gate,' 1846–1906." PhD diss., University of Michigan, 2015.

Fong, Eric W., and William T. Markham. "Anti-Chinese Politics in California in the 1870s: An Intercounty Analysis." *Sociological Perspectives* 45, no. 2 (2002), 183–210.

Frisken, Amanda. *Graphic News: How Sensational Images Transformed Nineteenth-Century Journalism*. Urbana: University of Illinois Press, 2020.

Fritz, Christian G. "A Nineteenth Century 'Habeas Corpus Mill': The Chinese before the Federal Courts in California." *American Journal of Legal History* 32, no. 4 (1988): 347–72.

Garrett, Charles Hiroshi. *Struggling to Define a Nation*. Publisher: University of California Press, 2008.

Gibb, Andrew. *Californios, Anglos, and the Performance of Oligarchy in the U.S. West: How the First Generation of Mexican Americans Fashioned a New Nation*. Carbondale: Southern Illinois University Press, 2018.

Gibbs, Jason. "Spoken Theater, La Scène Tonkinoise, and the First Modern Vietnamese Songs." *Asian Music* 31, no. 2 (2000): 1–33.

Gillenkirk, Jeff, and James Motlow. *Bitter Melon: Stories from the Last Rural Chinese Town in America*. Seattle: University of Washington Press, 1987.

Gin Lum, Kathryn. "Religion on the Road: How Chinese Migrants Adapted Popular Religion to an American Context." In *The Chinese and the Iron Road: Building the Transcontinental Railroad*, edited by Gordon H. Chang and Shelley Fisher Fishkin, 159–78. Stanford: Stanford University Press, 2019.

Graziano, John, ed. *European Music and Musicians in New York City, 1840–1900*. Rochester: University of Rochester Press, 2006.

Greene, Victor R. *A Singing Ambivalence: American Immigrants between Old World and New, 1830–1930*. Kent, OH: Kent State University Press, 2004.

Griego, Andrew. "Mayor of Chinatown: The Life of Ah Quin, Chinese Merchant and Railroad Builder of San Diego." Master's thesis, San Diego State University, 1979.

Gunning, Tom. "Foreword: The Same Old Tune, But with a Different Meaning." In Berthold Hoeckner, *Film, Music, Memory*, 1–15. Chicago: University of Chicago Press, 2019.

Haenni, Sabine. *The Immigrant Scene: Ethnic Amusements in New York, 1880–1920*. Minneapolis: University of Minnesota Press, 2008.

Hartman, Saidiya. *Lose Your Mother: A Journey along the Atlantic Slave Route*. New York: Farrar, Straus & Giroux, 2007.

——. "Venus in Two Acts." *Small Axe* 12, no. 2 (June 2008): 1–14.

——. *Wayward Lives, Beautiful Experiments: Intimate Histories of Social Upheaval*. New York: Norton, 2019.

Hoexter, Corinne K. *Canton to California: The Epic of Chinese Immigration*. New York: Four Winds Press, 1976.

Ho, Virgil Kit Yiu. *Understanding Canton: Rethinking Popular Culture in the Republican Period*. Oxford: Oxford University Press, 2006.

——. "'Why Don't We Take Drama as Facts?' Observations on Cantonese Opera in a Rural Setting." *Journal of the Royal Asiatic Society, Hong Kong Branch* 53 (2013): 183–214.

Hoeckner, Berthold. *Film, Music, Memory*. Berkeley: California University Press, 2019.

Hoes, Rose Gouveneur. "Historical Costumes of Famous American Women." *Daughters of the American Revolution Magazine* 47, no. 5 (November 1915): 283–90.

Hom, Marlon K. K. *Songs of Gold Mountain: Cantonese Rhymes from San Francisco Chinatown*. Berkeley: University of California Press, 1987.

Hoobler, Dorothy, and Thomas Hoobler. *The Chinese American Family Album*. New York: Oxford University Press, 1994.

Hoover, Catherine, and Robert Sawchuck. "'From the Place We Hear about . . .': A Descriptive Checklist of Pictorial Lithographs and Letter Sheets in the CHS Collection." *California Historical Quarterly* 56, no. 4 (1977/1978): 346–67.

Hsu, Hua. *A Floating Chinaman: Fantasy and Failure across the Pacific*. Cambridge, MA: Harvard University Press, 2016.

Hsu, Madeline Y. "Chinese and American Collaborations through Educational Exchange during the Era of Exclusion, 1872–1955." *Pacific Historical Review* 83, no. 2 (2014): 314–32.

Hudson, Janisch N. "The Chinese, the Courts, and the Constitution: A Study of the Legal Issues Raised by Chinese Immigration to the United States, 1850–1902," JSD diss., University of Chicago, 1971.

Jennex, Craig. "Diva Worship and the Sonic Search for Queer Utopia." In *Fan Identities and Practices in Context Dedicated to Music*, edited by Mark Duffett, 45–61. New York: Routledge, 2016.

Ji Dejun and He Shiying 紀德君 何詩瑩. 明清以來文學中的廣府風情研究 [A study of Guangfu style in literature since the Ming and Qing dynasties]. Beijing: Social Science Academy Press, 2018.

Jones, Adrew F. *Circuit Listening: Chinese Popular Music in the Global 1960s*. Minneapolis: University of Minnesota Press, 2020.

Kanazawa, Mark. "Immigration, Exclusion, and Taxation: Anti-Chinese Legislation in Gold Rush California." *Journal of Economic History* 65, no. 3 (2005): 779–805.

Kares, Jean L. "Performance, Adaptation, Identity: Cantonese Opera Costumes in Vancouver, Canada." *Textile Society of America Symposium Proceedings* 978 (2016), 242–51, http://digitalcommons.unl.edu/tsaconf/978.

Katrak, Ketu. "'Stripping Women of Their Wombs': Active Witnessing of Performances of Violence." *Theatre Research International* 39, no. 1 (2014): 31–46.

Killingray, David. "Introduction: Imperial Seas: Cultural Exchange and Commerce in the British Empire 1780–1900." In *Maritime Empires: British Imperial Maritime Trade in the Nineteenth Century*, edited by David Killingray, Margarette Lincoln, and Nigel Rigby, 1–12. Woodbridge, UK: Boydell Press, 2004.

Kim, Ju Yon. *The Racial Mundane: Asian American Performance and the Embodied Everyday*. New York: New York University Press, 2015.

——. "Trying on *The Yellow Jacket*: Performing Chinese Exclusion and Assimilation." *Theatre Journal* 62, no. 1 (March 2010): 75–92.

Ko Hsiang-Chun 柯香君. "明代職業戲班研究 [A study of the theatrical troupes in the Ming dynasty]." 國文學誌 *NCUE Journal of Chinese Studies* 14 (2007): 101–45.

Koegel, John. "*Canciones del país*: Mexican Musical Life in California after the Gold Rush." *California History* 78, no. 3 (Fall 1999): 160–87, 215–19.

——. "Mexican Music, Theater, and Circus at the Los Angeles Plaza, 1850–1900." In *De Nueva España a México: El universo musical mexicano entre centenarios (1517–1917)*, edited by Javier Marín López, 35–119. Seville: Universidad Internacional de Andalucía, 2020.

——. "Mexican Musical Theater and Movie Palaces in Downtown Los Angeles Before 1950." In *The Tide Was Always High: The Music of Latin America in Los Angeles*, ed. Josh Kun, 46–75. Berkeley: University of California Press, 2017.

——. *Music in German Immigrant Theater: New York City, 1840–1940*. Rochester: University of Rochester Press, 2009.

——. "Non-English-Language Musical Theater in the United States." In *The Cambridge Companion to the Musical*, 3rd ed., edited by Paul Laird and William Everett, 21–50. Cambridge: Cambridge University Press, 2017.

——. "What's in a Name? The Multiplicities of the Musical." In *The Routledge Companion to Musical Theatre*, edited by Laura MacDonald and Ryan Donovan, 502–20. New York: Routledge, 2022.

Kwon, Marci. Introduction to "Asian American Art, Pasts and Futures." *Panorama: Journal of the Association of Historians of American Art*, 7 no. 1 (2021), https://doi.org/10.24926/24716839.11446.

Lai, Him Mark. *Becoming Chinese American: A History of Communities and Institutions*. Walnut Creek, CA: Alta Mira Press, 2004.

——. "Chinese-American Press." in *The Ethnic Press in the United States: A Historical Analysis and Handbook*, edited by Sally M. Miller, 27–43. Westport, CT: Greenwood Press, 1987.

—— 陳依範. 從華僑到華人 [From overseas Chinese to Chinese American: History of development of Chinese American society during the twentieth century]. Hong Kong: Joint Publishing, 1992.

———. "Historical Development of the Chinese Consolidated Benevolent Association/Huiguan System." *Chinese America: History and Perspectives* 1 (1987): 13–51.

Lausent-Herrera, Isabelle. "The Chinatown in Peru and the Changing Peruvian Chinese Community(ies)." *Journal of Chinese Overseas* 7, no. 1 (2011): 69–113.

Lee, Anthony W. *Picturing Chinatown: Art and Orientalism in San Francisco.* Berkeley: University of California Press, 2001.

Lee, Erika. *At America's Gates: Chinese Immigration During the Exclusion Era, 1882–1943.* Chapel Hill: North Carolina University Press, 2003.

———. *The Making of Asian America: A History.* New York: Simon & Schuster, 2015.

Lee, Erika, and Judy Yung. *Angel Island: Immigrant Gateway to America.* New York: Oxford University Press, 2010.

Lee, Esther Kim. *Made-Up Asians: Yellowface During the Exclusion Era.* Ann Arbor: University of Michigan Press, 2022.

Lee, Josephine. "Between Immigration and Hyphenation: The Problems of Theorizing Asian American Theater." *Journal of Dramatic Theory and Criticism* 13, no. 1 (1998): 45–69.

———. *The Japan of Pure Invention: Gilbert and Sullivan's The Mikado.* Minneapolis: University of Minnesota Press, 2010.

———. *Oriental, Black, and White: The Formation of Racial Habits in American Theater.* Chapel Hill: University of North Carolina Press, 2022.

Lee, Robert G. *Orientals: Asian Americans in Popular Culture.* Philadelphia: Temple University, 1999.

Lee, Tong Soon. *Chinese Street Opera in Singapore.* Urbana: University of Illinois Press. 2009.

Lei, Daphne Pi-Wei. *Alternative Chinese Opera in the Age of Globalization: Performing Zero.* London: Palgrave Macmillan, 2011.

———. *Operatic China: Staging Chinese Identity Across the Pacific.* London: Palgrave, 2006.

———. *Uncrossing the Borders: Performing Chinese in Gendered (Trans)Nationalism.* Ann Arbor: University of Michigan Press, 2019.

Levine, Lawrence. *Highbrow/Lowbrow: The Emergence of Cultural Hierarchy in America.* Cambridge, MA: Harvard University Press, 1990.

Lew-Williams, Beth. "Before Restriction Became Exclusion: America's Experiment in Diplomatic Immigration Control." *Pacific Historical Review* 83, no. 1 (2014): 24–56.

———. *The Chinese Must Go: Violence, Exclusion, and the Making of the Alien in America.* Cambridge, MA: Harvard University Press, 2018.

Li, Hsiao-t'i. *Opera, Society, and Politics in Modern China.* Cambridge, MA: Harvard University Press, 2019.

——— 李孝悌. 昨日到城市：近世中國的逸樂與宗教 [Yesterday to the city: Entertainment and religion in China]. Taipei: Liangjin, 2008.

Li Jian 黎鍵. 香港粵劇口述史 [Discourse on Cantonese opera in Hong Kong]. Hong Kong: Joint Publishing, 2010.

Li, Siu Leung. *Cross-Dressing in Chinese Opera*. Hong Kong: Hong Kong University Press, 2003.

Liang Peijin 梁沛錦. 六國大封相 [Joint investiture of a prime minister of six warlords]. Hong Kong: Xiang Gang Shi Zheng Ju Gong Gong Tu Shu Guan, 1992.

Liang Peijin 梁沛錦. 粵劇劇目通檢 [Anthology of Cantonese opera titles]. Hong Kong: Joint Publishing, 1985.

Liao, Yvonne. "'Chinatown' and Global Operatic Knowledge." *Cambridge Opera Journal* 31, nos. 2–3 (2019): 280–90.

Lionnet, Françoise, and Shumei Shi. *Minor Transnationalism*. Durham, NC: Duke University Press, 2005.

Liu, April. *Divine Threads: The Visual and Material Culture of Cantonese Opera*. Vancouver: Figure 1 Publishing, 2019.

Liu Boji 劉伯驥. 美國華僑史 [History of the Chinese in the United States of America]. Taibei Shi: Xing zheng yuan qiao wu wei yuan hui: Zong fa xing suo Li ming wen hua shi ye gu fen you xian gong si, 1976.

Liu Guoxing 劉國興. 粵劇藝人在海外的生活及活動 [The lives and activities of Cantonese opera actors abroad]. *Guangdong wenshi ziliao*, 21 (1965):172–88.

Liu, Siyuan. *Transforming Tradition: The Reform of Chinese Theater in the 1950s and Early 1960s*. Ann Arbor: University of Michigan Press, 2021.

López, Kathleen. *Chinese Cubans: A Transnational History*. Chapel Hill: University of North Carolina Press, 2013.

Love, Harold. "Chinese Theatre on the Victorian Goldfields 1858–1870." *Australian Drama Studies* 3, no. 2 (April 1985): 47–86.

Lowe, Lisa. *Immigrant Acts: On Asian American Cultural Politics*. Durham, NC: Duke University Press, 1996.

Lum, Kathryn Gin. "Religion on the Road: How Chinese Migrants Adapted Popular Religion to an American Context." In *The Chinese and the Iron Road*, ed. Gordon H. Chang and Shelley Fisher Fishkin, 159–78. Palo Alto: Stanford University, 2019.

Luo Liming 羅澧銘. 顧曲談 [On appreciating music], edited by Zhu Shao-zhang, 朱少璋. Hong Kong: Joint Publishing Co. 2020.

Luo Zhaodong 駱昭東. 朝貢貿易與仗劍經商：全球經濟視角下的明清外貿政策 [Tribute-paying system and trade by force]. Taipei: Commercial Press, 2018.

Luozhu, Jufen. "Old Tale of Gold Mountain." *East-West Weekly*, January 7, 1970, 18.

Ma, L. Eve Armentrout. "The Big Business Ventures of Chinese in North America." In *The Chinese American Experience*, edited by Genny Lim. San Francisco: Chinese Historical Society of America and Chinese Culture Foundation, 1984.

Mackerras, Colin. "Theatre in Vietnam." *Asian Theatre Journal* 4, no. 1 (1987): 1–28.

Mai Xiaoxia 麥嘯霞. 廣東戲劇史略 [A brief history of opera theater in Guangdong]. In *Guangdong wenwu* 廣東文物 [Art and heritage in Guangdong], edited by Guangdong Wenwu Zhanlanhui 廣東文物展覽會 3: 8, 791–835. Hong Kong: Zhongguo Wenhua Xiejinhui, 1942.

Mandeles, Chad. "Theodore Wores's Chinese Fishmonger in a Cosmopolitan Context." *American Art Journal* 16, no. 1 (1984): 65–75, https://doi.org/10.2307/1594381.

Martin, George. *Verdi at the Golden Gate: Opera and San Francisco in the Gold Rush Years*. Berkeley: University of California Press, 1993.

Matthews, Glenna. *The Golden State in the Civil War: Thomas Starr King, the Republican Party, and the Birth of Modern California*. New York: Cambridge University Press, 2012.

McClain, Charles J., Jr. "The Chinese Struggle for Civil Rights in Nineteenth Century America: The First Phase, 1850–1870." *California Law Review* 72, no. 4 (1984): 529–68.

McKinnon, Dugal. "Materiality: The Fabrication of Sound." in *The Oxford Handbook of Sound Art*, edited by Jane Grant, John Matthias, and David Prior, 273–86. New York: Oxford University Press, 2021.

McKittrick, Katherine. *Dear Science and Other Stories*. Durham, NC: Duke University Press, 2021.

Meizel, Katherine. "A Powerful Voice: Investigating Vocality and Identity." *Voice and Speech Review* 7, no. 1 (2011): 267–74.

Metzger, Sean. "Charles Parsloe's Chinese Fetish: An Example of Yellowface Performance in Nineteenth-Century American Melodrama." *Theatre Journal* 56, no. 4 (2004): 627–51.

———. *The Chinese Atlantic: Seascapes and the Theatricality of Globalization*. Bloomington: Indiana University Press, 2020.

———. *Chinese Looks: Fashion, Performance, Race*. Bloomington: Indiana University Press, 2014.

Miles, Steven B. "Where Diasporas Met: Hunanese, Cantonese, and the State in Late-Qing Guangxi." *Journal of Chinese History* 5 (2021): 263–84.

Miller, Leta E. *Music and Politics in San Francisco: From the 1906 Quake to the Second World War*. Berkeley: University of California Press, 2011.

Minnick, Sylvia Sun. *Samfow: The San Joaquin Chinese Legacy*. Fresno, CA: Panorama West Publishing, 1988.

Moon, Krystyn R. "Lee Tung Foo and the Making of a Chinese American Vaudevillian, 1900s–1920s." *Journal of Asian American Studies* 8, no. 1 (2005): 23–48.

———. "On a Temporary Basis: Immigration, Labor Unions, and the American Entertainment Industry, 1880s-1930s." *Journal of American History* 99, no. 3 (2012): 771–92.

———. *Yellowface: Creating the Chinese in American Popular Music and Performance, 1850s-1920s*. New Brunswick, NJ: Rutgers University Press, 2005.

Mooney, Ralph James. "Matthew Deady and the Federal Judicial Response to Racism in the Early West." *Oregon Law Review* 63 (1985): 615–16.

Morgan, H. Wayne. *An Artist of the American Renaissance: The Letters of Kenyon Cox, 1883–1919*. Kent, OH: Kent State University Press, 2014.

Morrison, Toni. *The Source of Self-Regard: Selected Essays, Speeches, and Meditations*. New York: Vintage, 2020.

Moy, James S. *Marginal Sights: Staging the Chinese in America*. Iowa City: University of Iowa Press, 1993.

Myers, Red R. *Pintupi Country, Pintupi Self: Sentiment, Place, and Politics.* Washington, DC: Smithsonian Institution Press, 1991.

Ng, Wing Chung. *The Rise of Cantonese Opera: From Village Art to Global Phenomenon.* Urbana: University of Illinois Press, 2015.

Ngai, Mae M. *The Chinese Question: The Gold Rushes and Global Politics.* New York: Norton, 2021.

——. *Impossible Subjects: Illegal Aliens and the Making of Modern America.* Princeton, NJ: Princeton University Press, 2004.

——. *The Lucky Ones: One Family and the Extraordinary Invention of Chinese America.* New York: Houghton Mifflin Harcourt, 2010.

——. "Transnationalism and the Transformation of the 'Other': Response to the Presidential Address." *American Quarterly* 57, no. 1 (March 2005): 59–65.

Ngon, Yeng Pway. *Costume.* Translated by Jeremy Tang. London: Balestier Press, 2015.

Nichols, Roger. *The Life of Debussy.* Cambridge: Cambridge University Press, 1998.

Oakley, Eric Odell. "Columbia at Sea: America Enters the Pacific, 1787–1793." PhD diss., University of North Carolina, Greensboro, 2017.

Owens, Kenneth. *Gold Rush Saints: California Mormons and the Great Rush for Riches.* Norman: University of Oklahoma Press, 2005.

Palmquist, Peter E. *Carleton E. Watkins, Photographer of the American West.* Fort Worth: Amon Carter Museum of Western Art, 1983.

Pan Xiafeng. *The Stagecraft of Peking Opera.* Beijing: New World Press, 1995.

Pang, Cecilia J. "(Re)cycling Culture: Chinese Opera in the United States." *Comparative Drama* 39, nos. 3–4 (2005): 361–96.

Pasler, Jann. "Sonic Anthropology in 1900: The Challenge of Transcribing Non-Western Music and Language." *Twentieth-Century Music* 11, no. 1 (2014): 7–36.

Pauwels, Erin. "José María Mora and the Migrant Surround in American Portrait Photography." *Panorama: Journal of the Association of Historians of American Art* 6, no. 2 (2020), https://doi.org/10.24926/24716839.10613.

Pfaelzer, Jean. *Driven Out: The Forgotten War Against Chinese Americans.* Berkeley: University of California Press, 2008.

Platt, Steven. "The Military." In *China's Hidden Century: 1796–1912,* edited by Jessica Harrison-Hall and Julia Lovell, 86–129. Seattle: University of Washington Press, 2023.

Preston, Katherine. "American Musical Theatre before the Twentieth Century." In *The Cambridge Companion to the Musical,* edited by William A. Everett and Paul R. Laird, 19–20. Cambridge: Cambridge University Press, 2002.

——. *Opera for the People: English-Language Opera and Women Managers in Late Nineteenth-Century America.* New York: Oxford University Press, 2017.

——. *Opera on the Road: Traveling Opera Companies in the United States, 1825–1860.* Urbana: University of Illinois Press, 1993.

Qin, Yucheng. *The Cultural Clash: Chinese Traditional Native-Place Sentiment and the Anti-Chinese Movement.* Latham, MD: University Press of America, 2016.

——. *The Diplomacy of Nationalism: The Six Companies and China's Policy toward Exclusion.* Honolulu: University of Hawai'i Press, 2009.

Qiu, Z. Serena. "In the Presence of Archival Fugitives: Chinese Women, Souvenir Images, and the 1893 Chicago World's Fair." *Panorama: Journal of the Association of Historians of American Art* 7, no. 1 (Spring 2021), https://doi.org/10.24926/24716839.11645.

Rao, Nancy Yunhwa. "Anti-Asian Hate: It's Time to Stop Playing 'Chinatown, My Chinatown.'" *Musicology Now, An online platform for sounds, words, and ideas from the American Musicological Society*. August 2022. https://musicologynow.org/anti-asian-hate/

——. "Chinese Opera in Turn-of-the-century Canada: Local History and Transnational Circulation." *Nineteenth-century Music Review* 11, no. 2 (December 2014): 291–310.

——. *Chinatown Opera Theater in North America*. Urbana: University of Illinois Press, 2017.

——. "From Chinatown Opera to *The First Emperor*: Racial Imagination, the Trope of 'Chinese Opera,' and New Hybridity." In *Opera in a Multicultural World: Coloniality, Culture, Performance*, edited by Mary Ingraham, Joseph K. So, and Roy Moodley, 50–67. New York: Routledge, 2015.

——. "Inside Chinese Theatre: Cantonese Opera in Canada." *Intersections* 38, nos. 1–2 (2018): 81–104.

——. "Listening Practice and History: Sound, Erasure." *Kalfou: A Journal of Comparative and Relational Ethnic Studies* 8, no. 2 (2022): 307–17.

——. "The Public Face of Chinatown: Actresses, Actors, Playwrights, and Audiences of Chinatown Theaters in San Francisco of the 1920s." *Journal of the Society for American Music* 5, no. 2 (2011): 235–70.

——. "Racial Essences and Historical Invisibility: Chinese Opera in New York, 1930." *Cambridge Opera Journal* 12, no. 2 (2000): 135–62.

——. "Songs of the Exclusion Era: New York's Chinatown's Opera Theaters in the 1920s." *American Music* 20, no. 4 (2002): 399–444.

——. "Transnationalism and Everyday Practice: Chinatown Theaters of North America in the 1920s." *Ethnomusicology Forum* 26, no. 1 (2016): 107–30.

Rast, Raymond. "The Cultural Politics of Tourism in San Francisco's Chinatown, 1882–1917." *Pacific Historical Review* 76, no. 1 (2007): 39.

Rather, Lois Rodecape. "Chinese Theaters in America." Unpublished manuscript. San Francisco Performing Arts Library and Museum.

Rawls, James J., and Richard J. Orsi, eds. *A Golden State: Mining and Economic Development in Gold Rush California*. Berkeley: University of California Press, 1999.

Riddle, Ronald. *Flying Dragons, Flowing Streams: Music in the Life of San Francisco's Chinese*. Westport, CT: Greenwood Press, 1983.

Roberts, Tamara. *Resounding Afro Asia: Interracial Music and the Politics of Collaboration*. New York: Oxford University Press, 2016.

Rodecape, Lois. "Celestial Drama in the Golden Hills: The Chinese Theater in California, 1849–1869." *California Historical Society Quarterly* 23 (1944): 97–116.

Rohe, Randall. "Chinese Mining & Settlement at the Lava Beds, Ca." *Mining History Journal* 3 (1996): 51–60.

———. "Origins & Diffusion of Traditional Placer Mining in the West." *Material Culture* 18, no. 3 (1986): 127–66.

Sagne, Jean. "All Kinds of Portraits: The Photographer's Studio." In *The New History of Photography*, edited by Michel Frizot, 102–30. Cologne: Könemann, 1994.

Said, Edward. "Orientalism Reconsidered." *Cultural Critique* 1 (1985): 89–107.

Sandmeyer, Elmer. *The Anti-Chinese Movement in California*. Urbana: Illinois University Press, 1939.

Scott-Maxwell, Aline. "Australia and Asia: Tracing Musical Representations, Encounters and Connections." *Context* 35, no. 36 (2010/2011): 77–91.

Sears, Clare, *Arresting Dress: Cross-Dressing, Law, and Fascination in Nineteenth-Century San Francisco*. Durham, NC: Duke University Press, 2015.

Sebryk, Karrie M. "A History of Chinese Theatre in Victoria." Master's thesis, University of Victoria, 1995.

Seligman, Scott D. *The First Chinese American: The Remarkable Life of Wong Chin Foo*. Hong Kong: Hong Kong University Press, 2013.

Shah, Nayan. *Contagious Divides: Epidemics and Race in San Francisco's Chinatown*. Berkeley: California University Press, 2001.

Shaw, Bernard. "Rousolff and Wores." In *Bibliographical Shaw, Including a Supplement to Bernard Shaw: A Bibliography by Dan H. Laurence*, edited by Fred D. Crawford and Dan H. Laurence. University Park: Pennsylvania State University Press, 2000.

Shelton, Tamara Venit. *Herbs and Roots: A History of Chinese Doctors in the American Medical Marketplace*. New Haven: Yale University Press, 2019.

Sheppard, W. Anthony. "Puccini and the Music Boxes." *Journal of the Royal Musical Association* 140, no. 1 (2015): 41–92.

Shih, Shu-Mei. *Visuality and Identity: Sinophone Articulations across the Pacific*. Berkeley: Uiversity of California Press, 2007.

Shih, Shu-Mei, Brian Bernards, and Chien-hsin Tsai, eds. *Sinophone Studies: A Critical Reader*. New York: Columbia University Press, 2012.

Sieber, Patricia. "Whither Theatricality? Toward Traditional Chinese Drama and Theater (*Xiqu*) as World Theater." *Journal of Chinese Literature and Culture* 9, no. 1 (April 2022): 225–255.

Silberstein, Rachel. *A Fashionable Century: Textile Artistry and Commerce in the Late Qing*. Seattle: University of Washington Press, 2000.

Singal, Daniel Joseph. "Towards a Definition of American Modernism." *American Quarterly* 39, no. 1 (1987): 7–26.

Sinn, Elizabeth. *Pacific Crossing: California Gold, Chinese Migration, and the Making of Hong Kong*. Hong Kong: Hong Kong University Press, 2013.

———. "Pacific Ocean: Highway to Gold Mountain, 1850–1900." *Pacific Historical Review* 83, no. 2 (2014): 220–37.

Smith, Carl T. *Chinese Christians: Elites, Middlemen, and the Church in Hong Kong*. Hong Kong: Hong Kong University Press, 1985.

Smith, Thomas. "Hearing with American Law—On Music as Evidence and Offense in the Age of Mass Incarceration." PhD diss., Columbia University, 2021.

Spence, Jonathan. *The Chan's Great Continent: China in Western Minds*. New York: Norton, 1998.

Spiller, Henry. *Javaphilia: American Love Affairs with Javanese Music and Dance*. Honolulu: University of Hawai'i Press, 2015.

Spottswood, Richard K. *Ethnic Music on Records: A Discography of Ethnic Recordings Produced in the United States, 1893–1942*. 7 vols. Urbana: University of Illinois Press, 1990.

Starr, Kevin. *The Dream Endures: California Enters the 1940s*. New York: Oxford University Press, 2002.

Stenberg, Josh. "*Xiqu* in the Philippines: From Church Suppression to MegaMall Shows." *Journal of Chinese Overseas* 16, no. 1 (2020): 58–89.

Stoever, Jennifer Lynn. *The Sonic Color Line: Race and the Cultural Politics of Listening*. New York: New York University Press, 2016.

Stoler, Ann Laura. *Along the Archival Grain: Epistemic Anxiety and Colonial Commonsense*. Princeton, NJ: Princeton University Press, 2008.

Tan, Sooi Beng, and Nancy Yunhwa Rao. "Introduction: Emergent Sino-Soundscapes: Musical Pasts, Transnationalism and Identities." *Ethnomusicology Forum* 26, no. 1 (2016): 1–10.

Tanaka, Issei 田仲一成. 中國戲劇史 [The history of Chinese drama]. Translated by Yun Guibin and Yu Yun. Beijing: Beijing Broadcasting Institute Press, 2002.

——. 中國祭祀戲劇研究 [A study of Chinese religious drama]. Translated by Bu He. Bejing: Beijing University Press, 2008.

Tate, E. Mowbray. *Transpacific Steam: The Story of Steam Navigation from the Pacific Coast of North America to the Far East and the Antipodes, 1867–1941*. New York: Cornwall Books, 1986.

Taylor, Diane. *The Archive and the Repertoire: Performing Cultural Memory in the Americas*. Durham, NC: Duke University Press, 2003.

Tchen, John Kuo Wei. *New York Before Chinatown: Orientalism and the Shaping of American Culture, 1776–1882*. Baltimore: Johns Hopkins University Press, 2001.

Tenorio-Trillo, Mauricio. *Mexico at the World's Fairs: Crafting a Modern Nation*. Berkeley: University of California Press, 1996.

Thomas, John. *Illustrations of China and Its People: A Series of Two Hundred Photographs, with Letterpress Descriptive of the Places and People Represented*. London: Sampson Low, Marston, Low, and Searle, 1873.

Thorpe, Ashley. *Performing China on the London Stage: Chinese Opera and Global Power, 1759–2008*. London: Palgrave Macmillan, 2016.

Tiedemann, David Samuel. "Britain and the United States at the World's Fairs, 1851–1893." PhD diss., University College London, 2019.

Tillmany, Jack. *Theatres of San Francisco*. Charleston, NC: Arcadia Publishing, 2005.

Tom, Lawrence, and Brian Tom. *Gold Country's Last Chinatown: Marysville, California*. Charleston, SC: History Press, 2020.

Torok, John Hayakawa. "Reconstruction and Racial Nativism: Chinese Immigrants and the Debates on the Thirteenth, Fourteenth, and Fifteenth Amendments and Civil Rights Laws." *Asian Law Journal* 3 (1996): 55–104.

Trobits, Monika. *Antebellum and Civil War San Francisco: A Western Theater for Northern and Southern Politics*. Charleston, SC: History Press, 2014.

Tsai, Robert L. "Racial Purges." *Michigan Law Review* 118, no. 6 (2020): 1127–56.

Tsou, Judy. "Gendering Race: Stereotypes of Chinese Americans in Popular Sheet Music." *Repercussions* 6 (Fall 1997): 25–62.

Tsu, Jing. *Kingdom of Characters: The Language Revolution That Made China Modern*. New York: Riverhead, 2022.

Van Bueren, Thad M. "Late-Nineteenth-Century Chinese Farm Workers in the California Mother Lode." *Historical Archaeology* 42, no. 3 (2008): 80–96.

Vey, Shauna. *Childhood and Nineteenth-Century American Theatre: The Work of the Marsh Troupe of Juvenile Actors*. Carbondale: Southern Illinois University Press, 2015.

Wallace, Maurice. *King's Vibrato: Blackness, Modernism and the Sonic Life of Martin Luther King Jr.* Durham, NC: Duke University Press, 2022.

Walter, Helen Margaret. "'On and Off the Stage': Costume, Dress, and Locating the Actor-Manager's Identity, 1870–1900." In *Performance Costume: New Perspectives and Methods*, edited by Sofia Pantouvaki and Peter McNeil, 89–104. New York: Bloomsbury, 2021.

Wang, Grace. *Soundtracks of Asian America: Navigating Race through Musical Performance*. Durham, NC: Duke University Press, 2015.

Wang, Xiulu. "History of Translation and Reception of the Chinese Folk Opera *Pu Kang* in the 19th Century." *Compilation and Translation Review* 13, no. 1 (2020): 39–70.

Wang, Zheng Ting. *Chinese Music in Australia—Victoria: 1850s to mid-1990s*. Melbourne: Australia Asia Foundation, 1997.

Ward, Barbara E. "Not Merely Players: Drama, Art and Ritual in Traditional China." *Man* 14, no. 1 (1979): 18–39.

Weber, Samuel. *Theatricality as Medium*. New York: Fordham University Press, 2004.

Wei, S. Louisa, writer, dir., ed. *Havana Divas*. 2019. Feature documentary. Supported by the Hong Kong Art Development Council. Hong Kong: Blue Queen Cultural Communication Ltd. HD, 96 min.

——, writer, dir., ed. *Golden Gate Girls*. 2014. Feature documentary. Supported by the Hong Kong Art Development Council. Hong Kong: Blue Queen Cultural Communication Ltd., HD, 90 min.

Weinstein, Robert A. "North from Panama, West to the Orient: The Pacific Mail Steamship Company, as Photographed by Carleton E. Watkins." *California History* 57, no. 1 (1978): 46–57.

Wilcox, David R. "Anthropology in a Changing America: Interpreting the Chicago 'Triumph' of Frank Hamilton Cushing." In *Coming of Age in Chicago: The 1893 World's Fair and the Coalescence of American Anthropology*, edited by Curtis M. Hinsley and David Wilcox, 125–52. Lincoln: University of Nebraska Press, 2015.

Wilcox, Ruth Turner. *Five Centuries of American Costume*. New York: Dover, 2004.

Wills, John E. "A Very Long Early Modern? Asia and Its Ocean, 1000–1850." In *Pacific America: Histories of Transoceanic Crossings*, edited by Lon Kurashige, 15–28. Honolulu: University of Hawai'i Press, 2017.

Wong, Bernard P., and Chee-Beng Tan, eds. *Chinatowns around the World: Gilded Ghetto, Ethnopolis, and Cultural Diaspora*. Leiden: Brill, 2013.

Wong, Deborah. *Louder and Faster: Pain, Joy, and the Body Politic in Asian American Taiko*. Berkeley: University of California, 2019.

——. *Speak It Louder: Asian Americans Making Music*. New York: Routledge, 2004.

Wong, K. Scott, and Sucheng Chan. *Claiming America: Constructing Chinese American Identities during the Exclusion Era*. Philadelphia: Temple University Press, 1998.

Wong, Lily. "*Transpacific*—Transfiguring Asian North America and the Sinophonic in Jia Qing Wilson-Yang's *Small Beauty*." In *Keywords in Queer Sinophone Studies*, edited by Howard Chiang and Alvin K. Wong, 16–37. New York: Routledge, 2020.

Wong, Marie Rose. *Sweet Cakes, Long Journey: The Chinatowns of Portland, Oregon*. Seattle: University of Washington Press, 2004.

Wong, Oliver. *Legions of Boom: Filipino American Mobile Disc Jockey Crews in the San Francisco Bay Area*. Durham, NC: Duke University Press, 2015.

Wong, Sau-ling Cynthia. "Autobiography as Guided Chinatown Tour? Maxine Hong Kingston's *The Woman Warrior* and the Chinese-American Autobiographical Controversy." In *Critical Essays on Maxine Hong Kingston*, edited by Laura E. Skandera-Trombley, 146–67. New York: G. K. Hall and Co., 1998.

Wu Jen-shu 巫仁恕. 品味奢華：晚明的消費社會與士大夫 [Taste of luxury: Consumer society and the scholar-literati circle in the Late Ming Dynasty]. Taipei: Academia Sinica, 2007.

Wunder, John R. "Anti-Chinese Violence in the American West, 1850–1910." In *Law for the Elephant, Law for the Beaver: Essays in the Legal History of the North American West*, edited by John McLaren, 212–36. Pasadena, CA: Ninth Judicial Circuit Historical Society, 1992.

Yan, Yuan. "Historical Transition of Chinese Theaters in Cuba." [Chinese] *Journal of Latin American Studies* 33, no. 6 (2011): 37–42.

Yang, Hon-Lun, and Michael Saffle. *China and the West: Music, Representation, and Reception*. Ann Arbor: University of Michigan Press, 2017.

Yang, Mina. *California Polyphony: Ethnic Voices, Musical Crossroads*. Urbana: University of Illinois Press, 2008.

Yoshida, Masako. "Trade Stories: Chinese Export Embroideries in the Metropolitan Museum." *Metropolitan Museum Journal* 49 (2014): 165–85.

Yoshihara, Mari. *Musicians from a Different Shore: Asians and Asian Americans in Classical Music*. Philadelphia: Temple University Press, 2008.

Yu, Henry. "The Rhythms of the Trans-Pacific" and "The Intermittent Rhythms of the Cantonese Pacific." In *Connecting Seas and Connecting Ocean Rims: Indian, Atlantic, and Pacific Oceans and China Seas Migrations from the 1830s*, edited by by Donna R. Gabaccia and Dirk Hoerder, 393–414. Leiden: Brill, 2011.

Yu, Siu wah 余少華. "二十世紀初的粵劇樂隊觀念：太平戲院文獻的啟示 [Cantonese opera accompaniment of the early 20th century: Revelation from the sources of the Taiping Opera Theater]. In *A Study on the Taiping Theatre Collection*, edited by Yung Sai-shing, 134–53. Hong Kong: Hong Kong Heritage Museum, 2015.

Yu Yong 余勇. 明清時期粵劇的起源、形成和發展 [Cantonese opera in the Ming-Qing period: origin, formation, and development]. Beijing: Zhongguo Xiju Chubanshe, 2009.

Yue ju da ci dian 粵劇大辭典 [A dictionary of Cantonese opera]. Guangzhou Shi: Guangzhou chu ban she, 2008.

Yung, Bell. *Cantonese Opera: Performance as Creative Process*. Cambridge: Cambridge University Press, 1989.

Yung, Bell, and Eleanor S. Yung, eds. *Uncle Ng Comes to America: Chinese Narrative Songs of Immigration and Love*. Hong Kong: MCCM Creation Co., 2014.

Yung, Judy. *The Adventures of Eddie Fung: Chinatown Kid, Texas Cowboy, Prisoner of War*. Seattle: University of Washington Press. 2007.

——. *San Francisco's Chinatown*. Chicago: Arcadia Publishing, 2006.

——. *Unbound Feet: A Social History of Chinese Women in San Francisco*. Berkeley: University of California Press. 1995.

——. *Unbound Voices: A Documentary History of Chinese Women in San Francisco*. Berkeley: University of California Press, 1999.

Yung Sai-Shing 容世誠. 尋覓粵劇聲影：從紅船到水銀燈 [From opera boat to silver screen: Visual and sonic culture of Cantonese opera]. Hong Kong: Oxford University Press, 2012.

——. "Moving Body: The Interactions between Chinese Opera and Action Cinema." In *Hong Kong Connections: Transnational Imagination in Action Cinema*, edited by Meaghan Morris, Siu-leung Li, and Stephen Chan Ching-kiu, 21–34. Durham, NC: Duke University Press; Hong Kong: Hong Kong University Press, 2005.

——. "Mulian Rescues His Mother: Play Structure, Ritual, and Soundscapes." in *How To Read Chinese Drama: A Guided Anthology*, 349–66, edited by Patricia Sieber and Regina Llamas. New York: Columbia University Press, 2022.

——. 粵韻留聲：唱片工業與廣東曲藝 [Opera from the gramophone: A cultural history, 1903–1953]. Hong Kong: Institute for the Research of Humanities, Chinese University of Hong Kong, Cosmos Press, 2006.

——. "Preliminary Reflections about the History of Chinese Opera of Hong Kong: Theater, Steamship, and Gramophone (1860–1911)." In *Cross-Border, Exchange and Transformation of Chinese Opera in the Early Twentieth Century*, edited by Wu Wan-yi, 5–29. Conference at Department of Chinese Culture, Hong Kong Polytechnic University, 2021. Hong Kong: Joint Publishing, 2022.

——. "Recording Cantonese Opera and Music in the 1920s and 1930s from a Viewpoint of Cultural History." *Journal of Chinese Studies* 12 (2003): 473–502.

——, ed. 戲園・紅船・影畫:源氏珍藏「太平戲院文物」研究 [A study of the Tai Ping Theatre Collection]. Hong Kong: Hong Kong Heritage Museum, 2015.

——. "Taiping Theatre in the History of Cantonese Opera." In *Bonham Strand: East Meets West and South Meets West*, edited by Victor Cheng, 74–100. Hong Kong: Zhonghua Shuju, 2020.

——. "Territorialization and the Entertainment Industry of the Shaw Brothers in Southeast Asia." In *China Forever: The Shaw Brothers and Diasporic Cinema*, edited by Poshek Fu, 131–53. Urbana: University of Illinois Press, 2008.

Zarrilli, Phillip B. "Toward a Phenomenological Model of the Actor's Embodied Modes of Experience." *Theatre Journal* 56, no. 4 (2004): 653–66.

Zhang Yuanyuan 張圓圓. 《坦園日記》中的戲曲史料研究 [A study on historical materials of *xiqu* in Tanyuan Diary]. Master's thesis, Shanxi Normal University, 2013.

Zheng, Su. *Claiming Diaspora: Music, Transnationalism, and Cultural Politics in Asian/Chinese America.* New York: Oxford University Press, 2010.

Zhu Wei-bin and Jing Min 朱衛斌 敬敏. "論傅列秘對美國華僑的保護 [Research on Frederick Bee's protection of Chinese in America]" 學術研究 *Academic Studies* 8 (2019): 106–13.

Zukowski, Chelsea Tatham. "Reconnecting America: P. T. Barnum and the Trans-continental Railroad." *Saber and Scroll Journal* 8, no. 3 (2020): 3–15.

Index

Page numbers in italics refer to figures and tables.

actresses, Chinese, 102–3, 152, 209–10, 215, 236; on *Harper's Bazaar* cover, 227–29, *228*

Adelphi Theatre, 28–29, 50, 68; Chinese opera performances, 69–73, *70*; "Dutch act," 70, 289n7; *La sonnambula* (Bellini), 26–27, 38, 70

admission. *See* ticket prices

Ah Ching (merchant), 75, 77

Ah Ching (musician), 106–7, 176

Ah Chow, 82, *83*, *115*, *176*

Ah Fue, 295n21, 314n66

Ah Look (actor), 99

Ah Look (musician), 106, *115*

Ah Lum, 82, *176*

Ah Quin (Tom Chong-kwan): diary pages, *xiii*, *241*, 252; employment and filial responsibility, xii, 242, 272n14, 272n19, 324n10; theatergoing habits, ix–xv, 11, 132, 143–44, 148–49, 239–42

Ah Sam, 97, 103

Ah Sing, 154

Ah Sue (Bung Ah Soo), 16, 166, 175–77, *176*, 178–79, 240

Ah Wung Sing, 184–85

Ak Ling Tong Company, 99, *101*

Amador County, CA, 56

American Civil War, 41, 84

American Folklore Society, 12, 18, 233–34, 236, 322n90

American stages, Chinese actors on, 179, 184–85

American Theatre, 52, 53; revenues, *87*; Tong Hook Tong's debut at, 27–32, *28*, 37, 281n47

Angell Treaty (1880), 150, 154, 155

Annamite Theater, 231–32, 320nn64–65

anthropology, term usage, 232, 320n71, 320n74

anti-Chinese sentiment, 7, 116–17, 220, 244, 246; Canadian head tax and, 185; Chinese community leaders and, 23–24, 219; city ordinances and, 88, 103–8, *106*, 247–49, 250, 251, 325n35; in Los Angeles, 11, 298n70; in mining towns, 42, 43, 55–58; mockery of Chinese theater and music, 32–33, 131, 184, 190, 245, 249, 252, 256, 326n45; opium dens and, 226–27; restriction laws and bans, 153–56, 222–23; riots and expulsions, 18, 127–28, 131, 136, 137, 162, 307n42. *See also* sound erasure

architecture, 37, 90, 128, 129, 148–49

archives, xvi–xvii, 18, 244, 246, 249–52, 254

Arditi, Luigi, 182

arias, 186, 259–61

arrests and imprisonment, 141, 156, 160, 162, 249; for noise and curfew violations, 103, 106–7, 126–27, 247

art collectors, 187, 198–99, 312n34, 312n36, 313n49

Arthur, Chester, 153–54
Assing, Norman (Yuan Sheng), 8, 21–25, 26, 220, 282n48, 282n63; in *Daily Alta California*, *28*, 34
Auburn, CA, 43, 45–46, 50, 53, 54, 58–59, 74
audiences: adaptations for local, 112; American, 28, 30, 62, 91, 181–82, 230, 273n34; Becker's drawing of, 91, *92*, 93–94, 206; curfews and raids and, 126–27; eating and smoking, *73*, 75, 85, 185, *200*, 200–201, 217; elite Chinese women, 72, 93–94; emotional reactions, 242–43; enthusiasm, 108–9, 114; famous visitors and artists, 182; illustrations of Caucasian, 234, *235*; laughter, 177, 186; literacy of, 74; mixed-race, 58, 61; "porous socialization" and, 241, 323n6; reactions of Chinese, 69, 179, 183, 217, 224–25; separated by gender, 75, 76, 86, 201–2; social class and, 93, 132, 143, 214; throwing money on stage, 224

Bachner, Andrea, 252
backstage doors (*hudu men*), 69, 73–74, 112, 148, 171, 205, 216
Baldwin, Catherine, 188
Baldwin Theater, 17, 193–94
bangzi tune, 259, 261
banners, 19, *20*, 21, 147; in Chinese theaters, 172, *173*, 173–74, *174*
banquets, 76, 84, 89, 110, 146, 147, 294n6, 300n13
Barnum, Phineas T., 97, 222
Bar of a Gambling Saloon, The (Marryat), *51*, 51–52, 286n46
Beach, George W., 38
Becker, Joseph, 18, 194, 217, 295n15; Hing Chuen Yuen theater drawing, 97, *98*; "The Coming Man," 11, 91, *92*, 93–94, 96, 112, 132, 206
Belasco, David, 17, 179, 194
Bengya Qi, 118, *119*, 300n8
Berlioz, Hector, 324n18
Bernhardt, Sarah, 170, 230
Berson, Misha, 7, 10
Bert's New Idea Melodeon. *See* Union Theatre/New Idea Theatre

Bigler, Gov. John, 23–24, 31, 52, 282n48, 287n64, 291n41
"Birth Day Celebration of Three very Distinguished Men" (opera), 47, *48*
Birthday Greetings from Eight Immortals (opera), 65, 261. See also *Eight Genii* (opera)
boating scenes, 15–16, 178–79, 210
Bohemian Club, 11, 182, 277n52; members and theatrical productions, 188–89, 212, 310nn9–10, 314n64; Wores of, 193, 194, 212
Booth, Edwin, 62, 211
Borthwick, John David, 37, 52, 245
Boston: Chinese theater, 12, 134–35, 233–34, *235*, 236, 237; merchants, 6
Boston Daily Globe, 134–35, 211, 222, 225, 233–34, *235*
Brecht, Bertolt, 15, 16
Brignoli Italian Opera Troupe, 9, 64
British Columbia. *See* Victoria, BC
brothels, 45, 93, 290n14
Buddhism, 35, *36*, 64, 66, 219
Bung Ah Soo. *See* Ah Sue
Burlingame, Anson, 89, 294n3, 294n6
Burlingame Treaty (1868), 5, 88, 89, 99, 116, 150, 153–54, 294n3
Bush Street theater, 184

California: Chinese theater's development in, 2, 8–12; constitution, 24, 150; interior region, 41–42, 45–48, *46*, 66–67, *68*, 72–73, 74; mining towns, 42–45, 55–56; Oregon railroad link, 60, 61; population, 5, 82, 276n42, 285n21; socioeconomic transformation, 1, 88; statehood, 19, 21, 25, 275n27, 279n3
California Steam Navigation Company, 67
California Theatre, 102, 131
Cantonese opera: adaptations for American audiences, 112; boating scenes in, 15–16; cast lists and role types, 118, *119*, 120, *121*, 122–23, 195, *196*, 300n8, 301nn11–12; dialects, xv, 74, 175, 290n24, 308n25; in Foshan, 214; in Guangdong region, x, xv, 1, 2–3, 273n31; instruments

of the orchestra, 69, 74, 75, *76*; plot types, 65, 178, 192, 208–9, 285n30, 307n9; premiere in San Francisco, *27*, *28*, 29–32; prohibition of women performers, xvi, 102; religious events and, 3, 65–66, 260–61; in Sacramento, 47–48, *49*, 247; stylistic characteristics, 259–60; transpacific history of American music and, 254–55; venue types, 3–4, 36, 73, 274n9, 283n73

Carvalho, Charles, 75, 89, 294n6

Central Pacific Railroad Company (CPRR), 41, 58–59, 60, 90, 91

Central Valley, CA, 42, 44, 45, 47, 77, 276n42

Century Illustrated Magazine: "In a Chinese Theater" (Fitch), 190–93; "The Chinese Theater" (McDowell and artists), *167*, 168–69, 194–206, 238, 307n9

Certeau, Michel de, xvi, 252

certificates of entry, 154, 156–58, 159–61, 305n3; for returning laborers, 162, 317n31

Chae Chan Ping v. United States, 231, 319n61

Chan, Sau-yan, 65, 261

Chan, Sucheng, 42, 43–44, 285n15

Chang, Gordon H., 42, 55, 58–59, 65, 94

Chautauquan Monthly, 190, 213–17, *216*

Chen, Yong, xiv, 272n27, 302n53

Cheng, Anne Anlin, 14, 278n69

Chen Lanbin (Chun Lan Pin), 138–40, *140*

Chen Shutang, 146, 147

Che Young Kwong Builds a Ship That Sails on Land (opera), 209–10

Chicago, 221–22, 316n18; World's Columbian Exposition (1893), 12, 317n27, 323n95

Chicago Daily Inter Ocean, 221–22

Chicago Daily Tribune, 86, 89, 140, 221, 293n78

Chicago Opera Company, 222

Chico, CA, 50, 57, 58, 60, 66, 74

China Hill, CA, 54

Chinatown (Los Angeles), 11, 298n70

Chinatown (New York), 237. *See also* New York City

Chinatown (San Francisco), xii, 110, 164, 187, 197, 292n41, 314n66; Bohemian Club and, 188–89, 310n10; new Celestial Theatre, 37–38; police raids, 162; theater locations, xi, 98–100, *100*, *151*, 152, 171, *172*

China–US trade, 5–7, 25, 32–34, 116, 153. *See also* Chy Lung & Co.

Chinese-American identity, 18, 174–75, 219, 254–55

"Chinese Buddhistic Worship in San Francisco" (Nahl), 35, *36*, 283n71

Chinese characters, 73–74, 113, 213, 255, 296n41; in Ah Quin's diary, ix–x, xii, 242, 252; on banners, 172, *173*, 173–74, *174*; in newspapers, 118, *119*, 249, *250*; number of strokes, 272n17; on posters, 225, 318n47

Chinese Consolidated Benevolent Association (CCBA), 162. *See also* Six Companies

"Chinese Drama, The" (Masters), 189, 190, 213–17

Chinese Exclusion Act (1882). *See* Chinese Restriction Act (1882)

Chinese immigrants: arrival in California, xi, 41, 42, 73, 81, 154, 271n8; community and belonging, xvii, 36, 40, 55, 240, 254, 255; deportation, 162; free theater admission, 100; from Guangdong, x, 5, 175; illegality and identity papers, 159–62; importance of theater to, xvii–xviii, 25, 45, 132, 240–42, 250, 273n34; linguistic identity, 175, 253–54; miners, 41–45; participation in processions, 19, *20*, 21–22, 24–25, 40; restrictions and laws, 24, 128, 150, 153–63, 220, 305n3, 305n47; returning laborers, 158, 162, 223, 231, 317n31, 319n61; in Southeast Asian archipelago, 1, 4; transpacific crossing, 5–7, 32–34, 275n13; US population growth, 1, 5, 73, 116, 271n8, 274n1. *See also* anti-Chinese sentiment; Burlingame Treaty (1868); stereotypes

"Chineseness," 14, 220, 249
Chinese (or Chinese-English) newspapers, 18, 117–18, 139; *Chinese American*, 219; *Golden Hills' News*, 41, 299n7; *The Oriental*, 34, 118, *119*, *121*, 122–23, 249–50, *250*, 300n7; *San Francisco China News*, 110–11, 118, 300n7
Chinese New Year, 72, 89, 103, 150, 239, 294n7
Chinese opera theater, term usage, xv–xvi
Chinese Restriction Act (1882), xiv, 18, 153–56, 161–62, 305n3, 326n50; Chinese actors and, xviii, 156–58, 163, 170
"Chinese Theater, The" (McDowell): Cox's illustrations, 194–95, *196*, 197; impact on theater arts, 210–12; overview of, 194, *195*; Wores's illustrations, *167*, 168–69, 197–204, 217
Chu Fong, 237, 322n94, 323n96
Chung, Sue Fawn, 25, 275n13
Chy Lung & Co., *79*, 79–80, 291n41, 292n42, 294n6
citizenship, 43, 153–54, 284n11, 285n17
city ordinances: cubic air ordinance, 106, 107–8, 125–26, 249, 298n67; noise ordinance, 103–8, *106*, 115, 247–49; police enforcement, 126–27, 247; sidewalk ordinance, 106, 125–26
civil rights, 116, 135; advocate Wong Chin Foo, 12, 18, 218, 219–20, 237
Civil Rights Act (1875), 117
Clay, Henry, 25, 280n24
Collector of Customs (San Francisco), 154, 155, 156
comic roles, 15, 175, *176*, 177, 180–81, 184, 192
commercial theaters, 4, 10, 88, 135, 150, 283nn72–73, 325n22
competition. *See* rivalries and competition
construction workers, 33, 59
"coolies," 23, 57, 97
costumes: animal, 111–12, 113, 133, *134*; assistance for putting on, 114; cost or value of, 27, 75, 78, 222; emperor, 61, 62, 96, 180–81; European, 52;

of female impersonators, 183; of lead actors, *167*, 168–69, 176–77; nonlaborer immigration status and, 155–56, 158; at Paris Exposition, 232; for role types, 177, *178*; shipping of, 6; of spiritual leaders, 65; Tang dynasty, 227, *228*; visuality of, 2, 13–15; warrior, 14, 75, 123–24, *124*, *125*, 179–80, 213, 227. *See also* headdresses
Cox, Kenyon, 18, 312n26; illustrations, 194–95, *196*, 197, 200, 209, 210, 215, 226
criminalization, 7, 88, 106, 160, 247–48, 256
Crocker, Charles Templeton, 189, 212
crossdressing. *See* female impersonation
cubic air ordinance, 106, 107–8, 125–26, 249, 298n67
Culin, Stewart, 233, 320n71
cultural production, xiv, xvii, 8, 32, 188–89, 219, 253, 276n35; mining towns and, 42, 45, 55
curfew ordinance, 104, 107, 126, 301n26
Curlett, William, 128, 129
Cushing, Frank Hamilton, 210, 314n57, 320n71
cymbals, 19, *76*, 133, 180, 181, 186, 191, 260

daai hei (greater theater), xv–xvii
Daily Alta California, 7, 40, 50, 137; Adelphi Theatre ad, 69, *70*; on bringing Chinese theater to the East Coast, 210–11, 314n58; Chy Lung & Co. ad, *79*; on Donn Quai Yuen theater, 164–65; on El Dorado theatrical troupe, 55–56; on Fourth of July celebrations, 19, 21; on George Washington's birthday celebrations, 21–22; on Hing Chuen Yuen theater, 89–91; on Hong Gee Cheong, 159–60; letters to Gov. Bigler, 23–24, 52, 291n41; list of ships and passengers, 6, 275n27; Lyceum Theater ad, 81–82, *83*; on Maguire's Opera House, 76–77, *78*; Po Fung Nin Dramatic Company ad, *109*, 110; on Poo Hing Hee Yung theater, 128–29; Quon San Yok ad, 141, *142*, 143; Royal

Chinese Theatrical Company ad, *102*; Sacramento Theater ad, *48*; Tong Hook Tong ad, 27–30, *28*, 34, 281n47; on Wing Tie Ping theater merger, 144–45, *145*

Daily Evening Bulletin, 50, 61, 69, 75, 87, 99, 194, 310n9; on Donn Quai Yuen theater, 147–48; on Hing Chuen Yuen theater, 108–9; on Hong Gee Cheong identity case, 160–61; on Loo Chin Goon, 170; on Lyceum Theatre, 81–82; on Maguire's Opera house, 77–78; review of *Six Warlords*, 112; on Royal Chinese Theatre, 115; on San Francisco's cosmopolitan theater scene, 72–73

Dajia Sheng. *See* Ti Gar Sing

Dance of Promotion (opera), 65, 261

Dan Guei Yuan theater. *See* Donn Quai Yuen theater

Dan Shan Feng theater, 190, 200, 239, 313n45; audience experiences, 182–83; *Che Young Kwong Builds a Ship That Sails on Land* production, 209–10; costumes for role types, *178*; interior and location, *151*, *152*, 171–73, *172*, *173*, *204*, 204–5; personnel and roles, 175–77, *176*; *Six Warlords* production, 179–81; theatrical innovations, 178–79, 210

Dark Conspiracy, A (play), 224

Davidson, Harry, *195*, *199*, 200

Davis, Ronald L., 9, 27, 277n44

Deady, Matthew P., 156–57, 160, 306n18

Defeated Revenge (opera), 29–30

deities, 64, 130; opera performances as worship to, xv–xvi, 3, 30, 35, 57, 65, 207, 214, 260–61, 313n51; in opera plots, 69

dialects, xv, 32, 147, 254, 296n40, 300n12; of Guangdong immigrants, 175; Zhongzhou (Central dialect), 74, 207–8, 259, 290n24, 308n25

Di Ca Sing. *See* Ti Gar Sing

diplomacy, 136, 138–40, 149, 294n3

Donizetti, Gaetano, 38, 64, 80, 98

Donn Quai Yuen theater, xiii, 185, 200, 214, 313n45; arson incident, 164–65; construction and significance of, 147–50, 304n36; exterior, *205*, 205–6;

Fitch's article on, 190–93; interior, 148–49, *149*, 173–74, *174*, 182, *216*, 216–17, 315n74; location, *151*, 152, 171, *172*

Dragon Disputing Pearls, The (opera), 191–92

Edison Phonograph Company, 324n12

education. *See* mission schools

Eichin, Carolyn, 72, 290n14, 290n21

Eidsheim, Nina Sun, 245, 246, 252

Eighteen Grand Cantonese Operas, 47–48

Eight Genii (opera), *28*, 29–30, 38, 261

El Dorado, CA, 45, 56, 74

Elkhart Daily Review, 219–20

English-language theater, 70, 80, 82, 170, 209, 290n12

Era (London newspaper), 100, 152, 181

erasure. *See* sound erasure

erhuamian role type, *118*, 195, *196*, 197, 202, 227

erhuang tune, 259

erxian, *76*, 115, 212, *213*, 252, 260

ethnology, term usage, 232, 320n71

European Ravel troupe, 72

evil spirits, 6, 35, 123, 130, 289n113

exports, 33, 81, 116

face paint, 114, 195, 202–3

Fales, William E. S., 227, 229–30, 318nn49–50, 319n54

Fauser, Annegret, 231, 320n66

Fay-Yen-Fah (opera), 212

Feather River, 59

Fellezs, Kevin, 255

female impersonation, 16, 69, 70, 82, 85, 192, 322n84; of Dan Shan Feng theater actors, 175, *176*; Hong Gee Cheong's, 159–61, 306n30; Ti Gar Sing's, 122, 242. *See also* Ah Sue (Bung Ah Soo)

festivals, 3, 65–66, 189

Field, Kate, 210

Fitch, George Hamlin, 189–90, 190–93, 201, 215, 217, 311n15

Fok Yam Tang, 240

folk rites, 3, 4, 50

Folsom Theatre, 84

footwear, 31, 52, 133, 168, 176, 183

Foreign Miners' Tax (1850), 23, 43, 55–56, 280n17, 284n11, 287n64
Fourth of July, 19, *20*, 21, 40
Frank Leslie's Illustrated Magazine, 85, 132, 295n15, 295n24; "Chinese Drama in New York City," 225–27, *226*; circulation, 96–97; entry to the Hing Chuen Yuen theater, 97, *98*; "Interior of the Royal China Theatre," 132–33, *133*; "The All-Night Supper Spread in the Dressing Room of the Royal Theatre," 133–34, *134*; "The Coming Man," 11, 91, *92*, 93–94, 96, 112
Frank Leslie's Popular Monthly, 132
Frenzeny, Paul, 310n10

gambling, 45, *51*, 51–52, 85, 100, 117
Geary Act (1892), 161–62, 213
Gee Quuen Yung theater, 148, 239–41
Gerster, Etelka, 11, 159, 182
gesticulations, 75, 177; moving water and, 15–16, 178
Gibson, Rev. Otis, 136, 137, 240, 303n6
Gihon, John H., 27
Globe Hotel theater, 84–85, 86–87, *101*, 296n31; competition, 98–99, 293n78; location, *100*
Golden Era, 37
Golden Giant, The (play), 184–85
Golden Hills' News, 41, 299n7
Golden-leaved Chrysanthemum (opera): plot and significance of, 241–43; transcription of, 261, *262*–65; Victor Monarch recording, *243*, 243–44, 252, 261, 324nn11–12
gold rush, xvii, 33, 59, 275n15, 287n57; arrival of Chinese emigrants, 5, 6, 24, 41, 42, 64; in British Columbia, 81; saloons, *51*, 51–52
gongjiao role type, *118*, 195, *196*, 197, 261
gongs, 75, *76*, 93, 191, 245; ordinance on beating upon, 104–7, *106*, 248–49
Goong Bee, *176*, 177
Grand Opera House, 141, *142*, 143, *143*, 185
Grand Theatre. *See* Donn Quai Yuen theater
Grant, Ulysses S., 146–47, 193

Grass Valley, CA, 45, 50, 53–55, 57, 59, 65, 74
Great Rebellion, The (opera), 47, *49*
Guangdong: immigration, x, 5, 175; opera history, 2, 4, 300n8
Guangzhou: Cantonese opera, 3, 13, 120, 122, 300n11; dialect, 175; merchants, 2–3, 32; trade networks, 6
Guia T. Mot, 152

Hab Wa, 23, 291n41
Haenni, Sabine, 276n35
hairstyles, 93, 114, 229, 290n13; of elite Chinese women, 72, 94, *94*, 95; female impersonation and, 177
Harper's Bazaar, 12, 96, 227–29, *228*, 236, 319n51
Harper's Weekly, 227, 229–30
Hartman, Saidiya, 246, 252
Hauser, Miska, 11, 68
Hayes, Rutherford B., 11, 140, 149–50
headdresses, 113, 191; helmets, 168, 179–80; of warriors, 14, 75, 93, 123–24, *124*, *125*, *228*, 229
Heavenly Maiden Delivers a Son, The (opera), 65, 261
Helena, MT, 221, 316n20
heterogeneity, 255
Hing Chuen Yuen theater: construction and inaugural performance, 88, 89–91, 93, 130, 294n6, 325n22; entrance, 97, *98*; location, 99, *100*; new management and reopening, 108–9; stagecraft and critical reception, 96–97; success and competition, 98–99, 102
Hing Kig Chung theater, 239, 241
Hi-Yah-Tak-Kee (acrobatic troupe), 87
Ho, Virgil Kit Yiu, xiv
Ho King, xviii, 156–57, 163, 306n21
Holmes, Oliver Wendell, 233, 322n90
Hong Gee Cheong, 159–61, 306n30
Hong Kong, 4, 5, 10, 26; San Francisco trade, 5–7, 33–34, 275n17, 275n20
Hong Kong Gazette, 32–33
Honolulu, 145, 156, 304n28
Howe, George, 137
Howells, William Dean, 233, 236, 322n90

Hua Hsu, 255

huiguan, 6, 8, 23, 99, 139, 279n12; social influence, 24–25, 34; venues at, 3–4, 36

Hung Wah, 59, 287n77

Illustrated Sporting and Dramatic News, 212

imports, 79, 116, 292n41

"In a Chinese Theater" (Fitch), 189–90, 190–93, 201

Indianapolis Journal, 185, 218

In re Ho King, xviii, 156–57, 163, 306n21

interpreters, 47, 53, 75, 89, 149, 183, 184, 211

Israelite (newspaper), 100, 296n41

Issei, Tanaka, 35

Italian opera, 39, 73, 82, 99, 135, 182; Brignoli performances, 9, 64; Donizetti's, 38, 64, 80, 98

Jackson Street theaters (San Francisco), xi, 18, 87, 88, *101*, 308n20; Hing Kig Chung theater, 239, 241; maps of, *151*, 171, *172*; merger, 144–45; noise complaints from, 106, 107; Que Hing Log, ix–x, xii; Sing Ping Yuen, *109*, 109–15, 122, 130, 134, 141. *See also* Dan Shan Feng theater; Hing Chuen Yuen theater; Royal Chinese Theatre

Japanese immigrants, 253, 326n50

Jardine, Matheson & Co., 22, 33

Jenny Lind Theatre, 29

Jing Tsu, xii

jinks, 188–89, 212

Jiqing Gongsuo (guild), 3, 165–66, 260; cast lists of troupes, 118, *119*, 120, *121*, 122–23, 125, 140, 147

Joint Investiture of a Prime Minister of Six Warlords (opera), 38, 60–61, 70, 130, 148, 237, 317n27; cow characters, 111–12, 299n88; plot and popularity of, xxi, 29–30, 111–12, 260

Journalist, 219

Journey to the West (Wu Cheng'en), 30, 47

jugglers, 27, 28, 185

Kearney, Denis, 128, 131, 137, 146–47, 219, 230

Kin Yip Oak. See *Golden-leaved Chrysanthemum* (opera)

Knox, Thomas W., 91, 93, 96

Koegel, John, 7

kun and *yiyang* tunes, 32

Kwon, Marci, 256

labor shortage, 41, 58, 97

Lai ChuChuen, 292n41

Lai Fong, 123–25, *124*, *125*, 168, 301n20

Lai Yong, 94, *95*, 295n19

Lam Yap Ca (Lin Yuejiao), 241–42, 252

Land of Happiness, The (Redding and Crocker), 212

Langley's San Francisco City Directory, 171

Lau Ow Bew v. United States, 157

Lava Beds, CA, 56

Laver, Augustus, 128, 129

lead actors: community fervor for, 240; competition for, 165–66; description and duties of, 166, *167*, 168–70; professionalism, 230; salaries, 141, 144, 148, 159, 166, 192

Lee, Anthony, 188–89

Lee, Esther Kim, 220, 309n46, 315n11

Lee Bing, 316n17

Lee Kan (Mr. Likeoon), *28*, 34, 38, 282n63, 300n7

Lee Kay, 221–22

Lee Tin Toy Co., 84

Lee Tom, 138

Lee Young, 150

Lei, Daphne Pi-Wei, 273n34, 280n28

Leong Ahghue, 47

Leong Yow, 144, 166

Leslie, Miriam, 132

letter sheet, *36*, 283n71

Lew-Williams, Beth, 154, 275n18

licenses, theater, 104–5, 237, 247–48, 296n31

Li Hsiao-t'i, 3, 4

linguistic identity, 175, 253–54

Li Po Tai, 18, 110–11, *111*, 160, 171, 298n82

listening practice, 18, 244–53, 254, 326n40

literacy, 97
Liu, April, 123–24, 168
living arrangements, 103, 125–26
Loo Chin Goon, 163, 169–70, 218–19
Look Sun Fung theater, 130, 144, 145, *146*, 166, 272n17; Ah Quin's time at, ix, x. *See also* Poo Hing He Yuen theater
Los Angeles: Chinese theaters, xiv, 12, 237, 272n25, 277n54; mass lynching, 11, 108, 298n70
Los Angeles Herald, 135, 154–55
Lowe, Lisa, 255
Loyal Slave, The (opera), 219, 223
Lucia di Lammermoor (Donizetti), 80
Lung Quong Toy Dramatic Company, 98–99, 101, 245, 325n20
Lyceum Theatre, 10, 68, 72, 73, 81–82, *83*, 88

Madison Street Theater, 221, 222, 317n25
magicians, 27, 53
Maguire, Thomas, 75, 76–77, 194, 292n46
Maguire's Opera House, 131; billboard, *80*; Chinese operas, 10, 68, 70, 73, 76–81, *78*; competition, 81–82, 86; Italian and English operas, 80; revenues, *87*; Royal Chinese Theatrical Company at, *102*, 102–3
Manning, Rev. Samuel, 112, *113*, 194, 206, 299n88
Mariposa, CA, 45, 51, 53, 56, 74
Maritana (Wallace), 80
Markham, William, 116–17
Marryat, Frank, *51*, 51–52, 286n46
Marshall, Walter Gore, 189–90, 197, 245, 311nn12–13
Marsh Troupe of Juvenile Comedians, 72
Martinetti troupe, 72
Marysville, CA, 57, 66, 72; railroad construction and Chinese theater, 9, 45, 59–64; total population, 59, 277n47
Marysville Daily Appeal, 60–62, *61*, *63*, 64
Marysville Theater, 9, 45, 60–64, *101*

Masters, Rev. Frederic J., 189, 190, 213–17
material truth, 251, 252
McCullough, John, 62, 170
McDougal, John, 19, 284n11
McDowell, Henry Burden, 247, 311n20, 313n49, 322n90; influence on his contemporaries, 210–12, 218, 237; literary and theatrical interests, 189, 190, 193–94, 211, 311nn22–23; "The Chinese Theater" essay, 194–95, *196*, 197–210, 217; on Wores's *The Entry*, *167*, 168–69, 307n9
McDowell, Irvin, 146, 193, 197
McKittrick, Katherine, 246
Mender of Cracked Chinaware, The (opera), 214–15
merchants: anti-Chinese sentiments and, 23; in British Columbia, 81; Chy Lung & Co., *79*, 79–80, 292nn41–42, 295n6; engagement in US politics, 25, 146; Guangzhou, 2–3, 32; legal victories, 156–57; Ming dynasty, 274n3; Restriction Act (1882) and, 157–58; support for theater activities, 75, 77, 90, 97, 145–47, 221–22, 225, 237, 316n17; theater troupes and, xiv, 3, 4; transpacific trade and, 5, 6, 32–34
Meriwether, Lee, 234, 322n84
Metropolitan Theatre, 10, 64, 73, 86, 99, 245, 293n78; revenues, *87*
Mikado, The (opera), 184, 222, 317n25
Ming dynasty, 3–4, 47, 214, 274n3
Ming Sing, 53
mining companies, 44, 116
mining towns: Chinese miners and racial politics in, 42–45, 55–56, 81; circulation of opera troupes, 8–10, 17, 41, 45–55, 74; distribution of population in, 276n42; railroad lines and, 59–60. *See also* Foreign Miners' Tax (1850)
mission schools, 5, 18, 22, 122, 136–38, 213, 240
mixed-race socializing, *51*, 51–53, 57
"Mo li hua" (song), 234, 322n83
Moo Sung Jee, 230
Morrison, Toni, xvi–xvii
Mountain Wizard (opera), 47, *49*

Mulian Rescues His Mother (tale), 66
Mung Qua Choy, 183
musical instruments, 34, 138; in Cantonese opera accompaniment, 75, *76*, 90, *115*, 132–33, 180, 185–86, 191, 260; folk music, 236; noise complaints, 104–7, *106*, 247–49, 325n35. *See also individual instrument*
musical transcription, 231–32, 234, *235*, 322n84; of *Golden-leaved Chrysanthemum*, 261, *262–65*
musicians: arrests, 103, 106–7, 247, 250; census records of, 103, 297n46; earnings, 277n4; orchestral, 69, 74, 75, *76*, 180, 234, *235*, 236; for Po Fung Nin troupe, 114, *115*; spoken dialogue and, 185–86. *See also* singing
My Neighbor's Wife (opera), 31
My Partner (Campbell), 184, 316n11

Nahl, Charles Christian, 35, *36*, 283n71
Nevada City, CA, 53, 64, 74
New Chinese Theatre. *See* Sing Ping Yuen theater
New Idea Theatre. *See* Union Theatre/ New Idea Theatre
New York Amusement Gazette, 223, 317n32
New York City, 170, 198, 211, 212, 254, 300n12, 317n32; arrival of Chinese theater, 12, 218–20, 223–25, 232, 318n46, 321n75; Doyer Street theater, 237–38, 321n75, 322n94, 323n96; first Chinese-language newspaper, 219; merchants, 318n47; social elites ("400"), 233, 321n79; Tong Hook Tong performances in, 38–40, 225
New York Clipper, 73, 102, 103
New-York Daily Times, 75, 85, 147, 169, 223, 291n31, 321n79; Tong Hook Tong ad, 38, *39*
New York Herald, 31, 38–39, 85, 140, 157, 319n51; on Chinese theater in New York, 222–25, 238
New York Tribune, 38–39, 127, 224, 315n9
Ng, Wing Chung, 120, 125, 259, 274n9, 300n10

Ngai, Mae, 24, 116, 161, 277n43
Ngon, Yeng Pway, xv
Niblo's Garden, 39, 225
Nilsson, Christina, 159, 182
noise complaints: about the Globe Hotel theater, 98, 99, 296n31; city ordinances for, 103–7, 115, 247–49, 251, 325n35
nonlaborer status, 155, 156–58, 160, 305n3
nuisances, 105, 108, 247–49, 251

Oakland Theatre, 194, 211, 311n23
occupations, 44, 47, 97, 116. *See also* railroad workers
Ogden, Henry Alexander, 132, *133*, *134*, 194
opium dens, 226, 227
Oregon railroad line, 60, 61
Oriental (*Tangfan Gongbao*), 34, 249–50, *250*, 300n7; lists of Cantonese opera troupes, 118, *119*, 120, *121*, 122–23
Oroville, CA, 45, 52, 56, 60, 64, 66, 74
Orphan of China, The (opera), 273n34, 280n28

Page Act (1875), 244
pantomime, 82, 85, 96, 207–8, 310n46
Paris, 80, 84, 141, 143, 291n28, 323n6; Goupil & Cie. of, 198, 312n34; International Exposition (1867), 85; Universal Exposition (1889), 11–12, 18, 195, 218, 231–32, 320n74
Parsloe, Charles T., 220, 316n11
Parting at Park-Kew (opera), 29–30
Pasler, Jann, 11, 232, 234
Paul, Howard, 183–84
Pearl River Delta, x, 3, 8, *9*, 35, 57
Pellegrini Opera Company, 27, 70
People vs. Ah Tim and Ah Luck, 248
Pfaelzer, Jean, 43–44
Philadelphia, 163, 169–70, 198, 222
Piccadilly (1929), 14–15, 278nn68–69
placards, 53, 74, 96, 159
Placer County, CA, 43, 44, 45
playbills, 29–30, 209, 223, 236, 323n8
Po Fung Nin Dramatic Company, *109*, 110, 111–12, 114, *115*, 122

police raids, 117, 123, 126, 127, 160, 162, 249
Po Nge Yee dramatic company, 321n75
Poo Hing He Yuen theater, 127–32, 136–37, 144, 302n43. *See also* Look Sun Fung theater
Portland, OR: Chinese theater, 12, 156, 221, 237, 277n54, 316n17, 316n19; city ordinances, 251, 325n35
portraiture: of Cantonese opera performers, 123–25, *124*, *125*, 168, 301n20; Chinese names included in, 215–16; of high-society women and men, 94, *94*, *95*; of Li Po Tai, 110–11, *111*
Po Wah Ying theater, 322n84
Preemption Act (1841), 44, 285n17
Preston, Katherine, 84
printing technology, 11, 227
processions, 24–25, 34, 139, 280n24; Fourth of July, 19, *20*, 21–22, 40
programs. *See* playbills
prostitution, 72, 115, 290n14, 298n70
Pu Feng Nian troupe, *119*, *121*, 122, 300n13. *See also* Po Fung Nin Dramatic Company
puppet theater, 47, 58
purges, 43, 56, 162, 307n42

Qing dynasty, 3–4, 110, 113, 149, 280n24; Minister Chen's visit to the US, 136, 138–40
Quan Sun Yoke theater, ix, 144. *See also* Quon San Yok troupe
quartz mining, 53, 54, 287n57
Que Hing Log theater, ix–x, xii
Quon San Yok troupe, 140–41, *142*, 143, *143*, 304n22; cast lists for, *119*, *121*, 140
Quon Soon Tong Company, 99, *101*, 296n36
Quon Yet Tong Theatrical Company, 165, 166

racialization, 106, 134, 158–59; listening practices and, 246–49, 251–52. *See also* stereotypes; yellowface performance
railroad workers, 42, 64, 86; recruitment of, 58–59, 60, 91, 116, 288n79

Rankin, Mckee, 185
realism, 16–17, 178–79, 195, 240
Rebellion of Loo Fei, or the Chinese Joan of Arc (opera), 77
Redding, Joseph, 189, 212
Restriction Act (1882). *See* Chinese Restriction Act (1882)
Return of Sit Ping Quai, The (opera), 70–71, 260
revenues, theater, 38, 64, *87*, 108, 164
Rising of the Lions, or Looking at the Pictures (opera), 31–32, 282n50
ritual performances, xv, 3, 47, 55, 277n46, 313n51; community prosperity and, 9, 30; *matshed* structures for, 4, 50, 214; in mining and railroad town theaters, 64–66; for new temples, 34–35, 89; titles of operas for, 65, 260–61
rivalries and competition, 4, 29; Donn Quai Yuen and Dan Shan Feng theaters, 174, 190–91; Donn Quai Yuen and Wing Tie Ping theaters, 164–66; Hing Chuen Yuen and Globe Hotel theaters, 98–99; Maguire's Opera House and Lyceum Theatre, 81–82, 86; Royal Chinese Theatre, 122–23, 141, 144, 304n24
Rogers, William Allen, 227, *228*, 229, 319nn51–52
role types, 114, 195, *196*, 197, 204, 209, 261; of Dan Shan Feng personnel, 175–77, *176*, *178*; middle-aged warriors, 32, 123, *125*, 169, 183; summary and cast lists of, 118, *119*, 120, *121*, 122–23, 260
Rosebery, Lord, 198, 312n28, 312n36
Royal Chinese Theatre, 110, 114–15, 130, 132, 146, 171, *172*; rivalries, 122–23, 141, 144, 304n24; salaries of lead actors, 166; tragedy and deaths, 127, 129
Royal Chinese Theatrical Company, *102*, 102–3
Rusling, James, 84–85, 291n41, 293n69

Sacramento, 72, 145; Chinese theater in, 8, 9, 47–48, 62, 63, 66–67, 247–48, 326n37; location and population, 46–47, 63, 285n25; railway, 60

Sacramento Daily Union, 28, 32, *48*, 66–67, 247–48, 326n37

Sacramento News, 31

Sacramento River, 42, 57, 59

Sacramento Theater, 47–48, *48*, 49, 62, 73, 74, *101*

Sacrificial Offering to the White Tiger (opera), 260–61, 289n113

sailors, 154

Sala, George Augustus, 189–90, 197, 245, 311n13, 312n27

salaries: of actors, 10, 141, 144, 148, 159, 161, 166, 169, 192, 215; earnings of opera troupes, 38, 100, 221, 225; of musicians, 277n44; of personnel at Dan Shan Feng theater, 175, *176*; of theater proprietors, 103

Sam Kwok, 81, *83*

Sam Wang and the Pigs (opera), 183–84

Sam Yup (Yap) Association, 8, 99, 141

San Andreas, CA, 45, 50–51, 72, 74

Sandlot riot (1877), 18, 127–28, 136, 137

San Francisco: anti-Japanese campaign, 326n50; art scene, 188–89; Chinese consul general, 146–47, 150, 193; Chinese immigration, 6, 12, 34, 41, 81, 82, 86, 135, 154; Chinese theater's development in, 11–12, 17–18, 41–42, 257; cosmopolitan identity, 40, 80, 82, 98, 134–35; demand for Chinese theater, xiv–xv, 1, 81, 117, 164; first Chinese opera performances, 26–32, *28*; Fourth of July celebration (1852), 19, *20*, 21; Grant's visit to, 146–47, 193; merger of Chinese theaters, 144–47; Minister Chen's visit to, 138–40; non-English theater traditions, 7, 40; occupations of Chinese in, *44*; ordinances, 103–8, 125–27, 248–49; population, 10, 42, 97, 138, 272n27, 276n42; Presidio, xii, xiv; realism movement, 17; riots, 18, 127–28, 131, 136, 137; taxation, 138; theater competition, 97–99, 164–66; theater locations, x, xi, 98–100, *100*, *151*, 152, 171, *172*; theater revenues, *87*; total Chinese performers in, 103; trade with Hong Kong, 5–7, 33–34, 275n17, 275n20; unemployment rates, 116.

See also Jackson Street theaters; Washington Street theaters

San Francisco China News, 110, 118, 300n7

San Francisco Chronicle, 64, 97, *115*, 116, 122, 138, 185, 198; "Amusements" section, 130–31; on Chinese Mission School celebration, 136–37; on city ordinances, 105–8, 126; on Dan Shan Feng theater, 182–83; Fitch of, 190; on new Washington Street Chinese theater, 127–29, 302n43; review of Lung Quong Toy's performance, 245, 325n21; on Sing Ping Yuen theater, 113–14; *Six Warlords* plot, 111–12, 113

San Francisco Examiner, 16, 130, 155, 193, 240; on Dan Shan Feng theater, 174–75, 178–79, 179–81

San Francisco Fire Department Fund, 25

San Francisco Hall, 29, 38

San Francisco Herald, 23, 37, 76, 82

San Nang Foo troupe, *61*, 66, *101*

sanxian, 14, *76*, *115*, 133, 260, 279n69

Sawyer, Lorenzo, 160, 161

Scott Act (1888), 162, 222–23, 231, 317n31

Scribner's Monthly, 112, *113*, 206, 299n88

Seward, William, 294n3

shagu, *76*, *115*, 132, *133*, 212, *213*, 260, 302n56

Shakespeare, William, 7, 71, 72, 82, 170, 230

Shasta County, CA, 56

Shatuo Jiebing (*Borrowing Soldiers*) (opera), 31

Shatuo Moving the Army (opera), 285n30

Shaw, George Bernard, 313n38

Shegong Rong, *119*, 120, 300n8

Sheldon, Deacon, 52–53

Sheng Ping Theater, 10

ships. *See* steamships

Shy-Shy (Redding), 212

Sieber, Patricia, 15, 273n33

Siege of the House of Tso, The (opera), 69, 70

Sierra Nevada, 42, 45, 47, 53, 58, 91

silk embroidery: motifs and uses, 13–14; on opera costumes, 69, 75, 91, 123, 176, *178*, 180–81, 191, 227–29; ritual performances and, 35; on tapestry or curtains, 78, 90, 216, 236; trade, 27, 229, 281n33; worn by distinguished Chinese men, 22, 110–11; worn by wealthy Chinese women, 94, *94*, 95

singing, 65–66, 70, 137, 182, 192, 230; derision of, 190, 245, 249, 324n18; folk, 234, 236; stylistic characteristics, 259–60, 261

Sing Ping Yuen theater, *109*, 109–15, 122, 130, 134, 299n95; Quon San Yok troupe at, 141, 143

Sing Song Fung troupe, 98, *101*

Sinn, Elizabeth, 5–6, 33, 253

sinology, 214

Six Companies, 128, 139, 162, 169, 307n41

Six Warlords (or *Six Kings*). See *Joint Investiture of a Prime Minister of Six Warlords* (opera)

social class, 3; Boston elite, 234, *235*, 236, 322n90; hairstyles and attire and, 72, 93–94, 227; New York elite, 233, 321n79; ticket pricing and seating and, 132, 143, 182, 214. *See also* merchants

sonic color line, 158–59, 252

sonic ethnology, 11, 18, 190, 193, 218, 232, 234

Sonoma Democrat, 63

Son Son Fong troupe, 99, *101*, 296n34

sound erasure: act of listening through, 252, 253; Chinese American music history and, 254–55; mockery and criminalization and, 248–49, 256; prosperity in spite of, 250–51; types of, 244–47

Speer, Rev. William, 5, 22, 282n68, 299n7

Stage (London), 230

stagecraft, 50, 73–74, 112–13; bridge-crossing scenes, 71, 179; changing scenes, 208; lighting, 29, 88, 109, 182; minimalist settings, 15, 16, 178; placards, 74, 96; scenarios, 307n9; tables and chairs, 124–25, 216;

technological innovations, 15–16, 178–81

Stanford, Leland, 11, 60, 110, 197, 212, 311n20

star power. *See* lead actors

steamships, 81; *Berkshire*, 6, 32, 34; *Capital*, 66–67, 289n119; *Colorado*, 84; *Cortes*, 38; *Flora*, 60, 66, 67; *Moonlight*, 82; port of entry restrictions, 155, 156

stereotypes, xi, xviii, 144, 158–59, 160, 254; theater and artwork, 54, 184, 198, 225, 226–27, 312n27; Wong Chin Foo's challenges to, 230–31. *See also* yellowface performance

St. Louis Intelligencer, 29–30, 281n37

Stockton, CA, 45, 50, 58, 59, 72

Stoever, Jennifer, 158, 252

Stoler, Ann, 251

Sung Kong: The Robber Chief of the Laong Hills (opera), 31

Sun Heen Lok Theater Company, 103

Swentien Lok Royal Chinese dramatic company: disappearance of, 233; eastward tour, 221–23, 230, 316nn18–20; featured in magazines and newspapers, 225–30, *226*, *228*, 232; in Jiqing Gongsuo list, *119*; in New York City, 223–25, *224*, 300n12, 318n46

Syle, Rev. Edward, 45

symbolism, 16, 140, 203, 210; of Chinese opera, 1–2, 12; costumes and, 13–14, 177

Sze Yap (Siyi/Si Yup), 99

Sze Yup Association, 8, 47, 285n26

Taiping Rebellion (1851–64), 3

Tak-A-Wing, 230

Tanaka, Issei, 35

Tangfan Gongbao. See *Oriental* (*Tangfan Gongbao*)

Tang Xianzu, 214

Tchen, John, 220, 316n16

temples, 207, 214; construction of, 34–36, *36*, 110, 282n68; in goldmining towns, 64, 65; theater stages in, 3, 4–5, 36, 283n73

textiles, 124

Theatre of Arts and Letters, 211–12, 312n23, 322n90

theatricality, 1–2, 15–17; acrobatics or gymnastics, 75, 76, 85, 90, 102, 133, 141, 143; audience reactions to, xi, 252; pantomime, 82, 85, 96, 207–8, 310n46; use of feathers, 168

Thorpe, Ashley, 293n75

ticket prices, x, 37, 100, 114, 207, 214; Adelphi Theatre, 73; American Theater, 28, 281n47; Grand Opera House, 143; Lyceum Theatre, 82; Marysville Theater, 62; Poo Hing Hee Yung theater, 129, 132; Royal Chinese Theatre, 115; Sacramento Theater, 47, *48*; Windsor Theatre, 223

Tiersot, Julien, 232, 234

tigang xi practice, 307n9

Ti Gar Sing (Di Ca Sing/Daja Sheng), *119*, 122, 145, 147–48, 166, 173, 241–42

Toby Ho, *176*, 177, 180–81, 183, 308n28

Tom Chong-kwan. *See* Ah Quin

Tom Lee, 221, 225, 316n16, 321n75

Tong A-Chick (Tong Achick), 21, 22, 52, 79, 291n41; in *Daily Alta California*, *28*, 34; letter to Gov. Bigler, 23–24, 280n17, 282n48

Tong Hook Tong troupe: at the American Theater, 27–32, *28*, 37, 281n47; arrival in the US, 6, 8, 32–33; at Niblo's Garden, 38–40, *39*, 225, 283n89; North American tour, 281n34; theater construction and, 34–38

tong wars, 162

transcontinental railroad: Becker's illustrations and, 91, 295n15; Chinese laborers and contractors, 58–59, 86; completion of, 11, 18, 41, 59, 60, 88, 99, 245. *See also* Central Pacific Railroad Company (CPRR)

transpacific crossings, 1, 5–7, 14, 32–34, 82, 122, 255, 275n13; entry restrictions, 154, 156; Honolulu and, 145, 304n28; US census and, 253

transpacific history (of American music), xvii, xviii, 18, 253–56, 324n16

travelogues, 132, 189–90, 234, 245, 251

troupes: anti-Chinese hostility and, 55–58; cast lists and role types, 118, *119*, 120, *121*, 122–23, *176*, 300n8; circuit of California's interior, 8–10, 45–55, 66–67, 72–73, 74; competition among theaters and, 165–66, 293n78; continuous arrival of, 12, 27, 32–33, 81, 82, 86, 135; debut performances in San Francisco, 26–32, *28*, 41–42; dialects and, 74, 290n24; discipline, 177; eastward movement, 18, 38–40, 218, 221–25, 230–31, 233; family reunions, 239–40; immigration restrictions and, 155–56; living arrangements, 103; at Marysville Theater, 60–64; naming of, 250, 326n38; plaques for, 120, 300n10; recruitment of, xiv, 3, 47, 91, 98–99, 296n29; revenues, 38, 64; role of *huiguan*, 8; by size and city, 100, *101*; transpacific crossings, 5–7, 13, 34, 82, 84

Ung Yen, 166

Union Theatre/New Idea Theatre, 68, 73, 75, 76–77, 82, 84, 86–87, 131; destruction of, 296n36; location, 99, *100*; Yun Sing Ping Company at, 98, *101*, 296n29

United States, total Chinese population, 1, 5, 154, 163, 274n1

Vallejo Rail Company, 60

vessels. *See* steamships

Viceroy of Keang, The (opera), 77

Victoria, BC, 12, 81, 156, 158

Victor Monarch records, *243*, 243–44, 252, 261, 324nn11–12

Vietnamese opera, 231, 320n64

visuality, 1–2, 12–15, 134, 187; glamour, 229, 236. *See also* costumes

Wah Mee Company, 317n27

Ward, Barbara E., xii, 9, 30, 277n46

warriors, 26, 29, 69, 133, 183, 230; battle scenes, 97; costumes and headdresses, 14, 75, 123–24, *124*, *125*, 132, 179–81, *213*, 227; role types, 118, *119*, 120, 209, 300n8; weaponry, 90, 93

Washington Street theaters (San Francisco), *101*, 109, 110, 117, 145; Look Sun Fung, ix, x, 130, 144, 145, *146*, 166, 272n17; maps of, *151*, 171, *172*; opening of the new Chinese theater, 99, *100*; Poo Hing He Yuen, 127–32, 136–37, 144, 302n43

Watkins, Carleton, *94*, 96, 212, *213*, 295n21, 314n66

Weber, Samuel, 15–16

Wedded by Fate (McDowell and Field), 193–94, 311n22

Weekly Butte Record, 56–57, 66

Western dramas, 184–85, 273n34

Wilde, Oscar, 159, 182, 212

Williams, Samuel Wells, 38, 112, 214–15, 299n88

Windsor Theater, 12, 221, 223–25, *224*

Wing Tie Ping theater: Ah Quin's visits to, xiii, 148, 239; Grant's visit to, 146–47; merger and rivalries, 144–46, 165–66

Wong, Anna May, 14

Wong, Deborah, 255

Wong, Lily, xvii

Wong Chin Foo, 163, 315n2, 316n16, 317n27, 318n49; advocacy for civil rights and Chinese theater, 12, 18, 170, 218–20, 227, 230–31, 233, 237, 315n9; establishment of Doyer Street theater, 237–38, 322n94; Swentien Lok Royal dramatic company and, 221, 222, 223

Woodworth, Selim Edwin, 76, 275n27

Wores, Theodore, 18, 189, 310n9, 312n29; "A Candy Seller," *200*, 200–201, 217; "A Pirate," *203*, 203–4; *The Entry* ("An Entrance" or *Chinese Actor*), 166, *167*, 168–69, 197–200, *199*, 238, 313n40, 313nn44–45; "In the Women's Gallery," *201*, 201–2;

"Making Up," *202*, 202–3; reputation and early works, 197, 212, 312n36, 312n38; summary of works, 194, *195*

Workingmen's Party, 11, 128, 131, 150, 164, 311n12

world's fairs: Paris International Exposition (1867), 85; Paris Universal Exposition (1889), 11–12, 18, 195, 218, 231–32; in the United States, 319n62, 321n76; World's Columbian Exposition (1893), 12, 317n27, 323n95

xiqu, term usage, xv–xvi, 273n31

Yalan Trades Pigs (*Selling a Pig*) (opera), 31, 183–84, 224

Yang Enshou, xi, 13

Yang Fung Theater, 103

Yang Maojian, 13, 278n59

yangqin, 236

Yang Tse Kiang (Yangtze River), 16, 178–79

Yao Tian Cai. *See* Yu Henn Choy troupe

Yeager, Walter, 132, *133*, *134*, 194

yellowface performance, 184, 220, 290n12, 309n46, 315n11

Yoshihara, Mari, 255

Young Wo Association, 8, 23

youth, 138

Yuan dynasty, 15

Yuba City, CA, 59, 60

yueqin, *115*, 133, 212, *213*, 260

Yu Henn Choy troupe, 115, 123, 249, 301n15, 325n22

Yung, Bell, 283n70, 327n2

Yung, Judy, 292n41

Yun Sing Ping Company, 98, *101*, 296n29

Zhen Lan Bao, 300n11

Zuni drama, 210, 314n57

NANCY YUNHWA RAO is a distinguished professor of music at Rutgers University and the author of *Chinatown Opera Theater in North America*. An elected member of the American Academy of Arts and Sciences, she is also an Honorary Member of the American Musicological Society.

The University of Illinois Press
is a founding member of the
Association of University Presses.

————————————————

Composed in 10.5/13 Mercury Text G1
with Avenir LT Std display
by Kirsten Dennison
at the University of Illinois Press
Manufactured by Versa Press, Inc.

University of Illinois Press
1325 South Oak Street
Champaign, IL 61820-6903
www.press.uillinois.edu